MEANS
LANDSCAPE
ESTIMATING

Sylvia Hollman Fee

R.S. MEANS COMPANY, INC.
CONSTRUCTION CONSULTANTS & PUBLISHERS
100 Construction Plaza
P.O. Box 800
Kingston, Ma 02364-0800
(617) 747-1270

© 1987

In keeping with the general policy of R.S. Means Company, Inc., its authors, editors, and engineers apply diligence and judgment in locating and using reliable sources for the information published. However, no guarantee or warranty can be given, and all responsibility and liability for loss or damage are hereby disclaimed by the authors, editors, engineers and publisher of this publication with respect to the accuracy, correctness, value and sufficiency of the data, methods and other information contained herein as applied for any particular purpose or use.

The editors for this book were Mary P. Greene and Edward B. Wetherill; the production supervisor was Marion E. Schofield; and technical support was provided by Sharon L. Proulx.

Printed in the United States of America

10   9   8   7   6   5   4   3   2

Library of Congress Cataloging in Publication Data

ISBN 0-87629-064-0

MEANS LANDSCAPE ESTIMATING

Sylvia Hollman Fee

Illustrator
Carl W. Linde

Acknowledgements

The author wishes to express her appreciation for the creative and practical guidance she received from the many design professionals, nurserymen, landscape contractors and clients with whom she has been privileged to work in the dynamic and creative landscape industry. Many individuals and organizations have made specific contributions in this book, and are acknowledged as their contributions appear.

In addition, the author expresses a special thanks to: the American Association of Nurserymen (AAN), American Society of Landscape Architects (ASLA), Associated Landscape Contractors of Massachusetts (ALCM), Massachusetts Horticultural Society, University of Massachusetts, U.S.D.A. Cooperative Extension, and Bici Pettit, landscape architect, Cambridge, Massachusetts.

TABLE OF CONTENTS

FOREWORD

For over 45 years, R.S. Means Company, Inc. has been researching and publishing cost data for the building construction industry. *Means Landscape Estimating* applies that experience to aid the landscape professional in better understanding the estimating process.

The purpose of this book is to provide sound, practical methods and standards to achieve accurate estimates of landscape projects. The book provides an overview of the complete process — from the invitation to bid through job planning once the contract is signed. Included are the site visit, takeoff, material and labor pricing, calculating of overhead and profit, bidding, and scheduling.

A complete sample takeoff and estimate are provided in Chapter 6. This example is based on a set of plans for an actual landscape project. The procedures and forms explained and shown in earlier chapters are put into practice to complete a typical landscape estimate. Following the sample estimate are discussions of bidding and scheduling practices and a detailed explanation of how to use the annual cost reference, *Means Site Work Cost Data*, from which most costs in this book are taken.

In addition to its coverage of estimating procedures, *Means Landscape Estimating* includes an appendix with useful information in the form of tables and charts, definitions and illustrations. Topics covered include: materials, equipment, measurements, and earthwork calculations. A list of references provides a source for more information on plant materials. The names and addresses of trade and professional associations are also provided. In addition, there are a list of common abbreviations and a chart of symbols and graphics commonly used on landscape plans and drawings.

INTRODUCTION

The products of the landscape industry today are the result of experience, tradition, and research providing solutions to the changing uses for outdoor spaces. Within the landscape industry, several diverse professions contribute to each project. Each of these groups, whether contractors, architects, or suppliers, has its own role and its own perspective. Within these groups, project management and, in particular, estimating may be approached in as many different ways as there are landscape businesses. Among these diverse methods, there are certain sound estimating techniques that are used with the greatest share of success. The methods presented in the following chapters are suggested guidelines for effective estimating, and are supported by examples illustrating how the required procedures are carried out. The changes, challenges, and characteristics of the industry leave many openings for new possibilities and interpretations, but the theme that persists is organization as a means toward the goals of efficiency and profit.

The source of material for *Means Landscape Estimating* comes from the author's 15 years' experience as a landscape designer, combined with a selection of literature on landscape architecture and construction. The cost and productivity information in this book comes from reference data supported by the experienced staff of construction professionals at R.S. Means Company, Inc.

Chapter One

WHAT IS LANDSCAPE CONSTRUCTION?

Chapter One

WHAT IS LANDSCAPE CONSTRUCTION?

Landscape construction has become a major industry that ranges from metropolitan transportation projects - to neighborhood parks - to private residences. It has also proven to be an investment with a high rate of return. Landscape construction is the art and act of creating outdoor spaces that are functional and eye-catching. The criteria for each project are established by both the aesthetic and practical requirements of the client and the resolution of site problems. It is without overstatement that the president of a large New England construction company defines landscaping as "the 3% of the total construction job that makes a 30% difference."

Landscape design and construction is not only an art, but it is also a lively, growing business commanding an increasing share of attention and profit within the construction industry. Today, landscaping plays an integral part in real estate development. Zoning laws may require that trees and green, open spaces be incorporated into plans for new projects. Yet even when landscaping is not a legal requirement, real estate developers are always interested in outdoor spaces that attract prospective buyers or tenants to the property.

In landscaping, the needs of the client define the job. Considerations such as adequate access for pedestrians and vehicles must also be given attention. Appropriate distance must be allowed too, between people and such operations as heavy manufacturing and sewage treatment areas. Clients are interested not only in handsome spaces around structures, but also in open areas for recreation. Whether the client is a town government seeking a street tree planting, or a homeowner wanting a new lawn, attractive, economical green spaces are the goal. Figure 1.1, "The Development of a Landscape Plan", shows some of the factors that must be taken into account for a residential landscaping project. The planning process is shown, as are the design solutions.

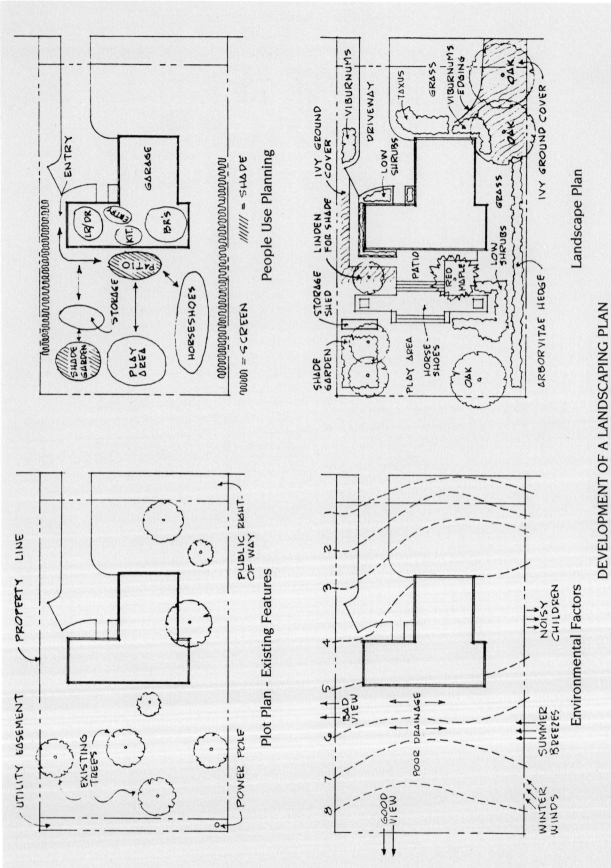

People Use Planning

00000 = SCREEN   ////// = SHADE

Landscape Plan

Plot Plan - Existing Features

Environmental Factors

DEVELOPMENT OF A LANDSCAPING PLAN

(courtesy U.S. Dept of Agriculture)

Figure 1.1

With the specialized skills and tremendous range of materials that are available today, the solutions offered by landscape professionals are limitless. However, success in the landscaping industry also requires good planning, expert performance, and familiarity with these new materials and methods. Up-to-date knowledge of industry costs and values is critical to effective estimating and business management. The sources of reliable cost information are discussed in detail in Chapter 4.

Divisions of Landscape Jobs

Landscape construction involves many construction disciplines. The jobs required for a typical project fit into four general categories:
- Site Work
- Hard Construction
- Planting
- Specialties

Site Work

Site Work includes clearing the land of excess trees and brush, digging utilities trenches, creating or leveling banks and slopes, grading, excavating and filling, and providing for proper drainage. Such work calls for decisions on the use of heavy equipment. This is a high cost item that must be effectively managed in order to keep project costs under control. The scope of site work for a landscape contractor is usually separated from the site work of a general contractor. That is to say, the landscape contractor may typically perform finish grade work, leaving the heavy equipment work to the general contractor.

Hard Construction

This category covers both the practical needs and the aesthetic requirements of a landscaping project. Included in this category is the construction of walls, steps, paved streets and walks, decks, fences, and other structures needed for the safe access and comfort of people. Designers and builders strive to combine beauty with utility while also responding to environmental concerns and regulations. A well placed wall, for example, serves as a sound barrier as well as a physical barrier. It may also control erosion of slopes and support flowering vines for screening and beauty. Likewise, a circular roadway can provide an elegant design feature, while serving as a practical access route for emergency vehicles. When effectively planned, hard construction resolves problems while it enhances the use of the land. Common landscape construction materials are defined in Chapter 2 -"Landscape Equipment and Materials".

Planting

Planting is performed for both practical and aesthetic reasons. Trees, shrubs, and hedges may control erosion, guide pedestrians and vehicles, provide shade in summer and shelter from the wind in winter. Plantings also act as architectural design features and of course, beautify. Since aesthetic concerns are so important to landscape construction, beautification belongs high on the list of concerns for planting, as it does for site work and hard construction. Some standards for plant materials are provided in Chapter 2, and more detailed reference information is included in the Appendix.

Specialties

Specialties make up an ever-expanding category that calls upon many different skills including landscape maintenance, irrigation, and the installation of play equipment. The need for outdoor lighting, recreation

facilities, street furniture, gardening, property design, and a host of other elements may call upon the skills of specialty subcontractors. Debate continues, however, on whether it is more economical for landscape contractors to perform these kinds of specialties as part of their own in-house services, or to delegate them to outside suppliers and tradesmen.

The creative latitude and independent decision-making permitted to the landscape architect and contractor varies with the size, characteristics, and management of a given project. In any case, it is the landscape specialist's knowledge and professional excellence that provide a workable solution for the optimum use of the site.

A View of Project Management

A great percentage of landscape work is for private residences. In most of these cases, the owner is the only party to be served by the work contract. Generally, the limited scope of a residential project calls for only one design professional or contractor to arrange and complete the work. It is on these relatively smaller, residential projects that the landscape architect or contractor is more likely to exercise total control and to take responsibility for most of the key decisions.

Unlike residential projects, commercial and industrial landscape projects usually involve the combined efforts of a group. Foremost in that group is the owner, who is to be either the principal user of the project or a representative of its tenants. It is the owner or developer who oversees matters of property acquisition and title, proposed land use, and finances for the project under discussion. Working closely with the owner are the architect and the landscape architect, jointly termed "design professionals", and the contractor. The design professionals conceive and prepare the plans of the project, and the contractor builds it.

The amount of responsibility that the owner delegates to designers and contractors varies greatly. For large commercial or industrial projects, the management picture can be complex, with the general contractor serving as manager of numerous subcontractors, the landscape contractor among them. On a smaller job, the landscape contractor might fulfill the contract under the direct supervision of the owner or the design professionals. No matter how the management of a project is delegated, contractors should have a clear agreement with the principal party for whom the work is being performed.

Before work begins on a project, each responsible party is called upon to handle certain preliminary arrangements and negotiations. These responsibilities entail meetings with businesses, governing boards, and other authorities whose consent or contribution is needed if the project is to proceed. Figure 1.2 shows the areas of involvement for each of the responsible parties in a typical commercial project.

The goals of the *owner* determine the character and scope of the project. As the figure illustrates, it is the responsibility of the owner to handle all legal and monetary matters involved in obtaining the property and financing its development. The owner may be working with bankers, realtors, and financiers in this phase of the project.

The *design professionals*, as the originators of the project's plans and specifications, produce a landscape plan that "fits" the ground, not one that "twists" the ground to fit the plan. Their experience makes them aware of the problems likely to be encountered as development

Figure 1.2

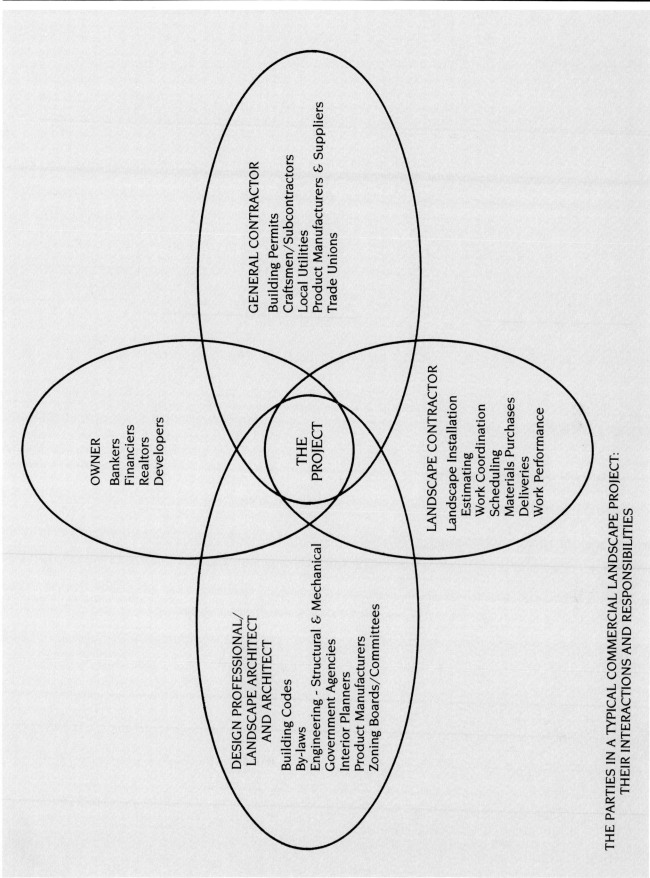

GENERAL CONTRACTOR
Building Permits
Craftsmen/Subcontractors
Local Utilities
Product Manufacturers & Suppliers
Trade Unions

OWNER
Bankers
Financiers
Realtors
Developers

THE PROJECT

LANDSCAPE CONTRACTOR
Landscape Installation
Estimating
Work Coordination
Scheduling
Materials Purchases
Deliveries
Work Performance

DESIGN PROFESSIONAL/
LANDSCAPE ARCHITECT
AND ARCHITECT

Building Codes
By-laws
Engineering - Structural & Mechanical
Government Agencies
Interior Planners
Product Manufacturers
Zoning Boards/Committees

THE PARTIES IN A TYPICAL COMMERCIAL LANDSCAPE PROJECT:
THEIR INTERACTIONS AND RESPONSIBILITIES

gets under way. These professionals may be called upon to meet with planning boards, zoning boards, conservation commissions, and other local or national regulatory agencies. It is also the responsibility of design professionals to consult and coordinate with interior planners, structural and mechanical engineers, and product manufacturers who are expected to participate in the project. Before plans are drawn, it is essential for the architect and landscape architect to familiarize themselves with the building codes and by-laws of the host community. Wasted moves in the planning stage can add thousands of dollars to project costs.

General contractors are problem solvers. It is their business to know which methods, materials, and equipment can be used most effectively to solve difficulties posed in the preparation and use of the land, to keep costs under control, and to bring the designer's concepts to reality. It is the contractor who seeks and procures building permits, negotiates with trade unions, carries out transactions with product manufacturers and suppliers, and arranges for power and water hook-ups with local utilities. The contractor also secures the services of craftsmen/subcontractors and oversees their performance of the work.

Through skillful application of the trade, the landscape contractor can quickly become a very visible asset to a project's general contractor, and a credit to the developer. As the landscape contractor becomes more familiar with methods and materials, the probability increases of obtaining desirable and profitable future contracts.

Business Enhancement

Staying up to date and working effectively with a general contractor are important aspects of landscape construction. Competitive bidding, however, calls for more than a sound reputation and the goodwill of the construction industry. It is a discipline in itself and involves experience, exhaustive research, planning, calculation, and a measure of good, intuitive judgement. Chapter 7 of this book is devoted to a detailed description of the bidding process. It includes an explanation of proper procedures and shows bid forms filled in for an example proposal.

Submitting Qualifications

Landscape contracts are secured by negotiation or by competitive bid. The bid is your proposal to complete a project for a stated sum. Before bids are accepted, however, the client may insist on knowing the qualifications of all prospective bidders. Landscape contractors who hope to compete must be prepared to provide owners and/or general contractors with all of the required information.

To assess contractors' qualifications, clients need to know the following:

- Type of landscape firm (corporation, partnership, sole proprietorship)
- How long in business
- Net worth (financial statement)
- Dollar volume (last three years)
- Bank references
- Certificate of insurance
- Bonding capacity
- Name of bonding company

- Licenses
- Trade affiliations
- References from clients for whom the company has completed work

In addition, the landscaping firm may be required to give information or to submit affidavits to prove that it is an equal opportunity employer and that it has complied with affirmative action programs established by the state and federal governments. Some projects also require a bid bond, which is a guarantee that a landscape contractor will sign a contract on the basis of the bid submitted.

Marketing Strategies

Most established firms doing commercial work are familiar with the process of submitting credentials. A promotional package is usually sent to clients, with pamphlets and advertising materials which emphasize the company's experience and highlight their specialties, along with a letter tailored specifically to the job.

Marketing materials for landscape construction services should be directed towards the person who is authorized to award the contract. Seek the person in charge of selecting subcontractors and address your information package to that individual's attention. In residential projects, this is frequently the property owner or an appointed representative. In other instances, the general contractor, construction manager, or the owner's architect is responsible for awarding the contract.

Successfully completed projects are the most compelling advertisements for your landscaping business. They let prospective clients see for themselves how well planned and executed outdoor spaces can conserve and beautify property while expanding on its use.

Another way to track down new work is to scan newspapers and trade publications that list starting dates of construction, new proposals, and invitations to bid. The law usually requires that public projects be advertised, giving all competitors a fair chance. Government projects are also open to all qualified companies and are almost always awarded to the low bidder, a consideration which challenges the aggressive young company to exercise shrewd judgment and planning skills in preparation of the bid.

By contrast, private clients often choose bidders from a selected list of qualified companies. Contracts do not necessarily go to the lowest bidder, but are awarded at the owner's discretion. Architects and construction companies often choose bidders from their own select list of qualified applicants. By complying with the highest standards of the trade, establishing a reputation for quality and goodwill, and advertising that fact, a landscaping company can establish a reliable reputation in the community and greatly improve its chance of winning a place on a list of select bidders.

Arrangements of this sort need not discourage the qualified newcomer; indeed, they can be a welcome challenge. There are always opportunities within the bidding process to remain competitive. For example, certain bid invitations encourage bidders to suggest changes and additions. This approach gives the landscape contractor an opportunity to show a measure of knowledge, skill, and creativity that may earn special consideration. In addition, projects large enough for

competitive bidding usually enter a phase of negotiations between management and the chosen bidder. Here again, the landscape contractor has a chance to win the confidence of the client.

The growth of a landscape related business requires both creative and business skills. Site work, hard construction, planting, and specialties comprise the general categories on a typical landscape project; experience in these essential areas is the cornerstone for growth and profit in the competitive landscape industry. Success also depends upon good planning, knowledge, and management.

Design professionals and contractors who want to expand their businesses should also develop marketing strategies. Selling one's skills is a new task for design pros and tradesmen alike. Formal and/or professional training often does not include marketing and accounting. Look for assistance in these areas from the many auxiliary organizations of the industry. Take advantage of these information sources to learn, grow, and prosper.

Planning the Landscape Proposal

Landscape architects and contractors must conduct extensive studies of all newly proposed projects before they are able to submit an appropriate proposal for the work. Architects use the term "program" to put a job into focus on a human scale. Their program defines who will use the newly created space and what activities the users will perform there. The requirements may be as down-to-earth as a playground or a baseball diamond for a housing project, or as abstract and dignified as the desire of a company to improve its corporate image. In either case, design professionals follow a carefully charted sequence of activities to determine the needs of the client and how those needs are best served.

A first step is a **survey** of the site where the project is to be executed. The design professional's survey encompasses more than the physical conditions of the site. Traffic studies, historical preservation values and ecological systems may also be considered. The landscape architect should determine what work will be needed to prepare the site for the proposed uses. For example, soil tests, pits or earth borings may be required. Will the parcel support the work from an ecological standpoint? Does water need to be retained or diverted? How much grading and excavation will be required? The survey gathers together all of the physical, environmental, and historical information that will come to bear on the project.

The next step is **analysis** of the project. Using the information gathered from the site survey, the landscape architect examines the owner's needs versus existing conditions for the proposed development. Consideration is given to such details as the time frame, the budget, building codes, and all zoning mandates, requirements, and restrictions. The scope of the project determines the degree of detail to be studied and included in further negotiations with the client.

It is on the basis of the survey and analysis that the landscape designer or contractor is finally able to submit a proposal to the client, stating the details of the services and/or work to be performed, and the total project cost. The proposal may be presented in direct negotiations with the owner, as is customary for smaller residential projects, or it may be submitted as a competitive bid, as part of a formal bidding procedure. In any event, the landscape professional should seek out the party

authorized to award the contract and, if possible, negotiate directly with that person.

When the job is estimated, bid and won, you can get on your way to building a functional and handsome landscape - that 3% of the job that makes a 30% difference.

National Landscaping Organizations

Landscape construction is a rapidly growing and changing industry. High quality work, adherence to local codes, accepted trade practices, and competitive bidding all play their part in making your landscaping business a continuing success. Yet to stay on top, landscapers must also keep up with the latest technological developments and confront challenging new demands within their field. It is here that they find strength in numbers.

National landscape trade and professional organizations exist to keep members informed of new materials and methods, as well as ways to cut costs, boost profits, and improve their practices. Among the many advantages provided by association memberships are: trade publications that offer up-to-date advice and information on every specialty, continuing education in seminars and workshops, representation in government, and conferences where members meet to share useful new ideas and developments in the field.

The best-known national associations are the *American Society of Landscape Architects, American Nurserymen's Association*, and *Associated Landscape Contractors of America*. Members include landscape architects, landscape contractors, and businesses that supply products and services to the industry. Also on the membership rolls are educators, technicians, and private citizens devoted to preservation and beautification of the land.

Professional groups provide and sponsor technical reports and monitor technical advances. They also publish manuals on industry practices, and trade journals filled with ideas to promote growth, profit, and savings in the landscaping industry. Conferences, symposia, and exhibits are among the services performed by the national associations.

In an age of urban sprawl and vanishing countryside, beautifying the landscape can be a battle. National landscape organizations are dedicated to this cause. The leaders of these groups are active in political lobbies and on industry awareness committees, where they remain alert to proposed laws that will affect the interests of the landscape business. Acting to promote what is best for the industry, they often exert a strong influence in the decisions reached by lawmakers.

Trade and professional organizations within the landscaping industry cooperate with local communities by encouraging their own high standards. Shows and exhibitions for design, building, and service trades bring new products and services to the attention of the entire landscape contracting industry. Each year, the national associations recognize citizens who underwrite outstanding landscaping projects and present awards to the professionals who design and perform the work.

Local and regional chapters of landscape organizations carry on the work of the national groups within the community. They are known to have a positive influence on towns and cities, winning the confidence of town boards and regulatory commissions by keeping standards high among all landscaping contractors practicing in the area.

For a complete list of landscaping trade associations in your area, contact these organizations at their national headquarters.

American Society of Landscape Architects   (202) 466-7730
1733 Connecticut Avenue, N.W.
Washington, D.C. 20009

American Association of Nurserymen, Inc.   (202) 789-2900
1250 I St., N.W., Suite 500
Washington, D.C. 20005

Associated Landscape Contractors of America   (703) 241-4004
405 Washington Street
North Falls Church, VA 22046

Chapter Two
LANDSCAPE
EQUIPMENT
AND MATERIALS

Chapter Two

LANDSCAPE EQUIPMENT AND MATERIALS

The range and versatility of landscape equipment and materials is nearly inexhaustible. The challenge lies in using these resources most efficiently and effectively, while working with highly vulnerable and constantly changing plant materials, exposed to all kinds of weather. The startling impact of 20' trees planted within one day often brings the delighted response, "It's like magic", but the designers and installers responsible are no magicians. Their "magic" results from a thorough knowledge of the methods, capacity and character of power equipment, tools, materials and supplies.

Site Work

The earthwork portion of a large job begins with the careful selection of cost effective equipment. Assuming the contractor does not own equipment, the options are equipment rental or subcontracting the work, coordinating it with any other work that can be accomplished at the same time. A listing of national average rental rates and operating costs of typical site work equipment and accessories is shown in Figure 2.1 (from *Means Site Work Cost Data*, 1987). The rental rates shown here pertain to late model, high quality machines in excellent working condition, rented from equipment dealers. Rental rates from contractors may be substantially lower than those of equipment dealers, depending on economic conditions. For a more detailed explanation of Means' format, costs, and productivity figures, see Chapter 9.

The selection of earthwork equipment depends on the type and quantity of materials being worked, as well as their moisture content. These factors will be discussed further, along with a quantity takeoff description in Chapter 5. The hauling distance and the type and condition of the road are other considerations, as are the time allowed and the availability of equipment. Short-haul cut-and-fill operations may require bulldozers only, while another operation may call for excavators, a fleet of trucks, and spreading and compaction equipment.

The contractor must determine the most cost effective use of equipment. Examples of excavating and hauling equipment are shown in Figures 2.2 and 2.3 from *Means Site Work Cost Data*, 1987 edition. Based on capacity, volume per hour, and haul distance, the proper excavating equipment can

1.5	Contractor Equipment		UNIT	HOURLY OPER. COST.	RENT PER DAY	RENT PER WEEK	RENT PER MONTH	CREW EQUIPMENT COST	
050 3300	Sheepsfoot roller, self-propelled, 4 wheel, 130 H.P.		Ea.	10.40	345	1,040	3,125	291.20	050
3320	300 H.P.			15.50	445	1,340	4,025	392	
3350	Vibratory steel drum & pneumatic tire, diesel, 18,000 lb.			11.70	310	925	2,775	278.60	
3400	29,000 lb.			14.60	370	1,115	3,350	339.80	
3410	Rotary mower, brush, 60", with tractor		↓	.90	240	725	2,170	152.20	
3430									
3450	Scrapers, towed type, 7 to 9 C.Y. capacity		Ea.	2.73	120	365	1,100	94.85	
3500	12 to 17 C.Y. capacity			4.54	155	460	1,375	128.30	
3550	Self-propelled, 4 x 4 drive, 2 engine, 14 C.Y. capacity			37	1,160	3,485	10,450	993	
3600	1 engine, 24 C.Y. capacity			44	1,265	3,800	11,400	1,112	
3650	Self-loading, 11 C.Y. capacity			33	605	1,815	5,450	627	
3700	22 C.Y. capacity		↓	50	930	2,790	8,375	958	
3850	Shovels, see Cranes division 1.5-200								
3860	Shovel front attachment, mechanical, ½ C.Y.	⑯	Ea.	.63	60	180	535	41.05	
3870	¾ C.Y.			2.60	95	285	855	77.80	
3880	1 C.Y.			2.82	145	435	1,300	109.55	
3890	1-½ C.Y.			3.07	165	490	1,475	122.55	
3910	3 C.Y.			5.70	305	910	2,725	227.60	
3950	Stump chipper, 18" deep, 30 H.P.			1.25	205	620	1,860	134	
4050	Tractor, 40 H.P.			3.35	210	625	1,880	151.80	
4110	Tractor, crawler, with bulldozer, torque converter, diesel 75 H.P.			6.80	255	765	2,300	207.40	
4150	105 H.P.			10.45	450	1,350	4,075	353.60	
4200	140 H.P.			13.90	550	1,650	4,950	441.20	
4260	200 H.P.			18.75	885	2,650	8,000	680	
4310	300 H.P.			26	1,150	3,450	10,400	898	
4360	410 H.P.			38	1,475	4,425	13,250	1,189	
4380	700 H.P.			67	2,340	7,165	21,500	1,969	
4400	Loader, crawler, torque conv., diesel, 1-½ C.Y., 80 H.P.			10.25	320	965	2,900	275	
4450	1-½ to 1-¾ C.Y., 95 H.P.			12.15	370	1,115	3,350	320.20	
4510	1-¾ to 2-¼ C.Y., 130 H.P.			15.90	510	1,525	4,550	432.20	
4530	2-½ to 3-¼ C.Y., 190 H.P.			24	675	2,025	6,100	597	
4560	4-½ to 5 C.Y., 275 H.P.			34	1,250	3,750	11,300	1,022	
4610	Tractor loader, wheel, torque conv 4 x 4, 1 to 1-¼ C.Y., 65 H.P.	⑰		8.05	245	740	2,225	212.40	
4620	1-½ to 1-¾ C.Y., 80 H.P.			10.40	315	940	2,825	271.20	
4650	1-¾ to 2 C.Y., 100 H.P.			12.20	380	1,135	3,400	324.60	
4710	2-½ to 3-½ C.Y., 130 H.P.			17.40	510	1,535	4,600	446.20	
4730	3 to 4-½ C.Y., 170 H.P.			21	560	1,675	5,025	503	
4760	5-¼ to 5-¾ C.Y., 270 H.P.			34	1,055	3,165	9,500	905	
4810	7 to 8 C.Y., 375 H.P.			58	1,210	3,635	10,900	1,191	
4870	12-½ C.Y., 690 H.P.			95	2,755	8,265	24,800	2,413	
4880	Wheeled, skid steer, 10 C.F., 30 H.P. gas			3.40	95	280	840	83.20	
4890	1 C.Y., 78 H.P., diesel			4.70	165	490	1,475	135.60	
4900	Trencher, chain, boom type, gas, operator walking, 12 H.P.			7.80	120	360	1,075	134.40	
4910	Operator riding, 40 H.P.			12.50	155	465	1,400	193	
5000	Wheel type, gas, 4' deep, 12" wide			11.25	250	750	2,250	240	
5100	Diesel, 6' deep, 20" wide			15	500	1,500	4,500	420	
5150	Ladder type, gas, 5' deep, 8" wide			8.55	315	950	2,850	258.40	
5200	Diesel, 8' deep, 16" wide			10.40	585	1,750	5,250	433.20	
5210	Tree spade, self-propelled		↓	4.25	435	1,310	3,930	296	
5230									
5250	Truck, dump, tandem, 12 ton payload		Ea.	12.75	190	575	1,725	217	
5300	Three axle dump, 16 ton payload			15.75	255	760	2,275	278	
5350	Dump trailer only, rear dump, 16-½ C.Y.			3.90	80	240	715	79.20	
5400	20 C.Y.			4.75	92	280	845	94	
5450	Flatbed, single axle, 1-½ ton rating			3.70	47	140	415	57.60	
5500	3 ton rating			4.25	57	170	505	68	
5550	Off highway rear dump, 25 ton capacity			25	750	2,250	6,750	650	
5600	35 ton capacity			34	1,055	3,160	9,475	904	
6000	Vibratory plow, 25 H.P., walking		↓	1.03	105	315	950	71.25	

For expanded coverage of these items see *Means Building Construction Cost Data 1987*

Figure 2.1

be most efficiently matched with the number and size of trucks to assure that all equipment is continuously in use - with no waiting, or "down" time.

In creating earthwork "systems", Means has matched various excavating equipment with the most efficient size and quantity of trucks. (see Chapter 9). An example is shown in Figure 2.4 from *Means Site Work Cost Data*, 1987. The same type of system, but for cut and fill (without hauling) is shown in Figure 2.5.

Site work consists primarily of earthwork, but can also include paving, drainage and piping. Site utilities and drainage involve the additional costs of pipe bedding, manholes, and catch basins. Electrical cables and ducts, though installed in the site work area, are more properly the work of others. The various kinds of site work may require different types of equipment (see the Appendix for illustrations).

Hard Construction

Hard construction includes a wide variety of materials. Selecting the proper materials while balancing aesthetics and cost effectiveness requires skill and ingenuity. Paving materials, for example, offer many options of shape, form, and cost. Various types can be coordinated. Concrete can be cast in place or used in the form of pre-cast paver units; it can be used on its own or in combination with other materials.

Bricks, blocks, and tiles are available in a wide range of sizes, colors, shapes, and textures. Other materials, such as water and earth, are not catalogued as "materials", but are instead defined as items like pools and fountains, or berms and mounds. Installation of these items may require work in the categories of both site work and construction. Much landscape construction involves paving for outdoor floor surfaces. There are specialized pavings for various recreational uses. Such "special" uses (ball fields, etc.) typically conform to agency and landscape architects' specifications and drawings. Within the landscape industry, many proprietary paving products are available. The most commonly used materials include: **asphalt, brick, concrete, stone, tile, and wood.**

2.3		Earthwork	CREW	DAILY OUTPUT	MAN-HOURS	UNIT	MAT.	LABOR	EQUIP.	TOTAL	TOTAL INCL O&P	
160	1500	Wheel mounted, ¾ C.Y. cap. = 45 C.Y./hr.	B-10R	360	.033	C.Y.		.64	.59	1.23	1.59	160
	1550	1-½ C.Y. cap. = 80 C.Y./hr.	B-10S	640	.019			.36	.43	.79	1	
	1601	3 C.Y. cap. = 100 C.Y./hr.	B-10T	800	.015			.29	.56	.85	1.04	
	1650	5 C.Y. cap. = 185 C.Y./hr.	B-10U	1,480	.008			.16	.61	.77	.90	
	1800	Gradall, 30 inch bucket, ½ C.Y. = 30 C.Y./hr.	B-12J	240	.067			1.29	1.86	3.15	3.93	
	1850	48 inch bucket, 1 C.Y. = 45 C.Y./hr.	B-12K	360	.044			.86	1.75	2.61	3.19	
	2400	Scrapers, towed, 10 C.Y. capacity, ¼ push dozer, 1500' haul	B-33B	600	.023			.45	2.08	2.53	2.96	
	2450	5000' haul	"	440	.032			.62	2.84	3.46	4.03	
	2600	15 C.Y. capacity, ¼ push dozer, 1500' haul	B-33C	800	.018			.34	1.56	1.90	2.22	
	2650	5000' haul	"	560	.025			.49	2.23	2.72	3.17	
	3000	Self-propelled scrapers, 15 C.Y. capacity, ¼ dozer, 1500' haul	B-33D	800	.018			.34	1.52	1.86	2.17	
	3050	5000' haul	"	560	.025			.49	2.17	2.66	3.10	
	3150	25 C.Y. capacity, ¼ push dozer, 1500' haul	B-33E	1,000	.014			.27	1.34	1.61	1.87	
	3200	5000' haul	"	600	.023			.45	2.23	2.68	3.11	
	3300	Elevating scrapers, self propelled, 10 C.Y., ¼ dozer, 1500' haul	B-33F	600	.023			.45	1.43	1.88	2.24	
	3350	5000' haul	"	440	.032			.62	1.95	2.57	3.05	
	3500	20 C.Y. capacity, ¼ push dozer, 1500' haul	B-33G	840	.017			.32	1.41	1.73	2.02	
	3550	5000' haul	"	680	.021			.40	1.74	2.14	2.50	
	3700	Shovel, ½ C.Y. capacity = 30 C.Y./hr. ⑯	B-12L	240	.067			1.29	1.34	2.63	3.36	
	3750	¾ C.Y. capacity = 50 C.Y./hr.	B-12M	400	.040			.78	1.11	1.89	2.35	
	3800	1 C.Y. capacity = 60 C.Y./hr. ⑰	B-12N	480	.033			.65	1.09	1.74	2.14	
	3850	1-½ C.Y. capacity = 90 C.Y./hr.	B-12O	720	.022			.43	.89	1.32	1.61	
	3900	3 C.Y. cap. = 150 C.Y./hr.	B-12T	1,200	.013			.26	.77	1.03	1.22	
	3950											
	4000	For soft soil or sand, deduct				C.Y.				15%	15%	
	4100	For heavy soil or stiff clay, add								60%	60%	
	4200	For wet excavation with clamshell or dragline, add								100%	100%	
	4250	All other equipment, add								50%	50%	
	4400	Clamshell in sheeting or cofferdam, minimum	B-12H	222	.072			1.40	2.03	3.43	4.28	
	4450	Maximum		59	.271			5.25	7.65	12.90	16.10	
163	0010	**EXCAVATING, BULK, DOZER** Open site										163
	2000	75 H.P., 50' haul, sand & gravel	B-10L	460	.026	C.Y.		.50	.45	.95	1.23	
	2020	Common earth		400	.030			.58	.52	1.10	1.41	
	2040	Clay		250	.048			.92	.83	1.75	2.26	
	2200	150' haul, sand & gravel		230	.052			1	.90	1.90	2.46	
	2220	Common earth		200	.060			1.15	1.04	2.19	2.83	
	2240	Clay		125	.096			1.84	1.66	3.50	4.52	
	2400	300' haul, sand & gravel		65	.185			3.54	3.19	6.73	8.70	
	2420	Common earth		55	.218			4.19	3.77	7.96	10.30	
	2440	Clay		35	.343			6.60	5.95	12.55	16.15	
	3000	105 H.P., 50' haul, sand & gravel	B-10W	700	.017			.33	.51	.84	1.04	
	3020	Common earth		610	.020			.38	.58	.96	1.19	
	3040	Clay		385	.031			.60	.92	1.52	1.89	
	3200	150' haul, sand & gravel		310	.039			.74	1.14	1.88	2.34	
	3220	Common earth		270	.044			.85	1.31	2.16	2.69	
	3240	Clay		170	.071			1.36	2.08	3.44	4.27	
	3300	300' haul, sand & gravel		140	.086			1.65	2.53	4.18	5.20	
	3320	Common earth		120	.100			1.92	2.95	4.87	6.05	
	3340	Clay		100	.120			2.30	3.54	5.84	7.25	
	4000	200 H.P., 50' haul, sand & gravel	B-10B	1,400	.009			.16	.49	.65	.78	
	4020	Common earth		1,230	.010			.19	.55	.74	.88	
	4040	Clay		770	.016			.30	.88	1.18	1.41	
	4200	150' haul, sand & gravel		595	.020			.39	1.14	1.53	1.82	
	4220	Common earth		516	.023			.45	1.32	1.77	2.10	
	4240	Clay		325	.037			.71	2.09	2.80	3.34	
	4400	300' haul, sand & gravel		310	.039			.74	2.19	2.93	3.50	
	4420	Common earth		270	.044			.85	2.52	3.37	4.02	
	4440	Clay		170	.071			1.36	4	5.36	6.40	
	5000	300 H.P., 50' haul, sand & gravel	B-10M	1,380	.009			.17	.65	.82	.96	
	5020	Common earth	"	1,200	.010			.19	.75	.94	1.10	

26

Figure 2.2

2.3 Earthwork

		CREW	DAILY OUTPUT	MAN-HOURS	UNIT	MAT.	LABOR	EQUIP.	TOTAL	TOTAL INCL O&P	
190	**2700**	12" wide trench and backfill, 12" deep	B-54	975	.008	L.F.		.16	.20	.36	.45	**190**
	2750	18" deep		860	.009			.18	.22	.40	.51	
	2800	24" deep		800	.010			.20	.24	.44	.55	
	2850	36" deep		725	.011			.22	.27	.49	.61	
	3000	16" wide trench and backfill, 12" deep		900	.009			.17	.21	.38	.49	
	3050	18" deep		750	.011			.21	.26	.47	.59	
	3100	24" deep	↓	700	.011	↓		.22	.28	.50	.63	
	3200	Compaction with vibratory plate, add								50%	50%	
200	**0010**	**FILL** Spread dumped material, no compaction, by dozer	B-10B	1,000	.012	C.Y.		.23	.68	.91	1.09	**200**
	0100	By hand	1 Clab	12	.667	"		10.75		10.75	15.75	
	0150	Spread fill, from stockpile with loader crawler,										
	0170	130 H.P. 300' haul	B-10P	600	.020	C.Y.		.38	1	1.38	1.66	
	0190	With dozer 300 H.P. 300' haul	B-10M	600	.020	"		.38	1.50	1.88	2.21	
	0500	Gravel fill, compacted, under floor slabs, 3" deep	B-14	10,000	.005	S.F.	.05	.08	.02	.15	.20	
	0600	6" deep		9,000	.005		.10	.09	.02	.21	.26	
	0700	9" deep		7,200	.007		.15	.11	.02	.28	.36	
	0800	12" deep	↓	6,000	.008	↓	.20	.14	.03	.37	.45	
	1000	Alternate pricing method, 3" deep		90	.533	C.Y.	8.50	9.10	1.80	19.40	25	
	1100	6" deep		160	.300		8.50	5.10	1.01	14.61	17.95	
	1200	9" deep		200	.240		8.50	4.08	.81	13.39	16.25	
	1300	12" deep	↓	220	.218	↓	8.50	3.71	.74	12.95	15.60	
	1501	For fill under exterior paving, see division 2.6-071										
220	**0010**	**GRADING** Site excav. & fill, not incl. mobilization, demobilization or										**220**
	0020	compaction. Includes ¼ push dozer per scraper.										
	0100	Dozer 300' haul, 75 H.P., = 20 C.Y./hr.	B-10L	160	.075	C.Y.		1.44	1.30	2.74	3.53	
	0200	300 H.P., 70 C.Y./hr.	B-10M	560	.021			.41	1.60	2.01	2.37	
	0400	Scraper, towed, 7 C.Y. 300' haul, 55 C.Y./hr.	B-33A	440	.032			.62	2.77	3.39	3.95	
	0500	1000' haul, 25 C.Y./hr.	"	200	.070			1.36	6.10	7.46	8.70	
	0700	10 C.Y. 300' haul, 85 C.Y./hr.	B-33B	680	.021			.40	1.84	2.24	2.61	
	0800	1000' haul, 50 C.Y./hr.	"	400	.035			.68	3.13	3.81	4.43	
	1000	Self-propelled scraper , 15 C.Y., 1000' haul, 95 C.Y./hr.	B-33D	760	.018			.36	1.60	1.96	2.29	
	1100	2000' haul, 70 C.Y./hr.	"	560	.025			.49	2.17	2.66	3.10	
	1300	25 C.Y. 1000' haul, 200 C.Y./hr.	B-33E	1,600	.009			.17	.84	1.01	1.17	
	1400	2000' haul, 160 C.Y./hr.	"	1,280	.011			.21	1.04	1.25	1.46	
	1600	For dozer with ripper, 200 H.P., add, minimum	B-11A	1,980	.008			.15	.34	.49	.60	
	1700	Add, maximum	"	990	.016			.30	.69	.99	1.19	
	1800	300 H.P., add, minimum	B-10M	3,670	.003			.06	.24	.30	.36	
	1900	Add, maximum	"	1,840	.007	↓		.13	.49	.62	.72	
	2100	Fine grade, 3 passes with motor grader	B-11L	1,600	.010	S.Y.		.18	.30	.48	.60	
	2200	With grader plus rolling	B-32	1,600	.020			.39	.83	1.22	1.49	
	2400	Hand grading, finish	1 Clab	75	.107	↓		1.72		1.72	2.52	
	2500	Rough		130	.062			.99		.99	1.45	
	2520	Alternate pricing method, finish		675	.012	S.F.		.19		.19	.28	
	2540	Rough		1,200	.007	"		.11		.11	.16	
250	**0010**	**GROUTING, CHEMICAL** Soil stabilization, phenolic resin,										**250**
	0020	medium gradation stone, minimum	B-61	10.50	3.810	C.Y.	105	66	26	197	240	
	0100	Average		5.90	6.780		130	115	46	291	365	
	0200	Maximum	↓	3	13.330	↓	140	230	90	460	590	
280	**0010**	**GROUTING, PRESSURE** Cement and sand, 1:1 mix, minimum		124	.323	Bag	6	5.55	2.18	13.73	17.15	**280**
	0100	Maximum		51	.784	"	6.85	13.50	5.30	25.65	33	
	0200	Cement and sand, 1:1 mix, minimum		120	.333	C.F.	4	5.75	2.26	12.01	15.30	
	0300	Maximum		51	.784		5	13.50	5.30	23.80	31	
	0400	Cement grout, minimum (1 bag = 1 C.F.)		137	.292		5.30	5	1.98	12.28	15.35	
	0500	Maximum	↓	57	.702	↓	6.25	12.05	4.75	23.05	30	
	0700	Alternate pricing method: (Add for materials)										
	0710	5 man crew and equipment	B-61	1	40	Day		690	270	960	1,300	
300	**0010**	**HAULING** Earth 6 C.Y. dump truck, ¼ mile round trip, 5.0 loads/hr.	B-34A	240	.033	C.Y.		.57	.90	1.47	1.81	**300**
	0030	½ mile round trip, 4.1 loads/hr.		197	.041			.69	1.10	1.79	2.21	
	0040	1 mile round trip, 3.3 loads/hr. ⑯		160	.050	↓		.85	1.36	2.21	2.72	
	0100	2 mile round trip, 2.6 loads/hr.	↓	125	.064			1.08	1.74	2.82	3.48	

29

Figure 2.3

| **12.1-414** | **Excavate Common Earth**

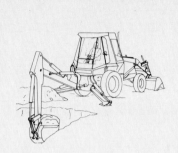

The Excavation of Common Earth System balances the productivity of the excavating equipment to the hauling equipment. It is assumed that the hauling equipment will encounter light traffic and will move up no considerable grades on the haul route. No mobilization cost is included. All costs given in these systems include a swell factor of 25% for hauling.

The Expanded System Listing shows Excavation systems using backhoes ranging from 1/2 Cubic Yard capacity to 3-1/2 Cubic Yards Power shovels indicated range from 1/2 Cubic Yard to 3 Cubic Yards. Dragline bucket rigs range from 1/2 Cubic Yard to 3 Cubic Yards. Truck capacities range from 6 Cubic Yards to 20 Cubic Yards. Each system lists the number of trucks involved and the distance (round trip) that each must travel.

System Components	QUANTITY	UNIT	COST PER C.Y.		
			EQUIP.	LABOR	TOTAL
SYSTEM 12.1-414-1000					
EXCAVATE COMMON EARTH, ½ CY BACKHOE, TWO 6 CY DUMP TRUCKS, 1 MRT					
Excavating, bulk hyd. backhoe wheel mtd., ½ C.Y.	1.000	C.Y.	1.24	1.79	3.03
Haul earth, 6 C.Y. dump truck, 1 mile round trip, 3.3 loads/hr	1.000	C.Y.	1.24	1.03	2.27
Spotter at dump or cut	.020	Hr.		.38	.38
TOTAL			2.48	3.20	5.68

12.1-414	Excavate Common Earth	COST PER C.Y.		
		EQUIP.	LABOR	TOTAL
1000	Excavate common earth, ½ C.Y. backhoe, two 6 C.Y. dump trucks, 1MRT	2.48	3.20	5.68
1200	Three 6 C.Y. dump trucks, 3 mile round trip	4.30	4.76	9.06
1400	Two 12 C.Y. dump trucks, 4 mile round trip	3.83	3.87	7.70
1600	¾ C.Y. backhoe, three C.Y. dump trucks, 1 mile round trip	2.25	2.48	4.73
1700	Five 6 C.Y. dump trucks, 3 mile round trip	3.95	4.07	8.02
1800	Two 12 C.Y. dump trucks, 2 mile round trip	2.95	2.81	5.76
1900	Two 16 C.Y. dump trailers, 3 mile round trip	3.30	2.28	5.58
2000	Two 20 C.Y. dump trailers, 4 mile round trip	3.46	2.43	5.89
2200	1-½ C.Y. backhoe, eight 6 C.Y. dump trucks, 3 mile round trip	3.95	3.44	7.39
2300	Four 12 C.Y. dump trucks, 2 mile round trip	2.73	2.13	4.86
2400	Six 12 C.Y. dump trucks, 4 mile round trip	3.39	2.51	5.90
2500	Three 16 C.Y. dump trailers, 2 mile round trip	3	1.72	4.72
2600	Two 20 C.Y. dump trailers, 1 mile round trip	2.46	1.46	3.92
2700	Three 20 C.Y. dump trailer, 3 mile round trip	3.15	1.74	4.89
2800	2-½ C.Y. backhoe, six 12 C.Y. dump trucks, 1 mile round trip	2.20	1.44	3.64
2900	Eight 12 C.Y. dump trucks, 3 mile round trip	2.88	1.94	4.82
3000	Four 16 C.Y. dump trailers, 1 mile round trip	2.49	1.24	3.73
3100	Six 16 C.Y. dump trailers, 3 mile round trip	3.21	1.60	4.81
3200	Six 20 C.Y. dump trailers, 4 mile round trip	3.24	1.57	4.81
3400	3-½ C.Y. backhoe, six 16 C.Y. dump trailers, 1 mile round trip	2.63	1.12	3.75
3600	Ten 16 C.Y. dump trailers, 4 mile round trip	3.63	1.54	5.17
3800	Eight 20 C.Y. dump trailers, 3 mile round trip	3.09	1.29	4.38
4000	½ C.Y. pwr. shovel, four 6 C.Y. dump trucks, 2 mile round trip	3.27	3.33	6.60
4100	Two 12 C.Y. dump trucks, 1 mile round trip	2.33	2.27	4.60
4200	Four 12 C.Y. dump trucks, 4 mile round trip	3.27	2.76	6.03
4300	Two 16 C.Y. dump trailers, 2 mile round trip	2.86	2.15	5.01
4400	Two 20 C.Y. dump trailers, 4 mile round trip	3.39	2.46	5.85
4500				

252

Figure 2.4

The Cut and Fill Common Earth System includes: moving common earth cut from an area above the specified grade to an area below the specified grade utilizing a bulldozer and/or scraper, with the addition of compaction equipment, plus a water wagon to adjust the moisture content of the soil.

The Expanded System Listing shows Cut and Fill operations with hauling distances that vary from 50' to 5000'. Lifts for compaction in the filled area vary from 4" to 8". There is no waste included in the assumptions.

System Components	QUANTITY	UNIT	COST PER C.Y.		
			EQUIP.	LABOR	TOTAL
SYSTEM 12.1-214-1000					
EARTH CUT & FILL, 75 HP DOZER & COMPACTOR, 50' HAUL, 4" LIFT, 2 PASSES					
Excavating, bulk, dozer & compactor, 50' haul, common earth	1.000	C.Y.	.57	.84	1.41
Water wagon, rent per day	.004	Hr.	.25	.10	.35
Backfill dozer, from existing stockpile, 75 H.P., 50' haul	1.000	C.Y.	.23	.35	.58
Compaction, roller, 4" lifts, 2 passes	1.000	C.Y.	.41	1.48	1.89
TOTAL			1.46	2.77	4.23

12.1-214	Cut & Fill Common Earth	COST PER C.Y.		
		EQUIP.	LABOR	TOTAL
1000	Earth cut & fill,75HP dozer & roller compact, 50' haul, 4" lift, 2 passes	1.46	2.77	4.23
1050	4 passes	2.11	4.35	6.46
1100	8" lift, 2 passes	1.14	2	3.14
1150	4 passes	1.46	2.77	4.23
1200	150' haul, 4" lift, 2 passes	2.26	3.96	6.22
1250	4 passes	2.91	5.55	8.46
1300	8" lift, 2 passes	1.94	3.19	5.13
1350	4 passes	2.26	3.96	6.22
1400	300' haul, 4" lift, 2 passes	5.50	8.75	14.25
1450	4 passes	6.15	10.35	16.50
1500	8" lift, 2 passes	5.20	8	13.20
1550	4 passes	5.50	8.75	14.25
1600	105 H.P. dozer and roller compactor, 50' haul, 4" lift, 2 passes	1.62	2.40	4.02
1650	4 passes	2.27	3.98	6.25
1700	8" lift, 2 passes	1.30	1.63	2.93
1750	4 passes	1.62	2.40	4.02
1800	150' haul, 4" lift, 2 passes	2.74	3.38	6.12
1850	4 passes	3.39	4.96	8.35
1900	8" lift, 2 passes	2.42	2.61	5.03
1950	4 passes	2.74	3.38	6.12
2000	300' haul, 4" lift, 2 passes	4.85	5.20	10.05
2050	4 passes	5.50	6.75	12.25
2100	8" lift, 2 passes	4.53	4.42	8.95
2150	4 passes	4.85	5.20	10.05
2200	200 H.P. dozer & roller compactor, 150' haul, 4" lift, 2 passes	2.86	1.90	4.76
2250	4 passes	3.60	2.82	6.42
2300	8" lift, 2 passes	2.50	1.43	3.93
2350	4 passes	2.86	1.90	4.76

246

Figure 2.5

Bituminous Paving

Asphalt, or bituminous paving, incorporates a number of methods and systems for the installation of walks, roadways and parking lots. Bituminous concrete is composed of carefully graded coarse and fine aggregates, bound together with asphaltic cement. Figure 2.6 shows cost and productivity information for bituminous and other sidewalks from *Means Site Work Cost Data.*

Brick

Brick is a material that has been used for paving for centuries. It is made from kiln-fired clay or shale. It is popular as a paving material because it is easy to produce and readily available in a wide range of sizes, shapes, colors and textures. Brick is graded by weather resistance, a measure of its porosity. Manufacturers also claim slip resistance for certain brick finishes. Most paving brick is suitable as a facing material, but many types of face brick are not appropriate for paving in northern climates. Continuous freeze-thaw cycles and heavy abrasion can damage brick that is not made for paving.

"Pavers" are a type of brick made specifically for outdoor walkway and floor surfaces. They are sized to permit a wide variety of paving patterns, as shown in Figure 2.7. Their thicknesses range from 1-1/8" to 2-1/4". Thin pavers are a cost-effective choice when specifications call for brick walks to be set in a mortar bed.

2.6	Roads & Walks	CREW	DAILY OUTPUT	MAN-HOURS	UNIT	MAT.	LABOR	EQUIP.	TOTAL	TOTAL INCL O&P	
370	0010	**SEALCOATING** 2 coat tar pitch emulsion, over 10,000 S.Y.	B-45	5,000	.003	S.Y.	.31	.06	.10	.47	.54	370
	0100	Under 1000 S.Y.	B-1	1,050	.023		.31	.38		.69	.90	
	0300	Petroleum resistant, over 10,000 S.Y.	B-45	5,000	.003		.45	.06	.10	.61	.70	
	0400	Under 1000 S.Y.	B-1	1,050	.023		.45	.38		.83	1.06	
	0600	Non-skid pavement renewal, over 10,000 S.Y.	B-45	5,000	.003		.50	.06	.10	.66	.75	
	0700	Under 1000 S.Y.	B-1	1,050	.023		.50	.38		.88	1.11	
	0800	Prepare and clean surface for above	A-2	8,545	.003			.05	.01	.06	.07	
	1000	Hand seal bituminous curbing	B-1	4,420	.005	L.F.	.19	.09		.28	.34	
	2000	Stone sealing, ⅜″ stone, asphalt emulsion, small area	B-91	5,000	.013	S.Y.	.50	.24	.18	.92	1.10	
	2040	Large area		10,000	.006		.45	.12	.09	.66	.78	
	2080	Sand sealing, sharp sand, asphalt emulsion, small area		10,000	.006		.40	.12	.09	.61	.72	
	2120	Large area		20,000	.003		.35	.06	.05	.46	.53	
	2200	Slurry sealing, 1 coat, small area	B-90	3,000	.021		.50	.37	.53	1.40	1.67	
	2240	Large area		16,000	.004		1	.07	.10	1.17	1.31	
	2300	2 coats, small area		2,000	.032		1.10	.56	.79	2.45	2.89	
	2340	Large area		11,000	.006		1.10	.10	.14	1.34	1.52	
	3000	Sealing random cracks, min ½″ wide, 1,000 L.F.	B-77	4,800	.007	L.F.	.30	.11	.05	.46	.55	
	3040	10,000 L.F.		7,800	.004	″	.24	.07	.03	.34	.39	
	3080	Alternate method, 1,000 L.F.		200	.160	Gal.	7.10	2.66	1.19	10.95	13	
	3120	10,000 L.F.		325	.098	″	5.70	1.63	.73	8.06	9.45	
	3200	Multi-cracks (flooding), 1 coat, small area	B-92	460	.070	S.Y.	1.65	1.15	.47	3.27	4.04	
	3240	Large area		2,850	.011		1.50	.19	.08	1.77	2.01	
	3280	2 coat, small area		230	.139		3.30	2.31	.95	6.56	8.05	
	3320	Large area		1,425	.022		3	.37	.15	3.52	4.02	
	3360	Alternate method, small area		115	.278	Gal.	6.40	4.62	1.89	12.91	15.90	
	3400	Large area		715	.045	″	6	.74	.30	7.04	8.05	
	3600	Waterproofing, membrane, tar and fabric, small area	B-63	233	.172	S.Y.	4.25	2.88	.36	7.49	9.30	
	3640	Large area		1,435	.028		3.95	.47	.06	4.48	5.10	
	3680	Preformed rubberized asphalt, small area		100	.400		5.30	6.70	.83	12.83	16.60	
	3720	Large area		367	.109		4.80	1.83	.23	6.86	8.20	
400	0010	**SIDEWALKS** Bituminous, no base included, 2″ thick	B-37	720	.067		3	1.13	.12	4.25	5.10	400
	0100	2-½″ thick	″	660	.073		3.75	1.24	.13	5.12	6.10	
	0110	Bedding for brick, mortar, 1″ thick	D-1	300	.053	S.F.	.22	.98		1.20	1.65	
	0120	2″ thick	″	200	.080		.44	1.47		1.91	2.59	
	0130	Sand, 2″ thick	B-18	8,000	.003		.07	.05		.12	.16	
	0140	4″ thick	″	4,000	.006		.14	.10	.01	.25	.31	
	0160	Brick pavers, 4.15 per S.F., 1-¾″ thick	D-1	240	.067		1.50	1.22		2.72	3.41	
	0170	2-¼″ thick		240	.067		1.62	1.22		2.84	3.54	
	0200	Laid on edge, 7.2 per S.F. (see also 2.6-150)		70	.229		2.92	4.19		7.11	9.25	
	0250	For 4″ thick concrete bed and joints, add		595	.027		.72	.49		1.21	1.50	
	0280	For steam cleaning, add	A-1	950	.008		.05	.14	.04	.23	.31	
	0290											
	0300	Concrete, 3000 psi, cast in place with 6 x 6 - #10/10 mesh,										
	0310	broomed finish, no base, 4″ thick	B-24	600	.040	S.F.	.86	.75		1.61	2.04	
	0350	5″ thick		545	.044		1.03	.83		1.86	2.33	
	0400	6″ thick		510	.047		1.20	.88		2.08	2.60	
	0450	For bank run gravel base, 4″ thick, add	B-18	2,500	.010		.10	.16	.02	.28	.36	
	0520	8″ thick, add	″	1,600	.015		.20	.25	.02	.47	.62	
	0550	Exposed aggregate finish, add to above, minimum	B-24	1,875	.013		.06	.24		.30	.42	
	0600	Maximum	″	455	.053		.18	.99		1.17	1.64	
	0710	Precast concrete patio blocks, 2″ thick, colors, 8″ x 16″	D-1	265	.060		.59	1.11		1.70	2.24	
	0720	16″ x 16″		335	.048		.86	.88		1.74	2.21	
	0730	24″ x 24″		510	.031		1.10	.58		1.68	2.04	
	0740	Green, 8″ x 16″		265	.060		.83	1.11		1.94	2.50	
	0750	Exposed local aggregate, natural		265	.060		1.90	1.11		3.01	3.68	
	0800	Colors		265	.060		2.10	1.11		3.21	3.90	
	0850	Exposed granite or limestone aggregate		265	.060		1.90	1.11		3.01	3.68	
	0900	Exposed white tumblestone aggregate		265	.060		1.94	1.11		3.05	3.72	
	0910	Paving stone, interlocking, 2-½″ thick		240	.067		1.84	1.22		3.06	3.78	
	0920	3-¼″ thick		240	.067		2.10	1.22		3.32	4.07	

65

Figure 2.6

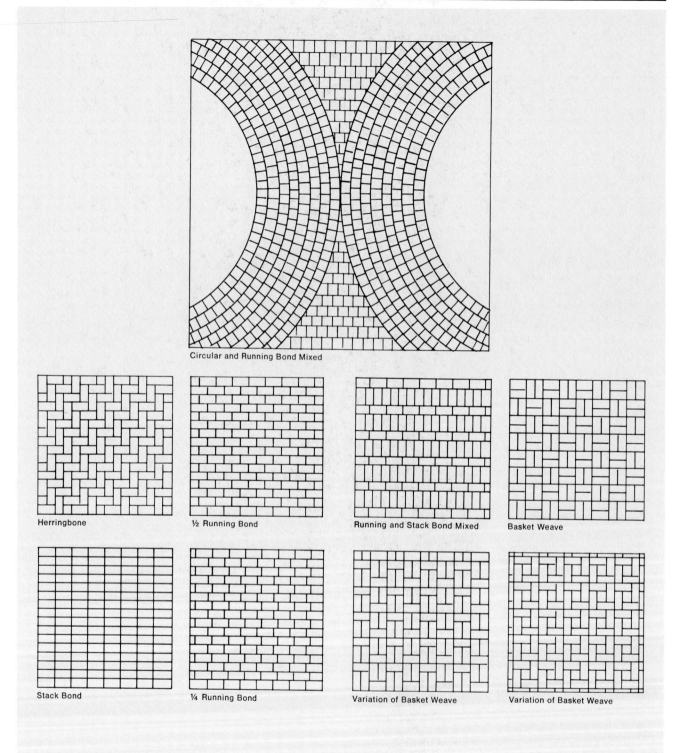

Circular and Running Bond Mixed

Herringbone

½ Running Bond

Running and Stack Bond Mixed

Basket Weave

Stack Bond

¼ Running Bond

Variation of Basket Weave

Variation of Basket Weave

Brick Paving Patterns

(courtesy Brick Institute of America)

Figure 2.7

Brick has many other applications in landscaping beyond its use for paving. The most obvious of these is its use for many types of walls. Some projects showing the versatility of brick in landscape design are shown in Figures 2.8, 2.9, and 2.10. Although brick is long-lasting, other materials are cheaper to purchase and apply. Brick does offer other advantages, such as the fact that it is easy to work with in small areas and can often be used in combination with other paving materials. It can also "match" brick buildings. In large areas, however, brick is costly to install and bulk materials such as concrete or asphalt paving are considerably less expensive. Figure 2.11, from *Means Site Work Cost Data*, 1987, shows the cost variation for different types of paving materials.

The terminology for brick surfaces, positions, and courses is illustrated in Figures 2.12 and 2.13.

Brick Enclosures

Figure 2.8

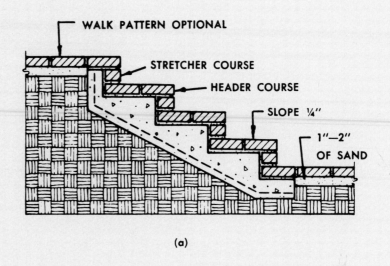

(a)

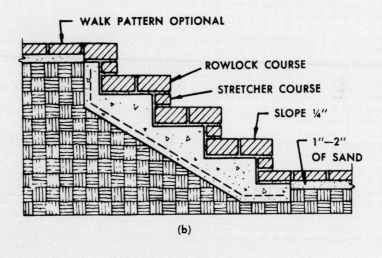

(b)

Brick Step Configurations

(courtesy Brick Institute of America)

Figure 2.9

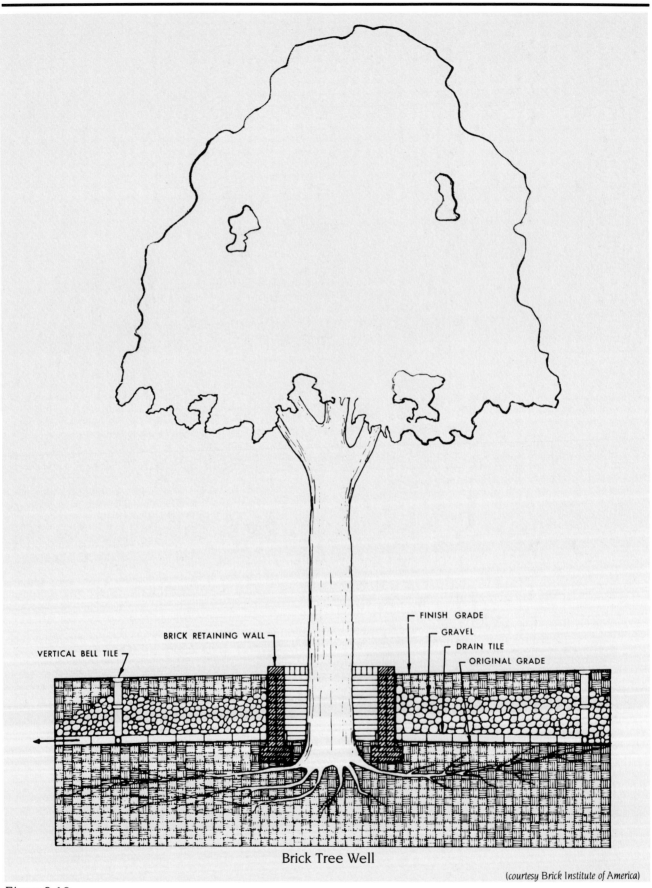

VERTICAL BELL TILE

BRICK RETAINING WALL

FINISH GRADE

GRAVEL

DRAIN TILE

ORIGINAL GRADE

Brick Tree Well

(courtesy Brick Institute of America)

Figure 2.10

28

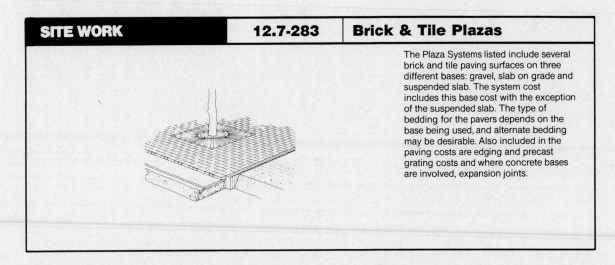

The Plaza Systems listed include several brick and tile paving surfaces on three different bases: gravel, slab on grade and suspended slab. The system cost includes this base cost with the exception of the suspended slab. The type of bedding for the pavers depends on the base being used, and alternate bedding may be desirable. Also included in the paving costs are edging and precast grating costs and where concrete bases are involved, expansion joints.

System Components	QUANTITY	UNIT	COST PER S.F.		
			MAT.	INST.	TOTAL
SYSTEM 12.7-283-2050					
PLAZA, BRICK PAVERS, 4″ X 8″ X 1-½″, GRAVEL BASE, STONE DUST BED					
Compact subgrade, static roller, 4 passes	.111	S.Y.		.07	.07
Bank gravel, 2 mi haul, dozer spread	.012	C.Y.	.05	.04	.09
Compact gravel base, vibrating plate	.012	C.Y.		.02	.02
Grading fine grade, 3 passes with grader	.111	S.Y.		.17	.17
Stone dust, 1″ thick, skid steer loader spread	.003	C.Y.	.03	.03	.06
Compact bedding, vibrating plate	.003	C.Y.		.01	.01
Brick paver, 4″ x 8″ x 1-¾″	4.150	Ea.	1.65	1.76	3.41
Brick edging, stood on end, 6 per L.F.	.060	L.F.	.12	.26	.38
Precast conc tree grating	.004	Ea.	.71	.13	.84
TOTAL			2.56	2.48	5.04

12.7-283	Brick & Tile Plazas	COST PER S.F.		
		MAT.	INST.	TOTAL
1050	Plaza, asphalt pavers, 6″ x 12″ x 1-¼″, gravel base, asphalt bedding	3.08	1.40	4.48
1100	Slab on grade, asphalt bedding	6.50	4.74	11.24
1150	Suspended slab, insulated & mastic bedding	7.20	6.70	13.90
1300	6″ x 12″ x 3″, gravel base, asphalt, bedding	5.80	2.18	7.98
1350	Slab on grade, asphalt bedding	5.85	4.52	10.37
1400	Suspended slab, insulated & mastic bedding	8.45	6.85	15.30
2050	Brick pavers, 4″ x 8″ x 1-½″, gravel base, stone dust bedding	2.56	2.48	5.04
2100	Slab on grade, asphalt bedding	3.63	3.02	6.65
2150	Suspended slab, insulated & no bedding	4.26	3.55	7.81
2300	4″ x 8″ x 2-¼″, gravel base, stone dust bedding	2.69	2.48	5.17
2350	Slab on grade, asphalt bedding	3.76	3.02	6.78
2400	Suspended slab, insulated & no bedding	4.39	3.55	7.94
2550	Brick shale pavers, 4″ x 8″ x 2-¼″, gravel base, stone dust bedding	2.45	2.83	5.28
2600	Slab on grade, asphalt bedding	3.52	3.37	6.89
2650	Suspended slab, insulated & no bedding	4.39	3.55	7.94
3050	Brick thin set tile, 4″ x 4″ x ⅜″, slab on grade, mortar bedding	4.16	2.76	6.92
3300	4″ x 4″ x ¾″, slab on grade, mortar bedding	5.70	2.85	8.55
3550	Concrete paving stone, 4″ x 8″ x 2-½″, gravel base, sand bedding	3.06	2.46	5.52
3600	Slab on grade, asphalt bedding	4.08	2.94	7.02
3650	Suspended slab, insulated & no bedding	4.50	3.89	8.39
3800	4″ x 8″ x 3-¼″, gravel base, sand bedding	3.35	2.46	5.81
3850	Slab on grade, asphalt bedding	4.37	2.94	7.31

288

Figure 2.11

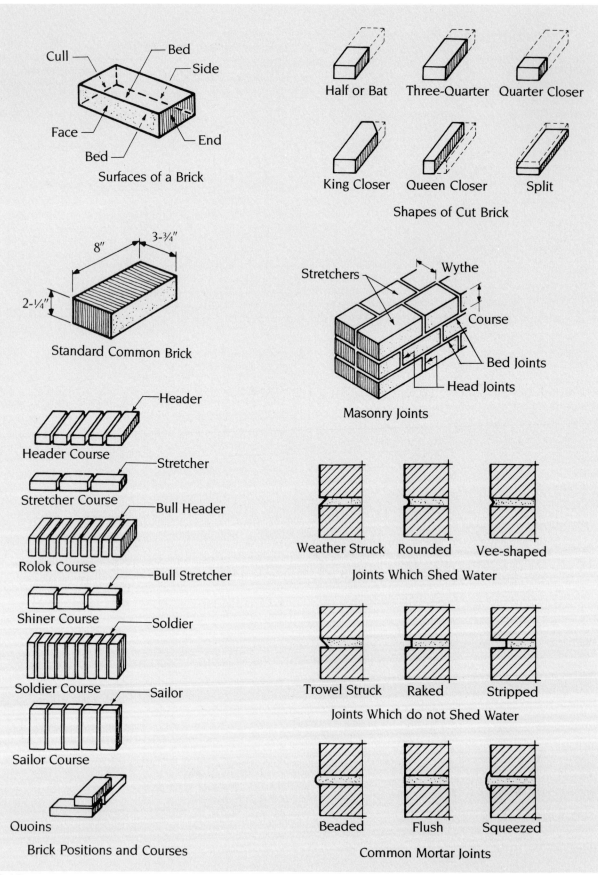

Surfaces of a Brick

Shapes of Cut Brick

Half or Bat Three-Quarter Quarter Closer

King Closer Queen Closer Split

Standard Common Brick

8" 3-¾" 2-¼"

Masonry Joints

Stretchers Wythe Course Bed Joints Head Joints

Brick Positions and Courses

Header Course — Header
Stretcher Course — Stretcher
Rolok Course — Bull Header
Shiner Course — Bull Stretcher
Soldier Course — Soldier
Sailor Course — Sailor
Quoins

Joints Which Shed Water

Weather Struck Rounded Vee-shaped

Joints Which do not Shed Water

Trowel Struck Raked Stripped

Common Mortar Joints

Beaded Flush Squeezed

Figure 2.12

Running or Stretcher Bond	The face brick are all stretchers and are tied to the backing by metal or reinforcing. Waste – 5%.
Common or American Bond	Every sixth course of stretcher bond is usually a header course. Waste – 4%.
Flemish Bond	Each course has alternate headers and stretchers with the alternate headers centered over the stretcher. Waste – 3 to 5%.
English Bond	Consists of alternate headers and stretchers with the vertical joints in the header and stretcher aligning or breaking over each other. Waste – 8 to 15%.
Stack Bond	Has no overlapping of units since all vertical joints are aligned. Usually this pattern is bonded to the backing with rigid steel ties. Waste – 3%.
English Cross or Dutch Bond	Built up of interlocking crosses. This wall consists of two headers and a stretcher forming a cross. Waste – 8%.

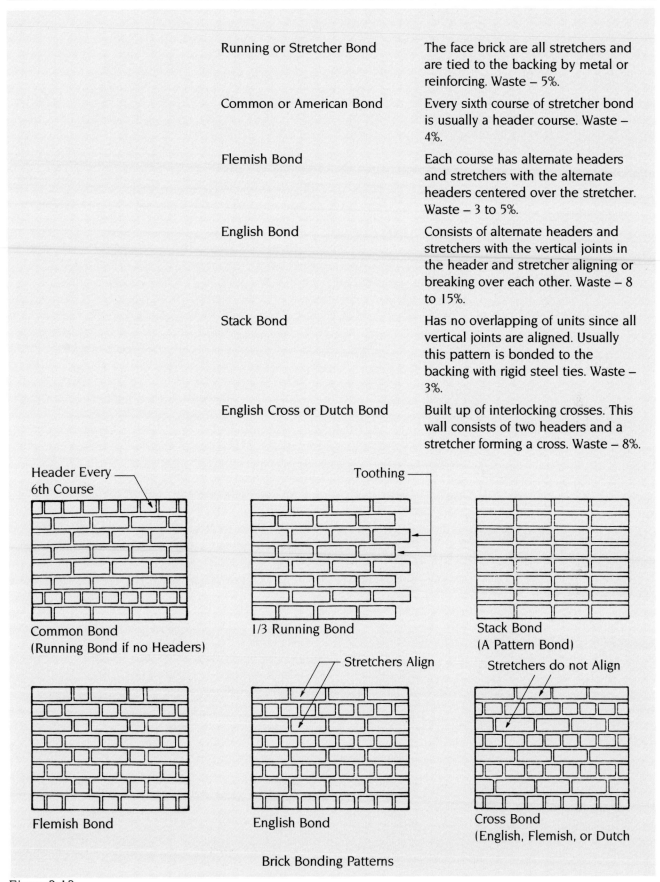

Header Every 6th Course

Common Bond
(Running Bond if no Headers)

Toothing

1/3 Running Bond

Stack Bond
(A Pattern Bond)

Flemish Bond

Stretchers Align

English Bond

Stretchers do not Align

Cross Bond
(English, Flemish, or Dutch

Brick Bonding Patterns

Figure 2.13

A table listing the dimensions of available brick sizes can be found in the Materials section of the Appendix.

Other masonry units have gained the interest and approval of designers and builders. Among the more popular types are building and paving blocks of concrete, adobe, and glass. Concrete block is functional for a range of uses - from rugged walls to lacy wall screens. "Turf blocks", a type of concrete paver with openings or slots for growing grass turf, are popular in appropriate climates and conditions. Glass block is available in a range of styles and functions. Adobe, a kind of mud brick, is also a good choice for decorative use or special effect. Manufacturers of these products may provide illustrations, literature, and samples. Trade shows are forums for these products.

Concrete

Concrete is a composite material. It consists essentially of a binding medium called cement, combined with sand, aggregate, and sufficient water to make the mixture workable. When cured, concrete attains a hardness not unlike stone. It is usually specified and ordered in the minimum compressive strength required (after curing for 28 days), varying from 2,500 p.s.i. to 6,000, or even 7,000 p.s.i. A rule of thumb for a field mixed 3000 p.s.i. concrete is one part cement, 2 parts sand, 4 parts stone, and no more than 6 gallons of water per 100 lbs of cement. An air entrainment additive is advised for exposed exterior concrete. Concrete is a good compressive material, but usually requires steel or glass fiber reinforcing to function in tension.

Concrete is a very versatile material. It may be mixed in bulk and placed in forms of wood, steel, aluminum or glass fiber to achieve any desired shape or surface. Concrete is also available in a great variety of precast units. The exposed surface may be finished with techniques such as steel trowel, wood float or broom, and the hardened concrete surface may be sand blasted or bush hammered to achieve various textures. Partially set concrete may be carved to achieve a sculpted effect.

Many concrete materials can be used for paving and other landscape applications. Concrete toppings or coatings are presented by manufacturers as solutions to problems generated by certain uses or conditions of paved surfaces. Patterned concrete may be cast in place by a number of proprietary systems used in the industry; one of these is "Bomanite", a specially finished concrete paving system. Concrete pavers can be formed in a wide range of textures and finishes. Interlocking concrete pavers find wide application and allow designers to use an arrangement other than parallel lines. Figure 2.14 is a concrete sidewalk system from *Means Site Work Cost Data*, 1987.

See Appendix D for references for concrete and masonry products and construction.

Stone

Stone is nature's most enduring material. Stone pavers are available as blocks and modules. Because of its beauty and durability, stone is often used for stair treads, borders, and coping. Stone is well suited to irregular floor patterns that can utilize "quarry run" irregular lines. Stone for paving is graded by:

- Hardness (U.S. Government standards)
- Porosity
- Abrasion resistance

Stone is used cut or uncut, and the varieties and applications of each type are many. See Figure 2.15 for some examples of stone face types. Uncut (rubble) stone is available with rough or smoothly worn surfaces. Examples are roughly broken quarry stone and smooth "river rock" stone. Both are usually measured and priced by weight (ton). Rubble stone is used for uncoursed work and often for fillings; river rock may be prized for Japanese garden effects. Cut stone is available in varieties ranging from roughly squared blocks to uniform ashlar; the latter may be laid like brick in walls or used for elegant paving. Ashlar may be squared and dressed in various finishes. Facing (veneer) applications are also common for costly finish stone. Fully trimmed ashlar is measured by the surface face in square feet or square yards. It is priced on these measurements as well as by its thickness. Stone block may be sold by unit price. Stone quarries and dealers may offer stone cut to measure, and can recommend sizes and corresponding thickness for paving. Unit price stone costs and a variety of stonework systems are included in *Means Site Work Cost Data*. An example, a stone retaining wall system, is shown in Figure 2.16.

Synthetic stone has many economical applications. Veneers made of concrete mixtures are often so like the real thing that most stoneyards promote their cost and labor saving qualities. The relatively light weight of synthetic stone veneers is a great economy feature as well. Imitation stone block resembles natural stone, costs much less, and is available in a variety of shapes, colors, and textures.

Tile

Tiles are baked clay units of various shapes, and can be glazed or unglazed. They are available in a wide range of colors, shapes and finishes, including skid-resistant finishes. The non-porous quality of glazed tile makes it very useful for certain kinds of applications. Small units, while labor intensive, are easy to handle and to work with in areas where space is limited. Tile has an ornamental character and is sometimes used as a decorative material. Like brick, it is graded for weather resistance.

Wood

Wood and wood products are used in the construction of many outdoor floors, walks, fences and steps. Wood is a strong and durable material for its weight. Pressure-treated wood or that which has specific decay-, insect-, and weather-resistant qualities, is most often specified for landscape construction. Plywood is a wood product, that may be used for outdoor projects. Depending on the application, "exterior" or "marine" grade plywood may be required. Hardboard, often called "HDO" or "MDO" (high or medium density overlay), is another wood product with many outdoor applications. It is tempered to resist moisture and weathering in outdoor use, and is commonly used for highway signage, both for traffic and advertising.

Figure 2.17 is a chart showing a broad classification of commonly used domestic woods according to their characteristics and properties. Many lumber species will provide good service in a wood deck. Still, some are better suited for the purpose than others. Usual wood characteristics necessary for decking and other outdoor applications include: high decay resistance, non-splintering grain, good stiffness, strength, wear-resistance, and freedom from warping. Woods with many of these characteristics include: cypress, white oak, locust, Douglas-fir, western larch, redwood, cedar, and southern pine.

SITE WORK	12.7-140	Concrete Sidewalks

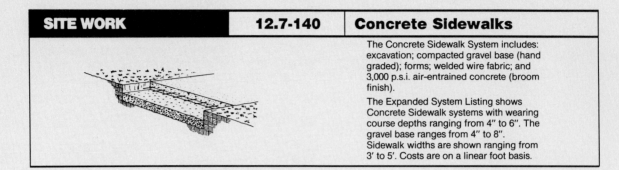

The Concrete Sidewalk System includes: excavation; compacted gravel base (hand graded); forms; welded wire fabric; and 3,000 p.s.i. air-entrained concrete (broom finish).

The Expanded System Listing shows Concrete Sidewalk systems with wearing course depths ranging from 4″ to 6″. The gravel base ranges from 4″ to 8″. Sidewalk widths are shown ranging from 3′ to 5′. Costs are on a linear foot basis.

System Components	QUANTITY	UNIT	COST PER L.F.		
			MAT.	INST.	TOTAL
SYSTEM 12.7-140-1580					
CONCRETE, SIDEWALK 4″ THICK, 4″ GRAVEL BASE, 3′ WIDE					
Excavation, box out with dozer	.100	C.Y.		.14	.14
Gravel base, haul 2 miles, spread with dozer	.037	C.Y.	.14	.13	.27
Compaction with vibrating plate	.037	C.Y.		.12	.12
Fine grade by hand	.333	S.Y.		.84	.84
Concrete in place including forms and reinforcing	.037	C.Y.	2.56	1.51	4.07
Backfill edges by hand	.010	C.Y.		.14	.14
TOTAL			2.70	2.88	5.58

12.7-140	Concrete Sidewalks	COST PER L.F.		
		MAT.	INST.	TOTAL
1580	Concrete sidewalk, 4″ thick, 4″ gravel base, 3′ wide	2.70	2.88	5.58
1600	4′ wide	3.59	3.75	7.34
1620	5′ wide	4.54	4.68	9.22
1640	6″ gravel base, 3′ wide	2.78	3.03	5.81
1660	4′ wide	3.68	3.95	7.63
1680	5′ wide	4.66	4.93	9.59
1700	8″ gravel base, 3′ wide	2.84	3.17	6.01
1720	4′ wide	3.78	4.15	7.93
1740	5′ wide	4.77	5.15	9.92
1800	5″ thick concrete, 4″ gravel base, 3′ wide	3.33	3.32	6.65
1820	4′ wide	4.49	4.36	8.85
1840	5′ wide	5.60	5.40	11
1860	6″ gravel base, 3′ wide	3.41	3.47	6.88
1900	5′ wide	5.70	5.65	11.35
1920	8″ gravel base, 3′ wide	3.47	3.61	7.08
1940	4′ wide	4.68	4.77	9.45
1960	5′ wide	5.80	5.85	11.65
2120	6″ thick concrete, 4″ gravel base, 3′ wide	3.84	2.97	6.81
2140	4′ wide	5.05	3.83	8.88
2160	5′ wide	6.40	4.74	11.14
2180	6″ gravel base, 3′ wide	3.92	3.12	7.04
2200	4′ wide	5.15	4.03	9.18
2220	5′ wide	6.50	4.99	11.49
2240	8″ gravel base, 3′ wide	3.98	3.27	7.25
2260	4′ wide	5.25	4.24	9.49
2280	5′ wide	6.60	5.25	11.85

284

Figure 2.14

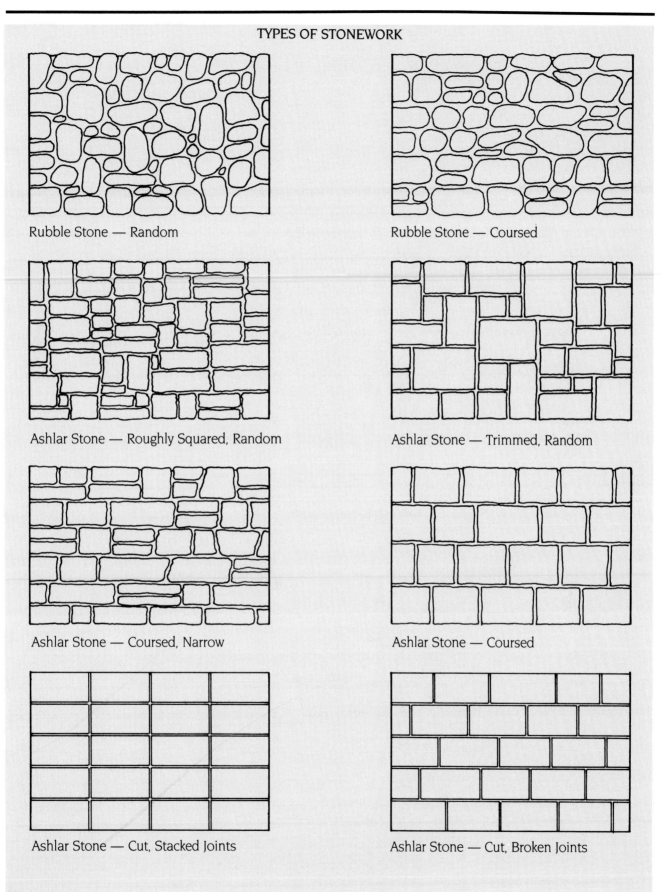

Rubble Stone — Random

Rubble Stone — Coursed

Ashlar Stone — Roughly Squared, Random

Ashlar Stone — Trimmed, Random

Ashlar Stone — Coursed, Narrow

Ashlar Stone — Coursed

Ashlar Stone — Cut, Stacked Joints

Ashlar Stone — Cut, Broken Joints

Figure 2.15

Stone Retaining Walls

The Stone Retaining Wall System is constructed of one of four types of stone. Each of the four types is listed in terms of cost per ton. Construction is either dry set or mortar set. System elements include excavation; concrete base; crushed stone; underdrain; and backfill.

The Expanded System Listing shows five heights above grade for each type, ranging from 3' above grade to 12' above grade.

System Components	QUANTITY	UNIT	COST PER L.F.		
			MAT.	INST.	TOTAL
SYSTEM 12.7-360-2400					
STONE RETAINING WALL, DRY SET, STONE AT $16.00/TON, 3' ABOVE GRADE					
Excavation, trench, hyd backhoe	.880	C.Y.		3	3
Concrete in place incl. forms and reinf. strip footings, 36" x 12"	.111	C.Y.	8.42	6.56	14.98
Setting stone wall, dry	6.550	C.F.	5.72	27.64	33.36
Stone borrow, delivered, ⅜", machine spread	.320	C.Y.	5.10	1.12	6.22
Piping, subdrainage, perforated bituminous fiber, 4" diameter	1.000	L.F.	1.54	1.41	2.95
Backfill with dozer, trench, up to 300' haul, no compaction	1.019	C.Y.		1.23	1.23
TOTAL			20.78	40.96	61.74

12.7-360	Stone Retaining Walls	COST PER L.F.		
		MAT.	INST.	TOTAL
2400	Stone retaining wall, dry set, stone at $16.00/ton, height above grade 3'	21	41	62
2420	Height above grade 4'	23	49	72
2440	Height above grade 6'	26	65	91
2460	Height above grade 8'	33	100	133
2480	Height above grade 10'	38	130	168
2500	Height above grade 12'	44	165	209
2600	$32.00/ton stone, height above grade 3'	27	41	68
2620	Height above grade 4'	30	49	79
2640	Height above grade 6'	37	65	102
2660	Height above grade 8'	49	100	149
2680	Height above grade 10'	60	130	190
2700	Height above grade 12'	72	165	237
2800	$48.00/ton stone, height above grade 3'	32	41	73
2820	Height above grade 4'	38	49	87
2840	Height above grade 6'	47	65	112
2860	Height above grade 8'	65	100	165
2880	Height above grade 10'	82	130	212
2900	Height above grade 12'	100	165	265
3000	$64.00/ton stone, height above grade 3'	38	41	79
3020	Height above grade 4'	45	49	94
3040	Height above grade 6'	58	65	123
3060	Height above grade 8'	81	100	181
3080	Height above grade 10'	105	130	235
3100	Height above grade 12'	125	165	290
5020	Mortar set, stone at $16.00/ton, height above grade 3'	21	36	57
5040	Height above grade 4'	23	43	66

295

Figure 2.16

Landscape timbers and railroad ties are sold by the unit. Lumber is priced and sold by the board foot. A board 1" thick by 12" wide and 12" long, equals one board foot. To find the number of board feet in a piece of lumber, multiply thickness in inches times width in inches, times length in feet. Then divide by twelve. For example, a 2x8 board that is 10 feet long has 13.3 board feet: 2"x8"x10' = 160 ÷ 12 = 13.3 Board Feet. Figure 2.18 is a chart of dimensional lumber converted to board feet.

Broad Classification of Woods According to Characteristics and Properties[1]										
	Working and Behavior Characteristics							Strength Properties		
Kind of Wood	Hardness	Freedom from Warping	Ease of Working	Paint Holding	Nail Holding	Decay Resistance of Heartwood	Proportion of Heartwood	Bending Strength	Stiffness	Strength as a Post	Freedom from Pitch
Ash	A	B	C	C	A	C	C	A	A	A	A
Western Red Cedar	C	A	A	A	C	A	A	C	C	B	A
Cypress	B	B	B	A	B	A	B	B	B	B	A
Douglas-fir, Larch	B	B	B-C	C	A	B	A	A	A	A	B
Gum	B	C	B	C	A	B	B	B	A	B	A
Hemlock, White Fir[2]	B-C	B	B	C	C	C	C	B	A	B	A
Soft Pine[3]	C	A	A	A	C	C	B	C	C	C	B
Southern Pine	B	B	B	C	A	B	C	A	A	A	C
Poplar	C	A	B	A	B	C	B	B	B	B	A
Redwood	B	A	B	A	B	A	A	B	B	A	A
Spruce	C	A-B	B	B	B	C	C	B	B	B	A

[1]A — among the woods relatively high in the particular respect listed; B — among woods intermediate in that respect; C — among woods relatively low in that respect. Letters do not refer to lumber grades.

[2]Includes west coast and eastern hemlocks.

[3]Includes the western and northeastern pines.

(courtesy U.S. Dept of Agriculture)

Figure 2.17

37

Perhaps the most prevalent use of wood in landscape construction today is for decks. Figure 2.19 shows an illustrated wood deck system from *Means Site Work Cost Data*, 1987.

Further data on the uses of wood can be obtained from many wood trade associations, universities, and wood research laboratories; some of these organizations and their addresses are listed in Appendix D.

Board Feet & Measure	
Nominal Dimension	Board Feet
1 x 1	.08
1 x 2	.17
1 x 3	.25
1 x 4	.33
1 x 6	.50
1 x 8	.67
1 x 10	.83
1 x 12	1.00
2 x 2	.33
2 x 4	.67
2 x 6	1.00
2 x 8	1.33
2 x 10	1.67
2 x 12	2.00
3 x 2	.50
3 x 4	1.00
3 x 6	1.50
3 x 8	2.00
3 x 10	2.50
3 x 12	3.00
3 x 16	4.00
4 x 2	.67
4 x 4	1.33
4 x 6	2.00
4 x 8	2.67
4 x 10	3.33
4 x 12	4.00
6 x 6	3.00
6 x 8	4.00
8 x 8	5.34

Figure 2.18

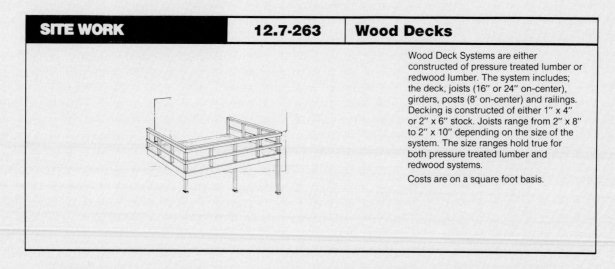

Wood Deck Systems are either constructed of pressure treated lumber or redwood lumber. The system includes; the deck, joists (16″ or 24″ on-center), girders, posts (8′ on-center) and railings. Decking is constructed of either 1″ x 4″ or 2″ x 6″ stock. Joists range from 2″ x 8″ to 2″ x 10″ depending on the size of the system. The size ranges hold true for both pressure treated lumber and redwood systems.

Costs are on a square foot basis.

System Components	QUANTITY	UNIT	COST PER S.F.		
			MAT.	INST.	TOTAL
SYSTEM 12.7-263-1000					
WOOD DECK, TREATED LUMBER, 2″X8″ JOISTS @ 16″ O.C., 2″X6″ DECKING					
Decking, planks, fir 2″ x 6″ treated	2.080	B.F.	1.06	2.11	3.17
Framing, joists, fir 2″ x 8″ treated	1.330	B.F.	.71	1.12	1.83
Framing, beams, fir 2″ x 10″ treated	.133	B.F.	.07	.10	.17
Framing, post, 4″ x 4″, treated	.333	B.F.	.21	.28	.49
Framing, railing, 2″ x 4″ lumber, treated	.667	B.F.	.33	.95	1.28
Footing, concrete, incl. excavation	.002	C.Y.	.16	.32	.48
TOTAL			2.55	4.87	7.42

12.7-263	Wood Decks	COST PER S.F.		
		MAT.	INST.	TOTAL
1000	Wood deck, treated lumber, 2″ x 8″ joists @ 16″ O.C., 2″ x 6″ decking	2.55	4.87	7.42
1004	2″ x 4″ decking	1.48	2.76	4.24
1008	1″ x 6″ decking	3.39	3.65	7.04
1012	1″ x 4″ decking	3.21	3.70	6.91
1500	2″ x 10″ joists @ 16″ O.C., 2″ x 6″ decking	2.73	5.15	7.88
1504	2″ x 4″ decking	2.79	6.30	9.09
1508	1″ x 6″ decking	3.57	4.08	7.65
1512	1″ x 4″ decking	3.39	3.99	7.38
1560	2″ x 10″ joists @ 24″ O.C., 2″ x 6″ decking	2.55	4.87	7.42
1564	2″ x 4″ decking	2.61	6	8.61
1568	1″ x 6″ decking	3.39	3.79	7.18
1572	1″ x 4″ decking	3.21	3.70	6.91
4000	Redwood lumber, 2″ x 8″ joists @ 16″ O.C., 2″ x 6″ decking	3.08	2.66	5.74
4004	2″ x 4″ decking	3.21	2.99	6.20
4008	1″ x 6″ decking	4.08	2.83	6.91
4012	1″ x 4″ decking	3.99	2.78	6.77
4500	2″ x 10″ joists @ 16″ O.C., 2″ x 6″ decking	3.77	2.74	6.51
4504	2″ x 4″ decking	3.89	3.07	6.96
4508	1″ x 6″ decking	4.76	2.91	7.67
4512	1″ x 4″ decking	4.67	2.86	7.53
4600	2″ x 10″ joists @ 24″ O.C., 2″ x 6″ decking	3.48	2.62	6.10
4612	2″ x 4″ decking	3.60	2.95	6.55
4616	1″ x 6″ decking	4.47	2.79	7.26
4620	1″ x 4″ decking	4.38	2.75	7.13

287

Figure 2.19

Earthen Materials

The type of earthen materials, such as sand, topsoil, and gravel will be a large factor in equipment selection. The other major factor is the work to be done, i.e., excavation, use on site, hauling away, "borrow" (brought to the site), and/or compacting. Characteristics such as weight and comparative volume of excavated material vary depending on moisture content and compaction. Soil volume is determined by its state in the earthmoving process. The three measures of soil volume are:

BCY - Bank Cubic Yard: one cubic yard of material as it lies undisturbed in the natural state.

LCY - Loose Cubic Yard: one cubic yard of material that has been disturbed and has swelled as a result of excavation.

CCY - Compacted Cubic Yard: one cubic yard of material that has been compacted and has thereby decreased in volume.

The illustration in Figure 2.20 shows comparative volumes for common earth. The tables show characteristics of various soil types. Additional charts on materials and measures can be found in the Appendix.

Crushed stone and gravel are measured and sold on the same basis as earthen materials, that is, by weight (ton) or by volume (cubic yard). Costs for loading and hauling earthen material are provided annually in *Means Site Work Cost Data* (see Figure 2.21 for a typical 1987 listing).

Planting

Plantings are among the first materials the landscape professional promotes. The selection of the right plant for the right place is both a technical and an aesthetic issue. Much horticultural information and many services are provided to the landscape industry from both public and private sources. Public information and services exist on a federal, state, and local level. The wise professional in the field keeps up to date with local agencies such as county offices of the U.S. Department of Agriculture, and with state university cooperative extension services and publications.

Ornamental plants chosen for landscaping must also pass horticultural requirements and fit specific site conditions and climate restrictions. Fortunately, the ornamental plant growing industries have their own information and promotion campaigns, and rely greatly on the needs and approval of the landscape industry. In addition, there are many excellent guides and references to the selection, use, function, and installation of plants; a list of recommended sources is given in Appendix C. Also consider advice from your local nurseryman, landscape architect, or landscape gardener. Some nurserymen's catalogues are widely used as references within the industry. A selection of these catalogues is included in the above mentioned reference list. The most accurate and relevant of all sources are local suppliers.

The nursery industry generally conforms to certain industry-wide classifications. One uniform classification is "plant hardiness", generally referred to in terms of geographical zones. Based on the USDA Plant Hardiness Zone Map, Figure 2.22, growers classify their plants by the farthest north zone where the plant may be expected to survive with vigor. The lower the zone number, the hardier the plant. Figure 2.23 (courtesy *Architectural Graphic Standards*, 6th edition, 1970), a chart of major and minor trees and shrubs, indicates the appropriate hardiness zones for each tree and shrub. The chart also shows tree shape and expected height at 10 years, mature height and spread, leaf color, latin names, and recommendations for use in street planting.

Regional climate has the greatest impact on the use of specific plants. Many fine books and gardening encyclopedias are available on the characteristics and culture of plants. No attempt will be made in this book to adequately cover this subject. Indeed, "horticulture is a very large field" General categories of plant types may be listed as:

> Trees — evergreen or deciduous
> Shrubs — evergreen or deciduous
> Herbaceous Plants, such as perennial and annual flowers
> Ground Covers and Vines, which may be evergreen, deciduous or herbaceous

The fact that plants are growing and changing over time gives them dramatic and unique characteristics that we may label and put into categories. Examples of these characteristics are described below.

Evergreen Plants

This category may include trees, shrubs, flowers and vines. The term "evergreen" is merely a broad definition meaning that leaves remain on the plant in a green condition throughout the year. Some are called "narrow-leaved", such as pines, and some are called "broad leaved", such as box and many types of rhododendron. Some plants will be evergreen in the south, but lose their leaves in the winter in the north. In addition, many low ground covers are evergreen in the north, as are some succulent plants in all climates.

Decidous Plants

Decidous plants have leaves that fall; they do not remain on the plant throughout the year. Examples are maple trees, lilac shrubs, and grape vines. Many useful lists of plants for special situations have been drawn up by horticulturists. Figure 2.23 is a good example. A list of other references is included in the Appendix.

Once the design has been created, certain standards are used as a basis for selecting and purchasing plant materials. The measurement of plants involves several approaches. For example, field-grown plants are measured differently than those grown in containers. Field-grown plants are specified by landscape architects as "balled and burlapped" ("B&B") and are dug from growing fields with their roots intact in an earthen ball. The ball is then protected and packaged with wire, ropes, and cloth as appropriate. Such "B&B" plants are measured by their height or width or a combination of both, exclusive of the earthen ball. For example, a juniper of upright growth habit (as shown in Figure 2.24 is measured by its height, while a juniper of spreading growth is measured by its width. Some plants are measured by both dimensions, such as a rhododendron 3' high and 2-1/2' wide.

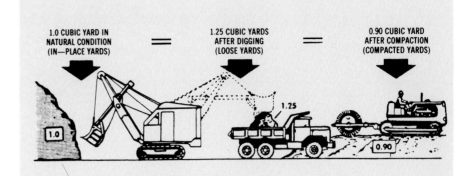

Approximate Material Characteristics*				
Material	Loose (lb/cu yd)	Bank (lb/cu yd)	Swell (%)	Load Factor
Clay, dry	2,100	2,650	26	0.79
Clay, wet	2,700	3,575	32	0.76
Clay and gravel, dry	2,400	2,800	17	0.85
Clay and gravel, wet	2,600	3,100	17	0.85
Earth, dry	2,215	2,850	29	0.78
Earth, moist	2,410	3,080	28	0.78
Earth, wet	2,750	3,380	23	0.81
Gravel, dry	2,780	3,140	13	0.88
Gravel, wet	3,090	3,620	17	0.85
Sand, dry	2,600	2,920	12	0.89
Sand, wet	3,100	3,520	13	0.88
Sand and gravel, dry	2,900	3,250	12	0.89
Sand and gravel, wet	3,400	3,750	10	0.91

*Exact values will vary with grain size, moisture content, compaction, etc. Test to determine exact values for specific soils.

Typical Soil Volume Conversion Factors				
Soil Type	Initial Soil Condition	Bank	Converted to: Loose	Compacted
Clay	Bank	1.00	1.27	0.90
	Loose	0.79	1.00	0.71
	Compacted	1.11	1.41	1.00
Common earth	Bank	1.00	1.25	0.90
	Loose	0.80	1.00	0.72
	Compacted	1.11	1.39	1.00
Rock (blasted)	Bank	1.00	1.50	1.30
	Loose	0.67	1.00	0.87
	Compacted	0.77	1.15	1.00
Sand	Bank	1.00	1.12	0.95
	Loose	0.89	1.00	0.85
	Compacted	1.05	1.18	1.00

Figure 2.20

The Loading and Hauling of Sand and Gravel System balances the productivity of loading equipment to hauling equipment. It is assumed that the hauling equipment will encounter light traffic and will move up no considerable grades on the haul route.

The Expanded System Listing shows Loading and Hauling systems that use either a track or wheel front-end loader. Track loaders indicated range from 1-1/2 Cubic Yards capacity to 4-1/2 Cubic Yards capacity. Wheel loaders range from 1-1/2 Cubic Yards to 5 Cubic Yards. Trucks for hauling range from 12 Cubic Yards capacity to 20 Cubic Yards capacity. Each system lists the number of trucks involved and the distance (round trip) that each must travel.

System Components	QUANTITY	UNIT	COST PER C.Y.		
			EQUIP.	LABOR	TOTAL
SYSTEM 12.1-612-1000					
LOAD & HAUL SAND & GRAVEL,1-½ CY LOADER, FOUR 12 CY TRUCKS, 1MRT					
Excavating bulk, F.E. loader, track mtd., ½ C.Y.	1.000	C.Y.	.34	.37	.71
Haul earth, 12 C.Y. dump truck, 1 mile round trip, 2.7 loads/hr	1.000	C.Y.	1.36	.86	2.22
Spotter at dump or cut	.040	Hr.		.10	.10
TOTAL			1.70	1.33	3.03

12.1-612	Load & Haul Sand & Gravel	COST PER C.Y.		
		EQUIP.	LABOR	TOTAL
1000	Load & haul sand&gravel,1-½CY tr.loader,four 12CY dump trucks,1MRT	1.70	1.33	3.03
1200	Six 12 C.Y. dump trucks, 3 mile round trip	2.26	1.81	4.07
1400	Four 16 C.Y. dump trailers, 3 mile round trip	2.60	1.48	4.08
1600	Three 20 C.Y. dump trailers, 2 mile round trip	2.05	1.23	3.28
1800	Four 20 C.Y.dump trailers, 4 mile round trip	2.63	1.45	4.08
2000	2-½ C.Y. track loader, six 12 C.Y. dump trucks, 2 mile round trip	2.10	1.55	3.65
2200	Eight 12 C.Y. dump trucks, 4 mile round trip	2.80	1.99	4.79
2400	Five 16 C.Y. dump trailers, 3 mile round trip	2.69	1.37	4.06
2600	Three 20 C.Y. dump trailers, 1 mile round trip	1.82	.98	2.80
3000	3-½ C.Y. track loader, six 12 C.Y. dump trucks, 1 mile round trip	1.85	1.25	3.10
3200	Six 16 C.Y. dump trailers, 2 mile round trip	2.35	1.21	3.56
3600	Eight 16 C.Y. dump trailers, 4 mile round trip	2.95	1.42	4.37
4000	4-½ C.Y. track loader, six 16 C.Y. dump trailers, 1 mile round trip	2.17	.96	3.13
4200	Eight 16 C.Y. dump trailers, 2 mile round trip	2.48	1.10	3.58
4400	Eight 20 C.Y. dump trailers, 3 mile round trip	2.61	1.12	3.73
4600	Nine 20 C.Y. dump trailers, 4 mile round trip	2.87	1.21	4.08
5000	1-½ C.Y. wheel loader, four 12 C.Y. dump trucks, 1 mile round trip	1.69	1.34	3.03
5200	Six 12 C.Y. dump trucks, 3 mile round trip	2.26	1.82	4.08
5400	Four 16 C.Y. dump trailers, 2 mile round trip	2.21	1.28	3.49
5600	Five 16 C.Y. dump trailers, 4 mile round trip	2.83	1.54	4.37
6000	3 C.Y. wheel loader, ten 12 C.Y.dump trucks, 3 mile round trip	2.25	1.60	3.85
6200	Five 16 C.Y. dump trailers, 1 mile round trip	1.87	.97	2.84
6400	Six 16 C.Y. dump trailers, 2 mile round trip	2.24	1.20	3.44
6600	Seven 20 C.Y. dump trailers, 4 mile round trip	2.61	1.28	3.89
7000	5 C.Y. wheel loader, eight 16 C.Y. dump trailers, 1 mile round trip	1.96	.88	2.84
7200	Twelve 16 C.Y. dump trailers, 3 mile round trip	2.63	1.16	3.79
7400	Nine 20 C.Y. dump trailers, 2 mile round trip	2.09	.92	3.01
7600	Twelve 20 C.Y. dump trailers, 4 mile round	2.67	1.14	3.81

256

Figure 2.21

ZONES OF PLANT HARDINESS

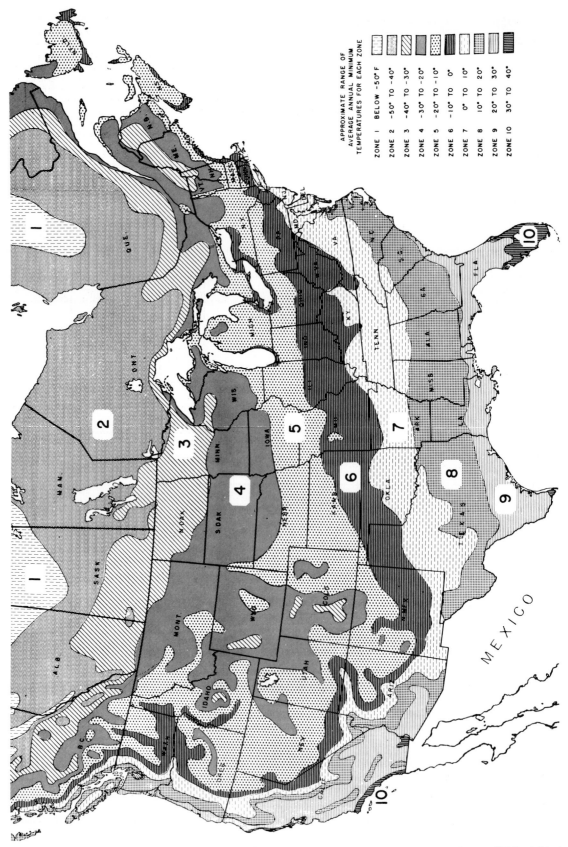

Figure 2.22

(courtesy U.S. Dept of Agriculture)

MAJOR TREES

Silhouettes indicate specimens of natural form, but varieties or forced forms possessing compact, spreading, columnar or pyramidal characteristics are available. The height at the ten year stage of development is given as an architectural design factor to be considered in the selection of tree sizes.

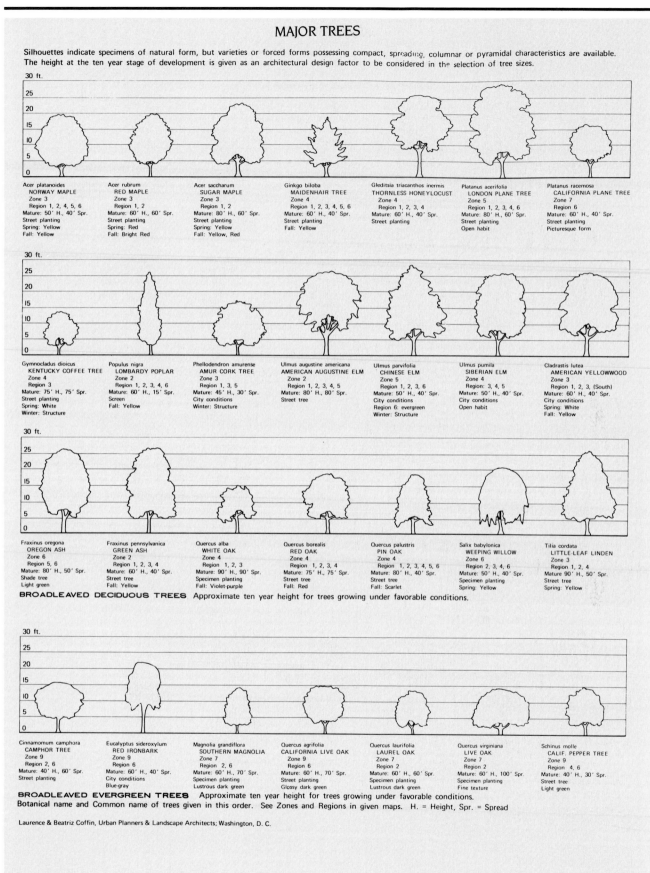

Acer platanoides
NORWAY MAPLE
Zone 3
Region 1, 2, 4, 5, 6
Mature: 50' H., 40' Spr.
Street planting
Spring: Yellow
Fall: Yellow

Acer rubrum
RED MAPLE
Zone 3
Region 1, 2
Mature: 60' H., 60' Spr.
Street planting
Spring: Red
Fall: Bright Red

Acer saccharum
SUGAR MAPLE
Zone 3
Region 1, 2
Mature: 80' H., 60' Spr.
Street planting
Spring: Yellow
Fall: Yellow, Red

Ginkgo biloba
MAIDENHAIR TREE
Zone 4
Region 1, 2, 3, 4, 5, 6
Mature: 60' H., 40' Spr.
Street planting
Fall: Yellow

Gleditsia triacanthos inermis
THORNLESS HONEYLOCUST
Zone 4
Region 1, 2, 3, 4
Mature: 60' H., 40' Spr.
Street planting

Platanus acerifolia
LONDON PLANE TREE
Zone 5
Region 1, 2, 3, 4, 6
Mature: 80' H., 60' Spr.
Street planting
Open habit

Platanus racemosa
CALIFORNIA PLANE TREE
Zone 7
Region 6
Mature: 60' H., 40' Spr.
Street planting
Picturesque form

Gymnocladus dioicus
KENTUCKY COFFEE TREE
Zone 4
Region 3
Mature: 75' H., 75' Spr.
Street planting
Spring: White
Winter: Structure

Populus nigra
LOMBARDY POPLAR
Zone 2
Region 1, 2, 3, 4, 6
Mature: 60' H., 15' Spr.
Screen
Fall: Yellow

Phellodendron amurense
AMUR CORK TREE
Zone 3
Region 1, 3, 5
Mature: 45' H., 30' Spr.
City conditions
Winter: Structure

Ulmus augustine americana
AMERICAN AUGUSTINE ELM
Zone 2
Region 1, 2, 3, 4
Mature: 80' H., 80' Spr.
Street tree

Ulmus parvifolia
CHINESE ELM
Zone 5
Region 1, 2, 3, 6
Mature: 50' H., 40' Spr.
City conditions
Region 6: evergreen
Winter: Structure

Ulmus pumila
SIBERIAN ELM
Zone 4
Region 3, 4, 5
Mature: 50' H., 40' Spr.
City conditions
Open habit

Cladrastis lutea
AMERICAN YELLOWWOOD
Zone 3
Region 1, 2, 3, (South)
Mature: 60' H., 40' Spr.
City conditions
Spring: White
Fall: Yellow

Fraxinus oregona
OREGON ASH
Zone 6
Region 5, 6
Mature: 80' H., 50' Spr.
Shade tree
Light green

Fraxinus pennsylvanica
GREEN ASH
Zone 2
Region 1, 2, 3, 4
Mature: 60' H., 40' Spr.
Street tree
Fall: Yellow

Quercus alba
WHITE OAK
Zone 4
Region 1, 2, 3
Mature: 90' H., 90' Spr.
Specimen planting
Fall: Violet-purple

Quercus borealis
RED OAK
Zone 4
Region 1, 2, 3, 4
Mature: 75' H., 75' Spr.
Street tree
Fall: Red

Quercus palustris
PIN OAK
Zone 4
Region 1, 2, 3, 4, 5, 6
Mature: 80' H., 40' Spr.
Street tree
Fall: Scarlet

Salix babylonica
WEEPING WILLOW
Zone 6
Region 2, 3, 4, 6
Mature: 50' H., 40' Spr.
Specimen planting
Spring: Yellow

Tilia cordata
LITTLE-LEAF LINDEN
Zone 3
Region 1, 2, 4
Mature 90' H., 50' Spr.
Street tree
Spring: Yellow

BROADLEAVED DECIDUOUS TREES Approximate ten year height for trees growing under favorable conditions.

Cinnamomum camphora
CAMPHOR TREE
Zone 9
Region 2, 6
Mature: 40' H., 60' Spr.
Street planting

Eucalyptus sideroxylum
RED IRONBARK
Zone 9
Region 6
Mature: 60' H., 40' Spr.
City conditions
Blue-gray

Magnolia grandiflora
SOUTHERN MAGNOLIA
Zone 7
Region 2, 6
Mature: 60' H., 70' Spr.
Specimen planting
Lustrous dark green

Quercus agrifolia
CALIFORNIA LIVE OAK
Zone 9
Region 6
Mature: 60' H., 70' Spr.
Street planting
Glossy dark green

Quercus laurifolia
LAUREL OAK
Zone 7
Region 2
Mature: 60' H., 60' Spr.
Specimen planting
Lustrous dark green

Quercus virginiana
LIVE OAK
Zone 7
Region 2
Mature: 60' H., 100' Spr.
Specimen planting
Fine texture

Schinus molle
CALIF. PEPPER TREE
Zone 9
Region 4, 6
Mature: 40' H., 30' Spr.
Street tree
Light green

BROADLEAVED EVERGREEN TREES Approximate ten year height for trees growing under favorable conditions.
Botanical name and Common name of trees given in this order. See Zones and Regions in given maps. H. = Height, Spr. = Spread

Laurence & Beatriz Coffin, Urban Planners & Landscape Architects; Washington, D. C.

(courtesy *Architectural Graphic Standards,* John Wiley & Sons, 6th edition, 1970)

Figure 2.23a

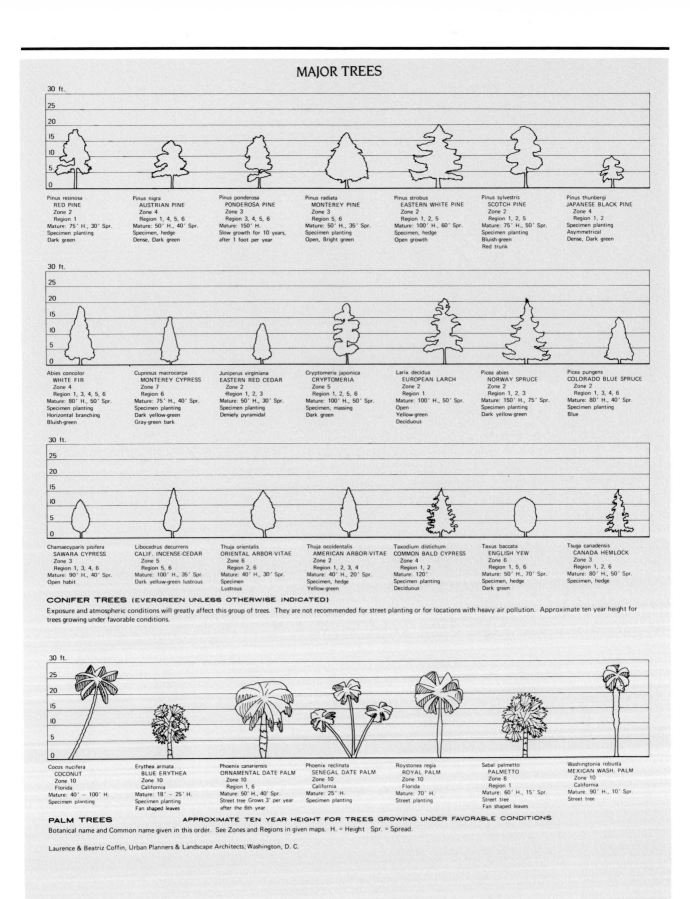

MAJOR TREES

30 ft.
25
20
15
10
5
0

Pinus resinosa	Pinus nigra	Pinus ponderosa	Pinus radiata	Pinus strobus	Pinus sylvestris	Pinus thunbergi
RED PINE	AUSTRIAN PINE	PONDEROSA PINE	MONTEREY PINE	EASTERN WHITE PINE	SCOTCH PINE	JAPANESE BLACK PINE
Zone 2	Zone 4	Zone 3	Zone 3	Zone 2	Zone 2	Zone 4
Region 1	Region 1, 4, 5, 6	Region 3, 4, 5, 6	Region 5, 6	Region 1, 2, 5	Region 1, 2, 5	Region 1, 2
Mature: 75' H., 30' Spr.	Mature: 50' H., 40' Spr.	Mature: 150' H.	Mature: 50' H., 35' Spr.	Mature: 100' H., 60' Spr.	Mature: 75' H., 50' Spr.	Specimen planting
Specimen planting	Specimen, hedge	Slow growth for 10 years,	Specimen planting	Specimen, hedge	Specimen planting	Asymmetrical
Dark green	Dense, Dark green	after 1 foot per year	Open, Bright green	Open growth	Bluish-green	Dense, Dark green
					Red trunk	

30 ft.
25
20
15
10
5
0

Abies concolor	Cupresus macrocarpa	Juniperus virginiana	Cryptomeria japonica	Larix decidua	Picea abies	Picea pungens
WHITE FIR	MONTEREY CYPRESS	EASTERN RED CEDAR	CRYPTOMERIA	EUROPEAN LARCH	NORWAY SPRUCE	COLORADO BLUE SPRUCE
Zone 4	Zone 7	Zone 2	Zone 5	Zone 2	Zone 2	Zone 2
Region 1, 3, 4, 5, 6	Region 6	Region 1, 2, 3	Region 1, 2, 5, 6	Region 1	Region 1, 2, 3	Region 1, 3, 4, 6
Mature: 80' H., 50' Spr.	Mature: 75' H., 40' Spr.	Mature: 50' H., 30' Spr.	Mature: 100' H., 50' Spr.	Mature: 100' H., 50' Spr.	Mature: 150' H., 75' Spr.	Mature: 80' H., 40' Spr.
Specimen planting	Specimen planting	Specimen planting	Specimen, massing	Open	Specimen planting	Specimen planting
Horizontal branching	Dark yellow-green	Densely pyramidal	Dark green	Yellow-green	Dark yellow-green	Blue
Bluish-green	Gray-green bark			Deciduous		

30 ft.
25
20
15
10
5
0

Chamaecyparis pisifera	Libocedrus decurrens	Thuja orientalis	Thuja occidentalis	Taxodium distichum	Taxus baccata	Tsuga canadensis
SAWARA CYPRESS	CALIF. INCENSE-CEDAR	ORIENTAL ARBOR-VITAE	AMERICAN ARBOR-VITAE	COMMON BALD CYPRESS	ENGLISH YEW	CANADA HEMLOCK
Zone 3	Zone 5	Zone 6	Zone 2	Zone 4	Zone 6	Zone 3
Region 1, 3, 4, 6	Region 5, 6	Region 2, 6	Region 1, 2, 3, 4	Region 1, 2	Region 1, 5, 6	Region 1, 2, 6
Mature: 90' H., 40' Spr.	Mature: 100' H., 35' Spr.	Mature: 40' H., 30' Spr.	Mature: 40' H., 20' Spr.	Mature: 120'	Mature: 50' H., 70' Spr.	Mature: 80' H., 50' Spr.
Open habit	Dark yellow-green lustrous	Specimen	Specimen, hedge	Specimen planting	Specimen, hedge	Specimen, hedge
	Lustrous		Yellow-green	Deciduous	Dark green	

CONIFER TREES (EVERGREEN UNLESS OTHERWISE INDICATED)

Exposure and atmospheric conditions will greatly affect this group of trees. They are not recommended for street planting or for locations with heavy air pollution. Approximate ten year height for trees growing under favorable conditions.

30 ft.
25
20
15
10
5
0

Cocos nucifera	Erythea armata	Phoenix canariensis	Phoenix reclinata	Roystonea regia	Sabal palmetto	Washingtonia robusta
COCONUT	BLUE ERYTHEA	ORNAMENTAL DATE PALM	SENEGAL DATE PALM	ROYAL PALM	PALMETTO	MEXICAN WASH. PALM
Zone 10	Zone 10	Zone 10	Zone 10	Zone 10	Zone 8	Zone 10
Florida	California	Region 1, 6	California	Florida	Region 1	California
Mature: 40' – 100' H.	Mature: 18' – 25' H.	Mature: 50' H., 40' Spr.	Mature: 25' H.	Mature: 70' H.	Mature: 60' H., 15' Spr.	Mature: 90' H., 10' Spr.
Specimen planting	Specimen planting	Street tree Grows 3' per year	Specimen planting	Street planting	Street tree	Street tree
	Fan shaped leaves	after the 6th year			Fan shaped leaves	

PALM TREES   **APPROXIMATE TEN YEAR HEIGHT FOR TREES GROWING UNDER FAVORABLE CONDITIONS**

Botanical name and Common name given in this order. See Zones and Regions in given maps. H. = Height Spr. = Spread.

Laurence & Beatriz Coffin, Urban Planners & Landscape Architects; Washington, D. C.

(courtesy Architectural Graphic Standards, John Wiley & Sons, 6th edition, 1970)

Figure 2.23b

MINOR TREES AND SHRUBS

Betula populifolia
GREY BIRCH
Zone 2
Region 1, 2, 3, 4, 5
Mature: 30' H., 20' Spr.
White bark
Fall: Yellow

Cornus florida
FLOWERING DOGWOOD
Zone 4
Region 1, 2, 3(East)
Mature: 20' H., 25' Spr.
Spring: White or Pink
Fall: Red

Cornus nutalli
PACIFIC DOGWOOD
Zone 7
Region 5, 6
Mature: 30' H., 30' Spr.
Spring: White
Fall: Scarlet and Yellow

Cercis canadensis
EASTERN REDBUD
Zone 4
Region 1, 2, 4
Mature: 30' H., 30' Spr.
Spring: Purplish Pink
Fall: Yellow

Crataegus phaenopyrum
WASHINGTON HAWTHORN
Zone 4
Region 1, 2
Mature: 30' H., 30' Spr.
Spring: White
Fall: Orange

Ilex opaca
AMERICAN HOLLY
Zone 5
Region 1, 2
Mature: 40' H., 25' Spr.
Dark green, Red fruit
Evergreen

Lagerstroemia indica
CRAPE MYRTLE
Zone 7
Region 2, 6
Mature: 20' H., 20' Spr.
Spring: Pink, Bluish
Dense

Acer palmatum
JAPANESE MAPLE
Zone 5
Region 1, 2, 6
Mature: 20' H., 20' Spr.
Spring: Red
Fall: Red

Delonix regia
FLAME TREE
Zone 10
Florida
Mature: 40' H., 40' Spr.
Summer: Red flowers
Fern-like folliage

Myrica californica
CALIFORNIA BAYBERRY
Zone 7
Region 5, 6
Mature: 30' H., 15' Spr.
Bronze colored
Evergreen

Magnolia soulangeana
SAUCER MAGNOLIA
Zone 5
Region 1, 2, 6
Mature: 25' H., 25' Spr.
Spring: White - Pink
Coarse texture

Malus (species)
FLOWERING CRAB
Zone 4
Region 1, 2, 4
Mature: 20' H., 25' Spr.
Spring: White, Pink, Red
Dense

Prunus serrulata
ORIENTAL CHERRY
Zone 5, 6
Region 1, 2, 5, 6
Mature: 25' H., 25' Spr.
Spring: White, Pink
Glossy bark

Photinia serrulata
CHINESE PHOTINIA
Zone 7
Region 2, 6
Mature: 36' H., 25' Spr.
Spring: New growth Red
Lustrous evergreen

Botanical name and Common name of trees and shrubs given in this order. See Zones and Regions in given maps.
H. = Height   Spr. = Spread
MINOR TREES—ADAPTED TO CITY CONDITIONS, DECIDUOUS UNLESS OTHERWISE SPECIFIED.

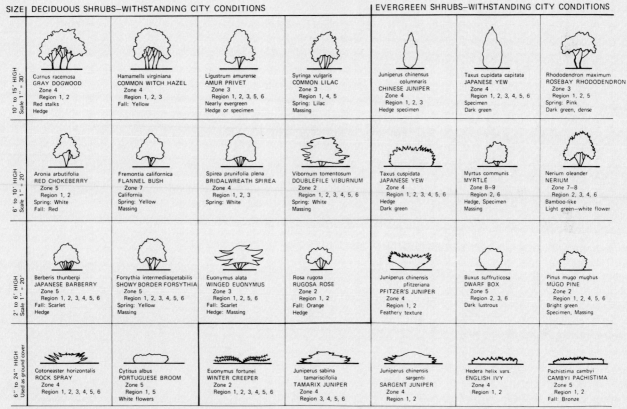

Silhouettes indicate specimens of natural form. Shrubs are adaptable to different height and forms by pruning. A wide range of varieties and exotic shrubs can be found throughout the plant regions. A few shrubs commonly used are listed here.

Laurence & Beatriz Coffin, Urban Planners & Landscape Architects; Washington, D. C.

(courtesy Architectural Graphic Standards, John Wiley & Sons, 6th edition, 1970)

Figure 2.23c

JUNIPER – CREEPING

JUNIPER–UPRIGHT

JUNIPER – MEDIUM SPREADER

(courtesy Monrovia Nursery Co.)

Figure 2.24

48

Container grown plants are measured by the size of the container in which they are sold. The American Nurseryman's Association standards for container size and volume are listed in Appendix B.

Trees are measured by the thickness of their trunks. The figure representing the tree trunk diameter is called a "caliper" measure. Trees of 1-1/2" to 4" caliper are measured 6" above the ground, and trees over 4" in caliper are measured 12" above ground. A tree caliper chart is provided in Appendix B.

Professional growers and landscape architects also urge the listing of color and use of proper latin names for plants. A cross reference list of common and latin plant names is provided in Appendix H.

Within the landscape industry, a separate a lawn care industry has been established. These specialists manage golf courses, parks, and places where lawns are significant. A great deal of materials and methods research, as well as the practice of lawn care are supported by university, government, and private research. A lawn system from *Means Site Work Cost Data* is illustrated in Figure 2.25.

The Lawn Systems listed include different types of seeding, sodding and ground covers for flat and sloped areas. Costs are given per thousand square feet for different size jobs; residential, small commercial and large commercial. The size of the job relates to the type and productivity of the equipment being used. Components include furnishing and spreading screened loam, spreading fertilizer and limestone and mulching planted and seeded surfaces. Sloped surfaces include jute mesh or staking depending on the type of cover.

System Components	QUANTITY	UNIT	COST PER M.S.F.		
			MAT.	INST.	TOTAL
SYSTEM 12.7-411-1000					
LAWN, FLAT AREA, SEEDED, TURF MIX, RESIDENTIAL					
Scarify subsoil, residential, skid steer loader	1.000	M.S.F.		11.35	11.35
Root raking, residential, no boulders	1.000	M.S.F.		14.75	14.75
Spread topsoil, skid steer loader	18.500	C.Y.	187.22	47.73	234.95
Spread limestone & fertilizer	110.000	S.Y.	11	2.20	13.20
Till topsoil, 26″ rototiller	110.000	S.Y.		25.30	25.30
Rake topsoil, screened loam	1.000	M.S.F.		12.60	12.60
Roll topsoil, push roller	18.500	C.Y.		.93	.93
Seeding, turf mix, push spreader	1.000	M.S.F.	8.14	22.86	31
Straw, mulch	110.000	S.Y.	24.20	44	68.20
TOTAL			230.56	181.72	412.28

12.7-411	Lawns	COST PER M.S.F.		
		MAT.	INST.	TOTAL
1000	Lawn, flat area, seeded, turf mix, residential	230	180	410
1040	Small commercial	230	130	360
1080	Large commercial	245	97	342
1200	Shade mix, residential	235	180	415
1240	Small commercial	235	130	365
1280	Large commercial	250	97	347
1400	Utility mix, residential	230	180	410
1440	Small commercial	235	130	365
1480	Large commercial	250	97	347
2000	Sod, bluegrass, residential	415	295	710
2040	Small commercial	380	265	645
2080	Large commercial	370	220	590
2200	Bentgrass, residential	595	185	780
2240	Small commercial	570	175	745
2280	Large commercial	540	140	680
2400	Ground cover, english ivy, residential	700	485	1,185
2440	Small commercial	700	420	1,120
2480	Large commercial	700	385	1,085
2600	Pachysandra, residential	865	2,525	3,390
2640	Small commercial	865	2,450	3,315
2680	Large commercial	865	2,425	3,290
2800	Vinca minor, residential	1,200	735	1,935

299

Figure 2.25

Specialties

Specialties include a diverse group of products, applications and systems. Specialties range from flagpoles and grandstands to street furnishings. Lighting and swimming pools are examples of specialties that may be installed by subcontractors. Street furniture, planters, recreational and playground items, benches, and bollards (short stone or concrete posts used to prevent vehicular access) are generally prefabricated products; examples are shown in Figure 2.26 and 2.27. Specialties may be installed on the site by the landscape contractor or others. Product manufacturers often provide technical information and assistance (as well as current prices) for the application and installation of their products.

Irrigation is an example of a specialty for which manufacturers provide detailed plans and information. Figure 2.28 is an illustration of three possible applications for football field irrigation.

The more information the landscape contractor has, the greater his ability to solve problems. Experience, combined with knowledge of materials, can generate greater creativity and innovation in landscape construction, and makes the landscape designer more effective in bringing a design concept to reality.

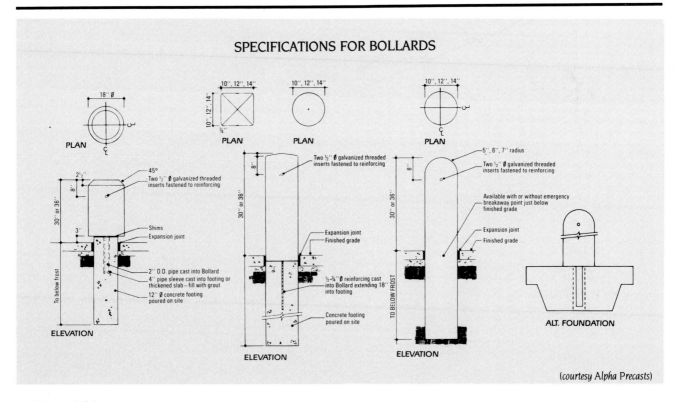

SPECIFICATIONS FOR BOLLARDS

(courtesy Alpha Precasts)

Figure 2.26

51

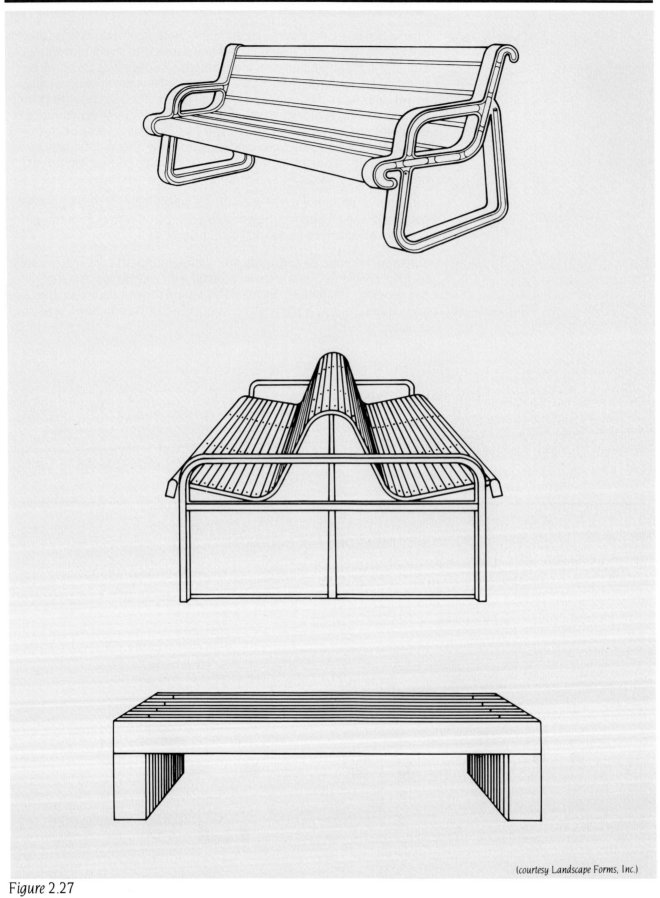

(courtesy Landscape Forms, Inc.)

Figure 2.27

FOOTBALL FIELD IRRIGATION SYSTEMS

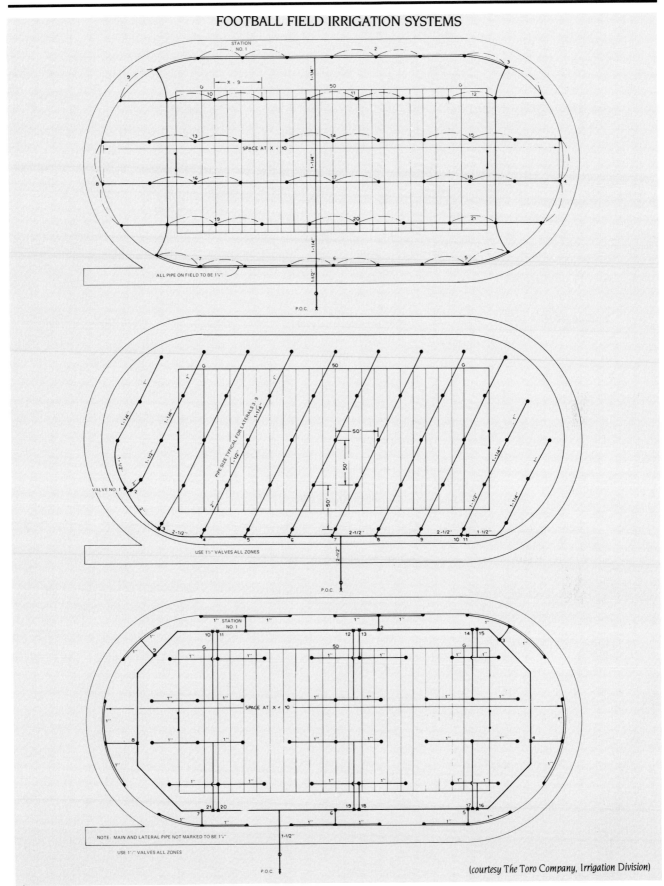

(courtesy The Toro Company, Irrigation Division)

Figure 2.28

Chapter Three

PROJECT ESTIMATING AND ANALYSIS

Chapter Three

PROJECT ESTIMATING AND ANALYSIS

Many landscaping companies fit the definition of small businesses. Owner/foremen are typical in the business, and many larger companies have evolved from the hands-on labor of their owners. In the competitive landscape business, it is the practical cost estimator who survives. Often this successful survivor has concentrated on the work he is best equipped to perform and the work on which the greatest profit can be made.

Initial interest in bidding a landscape contract is based on various factors. First of all, an analysis of all aspects of the proposed job is necessary to reveal the special conditions or features that could influence the landscape contractor's ability to do the contract work. Not all jobs should be bid by every landscape contractor.

To Bid or Not to Bid

The decision to bid a project should be well thought out by the experienced contractor. Before spending a lot of time estimating, it is wise to analyze the project objectively, looking at negative as well as positive aspects. Not all landscape projects in the vicinity are reasonably manageable. Factors to consider may include:

- Current job commitments
- Location of the job
- Employee expertise
- Labor restrictions
- Government regulations
- Need for work

Once the decision is made to bid or price the job, the estimating process begins. The landscape contractor may estimate and bid from plans and/or written specifications prepared by others. In other cases, the landscape bidder may be actively involved in the design proposal, and may submit a design with details, along with a price for the work. In *both* situations, it is critical that the entire scope of all the work be clearly defined. This complete definition of the project serves as a base, and enables the contractor to make informed decisions regarding bidding and estimating. Suggested procedures for estimating and analysis are described here and in the following chapters. Many of the steps are explained with the help of examples, charts, forms and diagrams.

Establishing a consistent routine for project analysis and estimating procedures and techniques is important. One advantage of a pre-established format is that everyone involved with the project can easily use and evaluate recorded information. Data compiled using familiar methods can be checked and traced easily.

The wise landscape contractor bases estimating decisions on an accumulated knowledge of several areas. While it may vary for each contractor, this knowledge base can generally be divided into three categories. These are **Information**, **Capability**, and **Capacity**.

Information
- Accepted trade practices
- Knowledge of materials
- Operating expenses/overhead costs
- Labor force (including subcontractors) required for a job
- Local conditions
- Constraints and incentives of a potential project

Capability
- Experience
- Skill
- Labor productivity
- Type of equipment available
- Mobilization capability

Capacity
- Labor force availability
- Amount of equipment available
- Purchasing power
- Time of year (seasonal limitations)

The landscape contractor relies on this knowledge base in making the decision to bid or perform the job.

Information

The Information categories can be further defined as follows:

Accepted Trade Practices are standards or norms within the industry. These standards are often determined from an analysis of the best overall results among different materials and methods over a wide range of conditions. Many of these results are published by product manufacturers, trade journals, and associations. In practice, some materials and methods are typical, or historically used for certain applications. The estimator must be familiar with these practices to ensure a complete and proper estimate.

Knowledge of Materials means knowing how and what items to use for specific applications and solutions; for example, knowing which plants will survive drought or other kinds of temperature or weather extremes. Knowing the full range, versatility and appropriate application of materials adds tremendously to the capability of the designer or contractor. Chapter 2, "Landscape Equipment and Materials", describes the kinds of materials used in the landscaping industry and explains their standards of measure.

Operating Expenses, or **Overhead**, is the cost of doing and maintaining a business. Such costs do not contribute directly to the physical costs of a project, but are necessary for the end achievement. They include, for example, management salaries, office and vehicle expenses, insurance, and advertising - many costly but required items - the costs of doing business. These expenses must be paid out of the income generated from the work of the landscape business and must therefore be included in the fees or estimated cost of the project. Overhead can be determined as the total annual cost of running the business, exclusive of direct project costs, i.e., field, or materials expenses. One way to estimate and recover these overhead costs is to distribute them over the total available work hours (your **capacity**), establishing an hourly rate that includes overhead. A detailed analysis and explanation of overhead costs are included in Chapter 5.

Labor Force information is needed to project your gross weekly payroll and to determine such items as project capacity. The complete labor burden is based on salary rates, estimated hours, and the following considerations:

- Worker's compensation and liability insurance
- Employer's contributions for social security
- State unemployment tax
- Federal unemployment tax
- Fringe benefits

Subcontractors are a segment of the labor force requiring separate consideration. Subcontracting for special skills has become an accepted and desirable way of responding to the need for these skills on a part time basis. The mason who specializes in stone walls or bluestone set in stonedust can provide quality work that is also cost effective. "Managability" of subcontractors is crucial for successful job performance. Even if extremely talented and skillful, a subcontractor who is unable to meet the schedule can be detrimental to the project.

Local Conditions are important factors. Among these considerations are prevailing wages and the ability to procure an adequate number of workers. The availability of materials and supplies must also be known. These important, specific conditions override any printed and suggested costs found in manuals. Local government regulations can also have a significant impact, not only on the design, but on the implementation of a project. The contractor (and designer) must be aware of applicable codes and zoning requirements.

Constraints and Incentives must also be considered in analyzing a landscape project. Past experience and present need will help you to reach a conclusion. Some judgment considerations are listed below.

- Location (travel distance)
- Character of project (simple or complex)
- Quality of drawings & specs
- Quality of supervision
- Quality of workers
- Expected level of cooperation between landscape architect and general contractor.
- Allowed completion time (ample or tight)
- Subcontractor availability
- Need for work
- Economic conditions

Capability

Capability translates easily into production, or the work a company is able to accomplish. The amount of skill and experience of designers, managers, foremen, and crew is a good indicator of overall capability. The availability of manpower and equipment also affects the contractor's ability to efficiently and effectively perform the job.

Experienced management not only increases employee production, but can also be a teaching tool, training employees for future responsibilities. Skill comes from practice and becomes more finely tuned with use. An accumulation of experience and skill increases the capability of apprentices. Everyone knows that "it's hard to get good help these days", and landscape contractors, like other good business managers, try to keep good, experienced workers. This aim can, however, be difficult to carry out due to the seasonal character of landscape work. Keeping workers through the winter can be an expensive proposition, but such a practice might pay off in the long run. By retaining a good work force, the contractor can be assured of higher productivity, and the estimator has a more reliable base from which to determine labor costs.

Determining the best equipment to have available requires careful, cost-effective analysis. Is it best to own certain equipment, or more cost effective to lease on a job by job basis? Such a decision is often based on how quickly a piece of equipment may become "needed" on projects. If equipment is often required on a moment's notice, ownership might be more practical. As with all cost questions, associated expenses such as insurance, depreciation, storage, and maintenance must enter into the analysis.

Mobilization capability is the ability to "respond" with appropriate manpower and equipment - in other words, all available manpower and equipment that can be placed on a job at a scheduled time. If the contractor does not have a well established mobilization capability, bidding certain jobs may not be feasible.

Capacity

In addition to the capability, or productivity, of the available labor force and equipment, the contractor (and estimator) must also know the *capacity* of the company's resources. Capacity involves the availability of resources, in the quantities needed. The availability of manpower is greatly dependent on regional economics. On a case by case basis, labor availability may be the prevailing factor in the decision to bid a project, or certain types of projects. Capacity also refers to the number of working hours or work days that are available for carrying out the required work in a project. A sample labor force capacity chart, in Figure 3.1, can help to anticipate available work hours. In this hypothetical case, the chart covers the period from March 15th to the middle of December and takes place in the Northeast U.S. The chart is based on a six day week with holidays off, and compensates for a certain percentage of loss time for any reason, including weather. Eight hours are suggested as the average working time per day. For help in determining anticipated loss time, always list weather conditions in a daily work diary. This sample chart suggests that for this hypothetical example, the total number of working hours in a typical season, for a full-time employee is 1600. This number times the number of full-time employees represents the total available work hours for the year. A similar chart could be created for equipment.

Distributing labor, trucks, equipment and tools effectively and choosing the most productive equipment to own, hire, or rent has a dramatic impact on productivity and costs. The purchasing power of a company may be assessed by its insurors, banks, and clients as well as by company management. Profitable business expansion is more likely to be sustained when it is properly and effectively planned.

Timing, within a project or over the course of a year, is an essential element in all business endeavors. This statement may have an even stronger meaning in the landscape industry, where many operations are restricted by weather and climate. In the New England region, for example, landscape contractors may postpone optional or non-essential tree removals until winter, when few other landscape operations can be done. Timing may also be essential to the finances of a business. Large investments or expenditures may be tied in to seasonal cash flow. If certain work (such as the tree removal mentioned above) is postponed for seasonal reasons, payments for that work may also be postponed. This possibility should be figured into the cash flow analysis of the company. In addition, the estimator must anticipate and include any incurred costs for such restrictions in the estimates.

Finally, a word should be said about subcontractors and vendors, a critical element in a contractor's capability *and* capacity. To insure reliability and quality work, the contractor must establish good relationships with these vital participants in the project.

	Available Work Hours		
	Number of Work Days	Loss Time	Work Time
March	14	2	12
April	26	4	22
May	26	4	22
June	27	4	23
July	26	4	23
August	26	4	22
September	26	4	22
October	27	4	21
November	25	4	21
December	13	2	11
	236	36 days	200 days
Average number of hours per work day			8 hrs./day
Total available work hours (per worker)			1600 hrs.

Figure 3.1

Before Starting the Estimate

To begin, every job proposal must receive a critical review. Ask questions to obtain a clear understanding of the total job. The landscape architect may refer to this understanding as the "scope of work". The complete scope of the work should be clear based on the plans and written specifications. A landscape checklist form can help both planners and contractors to accumulate and include all information, and provides a good starting place for the estimating process. A sample of such a form, a "Landscape Project Analysis" form, appears at the end of this chapter.

Carefully look over the site plans and written specifications. A chart listing plant materials and their sizes frequently appears directly on landscape plans. Drawings may note such items as fences and paving that may or may not be furnished and installed by others. Requirements may be listed for tests, samples, methods of delivery and storage. Methods of installation may be referenced to standards, for example: "according to standards of the American Nurserymen's Association". The estimator should be familiar with or reference any such information in order to properly estimate the project.

Be alert to the state of progress on the job. Find out when work can begin on the site and if the total site is accessible for inspection. Is the estimate being done at a conceptual stage? If so, considerable variation from the original project requirements should be anticipated. These changes may greatly alter the final landscape proposal. All of this information gathering will serve as a knowledge base for your cost estimate.

Accuracy in estimating depends on several factors we have discussed. Reliable sources of cost information, the availability of specific design details, and knowledge of proper methods and materials are all crucial elements. Another factor affecting estimating accuracy is the availability of adequate time in which to do the estimate. This is often a problem. When preparing an estimate for bidding, time must be allowed so that the project may be thoroughly reviewed. Be alert for omissions, ambiguities, or other defects in the drawings or specifications. Requests for clarification may result in an addendum to all bidders issued prior to the bidding. Contract documents often contain a paragraph stating the manner in which such addenda and interpretations must be handled.

Be sure to visit the site to confirm the data provided and to obtain additional information that may not appear in the plans or specifications. Sometimes plans, detail drawings, and written specs do not adequately highlight certain work components. Existing site conditions are not often detailed on plans. A checklist such as the "Landscape Project Analysis" form (Figures 3.2 - 3.6) can be very helpful in assuring that all pertinent information is obtained. Note additional information such as travel time to the job and access for machinery if it is needed. At the site, compare actual conditions to the drawings. This procedure includes reading contour lines that show existing and proposed grades and learning if soil tests or borings have revealed any useful information. Most sites change a great deal during building construction and before landscape operations begin, but the existing vegetation and site conditions can give you valuable information nonetheless.

For large jobs that have more paperwork and involve many subcontractors, a checklist like the one below can be helpful.

Job Checklist

1. Obtain plans and specs (including enough copies for subcontractors and vendors).

2. Check instructions to bidders for:
   Bid date, time and place
   Bid security required
   Pre-bid conference with owner, if any

   Mark dates on wall calendar to minimize conflicting job requirements. Be alert to the vital and unbendable guidelines regarding bid date, time and place. Public works bids that miss a deadline even by minutes are rejected and not considered. Likewise, required bid security must also be documented as required, or the bid may be invalidated. Pre-bid conferences with owners may explain or interpret specs and shed a new light on costs and requirements.

3. Examine the General and Special Conditions sections for completion time, liquidated damage dates and amounts, scope of the work, installation of owner-supplied items, allowances, alternates, retainage percentage and date of release, and any unusual payment requirements.

4. Make a special list of any questionable items for further clarification by owner or architect.

5. Estimate alternates separately from the primary scope of work.

Alternates are separate prices, or "subquotes", submitted for additional work or variations of the specified work. The owner or architect will often request alternates. They may want to compare the costs of different components for a particular project's requirements, or analyze the cost differences between bidders. For example, the landscape architect may feel that the landscape contractor knows more about the availability of specimen ornamental plants and may request suggestions for specific applications, along with the resulting cost variations.

The successful bidder/negotiator depends on the complete and accurate interpretation of plans and specifications. A careful review of documents, a site inspection, and if necessary, written clarification from the landscape architect and others are essential elements in an accurate estimation of costs.

The Landscape Project Analysis Form

A project analysis form may be used as an information gathering tool and a systematic checklist. It can provide a format for listing all specified products and work, and as a checklist, the form can ensure that all requirements (even those that may not be directly stated in the plans and specifications) are included. When the form is filled out, notes should be made of all relevant factors, using additional sheets as required. If the project is large or has unusual features, using this kind of form may reveal the need for cost contingencies. It may also be used as an on-site inspection checklist for the bidder to verify an estimate.

The site investigation accomplishes the following:

- Allows a comparison of drawings and specs to the facts and actual existing conditions.
- Provides new information that may explain (or contradict) that shown on the drawings and specs.
- Creates a space and dimension realization that may not be easily imagined from scaled drawings (the impact of slopes and obstacles, for example).

For the contractor, the project analysis form may help in deciding whether or not to bid the project. It may provide a format for recording and evaluating factors such as the suitability of equipment, the location and access of the project, and the expectations of both the prime contractor and the landscape architect or owner. The project analysis form can also be helpful with the scheduling of various work phases. For the planner, this form can serve as a detailed checklist for the specifications and drawings that are intended and required for a project. Both contractors and planners can use the form to ensure that all items affecting the project's costs are considered and included.

An example project analysis form is shown in the following pages, Figures 3.2 through 3.6.

LANDSCAPE PROJECT ANALYSIS FORM

Date _____

Travel Time From _____ To _____

Travel Minutes _____ Travel Miles _____

Project _____ Location _____

Owner _____ Project Manager _____

Landscape Architect _____

Contractor, General _____

Building Type _____
Quality: __ Economy __ Average __ Good __ Luxury

                Describe_____

Size: _____

      Ground floor area of bldg. _____ S.F.
      Outdoor surface parking _____ S.F.
      Number of parking spaces required _____
      Lawn area _____ S.F.
      Landscape planting area _____ S.F.
      Other area _____ S.F.

Zoning: __ Residential __ Commercial __ Industrial __ None __ Other
Zoning Requirements_____

*   *   *   *   *   *   *   *   *   *   *   *

ESTIMATE DATA

Budget due: ____ 19__ .
Schematic estimate due: ____ 19__ .
Preliminary estimate due: ____ 19__ .
Bid/Final estimate due: ____ 19__ , ____ a.m./p.m.
Working drawings _____

LABOR MARKET __ Highly competitive __ Normal __ Union __ Non-Union

Describe _____

TAXES
Tax Exempt: __ No __ Yes __% State __% County __% City __% Other

BOND __ Not required __ Required Type_____ Amount_____

BIDDING DATE _____ Start Date _____ Construction Duration _____
__ Open competitive __ Selected committee __ Negotiated __ Filed bids

CONTRACT __ Single __ Multiple Describe _____
Multiple type assigned to general contractor __ No __ Yes

Figure 3.2

65

SITE WORK, EARTHWORK, AND DRAINAGE

Date _____ Location_____

Project _____

DEMOLITION: __ No __ Yes Allowance _____ __ Separate contract

Removal
from site: __ No __ Yes Dump location _____ __ Separate contract

TOPOGRAPHY: __ Level __ Moderate grades __ Steep grades

Describe _____

SUBSURFACE EXPLORATION:

__ Borings __ Test Pits __ USDA maps __ Other

SITE AREA:

Total _____ Acres to clear _____ Acres to thin _____ Acres open _____

CLEARING & GRUBBING: __ No __ Light __ Medium __ Heavy

TOPSOIL: __ No __ Strip __ Stockpile __Dispose on site

__ Dispose off site _____ miles

__ Furnish:

Existing: __ inches deep Final depth: ____ inches

Describe _____

SOIL TYPE: __ Gravel __ Sand __ Clay __ Silt __ Rock __ Peat
Other

Describe _____

Rock expected: __ No __ Ledge __ Boulders __ Hardpan Describe _____

How paid _____

GROUND WATER EXPECTED: __ No __ Yes __ Depth or elevation _____

Disposal of _____ by _____

Figure 3.3

SITE WORK, EARTHWORK, AND DRAINAGE, CONT.

EXCAVATION: __ Grade and fill on site __ Dispose off site ____ Miles

__ Borrow expected ____ Miles

Quantity involved: Disposal _____ Borrow _____

BACKFILL: Paving area __ No __ Yes
Area _____
Material _____ Inches deep _____ % Compaction _____

Landscape area __ No __ Yes Area _____

Material _____ Inches deep _____ % Compaction _____

Source of materials _____

TERMITE CONTROL: _____

WATER CONTROL: Describe _____

STORM DRAINS: __ No __ Yes Type _____

Headwall: __ No __ Yes Type _____

Catch basins: __ No __ Yes __ Block __ Brick __ Concrete __ Precast

Size _____ Number ____

FRENCH DRAINS: __ No __ Yes Describe _____

RIP RAP: __ No __ Yes Describe _____

SPECIAL CONSIDERATIONS: _____

_____

_____

Figure 3.3 continued

UTILITIES, ROADS, AND WALKS

WATER SUPP1Y:
Existing Main ___ No ___ Yes   Location _____   Size _____

Service Piping ___ By Utility ___ By others ___ This contract

Water Pumping Station ___ No ___ Yes   Type _____

SPECIAL CONSIDERATIONS: _____

_____

DRIVEWAYS: ___ No ___ Yes ___ By others _____
Bituminous ___ Concrete ___ Gravel   Thickness _____

PARKING AREA: ___ No ___ Yes ___ By others _____
___ Bituminous ___ Concrete ___ Gravel   Thickness _____

Base Course: ___ No ___ Yes ___ By others ___ Gravel ___ Stone

CURBS: ___ No ___ Yes ___ By others
___ Bituminous ___ Concrete ___ Granite

PARKING BUMPERS: ___ No ___ Yes ___ By others
___ Concrete ___ Timber

PAINTING LINES: ___ No ___ Yes ___ By others

___ Paint ___ Thermoplastic ___ Traffic lines ___ Stalls

GUARD RAIL: ___ No ___ Yes ___ By others
___ Cable ___ Steel ___ Timber

SIDEWALKS: ___ No ___ Yes ___ By others
___ Bituminous ___ Concrete ___ Brick ___ Stone

Width _____   Thickness _____

STEPS: ___ No ___ Yes ___ Brick ___ Concrete ___ Stone ___ Timber

SIGNAGE: ___ No ___ Yes ___ By others

SPECIAL CONSIDERATIONS: _____

_____

_____

Figure 3.4

SITE IMPROVEMENTS AND SPECIALTIES

ARTWORK: __ No __ Yes __ By others

CARPENTRY: __ No __ Yes __ By others

FENCING: __ No __ Yes __ By others

__ Chain link __ Aluminum __ Steel Other _____

Height _____ Length _____ Gates _____

FLAGPOLES: __ No __ Yes __ By others

FOUNTAINS: __ No __ Yes __ By others

INTERIOR LANDSCAPING: __ No __ Yes __ By others

PATIOS AND TERRACES: __ No __ Yes __ By others

PLANTERS: __ No __ Yes __ By others Type _____

PLAYGROUND EQUIPMENT: __ No __ Yes __ By others

__ Benches __ Bleachers __ Bike Rack __ Goal Posts
__ Posts __ Running Track __ See Saw __ Shelters
__ Slides __ Swings

PLAYING FIELDS: __ No __ Yes __ By others

RETAINING WALLS: __ No __ Yes __ By others
__ C.I.P. __ Unit Masonry __ Brick __ Stone __ Timber
Other _____ Height _____ Length _____

STRUCTURES:

Benches   __ No __ Yes __ By others
Garden House __ No __ Yes __ By others
Greenhouse __ No __ Yes __ By others
Other   __ No __ Yes __ By others

POOLS: __ No __ Yes __ By others __ Swimming __ Other

IRRIGATION SYSTEM: __ No __ Yes __ By others

TENNIS COURTS: __ No __ Yes __ By others Surface Type _____
Number ____

TRASH ENCLOSURES: __ No __ Yes __ By others

Figure 3.5

LAWNS AND PLANTING

TOPSOIL: __ No __ Yes __ By others

Depth ____inches   Source _____

SHRUBS: __ No __ Yes __ By others

Number _____   Size Range: __ Small __ Medium __ Large

TREES: __ No __ Yes __ By others

Number Conifer _____   __ Small __ Medium __ Large

Number Deciduous _____   __ Small __ Medium __ Large

Tree Plazas: __ No __Yes __ By others

Describe _____

SEEDING: __ No __ Yes __ By others   Area: _____ S.F.

Describe _____

SOD: ___ No ___ Yes   S.F. Area _____

GROUND COVER: Type _____   S.F. Area _____

EDGING: Type _____   L.F. Area _____

WEED BARRIER: __ Physical __ Chemical

Describe _____

MULCHING: Material _____   Thickness _____

MAINTENANCE: __ No __ Yes __ By others

Describe _____

SPECIAL
CONSIDERATIONS: _____

_____

Figure 3.6

For projects with complete plans and specifications, cost estimating begins with a detailed quantity takeoff. This procedure is described in the following Chapter. A sample takeoff also appears in Chapter 6, where it is completed as part of the example estimate.

Types of Estimates

Estimating takes time and skill, and both are costly. The degree of accuracy required in the estimate must be balanced against the cost of creating it. The best, or most appropriate kind of estimate is determined by its purpose and just how much specific design detail is available when the estimate is done. For example: "around an acre or so" could vary two or three thousand square feet or more. There is no point in proposing exact figures when only an approximation of the site measurements is possible. The estimator must analyze various factors in order to choose the most appropriate estimating method.

The choice of estimating method is determined by several factors. Among these considerations are the amount and detail of the information given to the estimator, the amount of time available to complete the estimate, and the purpose of the estimate (e.g. project budget, construction bid, etc.). Whatever the method the estimator uses, all costs are derived from an established information base, using sources that are as accurate and relevant to the project as possible. Sources of cost information are discussed in Chapter 5.

No matter what the method, the estimating process involves breaking the landscape project down into various stages of detail. When the scope of the work is completely identified, the job categories, such as masonry, planting, and machine work should be listed separately and in as much detail as possible (or as necessary). By determining the quantities involved and the cost of each item, the estimator is able to complete a cost estimate.

Variables in both the estimating process and individual landscape project requirements are responsible for the spread in estimates. The two basic types of estimates that are most commonly used are:

- Systems, or "Assemblies" Estimates
- Unit Price Estimates

A third type, Square Foot Estimates, may also be used, usually for budgetary or cross-checking purposes.

Unit Price Estimates

Unit price estimates involve a careful breakdown of all the elements that go into the landscape project. In order to successfully perform a unit price estimate, detailed drawings and explicit specifications are necessary. This type of estimate is assembled item by item within each major category. Each component and associated unit price is matched to a specific quantity. To maintain accuracy, "ballparking" should not be used. In order to complete a unit price estimate, you need to know the specified or required unit prices for all material, equipment, and labor. Unit price estimates can provide the highest degree of accuracy, but require the most time, and therefore the greatest expense, to complete. For this reason, unit price estimates are typically performed on projects that are being competitively bid. This method is usually not cost effective for preliminary budget or design development pricing.

Systems Estimates

In systems estimating, various components of a landscape installation are grouped together in an "assembly". For example, Figure 3.7, from *Means Site Work Cost Data*, 1987 edition, illustrates tree pit "systems". Different tasks which could be estimated separately, are combined into one cost. Note that in this case, the tree is not included. Time is saved using systems costs because much of the detail work is eliminated. Figures 3.8 and 3.9 illustrate two other "typical" systems: lawns and site irrigation. In these cases, systems costs in *Means Site Work Cost Data* include overhead and profit. A full explanation of the derivation and use of Means cost information is included in Chapter 9.

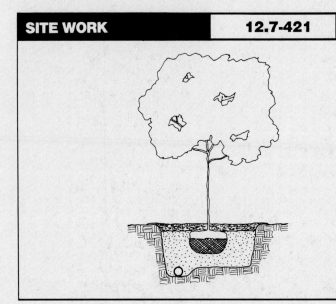

The Tree Pit Systems are listed for different heights of deciduous and evergreen trees, from 4' to 18'. Costs are given showing the pit size to accommodate the soil ball and the type of soil being excavated. In clay soils drainage tile has been included in addition to gravel drainage. Woven drainage fabric is applied before bark mulch is spread, assuming runoff is not harmful to roots.

System Components	QUANTITY	UNIT	COST EA. MAT.	COST EA. INST.	COST EA. TOTAL
SYSTEM 12.7-421-1220					
TREE PIT, 5' TO 6' TREE, DECIDUOUS, 2' X 1-¼' DEEP PIT, CLAY SOIL					
Excavate planting pit, backhoe, clay soil	.262	C.Y.		12.31	12.31
Fill in pit, screened gravel, ¾" to ½"	.050	C.Y.	.19	.79	.98
Drain tile 4"	3.000	L.F.	4.29	4.53	8.82
Mix planting soil, by hand, incl. loam, peat & manure	.304	C.Y.	6.59	1.92	8.51
Backfill planting pit, by hand, prepared mix	.304	C.Y.		6.38	6.38
Drainage fabric, woven	.500	S.Y.	.53	.08	.61
Bark mulch, hand spread, 3"	.346	C.Y.	.45	.65	1.10
TOTAL			12.05	26.66	38.71

12.7-421	Tree Pits	COST EACH MAT.	COST EACH INST.	COST EACH TOTAL
1000	Tree pit, 4' to 5' tree, evergreen, 2-½' x 1-½' deep pit, sandy soil	19.25	33	52.25
1020	Clay soil	20	35	55
1200	5' to 6' tree, deciduous, 2' x 1-¼' deep pit, sandy soil	10.45	16.90	27.35
1220	Clay soil	12.05	27	39.05
1300	Evergreen, 3' x 1-¾' deep pit, sandy soil	31	50	81
1320	Clay soil	31	56	87
1360	3-½' x 1-¾' deep pit, sandy soil	40	63	103
1380	Clay soil	38	65	103
1400	6' to 7' tree, evergreen, 4' x 1-¾' deep pit, sandy soil	48	74	122
1420	Clay soil	46	76	122
1600	7' to 9' tree, deciduous, 2-½' x 1-½' deep pit, sandy soil	19.25	40	59.25
1620	Clay soil	20	35	55
1800	8' to 10' tree, deciduous, 3' x 1-¾' deep pit, sandy soil	31	50	81
1820	Clay soil	31	56	87
1900	Evergreen, 4-½' x 2' deep pit, sandy soil, smaller ball	71	105	176
1910	Larger ball	69	105	174
1920	Clay soil, smaller ball	64	105	169
1930	Larger ball	62	100	162
2000	10' to 12' tree, deciduous, 3-½' x 1-¾' deep pit, sandy soil	40	62	102
2020	Clay soil	38	65	103

301

Figure 3.7

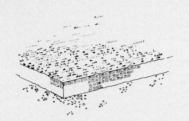

The Lawn Systems listed include different types of seeding, sodding and ground covers for flat and sloped areas. Costs are given per thousand square feet for different size jobs; residential, small commercial and large commercial. The size of the job relates to the type and productivity of the equipment being used. Components include furnishing and spreading screened loam, spreading fertilizer and limestone and mulching planted and seeded surfaces. Sloped surfaces include jute mesh or staking depending on the type of cover.

System Components	QUANTITY	UNIT	COST PER M.S.F.		
			MAT.	INST.	TOTAL
SYSTEM 12.7-411-1000					
LAWN, FLAT AREA, SEEDED, TURF MIX, RESIDENTIAL					
Scarify subsoil, residential, skid steer loader	1.000	M.S.F.		11.35	11.35
Root raking, residential, no boulders	1.000	M.S.F.		14.75	14.75
Spread topsoil, skid steer loader	18.500	C.Y.	187.22	47.73	234.95
Spread limestone & fertilizer	110.000	S.Y.	11	2.20	13.20
Till topsoil, 26″ rototiller	110.000	S.Y.		25.30	25.30
Rake topsoil, screened loam	1.000	M.S.F.		12.60	12.60
Roll topsoil, push roller	18.500	C.Y.		.93	.93
Seeding, turf mix, push spreader	1.000	M.S.F.	8.14	22.86	31
Straw, mulch	110.000	S.Y.	24.20	44	68.20
TOTAL			230.56	181.72	412.28

12.7-411	Lawns	COST PER M.S.F.		
		MAT.	INST.	TOTAL
1000	Lawn, flat area, seeded, turf mix, residential	230	180	410
1040	Small commercial	230	130	360
1080	Large commercial	245	97	342
1200	Shade mix, residential	235	180	415
1240	Small commercial	235	130	365
1280	Large commercial	250	97	347
1400	Utility mix, residential	230	180	410
1440	Small commercial	235	130	365
1480	Large commercial	250	97	347
2000	Sod, bluegrass, residential	415	295	710
2040	Small commercial	380	265	645
2080	Large commercial	370	220	590
2200	Bentgrass, residential	595	185	780
2240	Small commercial	570	175	745
2280	Large commercial	540	140	680
2400	Ground cover, english ivy, residential	700	485	1,185
2440	Small commercial	700	420	1,120
2480	Large commercial	700	385	1,085
2600	Pachysandra, residential	865	2,525	3,390
2640	Small commercial	865	2,450	3,315
2680	Large commercial	865	2,425	3,290
2800	Vinca minor, residential	1,200	735	1,935

299

Figure 3.8

There are three basic types of Site Irrigation Systems: pop-up, riser mounted and quick coupling. Sprinkler heads are spray, impact or gear driven. Each system includes: the hardware for spraying the water; the pipe and fittings needed to deliver the water; and all other accessory equipment such as valves, couplings, nipples, and nozzles. Excavation heads and backfill costs are also included in the system.

The Expanded System Listing shows a wide variety of Site Irrigation Systems.

System Components	QUANTITY	UNIT	COST PER S.F.		
			MAT.	INST.	TOTAL
SYSTEM 12.7-910-1000					
SITE IRRIGATION, POP UP SPRAY, PLASTIC, 10' RADIUS, 1000 S.F., PVC PIPE					
Excavation, chain trencher	54.000	L.F.		25.38	25.38
Pipe, plastic, PVC, schedule 40, 1" diameter	54.000	L.F.	11.88	116.64	128.52
Fittings PVC plastic	8.100	L.F.	1.78	17.50	19.28
Nipples, long PVC plastic, 1" diameter x 12" long	5.000	L.F.	1.10	10.80	11.90
Tees, PVC plastic, high pressure schedule, 40, 1" diameter	5.000	Ea.	10.90	169.10	180
Couplings PVC plastic, high pressure, 1" diameter	5.000	Ea.	1.70	74.55	76.25
Valves, bronze, globe, 125 lb. rising stem, threaded, 1" diameter	1.000	Ea.	33	14	47
Head & nozzle, pop-up spray, PVC plastic	5.000	Ea.	14.60	40.90	55.50
Backfill by hand with compaction	54.000	L.F.		15.66	15.66
Total cost per 1,000 S.F.			74.96	484.53	559.49
Total cost per S.F.			.07	.48	.55

12.7-910	Site Irrigation	COST PER S.F.		
		MAT.	INST.	TOTAL
1000	Site irrigation, pop up spray, plastic, 10' radius, 1000 S.F., PVC pipe	.07	.48	.55
1100	Polyethylene pipe	.07	.37	.44
1200	14' radius, 8000 S.F., PVC pipe	.03	.22	.25
1300	Polyethylene pipe	.03	.17	.20
1400	18' square, 1000 S.F. PVC pipe	.06	.37	.43
1500	Polyethylene pipe	.06	.25	.31
1600	24' square, 8000 S.F., PVC pipe	.02	.13	.15
1700	Polyethylene pipe	.02	.11	.13
1800	4' x 30' strip, 200 S.F., PVC pipe	.28	1.36	1.64
1900	Polyethylene pipe	.27	1.09	1.36
2000	6' x 40' strip, 800 S.F., PVC pipe	.08	.46	.54
2100	Polyethylene pipe	.08	.36	.44
2200	Economy brass, 11' radius, 1000 S.F., PVC pipe	.09	.48	.57
2300	Polyethylene pipe	.08	.37	.45
2400	14' radius, 8000 S.F., PVC pipe	.03	.22	.25
2500	Polyethylene pipe	.03	.17	.20
2600	3' x 28' strip, 200 S.F., PVC pipe	.32	1.36	1.68
2700	Polyethylene pipe	.31	1.09	1.40
2800	7' x 36' strip, 1000 S.F., PVC pipe	.07	.37	.44
2900	Polyethylene pipe	.07	.29	.36

305

Figure 3.9

Square Foot Estimates

Square Foot estimates primarily involve an overall project cost and should be based on experience as well as past, similar projects. Square Foot estimates are useful for establishing rough budget costs, usually before design development. Certain considerations should be taken into account when using square foot estimates: these include variations from the initial project requirements, and differences that occur from one project to another.

Square foot estimates are based on the concept that many jobs and small items involved in planting, hard construction, and landscape specialties can be grouped together into total project costs for "typical" installations. Care must be taken in using cost data from more than one source when preparing a square foot estimate. Be aware that a lawn that costs 36 cents per square foot to install under good working conditions may be considerably more costly under adverse conditions, such as steep slopes or locations that require extensive watering. Cost information taken from several sources should be applied only to jobs that are essentially identical to those used as the source of information.

Each estimator should choose an estimating method that experience has proven reliable, and which a particular project warrants. Landscape construction estimates commonly represent a combination of approaches. For example, trees and shrubs may be estimated using unit prices, while lawns, paving, some hard construction, and such specialties as irrigation may be estimated using the systems method. Whatever method is used by the estimator, costs should be derived from an established information base, using sources and resources that are as accurate and relevant to the circumstances as possible.

Chapter Four

THE QUANTITY TAKEOFF

Chapter Four

THE QUANTITY TAKEOFF

A quantity takeoff is a detailed and systematic list of the amounts of materials and the number of man-hours required to complete a particular project. The takeoff task, the initial step in the estimating process, is to separate, name, and describe the quantities for a primary purpose — to price out the cost of the job. In order to take off certain quantities, and to be sure that all items are included, the estimator must have an overall concept of how the job will be constructed. This is best achieved by visualizing the construction process and planning the work as the estimate is done.

The takeoff step is separate from and should not be confused with pricing or extending costs, a process described in Chapter 5. A takeoff primarily involves a list of items and quantities to which costs for material and labor are later applied — at the pricing stage. Some quantities which can easily be overlooked involve items that require costs for labor only, such as pruning and thinning of trees. A takeoff list of items includes not only amounts of materials and measurements of time (man-hours) but also should include equipment usage. Unusual conditions and special requirements that may abnormally influence materials, labor, or equipment are also noted, so that quantities (thus costs) may be adjusted accordingly. For example, traffic restrictions at the site of the project could adversely affect a normal project schedule, and therefore increase the costs. Another example is a tree installation project that is to be started in the fall and completed the following spring. Such a schedule should alert the estimator to divided work segments and the possibility of price changes from one year to the next.

The analysis recorded during the site visit can serve as a checklist to guard against oversights. Keep in mind how conditions may greatly influence costs and profitability. The estimator must consider all sorts of factors from travel time to equipment access. The analysis form can also help to identify and note items for pricing that might otherwise be overlooked.

When working with plans, try to approach each segment of a project in the same logical manner. For example, one might begin with the plant list from the plans. Lists that place plants in categories beginning with all deciduous trees, then conifer trees, deciduous shrubs, evergreen shrubs, flowers and ground covers are organized in the same manner in which the materials will be purchased. It makes sense to take off and list the plants similarly on the takeoff sheet. Putting individual species within these

groups into alphabetical order allows for handy and immediate reference to any particular plant.

As with all steps of the estimating process, it is very important to be consistent when it comes to plant list codes and keys. If the drawing or specs do not include a key, it is a good idea to create one, abbreviating plant names in order to save time. A simple approach is to use initials, such as "AR" for Acer rubrum, and to arrange the key alphabetically within categories on the plant list. (See Figure 6.1, the landscape plan for the sample estimate.) In addition to keys of abbreviated plant names, landscape architects also use many symbols and graphics on drawings and plans to provide information. A chart of typical symbols is found in Figure 4.1. Different designers may use different symbols for the same items. It is important to review each set of plans individually and carefully.

Landscape Systems and Graphics

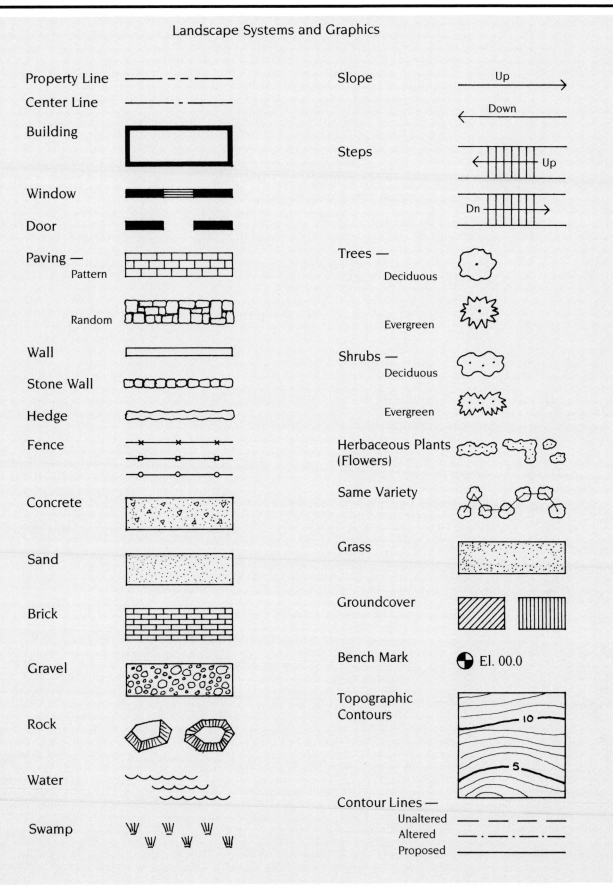

Figure 4.1

Experienced estimators often use pre-printed forms to list all of the costs involved in a project and to note the probable impact of particular working conditions. A standard form such as that shown in Figure 5.2 will work well for many sections of the takeoff. Some materials or work may, however, require a different or custom-made takeoff format. Preprinted forms can reduce errors and make reviews and corrections easier. Examples of printed forms (from *Means Forms for Building Construction Professionals*) are illustrated in Figures 4.2 and 4.3. A custom summary sheet such as one for planting may also serve as a reminder to include the costs of items that are normally included - whether they are listed or not for a particular project.

Figure 4.2 is a form designed specifically for quantity takeoff. The different columns allow for different quantities to be derived from the same dimensions. The form in Figure 4.3 combines takeoff and pricing on one sheet. This feature provides easy reference to data and helps to eliminate errors of transposition.

Means Forms

QUANTITY SHEET

SHEET NO.

PROJECT		ESTIMATE NO.
LOCATION	ARCHITECT	DATE
TAKE OFF BY	EXTENSIONS BY:	CHECKED BY:

DESCRIPTION	NO.	DIMENSIONS				UNIT		UNIT		UNIT		UNIT

Figure 4.2

▲ Means Forms

CONSOLIDATED ESTIMATE

					SHEET NO.	
PROJECT					ESTIMATE NO.	
ARCHITECT					DATE	
TAKE OFF BY	QUANTITIES BY	PRICES BY	EXTENSIONS BY		CHECKED BY	

DESCRIPTION	NO.	DIMENSIONS			QUANTITIES		UNIT			UNIT	MATERIAL UNIT COST	TOTAL	LABOR UNIT COST	TOTAL

Figure 4.3

Pre-printed forms are among the many resources the estimator uses to be sure that all items for a particular project are included in the estimate. The most reliable of all resources are experience and common sense. The estimator should visualize the step-by-step completion of the project while making a mental comparison to past projects. This is a good way to be sure that all requirements are included.

Mathematical errors are discovered and corrected with a simple review and calculation check of the estimate. However, "errors" due to omissions of items are much harder to remedy. In dealing with unfamiliar items, the estimator may rely on other sources. For example, one such source could be the Systems section of *Means Site Work Cost Data*. Figures 4.4 and 4.5, from the 1987 edition, show systems for a brick tree plaza and a retaining wall. Note that for each, all of the components (primary and associated) typically found in each type of construction are listed, along with required quantities. A quick review of such systems provides the estimator with another checklist to be sure that all required items are included.

The Plaza Systems listed include several brick and tile paving surfaces on three different bases: gravel, slab on grade and suspended slab. The system cost includes this base cost with the exception of the suspended slab. The type of bedding for the pavers depends on the base being used, and alternate bedding may be desirable. Also included in the paving costs are edging and precast grating costs and where concrete bases are involved, expansion joints.

System Components	QUANTITY	UNIT	COST PER S.F.		
			MAT.	INST.	TOTAL
SYSTEM 12.7-283-2050					
PLAZA, BRICK PAVERS, 4" X 8" X 1-½", GRAVEL BASE, STONE DUST BED					
Compact subgrade, static roller, 4 passes	.111	S.Y.		.07	.07
Bank gravel, 2 mi haul, dozer spread	.012	C.Y.	.05	.04	.09
Compact gravel base, vibrating plate	.012	C.Y.		.02	.02
Grading fine grade, 3 passes with grader	.111	S.Y.		.17	.17
Stone dust, 1" thick, skid steer loader spread	.003	C.Y.	.03	.03	.06
Compact bedding, vibrating plate	.003	C.Y.		.01	.01
Brick paver, 4" x 8" x 1-¾"	4.150	Ea.	1.65	1.76	3.41
Brick edging, stood on end, 6 per L.F.	.060	L.F.	.12	.26	.38
Precast conc tree grating	.004	Ea.	.71	.13	.84
TOTAL			2.56	2.48	5.04

12.7-283	Brick & Tile Plazas	COST PER S.F.		
		MAT.	INST.	TOTAL
1050	Plaza, asphalt pavers, 6" x 12" x 1-¼", gravel base, asphalt bedding	3.08	1.40	4.48
1100	Slab on grade, asphalt bedding	6.50	4.74	11.24
1150	Suspended slab, insulated & mastic bedding	7.20	6.70	13.90
1300	6" x 12" x 3", gravel base, asphalt, bedding	5.80	2.18	7.98
1350	Slab on grade, asphalt bedding	5.85	4.52	10.37
1400	Suspended slab, insulated & mastic bedding	8.45	6.85	15.30
2050	Brick pavers, 4" x 8" x 1-½", gravel base, stone dust bedding	2.56	2.48	5.04
2100	Slab on grade, asphalt bedding	3.63	3.02	6.65
2150	Suspended slab, insulated & no bedding	4.26	3.55	7.81
2300	4" x 8" x 2-¼", gravel base, stone dust bedding	2.69	2.48	5.17
2350	Slab on grade, asphalt bedding	3.76	3.02	6.78
2400	Suspended slab, insulated & no bedding	4.39	3.55	7.94
2550	Brick shale pavers, 4" x 8" x 2-¼", gravel base, stone dust bedding	2.45	2.83	5.28
2600	Slab on grade, asphalt bedding	3.52	3.37	6.89
2650	Suspended slab, insulated & no bedding	4.39	3.55	7.94
3050	Brick thin set tile, 4" x 4" x ⅜", slab on grade, mortar bedding	4.16	2.76	6.92
3300	4" x 4" x ¾", slab on grade, mortar bedding	5.70	2.85	8.55
3550	Concrete paving stone, 4" x 8" x 2-½", gravel base, sand bedding	3.06	2.46	5.52
3600	Slab on grade, asphalt bedding	4.08	2.94	7.02
3650	Suspended slab, insulated & no bedding	4.50	3.89	8.39
3800	4" x 8" x 3-¼", gravel base, sand bedding	3.35	2.46	5.81
3850	Slab on grade, asphalt bedding	4.37	2.94	7.31

288

Figure 4.4

There are four basic types of Concrete Retaining Wall Systems: reinforced concrete with level backfill; reinforced concrete with sloped backfill or surcharge; unreinforced with level backfill; and unreinforced with sloped backfill or surcharge. System elements include; all necessary forms (4 uses); 3,000 p.s.i. concrete with an 8" chute; all necessary reinforcing steel; and underdrain. Exposed concrete is patched and rubbed.

The Expanded System Listing shows walls that range in thickness from 10" to 18" for reinforced concrete walls with level backfill and 12" to 24" for reinforced walls with sloped backfill. Walls range from a height of 4' to 20'.

Unreinforced level and sloped backfill walls range from a height of 3' to 10'.

System Components	QUANTITY	UNIT	COST PER L.F. MAT.	INST.	TOTAL
SYSTEM 12.7-310-1000					
CONC.RETAIN. WALL REINFORCED, LEVEL BACKFILL 4' HIGH					
Forms in place, cont. wall footing & keyway, 4 uses	2.000	S.F.	.60	3.90	4.50
Forms in place, retaining wall forms, battered to 8' high, 4 uses	8.000	SFCA	5.52	30.08	35.60
Reinforcing in place, walls, #3 to #7	.004	Ton	2.29	1.47	3.76
Concrete ready mix, regular weight, 3000 psi	.204	C.Y.	11.42		11.42
Placing concrete and vibrating footing con., shallow direct chute	.074	C.Y.		.77	.77
Placing concrete and vibrating walls, 8" thick, direct chute	.130	C.Y.		1.81	1.81
Gravel drain and pipe installed, bank gravel, perf. pipe	1.000	L.F.	3.29	1.99	5.28
Finish walls and break ties, patch walls	4.000	S.F.	.04	1.68	1.72
TOTAL			23.16	41.70	64.86

12.7-310	Concrete Retaining Walls	COST PER L.F. MAT.	INST.	TOTAL
1000	Conc.retain.wall, reinforced, level backfill, 4' high x 2'-2" base,10"thick	23	42	65
1200	6' high x 3'-3" base, 10" thick	33	60	93
1400	8' high x 4'-3" base, 10" thick	43	78	121
1600	10' high x 5'-4" base, 13" thick	55	115	170
1800	12' high x 6'-6" base, 14" thick	68	135	203
2200	16' high x 8'-6" base, 16" thick	100	185	285
2600	20' high x 10'-5" base, 18" thick	150	235	385
3000	Sloped backfill, 4' high x 3'-2" base, 12" thick	27	43	70
3200	6' high x 4'-6" base, 12" thick	39	61	100
3400	8' high x 5'-11" base, 12" thick	51	80	131
3600	10' high x 7'-5" base, 16" thick	71	120	191
3800	12' high x 8'-10" base, 18" thick	92	145	237
4200	16' high x 11'-10" base, 21" thick	155	205	360
4600	20' high x 15'-0" base, 24" thick	235	275	510
5000	Unreinforced, level backfill, 3'-0" high x 1'-6" base	14.55	29	43.55
5200	4'-0" high x 2'-0" base	21	37	58
5400	6'-0" high x 3'-0" base	37	57	94
5600	8'-0" high x 4'-0" base	56	75	131
5800	10'-0" high x 5'-0" base	80	115	195
7000	Sloped backfill, 3'-0" high x 2'-0" base	16.75	30	46.75
7200	4'-0" high x 3'-0" base	26	39	65
7400	6'-0" high x 5'-0" base	51	60	111
7600	8'-0" high x 7'-0" base	83	81	164
7800	10'-0" high x 9'-0" base	125	125	250

290

Figure 4.5

Guidelines for Takeoff

The following guidelines are recommended to help organize the quantity takeoff. Most are common sense suggestions. However, in the haste of the estimating process, some of these steps may be overlooked. The use of these guidelines will help reduce errors and assure that all required items are included.

- Use preprinted forms for an orderly sequence of descriptions, dimensions, quantities, extensions, totals, etc.
- Be consistent when listing dimensions, for example, always describing length x width x height in the same sequence.
- Use printed dimensions where given. Since portions of a landscape plan may be schematic and/or curvilinear, it may be difficult to scale drawings in order to determine accurate quantities.
- Convert feet and inch measurements to decimal feet when you list them. A plant bed of 4' 6" should convert to 4.5 feet. Otherwise, dimensions in feet can be confused with dimensions in inches. The chart below (Figure 4.6) can be used to convert inches to decimal fractions of a foot. For further measurement references, see Appendix A.

Conversion of Inches to Decimal Parts per Foot												
	0	1"	2"	3"	4"	5"	6"	7"	8"	9"	10"	11"
0	0	.08	.17	.25	.33	.42	.50	.58	.67	.75	.83	.92
1/8"	.01	.09	.18	.26	.34	.43	.51	.59	.68	.76	.84	.93
1/4"	.02	.10	.19	.27	.35	.44	.52	.60	.69	.77	.85	.94
3/8"	.03	.11	.20	.28	.36	.45	.53	.61	.70	.78	.86	.95
1/2"	.04	.12	.21	.29	.37	.46	.54	.62	.71	.79	.87	.96
5/8"	.05	.14	.22	30	.39	.47	.55	.64	.72	.80	.89	.97
3/4"	.06	.15	.23	.31	.40	.48	.56	.65	.73	.81	.90	.98
7/8"	.07	.16	.24	.32	.41	.49	.57	.66	.74	.82	.91	.99

Figure 4.6

The Takeoff Process

What follows is an overview of the quantity takeoff process, using a few pertinent examples. More detailed information is included in the sample estimate in Chapter 6. Armed with site drawings, specifications, and information collected on-site, it is time to begin the takeoff. This process will include a systematic listing of all materials and work needed to complete the project. A great deal of information may already have been noted about amounts and types of materials from plant lists on plans or in the written specifications. Such data could be in the form of a project analysis (see Chapter 3).

Begin the takeoff using standard forms (see Figure 4.2 for an example), listing each broad category separately, such as site clearing, grading, retaining walls, etc. For each category, begin systematically listing materials that are noted or indicated on the plans. Constant reference to the other data sources, specs, project analysis, and checklist forms will be necessary. When doing a takeoff from a plan, read and make notations in a planned sequence. For example, one method is to always begin at the upper right quarter of a plan, listing the plants in this part of the drawing. Continue, working around the drawing in a consistent pattern, e.g., clockwise. Complete the takeoff for each group or category of materials by making separate searches around the plan. Be methodical. A typical sequence may proceed as follows: locate all lawn seed areas, then all sod areas, followed by all paved walkway areas of similar materials. Note each item on the plan when listed to prevent duplication or omissions. A different color pencil might be used for each category. Always use the same "path" through the plan that was followed in listing the other categories. Keep in mind the fact that the "low-ball" bidder may often be the one who left out an item.

For takeoff purposes, dimensions may appear in notations on the drawing or in detail drawings that accompany landscape plans. Unfortunately, landscape drawings are often sparsely dimensioned and sometimes not to scale. Be aware of the risks of measuring the length of a planting bed by "scaling" off a building. If quantities are difficult to determine, the contractor may qualify the estimate by stating certain assumed dimensions. In the contract bid, for example, "42,000 square feet of sod installed", may be stated, rather than simply, "grass sod installed". Field verification of measurements will be helpful, and is recommended if possible.

Many items that are mentioned briefly on the plans or in the specifications (or perhaps not mentioned, but required) may imply many different tasks and types of work. "Finish grade" is a typical specification for landscape contractors. The necessary methods are, however, rarely specified. Finish grade might be achieved by hand work, by York rake, or may require a significant amount of earthwork. The methods and the amount of work needed to achieve each specified portion of the project (and cleanup) must be determined and listed. This information will clearly have an impact on the estimate.

Wrapping Up The Takeoff

As the takeoff progresses, look over all of the quantities and compare the pieces of information that you have collected. Many items are a "natural check" against each other. For example, if specifications call for three inches of topsoil under grass sod, the relationship between square feet of sod and cubic yards of topsoil must be known, for purposes of comparison. Mulch may need to be similarly calculated, based on the square footage of planting beds. There are many relationships between materials, work areas, and equipment and installation costs, and these are cross referenced by the experienced estimator.

When estimating alternates, both at the takeoff and pricing stages, it is best to first list all of the items that are in the basic bid. Then figure the alternates separately. In this way, positive numbers are compared in both cases. Confusion is more likely when adds and deducts are both used. If any "outs", or exclusions are necessary, they should be *distinctly* noted so that it is clear that they should be deducted instead of added.

When figuring the time requirements for equipment, the estimator must plan how best to coordinate its use. This is especially true for extensive or heavy site work equipment, an expensive component in a landscape installation. The information in *Means Site Work Cost Data* can be used to determine the most cost effective use of equipment for various kinds of earthwork. See the example in Chapter 2, Figures 2.2 and 2.3.

When the quantity takeoff is complete and all material, labor, and equipment items have been identified and listed, the next step is to extend and summarize the quantities and price the estimate. Takeoff units should be converted to "pricing" units. For example, requirements for depths of topsoil or mulch over a given area can be converted to cubic yards (or cubic feet) of material - those units in which the material will be priced and purchased. The chart in Figure 4.7 is an example of a chart used for converting measurements for a few specific items. Each estimator should develop or become familiar with these kinds of references which facilitate the estimating process. Quantities of similar items from different areas of the plan should be totaled and summarized. Only then are prices applied and overhead and profit added, to arrive at the final estimated cost. A discussion of pricing follows in Chapter 5.

Conversion Chart for Loam, Baled Peat, and Mulch			
Loam Requirements		**Mulch Requirements** (Bulk Peat, Crushed Stone, Shredded Bark, Wood Chips)	
Depth per 10,000 S.F.	Cubic yards required	Depth per 1,000 S.F.	Cubic yards required
2 inches	70	1 inch	3-1/2
4 "	140	2 inches	7
6 "	210	3 "	10-1/2
		4 "	14
Per 1,000 S.F.		Per 100 S.F.	
2 inches	7	1 inch	1/3
4 "	14	2 inches	2/3
6 "	21	3 "	1
		4 "	1-1/3

Baled (or Compressed) Peat	
Per 100 S.F.	Bales Required
1 inch	one 4 cubic foot bale
2 inches	two 4 cubic foot bales
3 "	two 6 cubic foot bales
4 "	one 4 cubic foot bales and two 6 cubic foot bales

Note: Opened and spread, peat from bales will be about 2-1/2 times the volume of the unopened bale.

Figure 4.7

Chapter Five

PRICING THE ESTIMATE

Chapter Five

PRICING THE ESTIMATE

Once the quantities of material, equipment, and labor are determined, the estimate can be priced. This process involves first listing all items with their prices on cost analysis sheets, then summarizing this information on an estimate summary form.

Grouping the Items

Begin by entering or listing all of the categories that apply to the job (from the takeoff sheets). The breakdown and sequence should be the same as that used for the quantity takeoff. Such a routine and consistent pattern makes it easier to spot duplications, errors, or omissions. The list below provides an example of how this approach might be used, in this case, in the order of work on the site.

1. Demolition, clearing and grubbing
2. Excavation and backfill
3. Drainage
4. Utilities
5. Roads and walks
6. Site improvements
7. Planting

The planting category may be further broken down. Plant materials are typically priced on a separate sheet and summarized in groups such as trees, shrubs, grass, sod, etc. This approach helps to determine the types of equipment required and the sequence in which the work should be performed. Each type of plant material has its own installation requirements and methods, and these may vary depending upon the seasons. Special conditions such as temperature, typical rainfall, soil types, site grades, and access may also have a great influence on material, labor, and equipment costs. An experienced estimator takes all of these factors into consideration and makes notations on the takeoff sheets. All items must be priced — from tree wrap to backhoe.

As it is, some categories will become "systems" developed from a unit price basis. For example, a retaining wall may be figured by putting all components together to develop a systems price. Illustrated in Figure 5.1 is a retaining wall system which provides a cost per linear foot based on the quantities and costs of the individual components. Systems such as this may be developed for many other category items. Readers are referred to *Means Site Work Cost Data* which provides systems costs and other helpful examples (See Chapter 9).

For an estimate to be well organized, it must have a clear direction from the start. The various items to be priced should be transferred from the takeoff sheets to the pricing sheets. This can be done using the contractor's own forms and methods, or in the same general sequence as the work will take place. Examples are shown in Figures 5.2 and 5.3. Figure 5.2 is a "custom-made" form that might be appropriate for specific types of work, in this case, planting. Figure 5.3 is a generic form that can be tailored to each particular project. Examples of the use of such forms are illustrated in Chapter 6. Most firms would find it useful to develop custom forms that fit the type of work and methods familiar to their particular company.

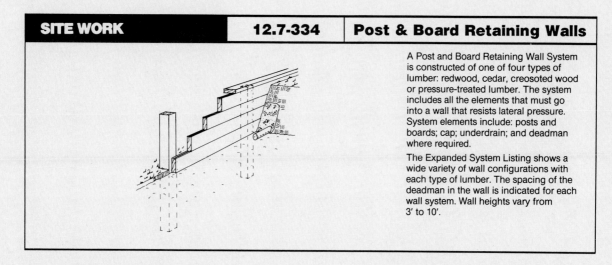

A Post and Board Retaining Wall System is constructed of one of four types of lumber: redwood, cedar, creosoted wood or pressure-treated lumber. The system includes all the elements that must go into a wall that resists lateral pressure. System elements include: posts and boards; cap; underdrain; and deadman where required.

The Expanded System Listing shows a wide variety of wall configurations with each type of lumber. The spacing of the deadman in the wall is indicated for each wall system. Wall heights vary from 3' to 10'.

System Components	QUANTITY	UNIT	COST PER L.F.		
			MAT.	INST.	TOTAL
SYSTEM 12.7-334-1000					
POST & BOARD RETAINING WALL, 2″ PLANKS, 4 X 4 POSTS, 3′ HIGH					
Redwood post 4″ x 4″	2.000	B.F.	2.02	1.93	3.95
Redwood joist 2″ x 10″	7.000	B.F.	6.31	2.09	8.40
Redwood cap 2″ x 10″	.167	B.F.	.90	.30	1.20
Gravel drain and pipe, bank run gravel, perf. pipe	1.000	L.F.	2.77	1.83	4.60
TOTAL			12	6.15	18.15

12.7-334	Post And Board Retaining Walls	COST PER L.F.		
		MAT.	INST.	TOTAL
1000	Post & board retaining wall, 2″ planking, redwood, 4 x 4 post, 4′ spacing, 3′ high	12	6.15	18.15
1200	2′ spacing, 4′ high	16.45	9.50	25.95
1400	6 x 6 post, 4′ spacing, 5′ high	22	11.55	33.55
1600	3′ spacing, 6′ high	30	15.75	45.75
1800	6 x 6 post with deadman, 3′ spacing, 8′ high	38	20	58
2000	8 x 8 post, 2′ spacing, 8′ high	68	39	107
2200	8 x 8 post with deadman, 2′ spacing, 9′ high	80	43	123
2400	Cedar, 4 x 4 post, 4′ spacing, 3′ high	9.90	5.95	15.85
2600	4 x 4 post with deadman, 2′ spacing, 4′ high	18.95	9.80	28.75
2800	6 x 6 post, 4′ spacing, 4′ high	15.90	9.60	25.50
3000	3′ spacing, 5′ high	21	13.45	34.45
3200	2′ spacing, 6′ high	32	21	53
3400	6 x 6 post with deadman, 3′ spacing, 6′ high	26	16.25	42.25
3600	8 x 8 post with deadman, 2′ spacing, 8′ high	64	40	104
3800	Pressure treated, 4 x 4 post, 4′ spacing, 3′ high	7.65	10.60	18.25
4000	3′ spacing, 4′ high	10.45	14.45	24.90
4200	4 x 4 post with deadman, 2′ spacing, 5′ high	18.25	19.15	37.40
4400	6 x 6 post, 3′ spacing, 6′ high	33	28	61
4600	2′ spacing, 7′ high	26	32	58
4800	6 x 6 post with deadman, 3′ spacing, 8′ high	27	31	58
5000	8 x 8 post with deadman, 2′ spacing, 10′ high	59	69	128
5200	Creosoted, 4 x 4 post, 4′ spacing, 3′ high	7.65	10.60	18.25
5400	3′ spacing, 4′ high	10.45	14.45	24.90
5600	4 x 4 post with deadman, 2′ spacing, 5′ high	18.25	19.15	37.40
5800	6 x 6 post, 3′ spacing, 6′ high	18.60	24	42.60
6000	2′ spacing, 7′ high	26	32	58
6200	6 x 6 post with deadman, 3′ spacing 8′ high	27	31	58
6400	8 x 8 post with deadman, 2′ spacing, 10′ high	59	69	128

293

Figure 5.1

LANDSCAPE ESTIMATE SHEET

Project _____   Date _____
Location _____   Sheet No. _____
Landscape Architect _____   Estimate No. _____
Takeoff by _____ Extensions by _____   Owner _____
                                                       Checked by _____

Category	Description	Qty	Price	Extension	Total
PLANTS Trees Shrubs Flowers Ground Cover Other Tax Subtotal					
HORTICULTURAL MATERIAL Mulch for Trees Mulch Soil Conditioner Fertilizer Other Tax Subtotal					
HARDWARE					
GRAVEL & BOULDERS					
LANDSCAPE TIMBERS					
SOIL					
SOD					
LAWN SEEDING					
OTHER MATERIALS					
LABOR					
TOOLS & EQUIPMENT Equipment on Job Rental Equipment Other					
FREIGHT					
DUMP CHARGES					
MAINTENANCE PROGRAM					
GRAND TOTAL					

Figure 5.2

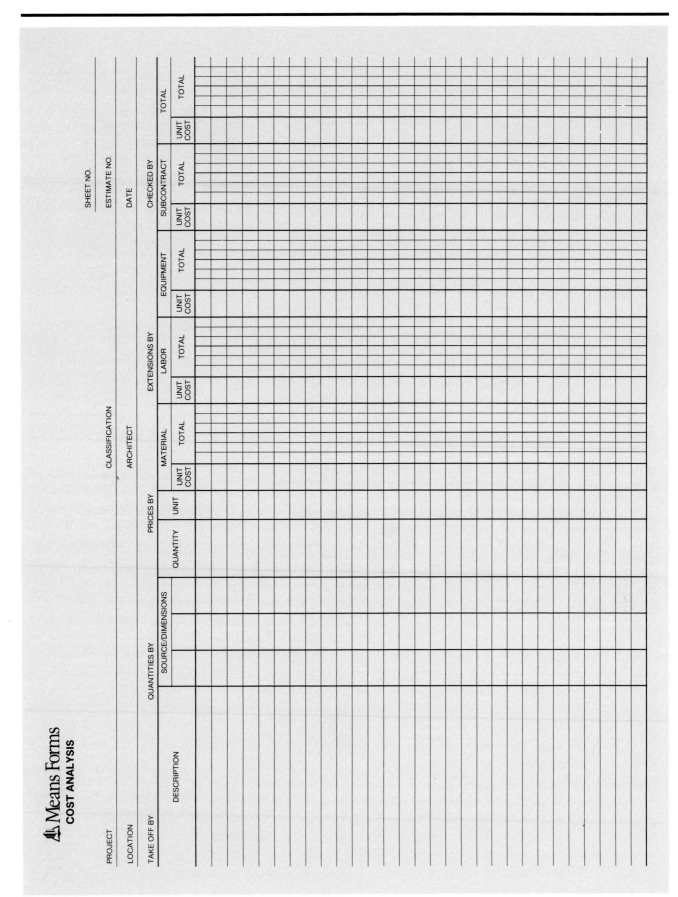

Figure 5.3

Sources of Cost Information

One of the most difficult parts of the estimator's job is determining accurate and reliable bare cost data. Sources for such data are varied, but can be categorized in terms of their relative reliability. The most reliable source of any cost information is the accurate, up to date, well kept records of the estimator's own company. There is no better cost for a particular construction item than the actual cost to the contractor of that item from another recent job, modified (if necessary) to meet the requirements of the project being estimated. Preprinted forms, such as those shown in Figures 5.4, 5.5, and 5.6, can simplify this kind of record keeping.

Bids from responsible subcontractors are the second most reliable source of cost data. A subcontract bid is a known, fixed cost, prior to the project. Whether the price is "right" or "wrong", does not matter (as long as it is a responsible bid with no gross errors). The bid provides the estimator with the cost of a designated portion of the work. No further estimating is required, except for possible verification of the quote. When pricing from a subcontractor's bid, it is essential to have a clear agreement between the parties on the complete scope of the work, and confidence that the subcontractor will be able to perform at the required time.

Quotations by nurseries or other suppliers for material costs are, for the same reasons, as reliable as subcontract bids. For these materials, the estimator must apply estimated labor costs. Thus the "installed" price for a particular item may be variable. Be sure the supplier's price will be "good" at the time of actual purchase. Whenever possible, all price quotations from vendors or subcontractors should be obtained in writing. Qualifications and exclusions should be clearly stated. Quoted prices should be checked to be sure that they are complete and as specified. One way to assure these requirements is to prepare a form on which all subcontractors and vendors must submit quotations. This form can ask all appropriate questions, such as "Is the price delivered or F.O.B.?" or "Is sales tax included?".

The above procedures are ideal, but often in the realistic haste of estimating and bidding, quotations are received verbally — in person or by telephone. The importance of gathering all pertinent information is heightened because omissions are more likely. A preprinted form, such as the one shown in Figure 5.7, can be extremely useful to assure that all required information and qualifications are obtained and understood. How often has the subcontractor stated, "I didn't know that I was supposed to include that"? With the help of such forms, the appropriate questions are asked and answered.

Means Forms

DAILY TIME SHEET

PROJECT _____

FO REMAN _____

WEATHER CONDITIONS _____

TEMPERATURE _____

DATE _____

SHEET NO. _____

NO.	NAME		DESCRIPTION OF WORK						TOTALS HOURS		COST INFORMATION			
									REG-ULAR	OVER-TIME	RATE	TOTAL		UNIT COST
		HOURS												
		UNITS												
		HOURS												
		UNITS												
		HOURS												
		UNITS												
		HOURS												
		UNITS												
		HOURS												
		UNITS												
		HOURS												
		UNITS												
		HOURS												
		UNITS												
		HOURS												
		UNITS												
		HOURS												
		UNITS												
		HOURS												
		UNITS												
		HOURS												
		UNITS												
		HOURS												
		UNITS												
		HOURS												
		UNITS												
		HOURS												
		UNITS												
	TOTALS	HOURS												
		UNITS												
	EQUIPMENT													

Figure 5.4

**MATERIAL
COST RECORD**

SHEET NO. _____

DATE FROM _____

PROJECT _____ DATE TO _____

LOCATION _____ BY _____

DATE	NUMBER	VENDOR/DESCRIPTION	QTY.	UNIT PRICE				QTY.	UNIT PRICE				QTY.	UNIT PRICE		

Figure 5.5

**LABOR
COST RECORD**

SHEET NO.

DATE FROM:

PROJECT

DATE TO:

LOCATION

BY:

DATE	CHARGE NO.	DESCRIPTION	HOURS	RATE	AMOUNT	HOURS	RATE	AMOUNT	HOURS	RATE	AMOUNT

Figure 5.6

If the estimator has no cost records for a particular item and is unable to obtain a quotation, then the next most reliable source of price information is a current cost book such as *Means Site Work Cost Data*. Means presents all such data in the form of national averages. These figures must be adjusted to local conditions, a procedure explained in Chapter 9. In addition to being a source of primary costs, such books can be useful as a reference or cross check for verifying costs obtained elsewhere. For example, a quote from a subcontractor for an unfamiliar item can be checked to assure that the bid is "in the ballpark".

Lacking cost information from any of the above-mentioned sources, the estimator may have to rely on data from old books or adjusted records from old projects. While these types of costs may not be very accurate, they may be better than the final alternative — guesswork.

No matter which source of cost information is used, the system and sequence of pricing should be the same as that used for the quantity takeoff. This consistent approach should continue through both accounting and cost control during construction of the project.

Types of Costs

The landscape project should first be broken down into categories and then into components within each category. Depending on the type of estimate and the amount of detail involved, each "item" can be broken down further into material, labor and equipment. Each of these categories involves different kinds of costs.

All costs included in a landscape estimate can be classified as direct or indirect. Direct costs are those directly linked to the physical construction of a project: work crew, plant material, and sod. The material, labor and equipment costs mentioned above, as well as subcontract costs are all direct costs. These may also be referred to as "bare" costs.

Indirect costs are usually added to the estimate at the summary stage and are most often calculated as a percentage of the direct costs. They include such items as administrative wages, overhead, profit and contingencies. It is the indirect costs that may account for a large variation in estimating. Methods for determining indirect costs are included later in this chapter.

Types of Costs in a Construction Estimate

Direct Costs	Indirect Costs
Material	Taxes
Labor	Overhead
Equipment	Profit
Subcontractors	Contingencies
Project Overhead	

Direct Costs

In the preceding list, Project Overhead is classified as a direct cost. Project Overhead represents those costs of a construction project which are usually included in Division One — General Requirements. Typical items are the job site office trailer, supervisory labor costs, daily and final cleanup, and temporary water. While these items may not be directly part of the "installed" work, the project could not be completed without them. Project Overhead, like all other direct costs, can be separated into material, labor and equipment components.

Material: When quantities have been carefully taken off, estimates of material cost can be very accurate. In order to maintain a high level of accuracy, the unit prices for materials must be reliable and current. The most reliable source of material costs is a quotation from a familiar local nursery, lumber yard, or gravel pit for the particular job in question. Ideally, the vendor should have access to the plans and specifications for verification of quantities and specified products. Current catalogues (e.g., for plant materials) may not account for actual availability in an industry that is often dependent on uncontrollable factors such as weather.

Material pricing appears relatively simple and straightforward. There are, however, certain considerations that the estimator must address when analyzing material quotations. The reputation of the vendor is a significant factor. Can the vendor "deliver", both figuratively and literally? Often estimators may choose not to rely on a "competitive" lower price from an unknown vendor, but will instead use a slightly higher price from a known, reliable vendor. Experience is the best judge for such decisions.

There are many questions that the estimator should ask. How long is the price guaranteed? How long are the plant materials guaranteed? At the end of that period, is there an escalation clause? Does the price include delivery or sales tax, if required? Note that most of these questions are addressed on the form in Figure 5.7. But more information should be obtained to assure that a quoted price is accurate and competitive.

The estimator must be sure that the quotation or obtained price is for the materials as per plans and specifications. Are the tree caliper sizes correct? Designers may write into the specifications that: a) the particular type of material or brand of product must be used *exactly* as specified, with no substitution, b) the particular type of material is recommended, but alternate materials or brands may be accepted *upon approval*, or c) no particular type or brand is specified. Depending upon the options, the estimator may be able to find an acceptable, less expensive alternative. In some cases, these substitutions can substantially lower the cost of a project.

When the estimator has received material quotations, there are still other considerations which should have a bearing on the final choice of a vendor. Lead time — the amount of time between order and delivery — must be determined and considered. It does not matter how competitive or low a quote is if the nursery cannnot deliver the plant material to the job site on time. If a delivery date is promised, is there a guarantee, or a penalty clause for late delivery?

The estimator should also determine if there are any unusual payment requirements. Cash flow for a company can be severely affected if a large material purchase, thought to be payable in 30 days is delivered C.O.D. Truck drivers may not allow unloading until payment has been received. Such requirements must be determined during the estimating stage so that the cost of borrowing money, if necessary, can be included.

If unable to obtain the quotation of a vendor from whom the material would be purchased, the estimator has other sources for obtaining material prices. These include, in order of reliability:

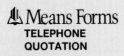
TELEPHONE
QUOTATION

DATE _____

PROJECT _____ TIME _____

FIRM QUOTING _____ PHONE (____) _____

ADDRESS _____ BY _____

ITEM QUOTED _____ RECEIVED BY _____

WORK INCLUDED	AMOUNT OF QUOTATION

DELIVERY TIME   **TOTAL BID**

DOES QUOTATION INCLUDE THE FOLLOWING: If ☐ NO is checked, determine the following:

STATE & LOCAL SALES TAXES	☐ YES	☐ NO	MATERIAL VALUE
DELIVERY TO THE JOB SITE	☐ YES	☐ NO	WEIGHT
COMPLETE INSTALLATION	☐ YES	☐ NO	QUANTITY
COMPLETE SECTION AS PER PLANS & SPECIFICATIONS	☐ YES	☐ NO	DESCRIBE BELOW

EXCLUSIONS AND QUALIFICATIONS

ADDENDA ACKNOWLEDGEMENT   **TOTAL ADJUSTMENTS**

ADJUSTED TOTAL BID

ALTERNATES

ALTERNATE NO.
ALTERNATE NO.
ALTERNATE NO.
ALTERNATE NO.
ALTERNATE NO.
ALTERNATE NO.
ALTERNATE NO.

Figure 5.7

1. Current price lists from manufacturer's catalogues. Be sure to check that the list is for "contractor prices".
2. Cost records from previous jobs. Historical costs must be updated for present conditions.
3. Reputable and current, annual unit price cost books, such as *Means Site Work Cost Data*. Such books usually represent national averages and must be factored to local markets.

No matter which price source is used, the estimator must be sure to include any costs (e.g., delivery, tax) over the actual cost of the material.

Labor: In order to determine the labor cost for each unit of construction, the estimator must know the following: first, the labor rate (hourly wage or salary) of the worker, and second, how many units this worker can produce or install in a given time period — in other words, the output or productivity. Wage rates are known going into a project, but productivity may be very difficult to determine. The best source of labor productivity (and therefore labor costs) is the estimator's well-kept records from previous projects. If no accurate labor cost records are available, the estimator has two basic alternatives for determining labor costs. The first alternative is to consult published data. Cost data books, such as *Means Site Work Cost Data*, provide national average labor rates by trade and base the unit costs for labor on these averages. Figure 5.8 shows national average *union* rates for the construction industry (based on January 1, 1987). Figure 5.9 lists national average *non-union* rates, again based on January 1, 1987.

CIRCLE REFERENCE NUMBERS

⑥ Contractor's Overhead & Profit (Div. 1.1)

Listed below in the last two columns are **average** billing rates for the installing contractor's labor.

The Base Rates are averages for the building construction industry and include the usual negotiated fringe benefits. Workers' Compensation is a national average of state rates established for each trade. Average Fixed Overhead is a total of average rates for U.S. and State Unemployment, 5.5%; Social Security (FICA), 7.15%; Builders' Risk, 1.14%; and Public Liability, 0.82%. These are analyzed in ② and ⑤ . All the rates except Social Security vary from state to state as well as from company to company. The installing contractor's overhead presumes annual billing of $500,000 and up. Overhead percentages may increase with smaller annual billing.

Overhead varies greatly within each trade. Some controlling factors are annual volume, job type, job size, location, local economic conditions, engineering and logistical support staff and equipment requirements. All factors should be examined carefully for each job.

Abbr.	Trade	Base Rate Incl. Fringes		Work-ers' Comp. Ins.	Average Fixed Over-head	Over-head	Profit	Total Overhead & Profit		Rate with O & P	
		Hourly	Daily					%	Amount	Hourly	Daily
Skwk	Skilled Workers Average (35 trades)	$20.80	$166.40	10.4%	14.6%	12.6%	10%	47.6%	$ 9.90	$30.70	$245.60
	Helpers Average (5 trades)	15.90	127.20	11.1		12.7		48.4	7.70	23.60	188.80
	Foremen Average, Inside (50¢ over trade)	21.30	170.40	10.4		12.6		47.6	10.15	31.45	251.60
	Foremen Average, Outside ($2.00 over trade)	22.80	182.40	10.4		12.6		47.6	10.85	33.65	269.20
Clab	Common Building Laborers	16.10	128.80	11.4		10.8		46.8	7.55	23.65	189.20
Asbe	Asbestos Workers	23.00	184.00	8.8		15.7		49.1	11.30	34.30	274.40
Boil	Boilermakers	23.00	184.00	7.2		16.0		47.8	11.00	34.00	272.00
Bric	Bricklayers	20.55	164.40	8.5		10.7		43.8	9.00	29.55	236.40
Brhe	Bricklayer Helpers	16.15	128.40	8.5		10.7		43.8	7.05	23.20	185.60
Carp	Carpenters	20.55	164.40	11.4		10.8		46.8	9.60	30.15	241.20
Cefi	Cement Finishers	19.70	157.60	6.6		10.8		42.0	8.30	27.95	223.60
Elec	Electricians	22.65	181.20	4.5		15.9		45.0	10.20	32.85	262.80
Elev	Elevator Constructors	23.05	184.40	6.0		15.9		46.5	10.70	33.75	270.00
Eqhv	Equipment Operators, Crane or Shovel	21.20	169.60	7.8		13.8		46.2	9.80	31.00	248.00
Eqmd	Equipment Operators, Medium Equipment	20.75	166.00	7.8		13.8		46.2	9.60	30.35	242.80
Eqlt	Equipment Operators, Light Equipment	19.60	156.80	7.8		13.8		46.2	9.05	28.65	229.20
Eqol	Equipment Operators, Oilers	17.55	140.40	7.8		13.8		46.2	8.10	25.65	205.20
Eqmm	Equipment Operators, Master Mechanics	22.00	176.00	7.8		13.8		46.2	10.15	32.15	257.20
Glaz	Glaziers	20.75	166.00	8.7		10.8		44.1	9.15	29.90	239.20
Lath	Lathers	20.50	164.00	7.2		10.8		42.6	8.75	29.25	234.00
Marb	Marble Setters	20.25	162.00	8.5		10.7		43.8	8.85	29.10	232.80
Mill	Millwrights	21.25	170.00	7.2		10.8		42.6	9.05	30.30	242.40
Mstz	Mosaic and Terrazzo Workers	20.05	160.40	6.0		10.7		41.3	8.30	28.35	226.80
Pord	Painters, Ordinary	19.55	156.40	8.9		10.8		44.3	8.65	28.20	225.60
Psst	Painters, Structural Steel	20.20	161.60	29.4		10.1		64.1	12.95	33.15	265.20
Pape	Paper Hangers	19.75	158.00	8.9		10.8		44.3	8.75	28.50	228.00
Pile	Pile Drivers	20.35	162.80	18.3		15.7		58.6	11.95	32.30	258.40
Plas	Plasterers	20.25	162.00	8.7		10.9		44.2	8.95	29.20	233.60
Plah	Plasterer Helpers	16.65	133.20	8.7		10.9		44.2	7.35	24.00	192.00
Plum	Plumbers	23.00	184.00	5.3		15.9		45.8	10.55	33.55	268.40
Rodm	Rodmen (Reinforcing)	22.10	176.80	18.6		13.3		56.5	12.50	34.60	276.80
Rofc	Roofers, Composition	19.15	153.20	20.8		10.4		55.8	10.70	29.85	238.80
Rots	Roofers, Tile & Slate	19.25	154.00	20.8		10.4		55.8	10.75	30.00	240.00
Rohe	Roofer Helpers (Composition)	14.20	113.60	20.8		10.4		55.8	7.90	22.10	176.80
Shee	Sheet Metal Workers	23.10	184.80	7.0		15.8		47.4	10.95	34.05	272.40
Spri	Sprinkler Installers	23.85	190.80	6.1		15.9		46.6	11.10	34.95	279.60
Stpi	Steamfitters or Pipefitters	23.30	186.40	5.3		15.9		45.8	10.70	33.95	271.60
Ston	Stone Masons	20.60	164.80	8.5		10.7		43.8	9.00	29.60	236.80
Sswk	Structural Steel Workers	22.10	176.80	21.5		13.7		59.8	13.20	35.30	282.40
Tilf	Tile Layers (Floor)	20.00	160.00	6.0		10.7		41.3	8.25	28.25	226.00
Tilh	Tile Layer Helpers	16.10	128.80	6.0		10.7		41.3	6.65	22.75	182.00
Trlt	Truck Drivers, Light	16.70	133.60	9.8		10.7		45.1	7.55	24.25	194.00
Trhv	Truck Drivers, Heavy	16.95	135.60	9.8		10.7		45.1	7.65	24.60	196.80
Sswl	Welders, Structural Steel	22.10	176.80	21.5		13.7		59.8	13.20	35.30	282.40
Wrck	*Wrecking	16.10	128.80	23.1		10.4		58.1	9.35	25.45	203.60

*Not included in Averages.

Figure 5.8

Installing Contractor's Overhead & Profit

Below are the **average** installing contractor's percentage mark-ups applied to base labor rates to arrive at typical billing rates.

Column A: Labor rates are based on average wages for 7 major U.S. regions. Base rates including fringe benefits are listed hourly and daily. These figures are the sum of the wage rate and employer-paid fringe benefits such as vacation pay and employer-paid health costs.

Column B: Workers' Compensation rates are the national average of state rates established for each trade.

Column C: Column C lists average fixed overhead figures for all trades. Included are Federal and State Unemployment costs set at 5.5%; Social Security Taxes (FICA) set at 7.15%; Builder's Risk Insurance costs set at 1.14%; and Public Liability costs set at 0.82%. All the percentages except those for Social Security Taxes vary from state to state as well as from company to company.

Column D and E: Percentages in Columns D and E are based on the presumption that the installing contractor has annual billing of $500,000 and up. Overhead percentages may increase with smaller annual billing. The overhead percentages for any given contractor may vary greatly and depend on a number of factors, such as the contractor's annual volume, engineering and logistical support costs, and staff requirements. The figures for overhead and profit will also vary depending on the type of job, the job location, and the prevailing economic conditions. All factors should be examined very carefully for each job.

Column F: Column F lists the total of columns B, C, D, and E.

Column G: Column G is Column A (hourly base labor rate) multiplied by the percentage in Column F (O&P percentage).

Column H: Column H is the total of Column A (hourly base labor rate) plus Column G (Total O&P).

Column I: Column I is Column H multiplied by eight hours.

Abbr.	Trade	A Base Rate Incl. Fringes Hourly	A Base Rate Incl. Fringes Daily	B Workers' Comp. Ins.	C Average Fixed Overhead	D Subs Overhead	E Subs Profit	F Subs Total Overhead & Profit %	G Subs Total Overhead & Profit Amount	H Rate with Subs O & P Hourly	I Rate with Subs O & P Daily
Skwk	Skilled Workers Average	$12.30	$ 98.40	10.4%	14.6%	22.8%	10%	57.8%	$ 7.10	$19.40	$155.20
	Helpers Average ($2.00 under trade)	10.30	82.40	11.1		23.0		58.7	6.05	16.35	130.80
	Foremen Average, ($2.00 over trade)	14.30	114.40	10.4		22.8		57.8	8.25	22.55	180.40
Clab	Laborers	9.70	77.60	11.4		21.0		57.0	5.55	15.25	122.00
Asbe	Pipe or Duct Insulators	13.55	108.40	8.8		26.0		59.4	8.05	21.60	172.80
Boil	Boilermakers	13.55	108.40	7.2		26.0		57.8	7.85	21.35	170.80
Bric	Brick or Block Masons	12.10	96.80	8.5		21.0		54.1	6.55	18.65	149.20
Carp	Carpenters	12.20	97.60	11.4		21.0		57.0	6.95	19.15	153.20
Cefi	Cement Finishers	11.70	93.60	6.6		21.0		52.2	6.10	17.80	142.40
Elec	Electricians	13.30	106.40	4.5		26.0		55.1	7.35	20.65	165.20
Elev	Elevator Constructors	13.50	108.00	6.0		26.0		56.6	7.65	21.15	169.20
Eqhv	Equipment Operators, Crane	12.50	100.00	7.8		24.0		56.4	7.05	19.55	156.40
Eqmd	Equipment Operators	12.25	98.00	7.8		24.0		56.4	6.90	19.15	153.20
Eqmm	Equipment Mechanics	13.00	104.00	7.8		24.0		56.4	7.35	20.35	162.80
Glaz	Glaziers	12.30	98.40	8.7		21.0		54.3	6.70	19.00	152.00
Lath	Lathers	12.20	97.60	7.2		21.0		52.8	6.45	18.65	149.20
Mill	Millwrights	12.50	100.00	7.2		21.0		52.8	6.60	19.10	152.80
Pord	Painters	11.60	92.80	8.9		21.0		54.5	6.30	17.90	143.20
Pile	Pile Drivers	12.05	96.40	18.3		26.0		68.9	8.30	20.35	162.80
Plas	Plasterers	11.95	95.60	8.7		21.0		54.3	6.50	18.45	147.60
Plum	Plumbers	13.45	107.60	5.3		26.0		55.9	7.50	20.95	167.60
Rodm	Rodmen (Reinforcing)	13.00	104.00	18.6		24.0		67.2	8.75	21.75	174.00
Rofc	Roofers	11.40	91.20	20.8		21.0		66.4	7.55	18.95	151.60
Shee	Sheet Metal Workers	13.50	108.00	7.0		26.0		57.6	7.75	21.25	170.00
Spri	Sprinkler Installers	13.85	110.80	6.1		26.0		56.7	7.85	21.70	173.60
Stpi	Pipefitters	13.65	109.20	5.3		26.0		55.9	7.65	21.30	170.40
Ston	Stone Masons	12.20	97.60	8.5		21.0		54.1	6.60	18.80	150.40
Sswk	Structural Steel Erectors	13.00	104.00	21.5		24.0		70.1	9.10	22.10	176.80
Tilf	Flooring Installers	11.90	95.20	6.0		21.0		51.6	6.15	18.05	144.40
Trhv	Truck Drivers	10.20	81.60	9.8	↓	21.0	↓	55.4	5.65	15.85	126.80
Wrck	Wreckers	9.75	78.00	23.1		21.0		68.7	6.70	16.45	131.60

Figure 5.9

If more accurate rates are required, the estimator has alternate sources. Union locals can provide rates (as well as negotiated increases) for a particular location. This source requires the estimator to call the union hall for each trade. Employer bargaining groups can usually provide labor cost data, but this data may not be continually updated. Means publishes *Labor Rates for the Construction Industry* on an annual basis. This book lists the union labor rates by trade for over 300 U.S. and Canadian cities.

Determination of specific, local non-union, or "open shop" rates is much more difficult. In some larger cities, there are organizations that represent non-union contractors. These groups may be a source of local pay scales, but ultimately the wage rates are determined by each contractor.

Productivity reference books, such as *Means Man-Hour Standards*, can be helpful. Included with the listing for each individual construction item is the designation of typical crew make-up, together with the productivity or output — the amount of work that the crew will produce. Figure 5.10, a typical page from *Means Man-Hour Standards*, includes this data and indicates the required number of man-hours for each "unit" of work for the appropriate task. The estimator can apply local, known labor rates to determine unit costs for labor. With known labor rates and proposed schedules (see Chapter 8 for a discussion of scheduling), the estimator can also develop weekly payroll estimates. This process will help to anticipate costs and the work crew that will be needed. In this way, the scheduled projects can be planned to meet budget and cash flow requirements. Weekly payroll estimates can then be compared to actual costs, and reliable productivity records can be made. An example is shown in Figure 5.11.

2.8 Lawns & Planting		CREW	MAKEUP	DAILY OUTPUT	MAN-HOURS	UNIT
1001	Wood, treated, 1" x 4"	F-2	2 Carpenters	500	.032	L.F.
			Power Tools			
1040	2" x 4"			330	.048	L.F.
1080	4" x 6"			250	.064	L.F.
1100	6" x 6"			200	.080	L.F.
1140	6" x 8"	↓	↓	170	.094	L.F.
070	EROSION CONTROL Jute mesh, 100 S.Y. per roll, 4' wide, stapled	B-1	1 Foreman (outside)	2,500	.010	S.Y.
			2 Building Laborers			
0100	Plastic netting, stapled			2,500	.010	S.Y.
0200	Polypropylene mesh, stapled			2,500	.010	S.Y.
0300	Tobacco netting, #2, stapled	↓	↓	2,500	.010	S.Y.
1000	Silt fence, polypropylene, ideal conditions	2 Clab	2 Building Laborers	1,600	.010	L.F.
1100	Adverse conditions	"	"	950	.017	L.F.
110	GROUND COVER planting only, no preparation					
0100	Ajuga, field division	B-1	1 Foreman (outside)	53	.453	C
			2 Building Laborers			
0150	Potted, 4"-6"			9	2.667	C
0200	Bearberry, potted			6	4.000	C
0250	Cottoneaster, 18"-24", shady areas			.80	30.000	C
0300	Boston ivy, on bank, 12"-18", bare root			9	2.667	C
0350	Potted, 2 year			6	4.000	C
0400	English ivy, rooted cutting			24	1.000	C
0450	Potted, 3"			12	2.000	C
0500	Halls honeysuckle, bare root, 1 year			9	2.667	C
0550	Potted, 2 year			6	4.000	C
0600	Memorial rose, 9"-12", 1 year			4.50	5.333	C
0650	Potted, 2 year			3	8.000	C
0700	Pachysandra, rooted cutting			53	453	C
0750	Potted, 3"			12	2.000	C
0800	Vinca minor, clumps, rooted cuttings			24	1.000	C
0850	Potted, 2 year			16	1.500	C
0900	Woodbine, on bank, 18"-24", seedling, 2 year			9	2.667	C
0950	Potted, 2 year	↓	↓	6	4.000	C
2000	Alternate method of figuring					
2100	Ajuga, field division	B-1	1 Foreman (outside)	1.33	18.045	M.S.F.
			2 Building Laborers			
2300	Boston ivy, 12"-18"			15	1.600	M.S.F.
2400	English ivy, rooted cutting			4.80	5.000	M.S.F.
2500	Halls honeysuckle, bare root			2.70	8.889	M.S.F.
2600	Memorial rose, 9"-12", 1 year			13.50	1.778	M.S.F.
2700	Pachysandra, rooted cutting			1.33	18.045	M.S.F.
2800	Vinca minor, rooted cutting			2.40	10.000	M.S.F.
2900	Woodbine, 18"-24"			15	1.600	M.S.F.
150	HEDGE PLANTS, barberry, 15" to 18" high			130	.185	Ea.
0200	Privet, 15" to 18" high			175	.137	Ea.
0400	Boxwood, 18" to 20" high			80	.300	Ea.
0600	Ilex, 8" to 10" high	↓	↓	52	.462	Ea.
250	LOAM OR TOPSOIL Remove and stockpile on site, using 200 H.P.					
0020	dozer, 6' deep, 200' haul	B-10B	1 Equipment Oper. (med.)	865	.014	C.Y.
			.5 Building Laborer			
			1 Dozer, 200 H.P.			
0100	300' haul			520	.023	C.Y.
0150	500' haul			225	.053	C.Y.
0200	Alternate method: 6" deep, 200' haul			5,090	.002	S.Y.
0250	500' haul	↓	↓	1,325	.009	S.Y.
0400	Spread from pile to rough finish grade, with 1-1/2 C.Y. F.E. loader	B-10S	1 Equipment Oper. (med.)	200	.060	C.Y.
			.5 Building Laborer			
			F.E. Loader, W.M., 1.5 C.Y.			
0500	200' by hand	1 Clab	1 Building Laborer	14	.571	C.Y.
0600	Top dress by hand, 1 C.Y. for 600 S.F.	"	"	11.50	.696	C.Y.

Figure 5.10

The estimator who has neither company records nor the published sources described takes the remaining alternative — judgment based on experience. In this case, the estimator must put together the appropriate crews and determine the expected output or productivity. This type of estimating should only be attempted if it is based on a solid foundation of experience and considerable exposure to landscape industry methods and practices.

Weekly Payroll Estimate							
Labor Data			Hours per Week		Weekly Payroll		
Worker	Number	Rate	Estimated	Actual	Estimated	Actual	Variance
Foreman "A"	1	14.30	40		$ 572.00		
Foreman "B"	1	13.00	20		260.00		
Workers "A"	2	12.30	40		492.00		
"B"	3	12.10	40		484.00		
"C"	1	10.50	25		262.50		
"D"	1	9.70	40		388.00		
Total Hours			205				
Total Wages					$2,458.50		
Payroll Taxes*					614.63		
TOTAL ESTIMATED PAYROLL					$3,073.13		

*For purposes of this example, 25% is added for payroll taxes. Actual percentages will vary from state to state and from company to company.

Figure 5.11

Equipment: There are four considerations for estimating the cost of equipment. These are:

- Choosing the proper type of equipment.
- Judging the amount of time it will be used.
- Applying the correct rental rate, including operator and fuel.
- Including the cost to move the equipment on and off the job.

The type of work to be done may suggest appropriate equipment. For example, large amounts of earthen materials to be moved in an easily accessible space may permit the largest equipment that is cost effective. Restricted access may require that materials be moved in a small tractor bucket or by hand with a wheel barrow. Excavating and hauling may require front-end loaders and dump trucks or dump trailers; cutting and filling suggests bulldozers and/or scrapers and a roller compactor, and a water wagon.

Equipment costs may be classified in the following way:

1. Bare equipment (without operator or fuel) priced as rented per hour, day, week or month. If operators and fuel (or any operating costs) are required, these may be priced out as separate labor and material items, respectively.

2. Bare equipment as above, but owned by the landscaper and charged to the job at an hourly depreciation rate figured by the owner for a fair return on the investment.

3. Operated equipment complete including fuel, priced by the hour, day, week, or month and entered, in its entirety, as an equipment expense.

Quotations for equipment rental or lease costs can be obtained from local dealers and suppliers, or even from manufacturers. These costs can fluctuate and should be updated regularly.

Ownership costs must be determined within a company. There are many considerations beyond the up-front purchase price; these factors must be taken into account when figuring the cost of owning equipment. Interest rates and amortization schedules should be studied prior to the purchase. Insurance costs, storage fees, maintenance, taxes and licenses, all added together, can become a significant percentage of the cost of owning equipment. Depreciation (a way of quantifying loss of value to the owner over time) is another important factor. All of these considerations should be reviewed prior to purchase in order to properly manage the ownership.

The operating costs of equipment, whether rented, leased or owned, are available from the following sources (listed in order of reliability):

1. The company's own records.
2. Annual cost books containing equipment operating costs, such as *Building Construction Cost Data.*
3. Manufacturers' estimates.
4. Text books dealing with equipment operating costs.

These operating costs consist of fuel, lubrication, expendable parts replacement, minor maintenance, transportation and mobilizing costs. For estimating purposes, the equipment ownership and operating costs can be listed separately. In this way, the decision to rent, lease, or purchase can be decided project by project.

There are two commonly used methods for including equipment costs in a landscape estimate. The first is to include the cost of equipment as a part of the task for which it is used. This method is obvious for subcontract items where the machine work is subcontracted as a separate price. The advantage of this method is that costs are allocated to the division or task that actually incurs the expense. As a result, more accurate records can be kept for each construction component.

The second method for listing equipment costs is to keep all such costs separate and to include them as a part of Project Overhead. The advantage of this method is that all equipment costs are grouped together. The disadvantage is that for future estimating purposes, equipment costs will be known only by job and not by unit of construction. Under these circumstances, omissions could possibly occur.

Whichever method is used, the estimator must be consistent, and must be sure that all equipment costs are included, but not duplicated. The estimating method should be the same as that chosen for cost monitoring and accounting, so that the data will be available for future projects.

Subcontractors: Subcontractor quotations should be carefully examined to insure the following:

- Are they complete as per the plans and specifications?
- Do they include sales tax?
- Do they involve any unusual scheduling requirements or constraints?
- Do they include a performance bond, or are they bondable?
- Do they include any unusual payment schedule?
- What is the experience of the subcontractor with the exact type of work involved?
- Is the price competitive or is it a "street" price?

Subcontractor quotations should be solicited and analyzed in the same way as material quotes. A primary concern is that the bid covers the work as per plans and specifications, and that all appropriate work alternates and allowances are included. Any exclusions should be clearly stated and explained. If the bid is received verbally, a form such as that in Figure 5.7 will help to assure that all items are included. Any unique scheduling or payment requirements must be noted and evaluated prior to submission of the prime bid. Such requirements could affect or restrict the normal progress of the the project, and have an impact on the costs.

The estimator should note how long the subcontract bid will be honored. This time period usually varies from 30 to 90 days and is often included as a condition in complete bids. The general contractor may have to define the time limits of the prime bid based upon certain subcontractors. The estimator must also note any escalation clauses that may be included in subcontractor bids.

Reliability is another factor to be considered when soliciting and evaluating subcontractor bids. Reliability cannot be measured or priced until the project is actually under construction. Most landscape contractors tend to stay with the same subcontractors for just this reason. A certain unspoken communication exists in these established relationships and usually has a positive effect on the performance of the work. Such familiarity, however, can often erode the competitive nature of the bidding. To be competitive with the landscape bid, the estimator should always obtain comparison subcontract (and vendor) prices, whether these prices come from another subcontractor or are prepared by the estimator.

The estimator may question and verify the bonding capability and capacity of unfamiliar subcontractors. Taking such action may be necessary when bidding in a new location. Other than word of mouth, these inquiries may be the only way to confirm subcontractor reliability.

For major subcontract items it may be necessary to make up spread sheets in order to list inclusions and omissions. This procedure ensures that there is an accounting for every item in the job. Time permitting, the estimator should make a takeoff and price these major subcontract items to compare with the sub-bids. If time does not permit a detailed takeoff, the estimator should at least budget the work. A systems estimate is ideal for this purpose.

Project Overhead: Some estimators list certain costs as project overhead. These are items required to perform the work but not necessarily a direct part of specific landscape tasks. Project overhead includes items from project supervision to clean-up, from temporary utilities to permits. Some estimators may not agree that certain items (such as equipment and tools) should be included as Project Overhead, and might prefer to list such items in another division. Ultimately, it is not important, *where* or *how* each item is incorporated into the estimate, but that *every item is included somewhere*.

Project overhead often includes time-related items; equipment rental, supervisory labor, and temporary utilities are examples. The cost for these items depends upon the duration of the project. A preliminary schedule should therefore be developed *prior* to completion of the estimate so that time-related items can be properly counted.

Bonds: Bonds — bid bonds, performance bonds, etc. — may also be considered as project overhead. Bond requirements for a project are usually specified in the General Conditions portion of the specification. Costs for bonds are based on total project cost and are determined at the estimate summary stage. Listed below are a few common types:

> *Bid Bond*: A form of bid security executed by the bidder or principle and by a surety (bonding company) to guarantee that the bidder will enter into a contract within a specified time and furnish any required Performance or Labor and Material Payment bonds.
> *Completion Bond*: Also known as ''Construction'' or ''Contract'' bond. The guarantee by a surety that the construction contract will be completed and that it will be clear of all liens and encumbrances.
> *Labor and Material Payment Bond*: The guarantee by a surety to the owner that the contractor will pay for all labor and materials used in the performance of the contract as per the construction documents. The claimants under the bond are those having direct contracts with the contractor or any subcontractor.

Performance Bond: (1) A guarantee that a contractor will perform a job according to the terms of the contracts. (2) A bond of the contractor in which a surety guarantees to the owner that the work will be performed in accordance with the contract documents. Except where prohibited by statute, the performance bond is frequently combined with the labor and material payment bond.

Surety Bond: A legal instrument under which one party agrees to be responsible for the debt, default or failure to perform of another party.

Indirect Costs

The direct costs of a project must be itemized, tabulated and totalled before the indirect costs can be applied to the estimate. The indirect costs are almost always defined as a percentage of direct costs and include:

- Sales tax (if required)
- Employment taxes
- Office or operating overhead (vs. project overhead)
- Profit
- Contingencies

Sales Tax: Sales tax varies from state to state and often from city to city within a state (see Figure 5.12). Larger cities may have a sales tax in addition to the state sales tax. Some localities also impose separate sales taxes on labor and equipment.

When bidding takes place in unfamiliar locations, the estimator should check with local agencies regarding the amount, and the method of payment of sales tax. Local authorities may require owners to withhold payments to out-of-state contractors until payment of all required sales tax has been verified. Sales tax is often taken for granted or even omitted and, as can be seen in Figure 5.12, can be as much as 7.5% of material costs. Indeed, this can represent a significant portion of the project's total cost. Conversely, some clients and/or their projects may be tax exempt. If this fact is unknown to the estimator, a large dollar amount for sales tax might be needlessly included in a bid.

State sales tax on materials is tabulated below (5 states have no sales tax). Many states allow local jurisdictions, such as a county or city, to levy additional sales tax. Some projects may be sales tax exempt, particularly those constructed with public funds.

Sales Tax

State	Tax	State	Tax	State	Tax	State	Tax
Alabama	4%	Illinois	5%	Montana	0%	Rhode Island	6%
Alaska	0	Indiana	5	Nebraska	3.5	South Carolina ...	5
Arizona	5	Iowa	4	Nevada	5.75	South Dakota	4
Arkansas	4	Kansas	3	New Hampshire ..	0	Tennessee	5.5
California	6	Kentucky	5	New Jersey	6	Texas	4
Colorado	3	Louisiana	4	New Mexico	3.75	Utah	5.5
Connecticut	7.5	Maine	5	New York	4	Vermont	4
Delaware	0	Maryland	5	North Carolina ...	3	Virginia	4
District of Columbia	6	Massachusetts ...	5	North Dakota	4	Washington	6.5
Florida	5	Michigan	4	Ohio	5.5	West Virginia	5
Georgia	3	Minnesota	6	Oklahoma	3	Wisconsin	5
Hawaii	4	Mississippi	6	Oregon	0	Wyoming	3
Idaho	4	Missouri	6.225	Pennsylvania	6	Average	4.25%

Figure 5.12

Employment taxes: As with sales taxes, the estimator must be familiar with local and federal regulations for amounts and payment of employment taxes. These may include, but are not limited to Workers Compensation, federal and state unemployment insurance, and employer paid social security tax (FICA). National average rates for these taxes are shown in Figure 5.8 as percentages of labor costs.

Office or Operating Overhead: Office overhead, or the cost of doing business, is perhaps one of the main reasons why so many contractors are unable to realize a profit, or even to stay in business. If a contractor does not know the costs of operating the business, then, more than likely, these costs will not be recovered. Many companies survive, and even turn a profit, by simply adding a certain percentage for overhead to each job, without knowing how the percentage is derived or what is included. When annual volume changes significantly, whether by increase or decrease, the previously used percentage for overhead may no longer be valid. Often when such a volume change occurs, the owner finds that the company is not doing as well as before and cannot determine the reasons. Chances are, overhead costs are not being fully recovered.

A list of typical types of operating costs for landscape contractors is found in Figure 5.13. Notice the columns of estimated annual costs. These estimates should be based upon records from prior years and should incorporate anticipated increases or decreases in costs for the coming year. At the end of a year, actual costs for each item should be determined, and variations between actual and estimated costs should be calculated and analyzed. This information can then be used, together with any other pertinent data, to predict the coming year's overhead figures.

Note the last category, "Cost per work hour". This figure should be based on the anticipated available work hours for a year (see Chapter 3 and Figure 3.1). The total annual overhead costs are divided by the total available work hours to determine the cost per hour that must be added to workers' wages in order to recover overhead costs. These overhead costs must be recovered (paid for) before any profit can be realized.

The estimator must also remember that if volume or manpower changes significantly, then the applicable costs for office overhead should be recalculated for current conditions. The same is true if there are changes in office staff. Remember that salaries are the major portion of office overhead costs.

Profit: Determining a fair and reasonable percentage to be included for profit is not an easy task. This responsibility is usually left to the owner or chief estimator. Experience is crucial in anticipating what profit the market will bear. The economic climate, competition, knowledge of the project, and familiarity with the landscape architect or owner all affect the way in which profit is determined.

Contingencies: Like profit, contingencies can be difficult to quantify. Especially appropriate in preliminary budgets, the addition of a contingency is meant to protect the contractor as well as to give the owner a realistic estimate of project costs.

OVERHEAD COST SHEET

ITEM	Previous Year Actual Costs	Current Year Est. Costs	Current Year Actual Costs	Next Year Est. Costs
OFFICE PERSONNEL: Salaries Payroll taxes Benefits				
SECRETARIAL SERVICE: ($___ per hr.)				
OFFICE COSTS: Rent Utilities Telephone Supplies Postage				
INSURANCE: Liability Vehicle				
LEGAL SERVICES:				
ACCOUNTING:				
ADVERTISING:				
TRAVEL:				
ENTERTAINING:				
VEHICLES: Gas Maint.& repairs Tax & license Depreciation				
EQUIPMENT Gas Maint.& repair Tax & license Depreciation				
HAND TOOLS:				
TOTAL COSTS:				
TOTAL AVAIL. WORK HOURS:				
COST PER WORK HOUR				

Figure 5.13

A contingency percentage should be based on the number of "unknowns" in a project. This percentage should be inversely proportional to the amount of planning detail that has been done for the project. If complete plans and specifications are supplied, and the estimate is thorough and precise, then there is little need for a contingency. Figure 5.14, from *Means Site Work Cost Data*, lists suggested contingency percentages that may be added to an estimate based on the stage of planning and design development.

A method that is not recommended for including contingencies is "padding" or "rounding up" each individual item as it is priced. This can cause problems because the cost sheets will not show the actual costs separate from the "padding". At the summary, the estimator cannot determine exactly how much has been included as a contingency for the whole project. A much more accurate and controllable approach is the precise pricing of the estimate and the addition of one contingency amount at the bottom line.

The takeoff and pricing methods discussed in the preceding pages can be carried out neatly and effectively when the appropriate forms are used as guidelines. First, the quantity sheets are used for the material takeoff. Next, the data may be transferred to a cost analysis or pricing sheets where items are priced and costs extended. Then, an estimate summary form can be used to summarize the price totals for the general categories of a project. An example is shown in Figure 5.15. This process, transferring from one sheet to another, should be checked very carefully, as errors of transposition can easily occur. All major categories, such as trees or irrigation and their totals can be listed on this form, and subtotals figured. Appropriate markups for the indirect costs described above are then applied to the total dollar values. Generally, the sum of each column has different percentages added near the end of the estimate for the indirect costs.

When entering the extended totals, ignore the cents column and round all totals to the nearest dollar. In a column of totals, the cents will average out and be of no consequence. Each division is added and the results checked, preferably by someone other than the person doing the extensions.

The estimating process as a whole calls upon an accumulation of knowledge and experience. The first decision is to bid or not to bid. Once the facts have been carefully weighed and a decision made in favor of bidding, the estimating process is begun. Checklists, forms and good working techniques aid in the process of information gathering and guard against oversights. The investigating and evaluation of a specific project and site conditions is one area in which effective communication between planners and contractors proves vital.

1.1 Overhead			CREW	DAILY OUTPUT	MAN-HOURS	UNIT	BARE COSTS				TOTAL INCL O&P	
							MAT.	LABOR	EQUIP.	TOTAL		
020	0011	**ARCHITECTURAL FEES**										020
	0020	For work to $10,000				Project					15%	
	0060	To $100,000 ⑩									10%	
	0090	To $1,000,000				↓					7%	
030	0011	**BOND PERFORMANCE** See 1.1-340										
040	0010	**CLEANING UP** After job completion, allow				Job					.30%	040
	0031	Rubbish removal, see division 2.1-430										
060	0013	**CITY COST INDEX** Location adjustment factor for 162 major U.S.										060
	0022	And Canadian cities, see division 19										
090	0010	**CONSTRUCTION MANAGEMENT FEES** $1,000,000 job, minimum				Project					4.50%	090
	0050	Maximum									7.50%	
	0300	$5,000,000 job, minimum									2.50%	
	0350	Maximum									4%	
110	0010	**CONTINGENCIES** Allowance to add at conceptual stage									15%	110
	0050	Schematic stage									10%	
	0100	Preliminary working drawing stage									7%	
	0150	Final working drawing stage				↓					2%	
120	0010	**CONTRACTOR EQUIPMENT** See division 1.5 ⑬ ⑰										120
140	0010	**CREWS** For building construction, see foreword										140
150	0011	**ENGINEERING FEES** ⑪										150
	0800	Landscaping & site development, minimum				Contrct					2.50%	
	0900	Maximum				"					6%	
180	0010	**INSURANCE** Builders risk, standard, minimum ②				Job					.19%	180
	0050	Maximum									1.14%	
	0200	All-risk type, minimum									.20%	
	0250	Maximum				↓					1.16%	
	0400	Contractor's equipment floater, minimum				Value					.50%	
	0450	Maximum				"					2.50%	
	0600	Public liability, average				Job					.82%	
	0610											
	0800	Workers' compensation & employer's liability, average										
	0850	by trade, carpentry, general ⑦				Payroll		11.41%				
	0900	Clerical						.42%				
	0950	Concrete						10.30%				
	1000	Electrical						4.46%				
	1050	Excavation						7.81%				
	1250	Masonry						8.53%				
	1300	Painting & decorating						8.91%				
	1350	Pile driving						18.33%				
	1450	Plumbing						5.31%				
	1600	Steel erection, structural						21.51%				
	1650	Tile work, interior ceramic						5.96%				
	1700	Waterproofing, brush or hand caulking						5.09%				
	1800	Wrecking						23.08%				
	2000	Range of 36 trades in 50 states, excl. wrecking, minimum						1.10%				
	2100	Average						10.42%				
	2200	Maximum				↓		96.40%				
200	0015	**LABOR INDEX** Location adjustment factor										200
	0016	see City Cost Indexes, division 19										
220	0010	**MAIN OFFICE EXPENSE** Average for General Contractors										220
	0020	As a percentage of their annual volume										
	0050	Annual volume under 1 million dollars				% Vol.				13.60%		
	0100	Up to 2.5 million dollars								8%		
	0150	Up to 4.0 million dollars								6.80%		
	0200	Up to 7.0 million dollars				↓				5.60%		

For expanded coverage of these items see *Means Building Construction Cost Data 1987*

1

Figure 5.14

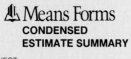

**CONDENSED
ESTIMATE SUMMARY**

PROJECT		SHEET NO.
LOCATION	TOTAL AREA/VOLUME	DATE
ARCHITECT	COST PER S.F./C.F.	NO. OF STORIES
PRICES BY:	EXTENSIONS BY:	CHECKED BY:

Figure 5.15

Chapter Six

THE SAMPLE TAKEOFF AND ESTIMATE

Chapter Six

THE SAMPLE TAKEOFF AND ESTIMATE

The estimator, whether designer or contractor, foreman or manager, has one basic goal — to compute a relatively accurate cost for constructing a project. Why then do formal bid openings bring such a wide range of bids? — because the skilled estimator does not merely compute the cost to construct a project; he or she computes the cost for his *particular company* to construct it. Estimators, even though they may use identical resources and the routines and methods outlined in earlier chapters, will still produce different true costs. Overhead, productivity, and purchasing power vary from company to company.

Estimating is a highly responsible job. Consideration must be given to the selection of suppliers and subcontractors; evaluations need to be made based on criteria such as reliability, price guarantees, and potential unexpected costs. When determining labor costs, it is more important to figure how much work is most likely to be accomplished in one day, rather than the amount that is possible under the best of circumstances. A good estimator knows his company's skills, costs, and capacity.

Not only does the estimator have to determine the costs for the project; he must also calculate the time required to complete the work. This determination is based on many factors: quantities derived from the estimate, time of year, availability of material, labor, and equipment resources.

The sample estimate in this chapter is based on an actual landscape project. A landscape plan (Figure 6.1) and the designer's specifications (referred to but not shown) are the basis of the estimate. The plan defines the sample landscape project and represents the major features of the job. This plan is provided for illustrative purposes only. In actuality, such a project might require additional drawings with more plans and details. A full set of specifications would also be provided.

An initial scan of the plans produces a general impression. In actual practice, this overview should be verified and corrected by the site survey visit and the process of gathering information — perhaps with a Landscape Project Analysis form (see Chapter 3, Figures 3.2 - 3.6). Together, these procedures can provide guidelines for proper estimating method and sequence, and set an attitude toward the project. A site visit and completed Landscape Project Analysis form may also reveal conditions not evident from the inspection of the plans alone. These

conditions may have a bearing upon the cost of labor, equipment, and materials.

In this example, the owner will be awarding the contract, with advice from the landscape architect. The bidding will be selected competitively, and no bond will be required. In actual projects, plans and specs would have been provided by the landscape architect for the complete site development.

The example project is located 12 miles from the contractor's garage, and company employees are capable of performing most of the required work. The contractor has reliable and known subcontractors available to perform certain specialized sections of the work.

The takeoff process begins with a careful review of the scope of the project. This example is a five acre site that is commercially zoned. The building on the site is owner-occupied. It is a two-story masonry building of good quality and serves as an office building and distribution center for a publishing company. All utilities are installed in the building. The site is located very near major highway access on good, paved roads. Soil tests and test pits identify a sandy soil. Fill and topsoil have been stockpiled on the site by the building excavating subcontractor.

The work area identified in the plans is only a part of the overall site and encompasses roughly 14,000 square feet, essentially all on the east side of the building. Special features and conditions include banks on both sides of a wet drainage ditch (stream) that will become a pond, an attractive focal point of the design. The steep sides of the stream banks are to be retained by stone rip-rap. The planted area is to blend into existing natural wooded areas. Access to the site is by paved road to both paved parking areas. Access to the building from the front parking lot is by a concrete footbridge (by the building contractor) that spans the steep banks and the stream. This unique entrance will be used by both employees and visitors. Another entrance and parking lot for trucks and service are located further along the access drive. The area of work includes both sides of the pond banks and all building terraces and walkways.

The plans, specs and Landscape Project Analysis form (based on the site visit) together form a "picture", or overall view of the work in the estimator's mind. An outline can now be made of the scope of the work. Such an outline could be set up on an Estimate Summary form to coincide with the organization of the project into basic "pricing categories". An example is shown in Figure 6.2.

This listing of the scope of the work can serve as a checklist of the major categories. The takeoff proceeds by breaking the categories down into various stages of detail. This is the process of defining the tasks and exactly what the work entails.

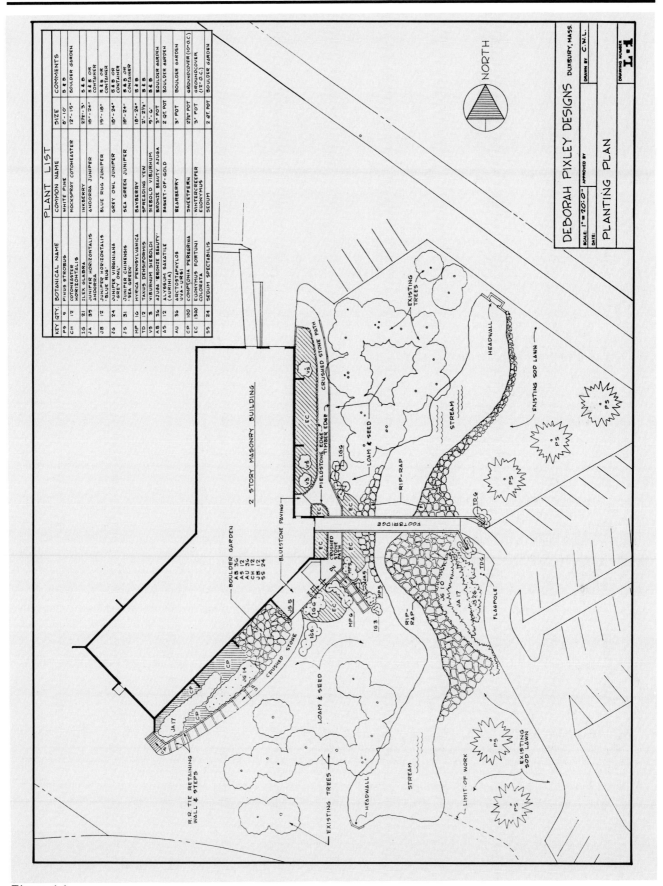

Figure 6.1

Means Forms

CONDENSED ESTIMATE SUMMARY

PROJECT Office Building		SHEET NO.
		ESTIMATE NO. 87-1
LOCATION	TOTAL AREA/VOLUME	DATE 1987
ARCHITECT	COST PER S.F./C.F.	NO. OF STORIES
PRICES BY:	EXTENSIONS BY:	CHECKED BY:

Description	Material	Labor	Equipment	Subcontract	Total
Site Work:					
Headwalls					
Rip-Rap					
Grading					
Hard Construction:					
Bluestone Patios					
RR tie Steps Walls & Edging					
Fieldstone Edging					
Crushed Stone Walks					
Plantings:					
Trees, Shrubs & Groundcover					
Horticultural material					
Lawn					
Miscellaneous:					
Pruning & Cleanup					

Figure 6.2

Area Measurements

Areas to be measured in landscape construction are often irregular and/or sloped. The estimator must perform various calculations in order to obtain the most accurate numbers.

There are three basic methods to determine area from a plan. The first is with a planimeter — a device which, when rolled along a designated perimeter, will measure area. The resulting measurement must then be converted to the scale of the drawing. Trigonometry can also be used to determine area. It is applied to the distances and bearings supplied by a survey. Sines and cosines are used to calculate coordinates, which are in turn used to calculate area. The planimeter may be used only if the drawing is to scale and the scale is known. The trigonometric method may be used on a drawing not to scale, but only if survey data is available. Both methods are accurate. A third method is less accurate but can be used whether or not the drawing is to scale. This method involves dividing the area into triangles, squares, and rectangles and determining the area of each. Some dimensions must be scaled. An example of this process is shown in Figure 6.3. This method can be performed quickly, and depending upon the scale of the site, it is accurate to within a few percent. Formulas for determining the areas of geometric and irregular shapes are included in Appendix A.

The above methods are used to determine "map" or plan area — the superimposition of an uneven surface onto a horizontal plane. If the surface is sloped, the actual area will differ from the area as shown on the map. When the slope is known, the map area is converted using a conversion factor. Such factors are shown in Figure 6.4. If a contour map is available, slope can be determined by measuring the change in elevation versus the horizontal distance.

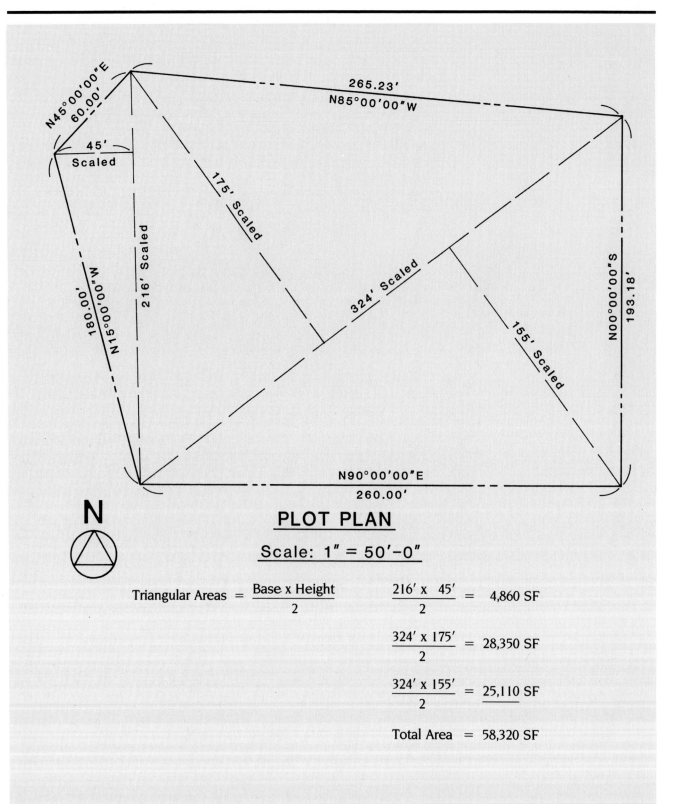

PLOT PLAN

Scale: 1" = 50'-0"

$$\text{Triangular Areas} = \frac{\text{Base x Height}}{2}$$

$$\frac{216' \times 45'}{2} = 4,860 \text{ SF}$$

$$\frac{324' \times 175'}{2} = 28,350 \text{ SF}$$

$$\frac{324' \times 155'}{2} = 25,110 \text{ SF}$$

Total Area = 58,320 SF

Figure 6.3

In addition to measuring area, materials must also be identified and quantified along with the labor and equipment needed in each outlined category. The estimator can record these measurements on a quantity sheet for extending, or directly list the quantities on a pricing sheet. For purposes of this sample estimate, both methods are illustrated.

Certain graphic symbols are commonly used on landscape plans. Landscape plans may or may not include a key of symbols, and different designers may use different codes for the same items. It is important to review each set of plans individually and carefully. See Chapter 4, Figure 4.1 for a chart of typical symbols.

Most costs used in the sample estimate are from *Means Site Work Cost Data*, 1987. In some cases, "local prices" are used where an estimator would be likely to solicit bids and/or labor costs from local suppliers and subcontractors. The methods shown in this sample estimate demonstrate how the estimator can use data such as that found in *Means Site Work Cost Data* to verify the subcontractor bids or to develop budget costs.

Factors to Convert		
Horizontal Plan Dimensions to Actual, Inclined Dimensions		
Angle	Rise/Run	Factor
0°	Flat	1.000
4.8°	1/12	1.003
9.5°	1/6	1.014
14°	1/4	1.031
18.4°	1/3	1.054
26.6°	1/2	1.118
45°	1/1	1.414

Figure 6.4

Site Work

The site work portion of the estimate involves the rip-rap slope, grading and spreading of topsoil, and the two headwalls of the pond. For purposes of this example, some items will be estimated as items that would normally be subcontracted, in other words, they will include the overhead and profit of the subcontractor. The landscape estimator would, in these cases, solicit bids from subcontractors for these certain portions of the work.

Rip Rap

The areas of placement of the rip rap slope for the project are shown in Figure 6.5. The actual "map" areas are measured from the plans using one of the methods described above. The dimensions and quantities can be entered on a quantity sheet as shown in Figure 6.6. From the site visit, the estimator has determined the average slope to be 1:2. The appropriate factor, (from Figure 6.4) is applied to determine the *actual* area for installation of the rip rap. The estimator has determined that this portion of the work is to be subcontracted. Costs (including the installing contractor's overhead and profit) are obtained from Figure 6.7 and entered on a cost analysis sheet (Figure 6.8).

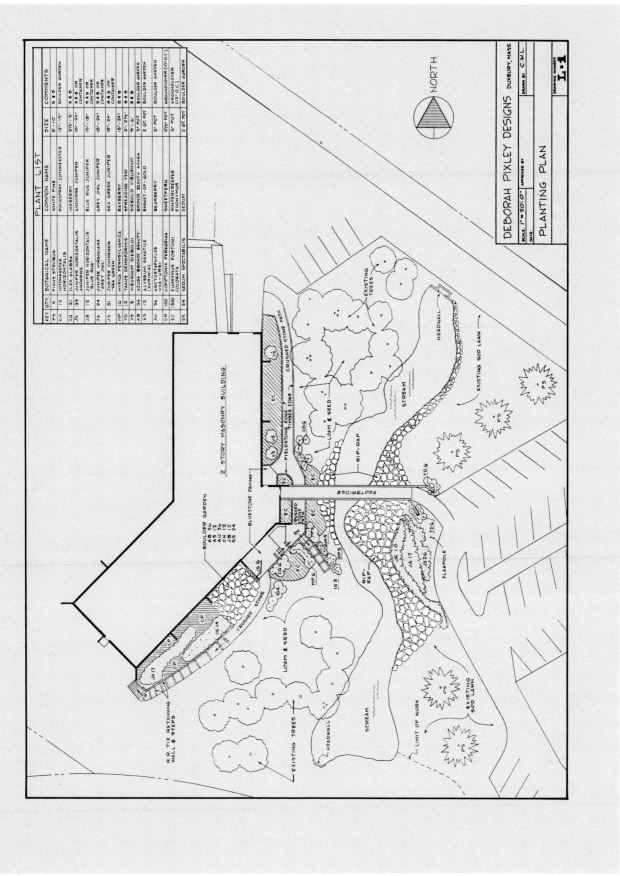

Figure 6.5

Means Forms
QUANTITY SHEET

SHEET NO. 1 of 7

PROJECT: Office Building
ESTIMATE NO. 87-1

LOCATION: ARCHITECT: DATE: 1987

TAKE OFF BY: SHF   EXTENSIONS BY: SLP   CHECKED BY: JDM

DESCRIPTION	NO.	L	W	Area	UNIT		UNIT	Volume	UNIT	Misc.	UNIT
Site Work											
Head walls										2	Ea
Rip- Rap		16'	11.5'	184	SF						
		29.5'	10.5'	310							
		15'	8'	120							
		13.5'	13'	176							
		24'	8'	192							
		90'	12'	1080							
				2062							
Slope Factor (x1.1180)				2305		256	SY				
Total											
Grading											
Plant Beds		88'	12'	1056							
		24'	6'	144							
		19'	5'	95							
		16'	11'	176							
		16'	8'	128							
		44'	12'	528							
		52'	20'	1040							
		31'	6'	186							
				3353	SF	373	SY				
Topsoil @ 6"								70	CY		
Lawns				5650	SF	628	SY				
Topsoil @ 6"								119	CY		
Misc. Prep.				4785	SF	532	SY				

Figure 6.6

134

2.3	Earthwork	CREW	DAILY OUTPUT	MAN-HOURS	UNIT	MAT.	LABOR	EQUIP.	TOTAL	TOTAL INCL O&P	
300	0150	3 mile round trip, 2.1 loads/hr.	B-34A	100	.080	C.Y.		1.36	2.17	3.53	4.36	**300**
	0200	4 mile round trip, 1.8 loads/hr.	"	85	.094			1.60	2.55	4.15	5.10	
	0310	12 C.Y. dump truck, ¼ mile round trip 3.7 loads/hr.	B-34B	356	.022			.38	.78	1.16	1.41	
	0320	½ mile round trip, 3.2 loads/hr.		308	.026			.44	.90	1.34	1.63	
	0330	1 mile round trip 2.7 loads/hr.		260	.031			.52	1.07	1.59	1.93	
	0400	2 mile round trip, 2.2 loads/hr.		210	.038			.65	1.32	1.97	2.39	
	0450	3 mile round trip, 1.9 loads/hr.		180	.044			.75	1.54	2.29	2.79	
	0500	4 mile round trip, 1.6 loads/hr.		150	.053			.90	1.85	2.75	3.35	
	0540	5 mile round trip, 1 load/hr.		98	.082			1.38	2.84	4.22	5.15	
	0550	10 mile round trip, .75 load/hr.		49	.163			2.77	5.65	8.42	10.25	
	0560	20 mile round trip, .5 load/hr.	↓	32	.250			4.24	8.70	12.94	15.70	
	0600	16.5 C.Y. dump trailer, 1 mile round trip, 2.6 loads/hr.	B-34C	340	.024			.40	1.22	1.62	1.92	
	0700	2 mile round trip, 2.1 loads/hr.		275	.029			.49	1.50	1.99	2.37	
	1000	3 mile round trip, 1.8 loads/hr.		235	.034			.58	1.76	2.34	2.77	
	1100	4 mile round trip, 1.6 loads/hr.		210	.038			.65	1.97	2.62	3.10	
	1110	5 mile round trip, 1 load/hr.		132	.061			1.03	3.13	4.16	4.94	
	1120	10 mile round trip, .75 load/hr.		100	.080			1.36	4.14	5.50	6.50	
	1130	20 mile round trip, .5 load/hr.	↓	66	.121			2.05	6.25	8.30	9.90	
	1150	20 C.Y. dump trailer, 1 mile round trip, 2.5 loads/hr.	B-34D	400	.020			.34	1.07	1.41	1.67	
	1200	2 mile round trip, 2 loads/hr.		320	.025			.42	1.34	1.76	2.09	
	1220	3 mile round trip, 1.7 loads/hr.		270	.030			.50	1.59	2.09	2.48	
	1240	4 mile round trip, 1.5 loads/hr.		240	.033			.57	1.79	2.36	2.78	
	1245	5 mile round trip, 1.1 load/hr.		172	.047			.79	2.49	3.28	3.89	
	1250	10 mile round trip, .85 load/hr.		136	.059			1	3.15	4.15	4.91	
	1255	20 mile round trip, .6 load/hr.	↓	96	.083	↓		1.41	4.46	5.87	6.95	
	1280											
	1300	Hauling in medium traffic, add				C.Y.				20%	20%	
	1400	Heavy traffic, add								30%	30%	
	1600	Grading at dump, if required, by dozer	B-10B	1,000	.012	↓		.23	.68	.91	1.09	
	1800	Spotter at dump or cut, if required	1 Clab	8	1	Hr.		16.10		16.10	24	
320	0010	**HORIZONTAL BORING** Casing only, 100' minimum,										**320**
	0020	not incl. jacking pits or dewatering										
	0100	Roadwork, ½" thick wall, 24" diameter casing	B-42	10	6.400	L.F.	35	115	95	245	315	
	0200	36" diameter		9.50	6.740		50	120	99	269	345	
	0300	48" diameter	↓	9	7.110	↓	85	125	105	315	400	
	0400											
	0500	Railroad work, 24" diameter	B-42	7	9.140	L.F.	35	165	135	335	430	
	0600	36" diameter		6.50	9.850		50	175	145	370	475	
	0700	48" diameter	↓	6	10.670		85	190	155	430	550	
	0900	For ledge, add								125	155	
	1000	Small diameter boring, 3", sandy soil	B-82	1,050	.015			.27	.03	.30	.43	
	1040	Rocky soil	"	550	.029			.52	.06	.58	.83	
350	0010	**MOBILIZATION AND DEMOBILIZATION** Dozer, 105 H.P.	B-34C	6.20	1.290	Ea.		22	67	89	105	**350**
	0100	300 H.P.		4.45	1.800			30	93	123	145	
	0300	Scraper, towed type (incl. tractor), 6 C.Y. capacity		5.85	1.370			23	71	94	110	
	0400	10 C.Y.		4.30	1.860			32	96	128	150	
	0600	Self-propelled scraper, 15 C.Y.		3.10	2.580			44	135	179	210	
	0700	24 C.Y.		1.90	4.210			71	220	291	345	
	0900	Shovel, backhoe or dragline, ¾ C.Y.		4.30	1.860			32	96	128	150	
	1000	1-½ C.Y.		2.90	2.760			47	145	192	225	
	1200	Tractor shovel or front end loader, 1 C.Y.		6.20	1.290			22	67	89	105	
	1300	2-¼ C.Y.	↓	4.45	1.800	↓		30	93	123	145	
360	0010	**RIP-RAP** Random, filter stone dumped from trucks										**360**
	0100	Machine placed slope protection	B-12G	62	.258	C.Y.	8	5	4.97	17.97	22	
	0110	⅜ to ¼ C.Y. pieces, grouted	B-13	80	.700	S.Y.	14	12.15	5.10	31.25	39	
	0200	18" minimum thickness, not grouted		53	1.060		10	18.30	7.70	36	46	
	0400	Gabions, galvanized steel mesh boxes, stone filled, 6" deep		190	.295		10.50	5.10	2.15	17.75	21	
	0500	9" deep		163	.344		13.25	5.95	2.50	21.70	26	
	0600	12" deep		153	.366		18	6.35	2.66	27.01	32	
	0700	18" deep	↓	102	.549	↓	24	9.50	4	37.50	45	

30

Figure 6.7

Means Forms
COST ANALYSIS

PROJECT **Office Building**

LOCATION

CLASSIFICATION

SHEET NO. **2 of 7**

ESTIMATE NO. **87-1**

DATE **1987**

TAKE OFF BY **SHF** QUANTITIES BY **SHF** PRICES BY **RSM** EXTENSIONS BY **SLP** CHECKED BY **JDM**

ARCHITECT

DESCRIPTION	SOURCE/DIMENSIONS			QUANTITY	UNIT	MATERIAL UNIT COST	MATERIAL TOTAL	LABOR UNIT COST	LABOR TOTAL	EQUIPMENT UNIT COST	EQUIPMENT TOTAL	SUBCONTRACT UNIT COST	SUBCONTRACT TOTAL	TOTAL UNIT COST	TOTAL
Site Work															
Headwalls	12.3	750	2020	2	Ea.							1645	3290		
Rip-Rap	2.3	360	0200	256	SY							46	11776		
Grading															
Plant Beds	2.8	240	3800	373	SY			1.12	418						
Lawns	2.8	240	5000	119	CY			1.53	182	.31	37				
Patio, Walk Prep.	2.3	220	2400	532	SY			1.72	915						
Place Topsoil	CREW			1	Day				230		275				
Total Site Work									1745		312		15066		

Figure 6.8

This procedure represents one choice of method and sequence, that can be used for all components of the estimate. No matter which procedure is used, the estimator should try to be consistent.

Grading

Various types of grading are required for this project. The estimator should consider: spreading and dressing topsoil for both planting beds and lawn areas, preparation for railroad tie edging and retaining walls, and preparation for patios and walks. Each of these different functions could be estimated individually, though the experienced estimator is likely to "lump" certain of the smaller items together. Measurements from the plan might yield the following quantities for the following basic grading work items:

Planting beds	3,353 S.F.
Lawn areas	5,650 S.F.
Patio, walk, and wall preparation	4,785 S.F.

Each of these areas will involve different types of work. Top soil will be placed in the planting beds and most likely spread and dressed by hand. Top soil for the lawn areas will be spread by machine and dressed by hand. Excavation and grading for the patio and walk areas will be completed by hand. For this example, the specifications require 6" of topsoil for the planting bed and lawn areas.

	Area (S.F.)	C.Y./M.S.F.	Total C.Y.
Planting beds	3,353	21	70.4
Lawns	5,650	21	118.6
6" topsoil required	9,003 S.F.	21	189.0

Figure 4.7 can be used to determine the amount of topsoil required. Sufficient quantities of topsoil have been stored on site so that costs required are for labor and equipment only. Quantities are derived in Figure 6.6 and costs are entered in Figure 6.8. Note that similar items, such as grading for plant beds and lawns, may be estimated in different ways. The grading for plant beds is priced by area (S.Y.) for a specific depth of topsoil, whereas grading for lawns is based on volume of material (C.Y.). See Figure 6.9 for the unit costs for these items. Both methods are equally valid. The choice is often a matter of personal preference. Note that much of the work is done by hand in either case. Equipment is required in order to place the topsoil for spreading and minor excavation. The cost of an appropriate crew (B-10N) is included (see Figure 6.10). Refer to Chapter 9 for a complete explanation of these crews and the use of *Means Site Work Cost Data.*

Headwalls

The headwalls in this case are part of the landscape portion of the project. This work is most likely be subcontracted. A "systems" cost (from Figure 6.11) is included in the estimate as a budget number until subcontractor bids are received.

2.8	Lawns & Planting	CREW	DAILY OUTPUT	MAN-HOURS	UNIT	BARE COSTS				TOTAL INCL O&P
						MAT.	LABOR	EQUIP.	TOTAL	
240 2400	Large commercial, no boulders	B-10B	400	.030	M.S.F.		.58	1.70	2.28	2.71	240
2500	With boulders	"	240	.050			.96	2.83	3.79	4.52
3000	Scarify subsoil, residential, skid steer loader w/scarifiers, 50 HP	B-66	32	.250			4.90	3.79	8.69	11.35
3050	Municipal, skid steer loader w/scarifiers, 50 HP	"	120	.067			1.31	1.01	2.32	3.02
3100	Large commercial, 75 HP, dozer w/ripper	B-10L	240	.050	↓		.96	.86	1.82	2.36
3110										
3500	Screen topsoil from stockpile, vibrating screen, wet material (organic)	B-10P	200	.060	C.Y.		1.15	2.99	4.14	4.97
3550	Dry material	"	300	.040			.77	1.99	2.76	3.31
3600	Mixing with conditioners, manure and peat	B-10R	550	.022	↓		.42	.39	.81	1.04
3650	Mobilization add for 2 days or less operation				Job					225
3800	Spread conditioned topsoil, 6" deep, by hand	B-1	360	.067	S.Y.	2.43	1.12		3.55	4.31
3850	300 HP dozer	B-38	27	.889	M.S.F.	324	15.35	13.90	353.25	395
4000	Spread soil conditioners, alum. sulfate, 1#/S.Y., push spreader	A-1	17,500		S.Y.	.17	.01		.18	.20
4050	Tractor spreader	B-66	700	.011	M.S.F.	18.75	.22	.17	19.14	21
4100	Fertilizer, 0.2#/S.Y., push spreader	A-1	17,500		S.Y.	.04	.01		.05	.05
4150	Tractor spreader	B-66	700	.011	M.S.F.	4.45	.22	.17	4.84	5.40
4200	Ground limestone, 1#/S.Y., push spreader	A-1	17,500		S.Y.	.05	.01		.06	.07
4250	Tractor spreader	B-66	700	.011	M.S.F.	5.50	.22	.17	5.89	6.55
4300	Lusoil, 3#/S.Y., push spreader	A-1	17,500		S.Y.	.31	.01		.32	.35
4350	Tractor spreader	B-66	700	.011	M.S.F.	34	.22	.17	34.39	38
4400	Manure, 18.#/S.Y., push spreader	A-1	2,500	.003	S.Y.	1.23	.05	.02	1.30	1.44
4450	Tractor spreader	B-66	280	.029	M.S.F.	135	.56	.43	135.99	150
4500	Perlite, 1" deep, push spreader	A-1	17,500		S.Y.	1.85	.01		1.86	2.05
4550	Tractor spreader	B-66	700	.011	M.S.F.	205	.22	.17	205.39	225
4600	Vermiculite, push spreader	A-1	17,500		S.Y.	1.70	.01		1.71	1.88
4650	Tractor spreader	B-66	700	.011	M.S.F.	190	.22	.17	190.39	210
5000	Spread topsoil, skid steer loader and hand dress	B-62	270	.089	C.Y.	9.20	1.53	.31	11.04	12.70
5100	Articulated loader and hand dress	B-100	320	.038		9.20	.72	1.35	11.27	12.65
5200	Articulated loader, 75 HP dozer	B-38	500	.048		9.20	.83	.75	10.78	12.15
5300	Road grader and hand dress	B-11L	1,000	.016	↓	9.20	.29	.47	9.96	11.05
6000	Tilling topsoil, 20 HP tractor w/6' disk, 2" deep	B-66	50,000		S.Y.				.01	.01
6050	4" deep		40,000						.01	.01
6100	6" deep	↓	30,000				.01		.01	.01
6150	26" rototiller, 2" deep	A-1	1,250	.006			.10	.03	.13	.19
6200	4" deep		1,000	.008			.13	.04	.17	.23
6250	6" deep	↓	750	.011	↓		.17	.05	.22	.31
6400	Lawn cutting, walking mower		4.40	1.820	Acre		29	9.15	38.15	53
6450	Riding mower	↓	7	1.140	"		18.40	5.75	24.15	33
310 0010	MULCH										310
0050										
0100	Aged barks, 3" deep, hand spread	1 Clab	100	.080	S.Y.	1.17	1.29		2.46	3.18
0150	Skid steer loader	B-63	13.50	2.960	M.S.F.	130	50	6.15	186.15	225
0200	Hay, 1" deep, hand spread	1 Clab	475	.017	S.Y.	.15	.27		.42	.56
0250	Power mulcher, small	B-64	180	.089	M.S.F.	17	1.46	.89	19.35	22
0350	Large	B-65	530	.030	"	17	.50	.41	17.91	19.85
0400	Humus peat, 1" deep, hand spread	1 Clab	700	.011	S.Y.	.51	.18		.69	.83
0450	Push spreader	A-1	2,500	.003	"	.51	.05	.02	.58	.65
0550	Tractor spreader	B-66	700	.011	M.S.F.	57	.22	.17	57.39	63
0600	Oat straw, 1" deep, hand spread	1 Clab	475	.017	S.Y.	.20	.27		.47	.62
0650	Power mulcher, small	B-64	180	.089	M.S.F.	23	1.46	.89	25.35	28
0700	Large	B-65	530	.030	"	23	.50	.41	23.91	26
0750	Add for asphaltic emulsion	B-45	1,770	.009	Gal.	1.45	.17	.28	1.90	2.16
0800	Peat moss, 1" deep, hand spread	1 Clab	900	.009	S.Y.	.75	.14		.89	1.04
0850	Push spreader	A-1	2,500	.003	"	.75	.05	.02	.82	.92
0950	Tractor spreader	B-66	700	.011	M.S.F.	83	.22	.17	83.39	92
1000	Polyethylene film, 6 mil.	2 Clab	2,000	.008	S.Y.	.14	.13		.27	.34
1100	Redwood nuggets, 3" deep, hand spread	1 Clab	150	.053	"	4.75	.86		5.61	6.50
1150	Skid steer loader	B-63	13.50	2.960	M.S.F.	530	50	6.15	586.15	665
1200	Stone mulch, hand spread, ceramic chips, economy	B-14	125	.384	S.Y.	5.10	6.55	1.29	12.94	16.60
1250	Deluxe	"	95	.505	"	7.50	8.60	1.70	17.80	23

76

Figure 6.9

CREWS

Crew B-10

Crew No.	Bare Costs Hr.	Daily	Incl. Subs O & P Hr.	Daily	Bare Costs	Incl. O&P
1 Equip. Oper. (med.)	$20.75	$166.00	$30.35	$242.80	$19.20	$28.11
.5 Building Laborer	16.10	64.40	23.65	94.60		
12 M.H., Daily Totals		$230.40		$337.40	$19.20	$28.11

Crew B-10A

Crew No.	Hr.	Daily	Hr.	Daily	Bare Costs	Incl. O&P
1 Equip. Oper. (med.)	$20.75	$166.00	$30.35	$242.80	$19.20	$28.11
.5 Building Laborer	16.10	64.40	23.65	94.60		
1 Roll. Compact., 2K Lbs.		75.60		83.15	6.30	6.92
12 M.H., Daily Totals		$306.00		$420.55	$25.50	$35.03

Crew B-10B

Crew No.	Hr.	Daily	Hr.	Daily	Bare Costs	Incl. O&P
1 Equip. Oper. (med.)	$20.75	$166.00	$30.35	$242.80	$19.20	$28.11
.5 Building Laborer	16.10	64.40	23.65	94.60		
1 Dozer, 200 H.P.		680.00		748.00	56.66	62.33
12 M.H., Daily Totals		$910.40		$1085.40	$75.86	$90.44

Crew B-10C

Crew No.	Hr.	Daily	Hr.	Daily	Bare Costs	Incl. O&P
1 Equip. Oper. (med.)	$20.75	$166.00	$30.35	$242.80	$19.20	$28.11
.5 Building Laborer	16.10	64.40	23.65	94.60		
1 Dozer, 200 H.P.		680.00		748.00		
1 Vibratory Roller, Towed		72.85		80.15	62.73	69.01
12 M.H., Daily Totals		$983.25		$1165.55	$81.93	$97.12

Crew B-10D

Crew No.	Hr.	Daily	Hr.	Daily	Bare Costs	Incl. O&P
1 Equip. Oper. (med.)	$20.75	$166.00	$30.35	$242.80	$19.20	$28.11
.5 Building Laborer	16.10	64.40	23.65	94.60		
1 Dozer, 200 H.P		680.00		748.00		
1 Sheepsft. Roller, Towed		81.10		89.20	63.42	69.76
12 M.H., Daily Totals		$991.50		$1174.60	$82.62	$97.87

Crew B-10E

Crew No.	Hr.	Daily	Hr.	Daily	Bare Costs	Incl. O&P
1 Equip. Oper. (med.)	$20.75	$166.00	$30.35	$242.80	$19.20	$28.11
.5 Building Laborer	16.10	64.40	23.65	94.60		
1 Tandem Roller, 5 Ton		84.20		92.60	7.01	7.71
12 M.H., Daily Totals		$314.60		$430.00	$26.21	$35.82

Crew B-10F

Crew No.	Hr.	Daily	Hr.	Daily	Bare Costs	Incl. O&P
1 Equip. Oper. (med.)	$20.75	$166.00	$30.35	$242.80	$19.20	$28.11
.5 Building Laborer	16.10	64.40	23.65	94.60		
1 Tandem Roller, 10 Ton		173.60		190.95	14.46	15.91
12 M.H., Daily Totals		$404.00		$528.35	$33.66	$44.02

Crew B-10G

Crew No.	Hr.	Daily	Hr.	Daily	Bare Costs	Incl. O&P
1 Equip. Oper. (med.)	$20.75	$166.00	$30.35	$242.80	$19.20	$28.11
.5 Building Laborer	16.10	64.40	23.65	94.60		
1 Sheepsft. Roll., 130 H.P.		288.20		317.00	24.01	26.41
12 M.H., Daily Totals		$518.60		$654.40	$43.21	$54.52

Crew B-10H

Crew No.	Hr.	Daily	Hr.	Daily	Bare Costs	Incl. O&P
1 Equip. Oper. (med.)	$20.75	$166.00	$30.35	$242.80	$19.20	$28.11
.5 Building Laborer	16.10	64.40	23.65	94.60		
1 Diaphr. Water Pump, 2"		21.15		23.25		
1-20 Ft. Suction Hose, 2"		4.00		4.40		
2-50 Ft. Disch. Hoses, 2"		8.00		8.80	2.76	3.03
12 M.H., Daily Totals		$263.55		$373.85	$21.96	$31.14

Crew B-10I

Crew No.	Hr.	Daily	Hr.	Daily	Bare Costs	Incl. O&P
1 Equip. Oper. (med.)	$20.75	$166.00	$30.35	$242.80	$19.20	$28.11
.5 Building Laborer	16.10	64.40	23.65	94.60		
1 Diaphr. Water Pump, 4"		41.95		46.15		
1-20 Ft. Suction Hose, 4"		7.40		8.15		
2-50 Ft. Disch. Hoses, 4"		14.80		16.30	5.34	5.88
12 M.H., Daily Totals		$294.55		$408.00	$24.54	$33.99

Crew B-10J

Crew No.	Hr.	Daily	Hr.	Daily	Bare Costs	Incl. O&P
1 Equip. Oper. (med.)	$20.75	$166.00	$30.35	$242.80	$19.20	$28.11
.5 Building Laborer	16.10	64.40	23.65	94.60		
1 Centr. Water Pump, 3"		25.25		27.80		
1-20 Ft. Suction Hose, 3"		5.00		5.50		
2-50 Ft. Disch. Hoses, 3"		10.00		11.00	3.35	3.69
12 M.H., Daily Totals		$270.65		$381.70	$22.55	$31.80

Crew B-10K

Crew No.	Hr.	Daily	Hr.	Daily	Bare Costs	Incl. O&P
1 Equip. Oper. (med.)	$20.75	$166.00	$30.35	$242.80	$19.20	$28.11
.5 Building Laborer	16.10	64.40	23.65	94.60		
1 Centr. Water Pump, 6"		63.20		69.50		
1-20 Ft. Suction Hose, 6"		12.40		13.65		
2-50 Ft. Disch. Hoses, 6"		23.60		25.95	8.26	9.09
12 M.H., Daily Totals		$329.60		$446.50	$27.46	$37.20

Crew B-10L

Crew No.	Hr.	Daily	Hr.	Daily	Bare Costs	Incl. O&P
1 Equip. Oper. (med.)	$20.75	$166.00	$30.35	$242.80	$19.20	$28.11
.5 Building Laborer	16.10	64.40	23.65	94.60		
1 Dozer, 75 H.P.		207.40		228.15	17.28	19.01
12 M.H., Daily Totals		$437.80		$565.55	$36.48	$47.12

Crew B-10M

Crew No.	Hr.	Daily	Hr.	Daily	Bare Costs	Incl. O&P
1 Equip. Oper. (med.)	$20.75	$166.00	$30.35	$242.80	$19.20	$28.11
.5 Building Laborer	16.10	64.40	23.65	94.60		
1 Dozer, 300 H.P.		898.00		987.80	74.83	82.31
12 M.H., Daily Totals		$1128.40		$1325.20	$94.03	$110.42

Crew B-10N

Crew No.	Hr.	Daily	Hr.	Daily	Bare Costs	Incl. O&P
1 Equip. Oper. (med.)	$20.75	$166.00	$30.35	$242.80	$19.20	$28.11
.5 Building Laborer	16.10	64.40	23.65	94.60		
F.E. Loader, T.M., 1.5 C.Y.		275.00		302.50	22.91	25.20
12 M.H., Daily Totals		$505.40		$639.90	$42.11	$53.31

Crew B-10O

Crew No.	Hr.	Daily	Hr.	Daily	Bare Costs	Incl. O&P
1 Equip. Oper. (med.)	$20.75	$166.00	$30.35	$242.80	$19.20	$28.11
.5 Building Laborer	16.10	64.40	23.65	94.60		
F.E. Loader, T.M., 2.25 C.Y.		432.20		475.40	36.01	39.61
12 M.H., Daily Totals		$662.60		$812.80	$55.21	$67.72

Crew B-10P

Crew No.	Hr.	Daily	Hr.	Daily	Bare Costs	Incl. O&P
1 Equip. Oper. (med.)	$20.75	$166.00	$30.35	$242.80	$19.20	$28.11
.5 Building Laborer	16.10	64.40	23.65	94.60		
F.E. Loader, T.M., 2.5 C.Y.		597.00		656.70	49.75	54.72
12 M.H., Daily Totals		$827.40		$994.10	$68.95	$82.83

Crew B-10Q

Crew No.	Hr.	Daily	Hr.	Daily	Bare Costs	Incl. O&P
1 Equip. Oper. (med.)	$20.75	$166.00	$30.35	$242.80	$19.20	$28.11
.5 Building Laborer	16.10	64.40	23.65	94.60		
F.E. Loader, T.M., 5 C.Y.		1022.00		1124.20	85.16	93.68
12 M.H., Daily Totals		$1252.40		$1461.60	$104.36	$121.79

Figure 6.10

12.3-750 | Headwalls

The Headwall Systems are listed in concrete and four different stone wall materials for two different backfill slope conditions. The backfill slope directly affects the length of the wing walls. Walls are listed for eight different culvert sizes from 30" diameter to 84" diameter. For pipes below 30" refer to 2.5-273 in the Unit Price section for reinforced concrete culvert with flared ends. Excavation and backfill are included in the system components.

System Components	QUANTITY	UNIT	COST PER EACH		
			MAT.	INST.	TOTAL
SYSTEM 12.3-750-2000					
HEADWALL C.I.P. CONCRETE FOR 30" PIPE, 3' LONG WING WALLS					
Excavation, hydraulic backhoe, ⅜ C.Y. bucket	2.500	C.Y.		65.24	65.24
Formwork, 2 uses	157.000	SFCA	152.05	827.64	979.69
Reinforcing in place including dowels	45.000	Lb.	17.55	54.90	72.45
Concrete, 3000 psi, in place	2.600	C.Y.	145.60	59.80	205.40
Backfill, dozer	2.500	C.Y.		25.20	25.20
TOTAL			315.20	1,032.78	1,347.98

12.3-750	Headwalls	COST PER EACH		
		MAT.	INST.	TOTAL
2000	Headwall, 1-½ to 1 slope soil, C.I.P. conc, 30"pipe, 3'long wing walls	315	1,025	1,340
2020	Pipe size 36", 3'-6" long wing walls	395	1,250	1,645
2040	Pipe size 42", 4' long wing walls	480	1,450	1,930
2060	Pipe size 48", 4'-6" long wing walls	575	1,700	2,275
2080	Pipe size 54", 5'-0" long wing walls	685	1,975	2,660
2100	Pipe size 60", 5'-6" long wing walls	800	2,275	3,075
2120	Pipe size 72", 6'-6" long wing walls	1,075	2,925	4,000
2140	Pipe size 84", 7'-6" long wing walls	1,375	3,600	4,975
2500	$16/ton stone, pipe size 30", 3' long wing walls	57	340	397
2520	Pipe size 36", 3'-6" long wing walls	74	410	484
2540	Pipe size 42", 4' long wing walls	92	490	582
2560	Pipe size 48", 4'-6" long wing walls	115	585	700
2580	Pipe size 54", 5' long wing walls	140	685	825
2600	Pipe size 60", 5'-6" long wing walls	165	795	960
2620	Pipe size 72", 6'-6" long wing walls	225	1,075	1,300
2640	Pipe size 84", 7'-6" long wing walls	295	1,375	1,670
3000	$32/ton stone, pipe size 30", 3' long wing walls	115	340	455
3020	Pipe size 36", 3'-6" long wing walls	145	410	555
3040	Pipe size 42", 4' long wing walls	185	490	675
3060	Pipe size 48", 4'-6" long wing walls	230	585	815
3080	Pipe size 54", 5' long wing walls	275	685	960
3100	Pipe size 60", 5'-6" long wing walls	325	795	1,120
3120	Pipe size 72", 6'-6" long wing walls	450	1,075	1,525
3140	Pipe size 84", 7'-6" long wing walls	595	1,375	1,970
3500	$48/ton stone, pipe size 30", 3' long wing walls	170	340	510
3520	Pipe size 36", 3'-6" long wing walls	220	410	630

273

Figure 6.11

Hard Construction

A majority of the hard construction in this sample project is to be subcontracted. For those designated items — the bluestone patios and the railroad tie walls, steps, and edging — the costs include the subcontractors' overhead and profit.

It is sound estimating practice, even if a bid is solicited for a certain item, for the estimator to perform a takeoff and to price this same item. This approach allows the estimator to not only verify and cross check costs (against past jobs as well as bids for the current project), but also to schedule the work based on the derived quantities. Note that the productivity data in *Means Site Work Cost Data* is presented both as daily output (for a designated crew) and as man-hours per unit. (See Figure 6.9 and Chapter 9.) Productivity information in both formats can be used to determine duration times for scheduling. Figures 6.12 and 6.13 demonstrate the use of this data in calculating the time required for the bluestone patios.

2.6 Roads & Walks	CREW	DAILY OUTPUT	MAN-HOURS	UNIT	BARE COSTS MAT.	BARE COSTS LABOR	BARE COSTS EQUIP.	BARE COSTS TOTAL	TOTAL INCL O&P	
400	**0010** SIDEWALKS Bituminous, no base included, 2" thick	B-37	720	.067		3	1.13	.12	4.25	5.10	**400**
0100	2-½" thick	"	660	.073	↓	3.75	1.24	.13	5.12	6.10	
0110	Bedding for brick, mortar, 1" thick	D-1	300	.053	S.F.	.22	.98		1.20	1.65	
0120	2" thick	"	200	.080		.44	1.47		1.91	2.59	
0130	Sand, 2" thick	B-18	8,000	.003		.07	:05		.12	.16	
0140	4" thick	"	4,000	.006		.14	.10	.01	.25	.31	
0160	Brick pavers, 4.15 per S.F., 1-¾" thick	D-1	240	.067		1.50	1.22		2.72	3.41	
0170	2-¼" thick		240	.067		1.62	1.22		2.84	3.54	
0200	Laid on edge, 7.2 per S.F. (see also 2.6-150)		70	.229		2.92	4.19		7.11	9.25	
0250	For 4" thick concrete bed and joints, add	↓	595	.027		.72	.49		1.21	1.50	
0280	For steam cleaning, add	A-1	950	.008	↓	.05	.14	.04	.23	.31	
0290											
0300	Concrete, 3000 psi, cast in place with 6 x 6 - #10/10 mesh,										
0310	broomed finish, no base, 4" thick	B-24	600	.040	S.F.	.86	.75		1.61	2.04	
0350	5" thick		545	.044		1.03	.83		1.86	2.33	
0400	6" thick	↓	510	.047		1.20	.88		2.08	2.60	
0450	For bank run gravel base, 4" thick, add	B-18	2,500	.010		.10	.16	.02	.28	.36	
0520	8" thick, add	"	1,600	.015		.20	.25	.02	.47	.62	
0550	Exposed aggregate finish, add to above, minimum	B-24	1,875	.013		.06	.24		.30	.42	
0600	Maximum	"	455	.053		.18	.99		1.17	1.64	

		CREW	DAILY OUTPUT	MAN-HOURS	UNIT	MAT.	LABOR	EQUIP.	TOTAL	INCL O&P	
400	**1100** Flagging, bluestone, irregular, 1" thick,	D-1	81	.198	S.F.	1.45	3.62		5.07	6.80	**400**
1110	1-½" thick		90	.178		1.70	3.26		4.96	6.55	
1120	Pavers, ½" thick		110	.145		2.40	2.67		5.07	6.50	
1130	¾" thick		95	.168		3.25	3.09		6.34	8	
1140	1" thick		81	.198		3.25	3.62		6.87	8.80	
1150	Snapped random rectangular, 1" thick		92	.174		2.10	3.19		5.29	6.90	
1200	1-½" thick		85	.188		2.50	3.45		5.95	7.70	
1250	2" thick	↓	83	.193	↓	2.85	3.54		6.39	8.20	

		CREW	DAILY OUTPUT	MAN-HOURS	UNIT	MAT.	LABOR	EQUIP.	TOTAL	INCL O&P	
450	**0010** STEPS Incl. excav., borrow & concrete base, where applicable										**450**
0100	Bricks	B-24	35	.686	LF Rsr	19	12.90		31.90	40	
0200	Railroad ties	2 Clab	25	.640		6.65	10.30		16.95	22	
0300	Bluestone treads, 12" x 2" or 12" x 1-½"	B-24	30	.800	↓	11.30	15.05		26.35	34	
0501	Concrete, cast in place, see division 3.3-140-6800										
0601	Precast concrete, see division 3.4-500										

Figure 6.12

142

As the quantities of work can be used to estimate the time required for certain items, so can the estimated time be used to determine the costs for other items. Such is the case for the fieldstone edging and crushed bluetone walks. See also the "plantings" estimate in Figure 6.17.

The quantity takeoff and costs analysis sheets for the hard construction portion of the project are shown in Figures 6.14 and 6.15.

Plantings

The takeoff for plant materials is primarily a counting process. A plant list is often provided on the landscape plan or in the specifications. The quantities required may or may not be listed. In either case, the estimator should verify counts carefully to avoid omissions or duplication when determining quantities of plant material.

Item	Line #	Quantity	Unit	Man-hours/Unit	Total Man-hours
Gravel Base	2.6-400-0450	453	SF	.010	4.53
Concrete Slab	2.6-400-0310	453	SF	.040	18.12
Blue Stone Bedding	2.6-400-0110	453	SF	.053	24.01
Flogging	2.6-400-1250	453	SF	.193	87.43
Steps	2.6-450-0300	25	LF	.800	20.00
				Total Man-hours	154.09
				Total Man-days (÷ 8)	19.26
				Total Days (2 workers)	10 days

Figure 6.13

Means Forms
QUANTITY SHEET

PROJECT **Office Building**

LOCATION   ARCHITECT   DATE **1987**

TAKE OFF BY: **SHF**   EXTENSIONS BY: **SLP**   CHECKED BY: **JDM**

DESCRIPTION	NO.	L	W	D	Area	UNIT	Risers	UNIT	Length	UNIT	Volume	UNIT
Hard Construction												
Bluestone												
Flagging		20'	8.5'		170	SF						
		16.5'	5'		83							
		12.5'	6.5'		81							
		Irreg.			25							
		9'	8'		72							
					431	SF						
5% waste					22							
Total					453	SF						
Steps	5	5'					25	LF				
Concrete Slab				4"	453	SF						
Gravel Base				4"	453	SF						
RR Tie												
Steps	14	4'					56	LF				
Edging		241'							241	LF		
Retaining Wall 2'		25'							25	LF		
4'		60'							60	LF		
Fieldstone Edging		137'							137	LF		
Crushed Bluestone		227'	5'	3"	1135	SF					10½	CY

Figure 6.14

144

Means Forms
COST ANALYSIS

PROJECT Office Building	
LOCATION	
TAKE OFF BY SHF	QUANTITIES BY SHF
	PRICES BY RSM
CLASSIFICATION	
ARCHITECT	
EXTENSIONS BY SLP	
CHECKED BY JDM	
ESTIMATE NO. 87-1	DATE 1987

DESCRIPTION	SOURCE/DIMENSIONS		QUANTITY	UNIT	MATERIAL UNIT COST	MATERIAL TOTAL	LABOR UNIT COST	LABOR TOTAL	EQUIPMENT UNIT COST	EQUIPMENT TOTAL	SUBCONTRACT UNIT COST	SUBCONTRACT TOTAL	TOTAL UNIT COST	TOTAL
Hard Construction														
Concrete														
4" Slab	400 0310	2.6	453	SF							2.04	924		
4" Gravel Base	400 0450	2.6	453	SF							.36	163		
Bluestone														
Bedding	400 0110	2.6	453	SF							1.65	747		
Flagging	400 1250	2.6	453	SF							8.20	3715		
Steps	450 0300	2.6	25	LF							34	850		
RR Tie														
Steps	450 0200	2.6	56	LF							22	1232		
Edging	060 0600	2.8	241	LF							5.15	1241		
Retaining Wall 2'	336 5000	12.7	25	LF							26.40	660		
Systems 4'	336 5400	12.7	60	LF							56	3360		
Fieldstone Edge	2 Laborers 4 Hrs		137	LF		—		129						
Crushed Bluestone 3"														
Material	400 1050	2.6	1135	SF	.21	238								
Labor	B-62 Crew	0.5		Day				207		42				
Total Hard Construction						238		336		42		12892		

Figure 6.15

Plant Material

In the sample estimate, the plant list and quantities have been provided by the designer. When the quantities are checked, these items can be transferred to a form that will allow for comparative pricing. Costs for plant material can vary greatly by region and season and should be obtained from local sources. An example of plant pricing is shown in Figure 6.16. Three vendors are used and, where possible, costs are compared.

In this example, material and labor costs for plantings are estimated separately. To figure labor costs, the plant material is first divided into size categories so that appropriate costs can be applied to each size. Installation costs are dependent on root ball size and weight. An example of a labor estimate for plant material is shown in Figure 6.17. Unit costs are obtained from *Means Site Work Cost Data*. Also useful is the appropriate crew and daily output data from *Means Site Work Cost Data* which can be used for scheduling purposes. See Chapter 9 of this book, "Using *Means Site Work Cost Data*," for more information on the practical applications of crew and daily output data.

With simple calculations, the estimator can plan the duration of the planting activities as shown. The durations for all activities should be calculated in the same manner to be used for scheduling the project and determining manpower allocation. Chapter 8, "Job Planning", of this book provides a further explanation of scheduling methods.

Means Forms
QUANTITY SHEET

PROJECT Office Building - Plantings

ESTIMATE NO. 87-1

LOCATION   ARCHITECT   DATE 1987

TAKE OFF BY SHF   EXTENSIONS BY: SLP   CHECKED BY: JDM

DESCRIPTION	NO.	DIMENSIONS		Vendor A	UNIT	Vendor B	UNIT	Vendor C	UNIT	Total	UNIT
Trees											
Pinus Strobus	5	8'-10'	B&B	(95)			110			475	
Shrubs											
Cotoneaster horizontalis	12	12"-15"	Pot	(9)						108	
Ilex glabra	21	2'6"-3'	B&B	(25)						525	
Juniper											
horizontalis Andorra	39	18"-24"	B&B or Cont	(16)						624	
horizontalis Blue Rug	12	15"-18"	B&B or Cont.	(11)						132	
Virginia Grey Owl	24	18"-24"	B&B or Cont.	(14)						336	
Chinensis Sea Green	31	18"-24"	B&B or Cont.	(14)						434	
Myrica pennsylvanica	16	18"-24"	B&B or Cont.	(18)						288	
Taxus densiformis	12	2'-2'6"	B&B	(28)						336	
Viburnum sieboldi	3	5'-6'	B&B	(46)						138	
Groundcover											
Ajuga "Bronze Beauty"	36	3" Pot			.80		.75	(.65)		23 40	
Alyssum saxatile	12	2 Qt. Pot			3 25	(2 50)		3		30	
Arctostaphylos uva-ursi	36	3" Pot						(.95)		34 20	
Comptonia peregrina	100	2'6" Pot						(.95)		95	
Euonymus f. Colorata	1300	3" Pot			.85		1	(.65)		845	
Sedum spectabilis	24	2 Qt. Pot				(2 50)				60	
Subtotal										4483 60	
Delivery					85		10		30	125	
Total										4608 60	

Figure 6.16

147

Horticultural Material

Quantities of horticultural materials can be determined from several different sources. The specifications often state required quantities, such as "five pounds of ground limestone per hundred square feet". Quantities and costs for the sample project are shown in Figure 6.18, where they are listed by total area.

For plant beds and tree pits, excavation volumes must be measured and then offset by the root ball volumes in order to determine the required volume (quantity) of topsoil. This can be a tedious task requiring numerous repetitive calculations. The use of estimating aids such as the Surtees' Charts will help cut down the number of such calculations. An excerpt from the Surtees' Charts is shown in Figure 6.19. See Appendix A for a more extensive listing.

Plant	Quantity	Unit Labor Cost	Total Cost	Crew	Daily Output	Time
Groundcover	1472	$ 0.67	$ 986	B-1	600	2.5 days
Potted Plants (approx. 1 gal.)	48	3.10	149	B-1	130	0.4
Potted Plants (approx. 3 gal.)	122	5.05	616	B-1	80	1.5
B & B Plants (approx. 18" ball)	15	13.40	201	B-1	30	0.5
Trees	5	55.00	275	B-17	10	0.5
		38.00*	190			
			$2,417			5.4

*Equipment cost

Figure 6.17

Means Forms
COST ANALYSIS

PROJECT: Office Building
LOCATION:

TAKE OFF BY: SHF QUANTITIES BY: SHF PRICES BY: RSM EXTENSIONS BY: SLP

CLASSIFICATION:
ARCHITECT:

DESCRIPTION	SOURCE/DIMENSIONS		QUANTITY	UNIT	MATERIAL		LABOR		EQUIPMENT		SUBCONTRACT		TOTAL	
					UNIT COST	TOTAL	UNIT COST	TOTAL	UNIT COST	TOTAL	UNIT COST	TOTAL	UNIT COST	TOTAL
Plantings														
Trees														
Shrubs						4609		2227		190				
Groundcover														
Horticultural materials (mat. only)														
Plant Beds - Peat	4 CY Bales		3	Ea.	4.50	14								
- Fertilizer	50# 5-10-10		1	Ea.	8.90	9								
- Bone meal	25# Bag		1	Ea.	14.50	15								
- Pine Bark Mulch	310 0100	2.8	373	SY	1.17	436	1.29	481						
Lawn - 5650 SF														
- Seed	25# Bag		1	Ea.	48	48								
- Fertilizer	50# Bag		2	Ea.	9.50	19								
- Lime	50# Bag		6	Ea.	1.90	11								
- Installation	B-6 Crew		1	Day				414		291				
Total Plantings						5161		3122		352				

Figure 6.18

Surtee's Tree Pits and Tree Balls
Cubic Feet Per Tree
For Estimating Excavation and Top Soil

Diameters Depths		1'	1¼'	1½'	1¾'	2'	2¼'	2½'	2¾'	3'	3¼'	3½'
Tree Pit Ball	1'	.94 .68	1.47 1.07	2.13 1.54	2.88 2.10	3.77 2.73	4.78 3.42	5.89 4.30	7.13 5.20	8.48 6.19	9.96 7.38	11.5 8.4
Tree Pit Ball	1¼'	1.16 .85	1.85 1.35	2.65 1.93	3.60 2.63	4.71 3.42	5.93 4.29	7.37 5.36	8.90 6.49	10.6 7.7	12.4 9.2	14.4 10.5
Tree Pit Ball	1½'	1.40 1.02	2.22 1.62	3.08 2.32	4.32 3.15	5.65 4.10	7.16 5.19	8.83 6.39	10.7 7.8	12.7 9.2	15.0 10.9	17.3 12.7
Tree Pit Ball	1¾'	1.65 1.20	2.58 1.88	3.70 3.72	5.04 3.68	6.60 4.78	8.20 6.03	10.3 7.5	12.5 9.1	14.8 10.7	17.4 12.7	20.2 14.7
Tree Pit Ball	2'	1.87 1.38	2.95 2.15	4.26 3.10	5.76 4.20	7.54 5.49	9.55 6.92	11.8 8.5	14.3 10.4	17.0 12.3	19.9 14.5	23.0 16.8
Tree Pit Ball	2¼'	2.10 1.55	3.32 2.43	4.78 3.48	6.48 4.73	8.48 6.19	10.7 7.5	13.2 9.6	16.0 11.7	19.1 13.8	22.4 16.4	26.0 18.9
Tree Pit Ball	2½'	2.34 1.70	3.69 2.70	5.30 3.87	7.20 5.25	9.42 6.89	11.9 8.7	14.7 10.7	17.8 13.0	21.2 15.4	24.9 18.2	28.9 21.0
Tree Pit Ball	2¾'	2.57 1.87	4.06 2.98	5.83 4.25	7.92 5.77	10.3 7.6	13.1 9.6	16.2 11.8	19.6 14.3	23.3 17.0	27.4 20.0	31.8 23.1
Tree Pit Ball	3'	2.81 2.05	4.43 3.24	6.37 4.65	8.64 6.30	11.3 8.3	14.3 10.5	17.7 12.9	21.4 15.6	25.4 18.6	29.9 21.8	34.6 25.2
Tree Pit Ball	3¼'	3.00 2.21	4.80 3.50	6.90 5.03	9.36 6.83	12.2 8.9	15.5 11.4	19.2 14.0	23.2 16.9	27.5 20.1	32.4 23.6	37.5 27.3
Tree Pit Ball	3½'	3.28 2.39	5.17 3.77	7.41 5.42	10.1 7.4	13.2 9.6	16.7 12.2	20.7 15.0	25.0 18.2	29.6 21.7	34.9 25.4	40.4 29.4
Tree Pit Ball	3¾'	3.50 2.56	5.53 4.04	7.96 3.80	10.8 7.9	14.2 10.3	17.9 13.1	22.2 16.1	26.7 19.5	31.7 23.2	37.1 27.2	43.3 31.5
Tree Pit Ball	4'	3.74 2.73	5.90 4.31	8.50 6.19	11.5 8.4	15.1 11.0	19.1 14.0	23.7 17.2	28.5 20.8	33.8 24.8	39.9 29.0	46.2 33.6
Tree Pit Ball	4¼'	3.97 2.90	6.28 4.58	9.01 6.58	12.3 8.9	16.0 11.8	20.3 14.8	25.1 18.3	30.3 22.1	36.0 26.3	42.3 30.8	49.1 35.7
Tree Pit Ball	4½'	4.20 3.07	6.64 4.85	9.55 6.97	13.0 9.5	17.0 12.4	21.5 15.7	26.6 19.4	32.0 23.4	38.1 27.8	44.8 32.6	52.0 37.8
Tree Pit Ball	4¾'	4.43 3.24	7.00 5.12	10.0 7.4	13.7 10.0	17.9 13.0	22.7 16.5	28.0 20.4	33.8 24.7	40.2 29.1	47.3 34.2	54.9 40.0
Tree Pit Ball	5'	4.68 3.41	7.38 5.38	10.6 7.8	14.4 10.5	18.8 13.7	23.9 17.4	29.8 21.5	35.6 26.0	42.3 30.9	49.9 36.1	57.7 42.1
Tree Pit Ball	5½'	5.14 3.76	8.12 5.93	11.7 8.5	15.8 11.6	20.7 15.1	26.3 19.1	32.4 23.7	39.2 28.6	46.7 34.0	54.8 40.0	63.5 46.3
Tree Pit Ball	6'	5.41 4.10	8.86 6.46	12.7 9.3	17.3 12.6	22.6 16.5	28.7 20.9	35.4 25.9	42.8 31.2	50.9 37.1	57.8 43.6	69.3 50.5

Figure 6.19

The measured area of the planting beds is also used to determine the volume of mulch needed. For the sample project, three inches of pine bark is specified for all planting beds. The chart in Figure 4.7 can be used to determine the quantity of mulch required. Costs can be determined by volume or by area (based on specific depth).

Mulch depth	3 inches
Planting bed area	3,353 S.F.
Cubic yards per M.S.F. (at 1″ depth)	3.5 C.Y.
Total C.Y. required	35 C.Y.

For the sample project, the costs are from Figure 6.20, line 2.8-310-0100. For the mulch requirements of individual tree pits, the surface area can be determined using the Surtees' Charts.

Lawns

In the sample estimate, costs for the seeded lawn have been determined by estimating the separate components: grading, spreading topsoil, horticultural material, and labor. The experienced landscape estimator will often have developed a complete "system" price based on the costs from past projects. This complete cost can be used as a comparison to assure that the unit price estimate is complete. For example, systems costs for lawns are shown in Figure 6.21, from *Means Site Work Cost Data*. The most appropriate "system" for the project is line 1240. The complete system cost is $365 per thousand square feet. (See Chapter 9 for a complete discussion of the information presented in *Means Site Work Cost Data*.) This figure can be used as a cross check for the costs as determined in the sample estimate.

2.8 Lawns & Planting		CREW	DAILY OUTPUT	MAN-HOURS	UNIT	BARE COSTS				TOTAL INCL O&P
						MAT.	LABOR	EQUIP.	TOTAL	
240	2400	Large commercial, no boulders	B-10B	400	.030	M.S.F.		.58	1.70	2.28	2.71	240
	2500	With boulders	"	240	.050			.96	2.83	3.79	4.52
	3000	Scarify subsoil, residential, skid steer loader w/scarifiers, 50 HP	B-66	32	.250			4.90	3.79	8.69	11.35
	3050	Municipal, skid steer loader w/scarifiers, 50 HP	"	120	.067			1.31	1.01	2.32	3.02
	3100	Large commercial, 75 HP, dozer w/ripper	B-10L	240	.050			.96	.86	1.82	2.36
	3110										
	3500	Screen topsoil from stockpile, vibrating screen, wet material (organic)	B-10P	200	.060	C.Y.		1.15	2.99	4.14	4.97
	3550	Dry material	"	300	.040			.77	1.99	2.76	3.31
	3600	Mixing with conditioners, manure and peat	B-10R	550	.022			.42	.39	.81	1.04
	3650	Mobilization add for 2 days or less operation				Job					225
	3800	Spread conditioned topsoil, 6" deep, by hand	B-1	360	.067	S.Y.	2.43	1.12		3.55	4.31
	3850	300 HP dozer	B-38	27	.889	M.S.F.	324	15.35	13.90	353.25	395
	4000	Spread soil conditioners, alum. sulfate, 1#/S.Y., push spreader	A-1	17,500		S.Y.	.17	.01		.18	.20
	4050	Tractor spreader	B-66	700	.011	M.S.F.	18.75	.22	.17	19.14	21
	4100	Fertilizer, 0.2#/S.Y., push spreader	A-1	17,500		S.Y.	.04	.01		.05	.05
	4150	Tractor spreader	B-66	700	.011	M.S.F.	4.45	.22	.17	4.84	5.40
	4200	Ground limestone, 1#/S.Y., push spreader	A-1	17,500		S.Y.	.05	.01		.06	.07
	4250	Tractor spreader	B-66	700	.011	M.S.F.	5.50	.22	.17	5.89	6.55
	4300	Lusoil, 3#/S.Y., push spreader	A-1	17,500		S.Y.	.31	.01		.32	.35
	4350	Tractor spreader	B-66	700	.011	M.S.F.	34	.22	.17	34.39	38
	4400	Manure, 18.#/S.Y., push spreader	A-1	2,500	.003	S.Y.	1.23	.05	.02	1.30	1.44
	4450	Tractor spreader	B-66	280	.029	M.S.F.	135	.56	.43	135.99	150
	4500	Perlite, 1" deep, push spreader	A-1	17,500		S.Y.	1.85	.01		1.86	2.05
	4550	Tractor spreader	B-66	700	.011	M.S.F.	205	.22	.17	205.39	225
	4600	Vermiculite, push spreader	A-1	17,500		S.Y.	1.70	.01		1.71	1.88
	4650	Tractor spreader	B-66	700	.011	M.S.F.	190	.22	.17	190.39	210
	5000	Spread topsoil, skid steer loader and hand dress	B-62	270	.089	C.Y.	9.20	1.53	.31	11.04	12.70
	5100	Articulated loader and hand dress	B-100	320	.038		9.20	.72	1.35	11.27	12.65
	5200	Articulated loader, 75 HP dozer	B-38	500	.048		9.20	.83	.75	10.78	12.15
	5300	Road grader and hand dress	B-11L	1,000	.016		9.20	.29	.47	9.96	11.05
	6000	Tilling topsoil, 20 HP tractor w/6' disk, 2" deep	B-66	50,000		S.Y.				.01	.01
	6050	4" deep		40,000						.01	.01
	6100	6" deep		30,000				.01		.01	.01
	6150	26" rototiller, 2" deep	A-1	1,250	.006			.10	.03	.13	.19
	6200	4" deep		1,000	.008			.13	.04	.17	.23
	6250	6" deep		750	.011			.17	.05	.22	.31
	6400	Lawn cutting, walking mower		4.40	1.820	Acre		29	9.15	38.15	53
	6450	Riding mower		7	1.140	"		18.40	5.75	24.15	33
310	0010	MULCH										310
	0050										
	0100	Aged barks, 3" deep, hand spread	1 Clab	100	.080	S.Y.	1.17	1.29		2.46	3.18
	0150	Skid steer loader	B-63	13.50	2.960	M.S.F.	130	50	6.15	186.15	225
	0200	Hay, 1" deep, hand spread	1 Clab	475	.017	S.Y.	.15	.27		.42	.56
	0250	Power mulcher, small	B-64	180	.089	M.S.F.	17	1.46	.89	19.35	22
	0350	Large	B-65	530	.030	"	17	.50	.41	17.91	19.85
	0400	Humus peat, 1" deep, hand spread	1 Clab	700	.011	S.Y.	.51	.18		.69	.83
	0450	Push spreader	A-1	2,500	.003	"	.51	.05	.02	.58	.65
	0550	Tractor spreader	B-66	700	.011	M.S.F.	57	.22	.17	57.39	63
	0600	Oat straw, 1" deep, hand spread	1 Clab	475	.017	S.Y.	.20	.27		.47	.62
	0650	Power mulcher, small	B-64	180	.089	M.S.F.	23	1.46	.89	25.35	28
	0700	Large	B-65	530	.030	"	23	.50	.41	23.91	26
	0750	Add for asphaltic emulsion	B-45	1,770	.009	Gal.	1.45	.17	.28	1.90	2.16
	0800	Peat moss, 1" deep, hand spread	1 Clab	900	.009	S.Y.	.75	.14		.89	1.04
	0850	Push spreader	A-1	2,500	.003	"	.75	.05	.02	.82	.92
	0950	Tractor spreader	B-66	700	.011	M.S.F.	83	.22	.17	83.39	92
	1000	Polyethylene film, 6 mil.	2 Clab	2,000	.008	S.Y.	.14	.13		.27	.34
	1100	Redwood nuggets, 3" deep, hand spread	1 Clab	150	.053	"	4.75	.86		5.61	6.50
	1150	Skid steer loader	B-63	13.50	2.960	M.S.F.	530	50	6.15	586.15	665
	1200	Stone mulch, hand spread, ceramic chips, economy	B-14	125	.384	S.Y.	5.10	6.55	1.29	12.94	16.60
	1250	Deluxe	"	95	.505	"	7.50	8.60	1.70	17.80	23

Figure 6.20

The Lawn Systems listed include different types of seeding, sodding and ground covers for flat and sloped areas. Costs are given per thousand square feet for different size jobs; residential, small commercial and large commercial. The size of the job relates to the type and productivity of the equipment being used. Components include furnishing and spreading screened loam, spreading fertilizer and limestone and mulching planted and seeded surfaces. Sloped surfaces include jute mesh or staking depending on the type of cover.

System Components	QUANTITY	UNIT	COST PER M.S.F.		
			MAT.	INST.	TOTAL
SYSTEM 12.7-411-1000					
LAWN, FLAT AREA, SEEDED, TURF MIX, RESIDENTIAL					
Scarify subsoil, residential, skid steer loader	1.000	M.S.F.		11.35	11.35
Root raking, residential, no boulders	1.000	M.S.F.		14.75	14.75
Spread topsoil, skid steer loader	18.500	C.Y.	187.22	47.73	234.95
Spread limestone & fertilizer	110.000	S.Y.	11	2.20	13.20
Till topsoil, 26″ rototiller	110.000	S.Y.		25.30	25.30
Rake topsoil, screened loam	1.000	M.S.F.		12.60	12.60
Roll topsoil, push roller	18.500	C.Y.		.93	.93
Seeding, turf mix, push spreader	1.000	M.S.F.	8.14	22.86	31
Straw, mulch	110.000	S.Y.	24.20	44	68.20
TOTAL			230.56	181.72	412.28

12.7-411	Lawns	COST PER M.S.F.		
		MAT.	INST.	TOTAL
1000	Lawn, flat area, seeded, turf mix, residential	230	180	410
1040	Small commercial	230	130	360
1080	Large commercial	245	97	342
1200	Shade mix, residential	235	180	415
1240	Small commercial	235	130	365
1280	Large commercial	250	97	347
1400	Utility mix, residential	230	180	410
1440	Small commercial	235	130	365
1480	Large commercial	250	97	347
2000	Sod, bluegrass, residential	415	295	710
2040	Small commercial	380	265	645
2080	Large commercial	370	220	590
2200	Bentgrass, residential	595	185	780
2240	Small commercial	570	175	745
2280	Large commercial	540	140	680
2400	Ground cover, english ivy, residential	700	485	1,185
2440	Small commercial	700	420	1,120
2480	Large commercial	700	385	1,085
2600	Pachysandra, residential	865	2,525	3,390
2640	Small commercial	865	2,450	3,315
2680	Large commercial	865	2,425	3,290
2800	Vinca minor, residential	1,200	735	1,935

299

Figure 6.21

Sample estimate costs:

	Material	Labor	Equipment
Grading		$182	$ 37
Place Topsoil (40% of total)		$ 92	$110
Seed, Fertilizer, Lime	$78		
Installation		$414	$162
	$78	$688	$309

Total cost	$1,075
Total area	5,650 S.F.
Cost per M.S.F.	$ 190

Note that the system cost in Figure 6.21 includes $187.22 as a material cost for topsoil. This component is not required in the sample project. When the cost for topsoil is deducted, the system price is $178 per thousand square feet, well within tolerable variances from the "actual" cost. Systems costs are useful not only for cross checking purposes, but also for establishing budgets. However, for detailed estimating, the systems method may not allow for the variation needed to meet specific project requirements.

Estimate Summary

At this point in the estimating process, all of the work has been identified, listed, and priced. All vendor quotes and subcontractor bids should be in hand (ideally, but not always realistically) and all costs should be determiend "in house".

The costs for the major portions of the landscape work can now be transferred to an Estimate Summary form as shown in Figure 6.22. In addition to the items listed in the pricing sheets, certain other types of work may be specified. In this case, tree pruning (for all trees within the work area) and general site clean-up are required. The estimator must determine the extent of the work, as well as the appropriate crew and duration. For the sample project the equivalent of a B-85 crew (see Figure 6.23) is chosen for one day. Based on the site visit, the estimator feels that two laborers are required. One is added in addition to the daily crew cost in Figure 6.22.

For this example, overhead and profit are applied as in *Means Site Work Costs Data*, and explained in Chapter 9. Ten percent is added to material and equipment costs for handling and ten percent is added to subcontract costs to cover supervision, management, and profit. However, 47.6 percent is added to the bare labor costs (shown in Figure 6.24) to cover employment taxes, insurance, office overhead and profit.

Means Forms

CONDENSED ESTIMATE SUMMARY

PROJECT **Office Building**

ESTIMATE NO. **87-1**

LOCATION	TOTAL AREA/VOLUME	DATE **1987**
ARCHITECT	COST PER S.F./C.F.	NO. OF STORIES

PRICES BY: **RSM**   EXTENSIONS BY: **SLP**   CHECKED BY: **JDM**

Description	Material	Labor	Equipment	Subcontract	Total
Site Work:	1745	312		15066	17123
Headwalls					
Rip-Rap					
Grading					
Hard Construction:	238	336	42	12892	13508
Bluestone Patios					
RR Tie Steps Walls & Edging					
Fieldstone Edging					
Crushed Stone Walks					
Plantings:	5161	3122	352		8635
Trees, Shrubs & Groundcover					
Horticultural material					
Lawn					
Miscellaneous:					
Pruning & Cleanup (B-85 & one laborer – 1 Day)		559	432		991
Sales Tax 5%	357				357
Direct Costs Subtotal	7501	4329	826	27958	40614
Overhead & Profit 10% M, 47.6% L, 10% E, 10% S	750	2061	83	2796	5690
Total	8251	6390	909	30754	46304

Figure 6.22

CREWS

Crew B-75

Crew B-75	Hr.	Daily	Hr.	Daily	Bare Costs	Incl. O&P
1 Labor Foreman (outside)	$18.10	$144.80	$26.55	$212.40	$19.16	$28.02
1 Highway Laborer	16.10	128.80	23.65	189.20		
4 Equip. Oper. (med.)	20.75	664.00	30.35	971.20		
1 Truck Driver (heavy)	16.95	135.60	24.60	196.80		
1 Motor Grader, 30,000 Lb.		473.40		520.75		
1 Grader Attach., Ripper		39.15		43.05		
2 Stabilizers, 310 H.P.		1554.00		1709.40		
1 Dist. Truck, 3000 Gal.		221.20		243.30		
1 Vibr. Roller, 29,000 Lb.		339.80		373.80	46.92	51.61
56 M.H., Daily Totals		$3700.75		$4459.90	$66.08	$79.63

Crew B-76

Crew B-76	Hr.	Daily	Hr.	Daily	Bare Costs	Incl. O&P
1 Dock Builder Foreman	$22.35	$178.80	$35.45	$283.60	$20.45	$31.62
5 Dock Builders	20.35	814.00	32.30	1292.00		
2 Equip. Oper. (crane)	21.20	339.20	31.00	496.00		
1 Equip. Oper. Oiler	17.55	140.40	25.65	205.20		
1 Crawler Crane, 60 Ton		593.20		652.50		
1 Barge, 400 Ton		360.95		397.05		
1 Hammer, 15K. Ft. Lbs.		199.00		218.90		
60 L.F. Leads, 15K. Ft. Lbs.		48.00		52.80		
1 Air Compr., 600 C.F.M.		238.80		262.70		
2-50 Ft. Air Hoses, 3" Dia.		19.10		21.00	20.26	22.29
72 M.H., Daily Totals		$2931.45		$3881.75	$40.71	$53.91

Crew B-77

Crew B-77	Hr.	Daily	Hr.	Daily	Bare Costs	Incl. O&P
1 Labor Foreman (outside)	$18.10	$144.80	$26.55	$212.40	$16.60	$24.37
3 Highway Laborers	16.10	386.40	23.65	567.60		
1 Crack Cleaner, 25 H.P.		63.40		69.75		
1 Crack Filler, Trailer Mtd.		105.60		116.15		
1 Flatbed Truck, 3 Ton		68.00		74.80	7.40	8.14
32 M.H., Daily Totals		$768.20		$1040.70	$24.00	$32.51

Crew B-78

Crew B-78	Hr.	Daily	Hr.	Daily	Bare Costs	Incl. O&P
1 Labor Foreman (outside)	$18.10	$144.80	$26.55	$212.40	$16.50	$24.23
4 Highway Laborers	16.10	515.20	23.65	756.80		
1 Paint Striper, S.P.		158.40		174.25		
1 Flatbed Truck, 3 Ton		68.00		74.80		
1 Pickup Truck, 3/4 Ton		63.40		69.75	7.24	7.97
40 M.H., Daily Totals		$949.80		$1288.00	$23.74	$32.20

Crew B-79

Crew B-79	Hr.	Daily	Hr.	Daily	Bare Costs	Incl. O&P
1 Labor Foreman (outside)	$18.10	$144.80	$26.55	$212.40	$16.60	$24.37
3 Highway Laborers	16.10	386.40	23.65	567.60		
1 Thermo. Striper, T.M.		198.00		217.80		
1 Flatbed Truck, 3 Ton		68.00		74.80		
2 Pickup Trucks, 3/4 Ton		126.80		139.50	12.27	13.50
32 M.H., Daily Totals		$924.00		$1212.10	$28.87	$37.87

Crew B-80

Crew B-80	Hr.	Daily	Hr.	Daily	Bare Costs	Incl. O&P
1 Labor Foreman (outside)	$18.10	$144.80	$26.55	$212.40	$17.93	$26.28
1 Highway Laborer	16.10	128.80	23.65	189.20		
1 Equip. Oper. (light)	19.60	156.80	28.65	229.20		
1 Flatbed Truck, 3 Ton		68.00		74.80		
1 Post Driver, T.M.		192.00		211.20	10.83	11.91
24 M.H., Daily Totals		$690.40		$916.80	$28.76	$38.19

Crew B-81

Crew B-81	Hr.	Daily	Hr.	Daily	Bare Costs	Incl. O&P
1 Equip. Oper. (med.)	$20.75	$166.00	$30.35	$242.80	$18.85	$27.47
1 Truck Driver (heavy)	16.95	135.60	24.60	196.80		
1 Hydromulcher, T.M.		136.20		149.80		
1 Tractor Truck, 4x2		243.20		267.50	23.71	26.08
16 M.H., Daily Totals		$681.00		$856.90	$42.56	$53.55

Crew B-82

Crew B-82	Hr.	Daily	Hr.	Daily	Bare Costs	Incl. O&P
1 Highway Laborer	$16.10	$128.80	$23.65	$189.20	$17.85	$26.15
1 Equip. Oper. (light)	19.60	156.80	28.65	229.20		
1 Horiz. Borer, 6 H.P.		33.00		36.30	2.06	2.26
16 M.H., Daily Totals		$318.60		$454.70	$19.91	$28.41

Crew B-83

Crew B-83	Hr.	Daily	Hr.	Daily	Bare Costs	Incl. O&P
1 Tugboat Captain	$20.75	$166.00	$30.35	$242.80	$18.42	$27.00
1 Tugboat Hand	16.10	128.80	23.65	189.20		
1 Tugboat, 250 H.P.		396.00		435.60	24.75	27.22
16 M.H., Daily Totals		$690.80		$867.60	$43.17	$54.22

Crew B-84

Crew B-84	Hr.	Daily	Hr.	Daily	Bare Costs	Incl. O&P
1 Equip. Oper. (med.)	$20.75	$166.00	$30.35	$242.80	$20.75	$30.35
1 Rotary Mower/Tractor		146.20		160.80	18.27	20.10
8 M.H., Daily Totals		$312.20		$403.60	$39.02	$50.45

Crew B-85

Crew B-85	Hr.	Daily	Hr.	Daily	Bare Costs	Incl. O&P
1 Highway Laborer	$16.10	$128.80	$23.65	$189.20	$17.93	$26.20
1 Equip. Oper. (med.)	20.75	166.00	30.35	242.80		
1 Truck Driver (heavy)	16.95	135.60	24.60	196.80		
1 Aerial Lift Truck		282.40		310.65		
1 Brush Chipper, 130 H.P.		133.40		146.75		
1 Pruning Saw, Rotary		16.30		17.95	18.00	19.80
24 M.H., Daily Totals		$862.50		$1104.15	$35.93	$46.00

Crew B-86

Crew B-86	Hr.	Daily	Hr.	Daily	Bare Costs	Incl. O&P
1 Equip. Oper. (med.)	$20.75	$166.00	$30.35	$242.80	$20.75	$30.35
1 Stump Chipper, S.P.		160.00		176.00	20.00	22.00
8 M.H., Daily Totals		$326.00		$418.80	$40.75	$52.35

Crew B-87

Crew B-87	Hr.	Daily	Hr.	Daily	Bare Costs	Incl. O&P
1 Common Laborer	$16.10	$128.80	$23.65	$189.20	$19.82	$29.01
4 Equip. Oper. (med.)	20.75	664.00	30.35	971.20		
2 Feller Bunchers, 50 H.P.		527.60		580.35		
1 Log Chipper, 22" Tree		1554.00		1709.40		
1 Dozer, 105 H.P.		207.40		228.15		
1 Chainsaw, Gas, 36" Long		27.05		29.75	57.90	63.69
40 M.H., Daily Totals		$3108.85		$3708.05	$77.72	$92.70

Crew B-88

Crew B-88	Hr.	Daily	Hr.	Daily	Bare Costs	Incl. O&P
1 Common Laborer	$16.10	$128.80	$23.65	$189.20	$20.08	$29.39
6 Equip. Oper. (med.)	20.75	996.00	30.35	1456.80		
2 Feller Bunchers, 50 H.P.		527.60		580.35		
1 Log Chipper, 22" Tree		1554.00		1709.40		
2 Log Skidders, 50 H.P.		472.00		519.20		
1 Dozer, 105 H.P.		207.40		228.15		
1 Chainsaw, Gas, 36" Long		27.05		29.75	49.78	54.76
56 M.H., Daily Totals		$3912.85		$4712.85	$69.86	$84.15

Figure 6.23

Installing Contractor's Overhead & Profit

Below are the **average** installing contractor's percentage mark-ups applied to base labor rates to arrive at typical billing rates.

Column A: Labor rates are based on union wages averaged for 30 major U.S. cities. Base rates including fringe benefits are listed hourly and daily. These figures are the sum of the wage rate, employer-paid fringe benefits such as vacation pay, employer-paid health and welfare costs, pension costs, plus appropriate training and industry advancement funds costs.

Column B: Workers' Compensation rates are the national average of state rates established for each trade.

Column C: Column C lists average fixed overhead figures for all trades. Included are Federal and State Unemployment costs set at 5.5%; Social Security Taxes (FICA) set at 7.15%; Builder's Risk Insurance costs set at 1.14%; and Public Liability costs set at 0.82%. All the percentages except those for Social Security Taxes vary from state to state as well as from company to company.

Column D and E: Percentages in Columns D and E are based on the presumption that the installing contractor has annual billing of $500,000 and up. Overhead percentages may increase with smaller annual billing. The overhead percentages for any given contractor may vary greatly and depend on a number of factors, such as the contractor's annual volume, engineering and logistical support costs, and staff requirements. The figures for overhead and profit will also vary depending on the type of job, the job location, and the prevailing economic conditions. All factors should be examined very carefully for each job.

Column F: Column F lists the total of columns B, C, D, and E.

Column G: Column G is Column A (hourly base labor rate) multiplied by the percentage in Column F (O&P percentage).

Column H: Column H is the total of Column A (hourly base labor rate) plus Column G (Total O&P).

Column I: Column I is Column H multiplied by eight hours.

		A		B	C	D	E	F		G	H	I
		Base Rate Incl. Fringes		Work-ers' Comp. Ins.	Average Fixed Over-head	Over-head	Profit	Total Overhead & Profit			Rate with O & P	
Abbr.	Trade	Hourly	Daily					%	Amount		Hourly	Daily
Skwk	Skilled Workers Average (35 trades)	$20.80	$166.40	10.4%	14.6%	12.6%	10%	47.6%	$ 9.90	$30.70	$245.60
	Helpers Average (5 trades)	15.90	127.20	11.1		12.7		48.4	7.70	23.60	188.80
	Foremen Average, Inside (50¢ over trade)	21.30	170.40	10.4		12.6		47.6	10.15	31.45	251.60
	Foremen Average, Outside ($2.00 over trade)	22.80	182.40	10.4		12.6		47.6	10.85	33.65	269.20
Clab	Common Building Laborers	16.10	128.80	11.4		10.8		46.8	7.55	23.65	189.20
Asbe	Asbestos Workers	23.00	184.00	8.8		15.7		49.1	11.30	34.30	274.40
Boil	Boilermakers	23.00	184.00	7.2		16.0		47.8	11.00	34.00	272.00
Bric	Bricklayers	20.55	164.40	8.5		10.7		43.8	9.00	29.55	236.40
Brhe	Bricklayer Helpers	16.15	128.40	8.5		10.7		43.8	7.05	23.20	185.60
Carp	Carpenters	20.55	164.40	11.4		10.8		46.8	9.60	30.15	241.20
Cefi	Cement Finishers	19.70	157.60	6.6		10.8		42.0	8.30	27.95	223.60
Elec	Electricians	22.65	181.20	4.5		15.9		45.0	10.20	32.85	262.80
Elev	Elevator Constructors	23.05	184.40	6.0		15.9		46.5	10.70	33.75	270.00
Eqhv	Equipment Operators, Crane or Shovel	21.20	169.60	7.8		13.8		46.2	9.80	31.00	248.00
Eqmd	Equipment Operators, Medium Equipment	20.75	166.00	7.8		13.8		46.2	9.60	30.35	242.80
Eqlt	Equipment Operators, Light Equipment	19.60	156.80	7.8		13.8		46.2	9.05	28.65	229.20
Eqol	Equipment Operators, Oilers	17.55	140.40	7.8		13.8		46.2	8.10	25.65	205.20
Eqmm	Equipment Operators, Master Mechanics	22.00	176.00	7.8		13.8		46.2	10.15	32.15	257.20
Glaz	Glaziers	20.75	166.00	8.7		10.8		44.1	9.15	29.90	239.20
Lath	Lathers	20.50	164.00	7.2		10.8		42.6	8.75	29.25	234.00
Marb	Marble Setters	20.25	162.00	8.5		10.7		43.8	8.85	29.10	232.80
Mill	Millwrights	21.25	170.00	7.2		10.8		42.6	9.05	30.30	242.40
Mstz	Mosaic and Terrazzo Workers	20.05	160.40	6.0		10.7		41.3	8.30	28.35	226.80
Pord	Painters, Ordinary	19.55	156.40	8.9		10.8		44.3	8.65	28.20	225.60
Psst	Painters, Structural Steel	20.20	161.60	29.4		10.1		64.1	12.95	33.15	265.20
Pape	Paper Hangers	19.75	158.00	8.9		10.8		44.3	8.75	28.50	228.00
Pile	Pile Drivers	20.35	162.80	18.3		15.7		58.6	11.95	32.30	258.40
Plas	Plasterers	20.25	162.00	8.7		10.9		44.2	8.95	29.20	233.60
Plah	Plasterer Helpers	16.65	133.20	8.7		10.9		44.2	7.35	24.00	192.00
Plum	Plumbers	23.00	184.00	5.3		15.9		45.8	10.55	33.55	268.40
Rodm	Rodmen (Reinforcing)	22.10	176.80	18.6		13.3		56.5	12.50	34.60	276.80
Rofc	Roofers, Composition	19.15	153.20	20.8		10.4		55.8	10.70	29.85	238.80
Rots	Roofers, Tile & Slate	19.25	154.00	20.8		10.4		55.8	10.75	30.00	240.00
Rohe	Roofer Helpers (Composition)	14.20	113.60	20.8		10.4		55.8	7.90	22.10	176.80
Shee	Sheet Metal Workers	23.10	184.80	7.0		15.8		47.4	10.95	34.05	272.40
Spri	Sprinkler Installers	23.85	190.80	6.1		15.9		46.6	11.10	34.95	279.60
Stpi	Steamfitters or Pipefitters	23.30	186.40	5.3		15.9		45.8	10.70	33.95	271.60
Ston	Stone Masons	20.60	164.80	8.5		10.7		43.8	9.00	29.60	236.80
Sswk	Structural Steel Workers	22.10	176.80	21.5		13.7		59.8	13.20	35.30	282.40
Tilf	Tile Layers (Floor)	20.00	160.00	6.0		10.7		41.3	8.25	28.25	226.00
Tilh	Tile Layer Helpers	16.10	128.80	6.0		10.7		41.3	6.65	22.75	182.00
Trlt	Truck Drivers, Light	16.70	133.60	9.8		10.7		45.1	7.55	24.25	194.00
Trhv	Truck Drivers, Heavy	16.95	135.60	9.8		10.7		45.1	7.65	24.60	196.80
Sswl	Welders, Structural Steel	22.10	176.80	21.5		13.7		59.8	13.20	35.30	282.40
Wrck	*Wrecking	16.10	128.80	23.1		10.4		58.1	9.35	25.45	203.60

*Not included in Averages.

Figure 6.24

The "markups" for each individual company will vary and should be calculated based on specific requirements and conditions. A discussion of these types of costs is included in Chapter 5.

At this stage, the estimator has a final number ("subtotal" in Figure 6.22) to "work with". Now is the time when sound judgment and experience are used to determine the bid price. Adjustments can be made (up or down) depending upon certain factors that may affect a final decision: the risk involved, competition from other bidders, thoroughness of the plans and specs, and above all, the years of experience — the qualification to make such a judgment. Some firms are so scientific and calculating that every quoted price includes a lucky number.

A great deal of success in bidding can be attributed to the proper choice of jobs to bid. A landscape firm can go broke estimating every available job. The company must be able to recognize which jobs are too risky and when the competition is too keen, while not overlooking those which can be profitable. Again, knowledge of the marketplace and *experience* are the keys to successful bidding.

The primary purpose of this sample estimate (and this text) has not been to tell the reader how much an item will cost, but instead, how to develop a consistent and thorough approach to the estimating process. If such a pattern is developed, employing consistency, attention to detail, experience and above all, common sense, accurate estimates will follow.

If an estimate is thorough, organized, neat and concise, the benefits go beyond winning contracts. The information and data that is developed will be useful throughout a project — for purchasing, change orders, cost accounting and control, and development of historical costs.

THE
LANDSCAPE
PROPOSAL

Chapter Seven

THE LANDSCAPE PROPOSAL

All previous activities aimed at producing an estimate are now directed to the goal of putting forth a bid. That bid will be an offer to complete a job for a stated sum of money. This bid amount is the result of carefully figured costs for materials, equipment, and labor, and includes the necessary markups for overhead and profit. Under some circumstances, that offer may be a legal binder to perform.

Bidding is a systematic process aimed at gaining a desirable work contract. It is also a strategy, and like all good strategies, should incorporate both advance preparations and final stage flexibility.

Bidding is also hard work. Putting a bid together is a job, simplified by proper organization. Routine and systematic procedures or methods can be valuable organizational tools, as they make bidding easier and help guard against costly errors.

The importance of proper bidding methods and skills is demonstrated by the interest this topic generates within the industry. Trade associations run bidding workshops as a part of their educational and training programs. The key to successful bidding and competition is obtaining precise cost information for all direct costs. Good productivity data is also essential for producing competitive landscape project bids. The best source of such data is well-kept records from previous jobs. Collecting accurate productivity data is a joint effort of management and landscape foreman, and should be based on work over a substantial period of time for greater accuracy.

The bidding procedure can be viewed from several different perspectives. The client's goal is to obtain the best work for the lowest price. A client puts together a bid package with these aims in mind. The bidders' qualifications as well as prices are carefully analyzed by the client who wants quality work, a conscientious performance, and follow-up corrections if necessary.

From the bidder's point of view, the goal is not only winning the contract, but subsequently, profitable and timely completion of the project. The exact percentage or amount of the profit may be one of the "estimated" items in a bid package. Many experienced contractors do not use a predetermined mark-up for overhead and profit for every job, but determine such costs on a job-by-job basis. After all, many variables may influence the costs applicable to any particular project. The size of the job

and its desirability are obvious factors. Other points to consider are:
- Economic circumstances
- Number and quality of competitors
- Need for work

The contractor must take into account competition from other bidders. Strong competition puts pressure on the bidder to lower his profit percentage. Other factors that limit profit include the possibility of increased overhead, and self-imposed limitations, such as those required for a company growth plan. In other words, the need for work may outweigh the "need" for large profits (on a short term basis).

With the large number of small owner/foreman businesses in the landscape industry, there is a particularly large pitfall open for struggling contractors entering the competitive bidding scene. Caution must be taken against inadvertantly "buying a contract", that is to say, working at no profit — or possibly at a loss. Too much optimism may be costly. Caution is advised against bids that are based on imagined maximum labor production and lowest possible material costs. Even large established firms must carefully scrutinize their bids to be sure they are based on sound estimating practice, guaranteed price quotes, and firm bids from known subcontractors. Advantages shift back and forth among bidders, and there will be highly desirable work prospects at certain times. The profit on a job should be large enough to permit the growth of company assets. Too low, and the company does not prosper; too high, and the company will not win contracts.

The bidder wants to bid as low as possible and hopefully close to the next lowest bid. A large gap between his bid and next lowest bid shows that the bidder has failed to see the advantages he had over his competitors. The bidder needs to procure the contract with a low bid AND make a profit.

Activities and requirements for successful bidding include:
- Accurate quantity takeoff
- Accurate pricing (good source of cost data)
- Dependable subcontractors
- Careful planning for realistic time scheduling
- Anticipation of the methods used to perform the work

While many landscape decisions are inevitably made in the field, as much project planning as possible should be outlined before bidding. By highlighting options and strategies, unanticipated problems can be minimized. Bidding is a time to sort and analyze information and determine answers.

Bid Strategies

The strategies of bidding are well charted by Paul J. Cook in his book *Bidding for the General Contractor*, published by R.S. Means Co., Inc., 1985. The need for work is always the major determining factor that influences bidding for a contract. But other factors, such as desirability, should also be critically analyzed. Author Paul Cook lists and explains 14 different conditions that may influence bidding decisions:
1. Size (cost of the project in dollars)
2. Location of project (travel distance)
3. Relationship with client
4. Type of and familiarity with construction
5. Probable level of competition

6. Labor market
7. Subcontractor market
8. Quality of drawings and specifications
9. Quality of supervision
10. Special risks
11. Completion time and penalty
12. Estimating and bidding time
13. Need for work
14. Other special advantages or disadvantages

If all conditions are primarily positive, the project should be highly desirable and the bidding competitive. If most of these conditions are negative, the project should be less desirable and the bidding conservative.

The Bid Package

Professionally managed and government (federal, state, county, city) landscape projects often have prepared bid packages. The bid package has two main parts, one for the client and one for the bidder. The client's responsibility is to provide:

- Drawings and plans, including graphic details.
- Written information and specifications as a part of the drawings.

When this information is extensive (as is typical in the case of government projects), the specifications may be called the "Project Manual" and may consist of the following segments:

- Advertisement for bids, or Invitation to bid
- Bid and contract requirements
  — Instructions to bidders
  — Bid forms
  — Bond forms
  — Experience qualification forms
  — Contract forms (agreement)
- Standard clauses
  — Labor laws
  — Miscellaneous laws, rules, regulations
  — Taxes, permits, licenses, inspections
- General and special conditions
- Technical specifications pertaining to the various trades and sub-trades (often organized by Index Divisions)
- Requirements for acceptance of the completed work by the owner and release by the contractor

The American Society of Landscape Architects (ASLA) *Handbook of Professional Practice* suggests that the formality of the bid procedure and documents should correspond with the size of the job. Simple jobs should be simply documented. Large, highly detailed, costly jobs should be appropriately detailed and documented. Generally, good specifications are brief while remaining complete and adequate so as not to discourage the competing contractors and/or increase the bid. The ASLA recommends, as a minimum, simple and concise drawings, specifications offering a clear understanding of the work to be done, the amount and schedule of payments, and the completion date.

Simple bid packages may consist of the client's requirements written on a standard proposal form. An example of how a simple, minimum bid proposal should be presented is shown in Figure 7.1. The project

requirements should be clearly and completely presented as an integral part of the proposal.

The American Society of Landscape Architects suggests the use of certain standard forms, contract documents and specifications for landscape professionals. There are many ASLA examples of bid documents; their "Invitation for Bids" and "Instruction to Bidders" are shown in Figures 7.2, 7.3 and 7.4. A simple bid form, a Lump Sum Bid form and a Unit Price Bid form appear in Figures 7.5 through 7.7. Each is explained by guidelines and specifications on the form itself. Both require a total price for all of the work as included in the plans and specifications.

Unit Price proposals are typically divided into separate, task-related categories or systems which can be used by the client for comparative purposes. The "units" in a Unit Price proposal are typically those items estimated as systems. This type of bid is also appropriate if the project parameters have not been completely detailed. The bidder can provide costs based on "estimated" quantities. Total costs can then vary based on actual installed quantities. An example of the use of this form is shown in Figure 7.8. An actual bid would include a total price and most likely many more items.

Overhead and profit are usually included in the costs for each item in this type of unit pricing. The same total bid amount is reached as would be in a lump sum bid for the same quantities of materials and work, but in this case, the project is broken down. Unit Price bids are legitimate methods and should provide reliable estimates. Unfortunately, the Unit Price method is sometimes used by the client or designer as a basis for cancelling or manipulating individual costly items; in such cases, serious doubt can be cast upon the integrity of the proposed design solution if items are detailed solely on the basis of cost. The character of a particular material or item may be integral to the unity or beauty of a project. When such an item is changed or deleted, the entire project may lose its intended value.

Lump Sum Bids provide one price for all the materials and labor required according to the plans and specs. In many cases, the bidder may wish to list some unit prices in his Lump Sum bid, especially if work areas are subject to individual interpretation or if certain items are excluded from the bid. For example, an area that is difficult to estimate for seeding could be safely bid by stating that the bid price is based on "not more than 15,000 square yards of grass seeding".

⚓ Means Forms
PROPOSAL

FROM: _____

_____

_____

_____

TO: _____

_____

_____

_____

PROPOSAL NO. _____

DATE _____

PROJECT _____

LOCATION _____

_____

CONSTRUCTION TO BEGIN _____

COMPLETION DATE _____

Gentlemen:

The undersigned proposes to furnish all materials and necessary equipment and perform all labor necessary to complete the following work:

_____

_____

_____

_____

_____

_____

_____

_____

_____

_____

_____

_____

All of the above work to be completed in a substantial and workmanlike manner

☐ for the sum of _____ dollars ($_____)

☐ to be paid for at actual cost of Labor, Materials and Equipment plus_____ percent (_____ %)

Payments to be made as follows:_____

_____

_____The entire amount of the contract to be paid within_____ after completion.

Any alteration or deviation from the plans and specifications will be executed only upon written orders for same and will be added to or deducted from the sum quoted in this contract. All additional agreements must be in writing.

The Contractor agrees to carry Workmen's Compensation and Public Liability Insurance and to pay all taxes on material and labor furnished under this contract as required by Federal laws and the laws of the State in which this work is performed.

Respectfully submitted,

Contractor_____

By_____

ACCEPTANCE

You are hereby authorized to furnish all material, equipment and labor required to complete the work described in the above proposal, for which the undersigned agrees to pay the amount stated in said proposal and according to the terms thereof.

Date _____ 19_____   _____

_____

Figure 7.1

INVITATION FOR BIDS

The _____ will receive bids for the

_____

_____

_____

until_____ A.M. _____time on the _____
              P.M.

day of _____ 19 ____ at the _____

_____

at which time and place all Bids will be publicly opened and read aloud.

Sealed Bids are invited upon the several items and quantities as follows:

_____

_____

_____

_____

_____

_____

Contract Documents, including Drawings and Specifications, are on file at the office of the

Landscape Architect, _____

and at the _____

_____

Copies of the Contract Documents may be obtained at the office of _____

_____ on payment of $ _____
for each set of Documents so obtained. Said sum is refundable upon return of all Documents in
good condition not later than seven (7) days following opening of Bids. Plans may be examined
without cost.

A certified check or bank draft, payable to the _____
or a satisfactory Bid Bond executed by the Bidder and an acceptable surety, in an amount equal to

_____ (_____ %) percent of the total Base Bid shall be submitted with each bid as a
guaranty that if the Proposal is accepted the Bidder will execute the Contract and file acceptable
Performance and Labor and Material Bonds within ten (10) days after award of the Contract.

The _____ hereinafter called the Owner, reserves the
right to reject any and all Proposals and waive any formality or technicality in any Proposal in the
interest of the Owner.

Bids may be held by the Owner for a period not to exceed thirty (30) days from the date of Bids
for the purpose of reviewing the Bids and investigating the qualifications of the Bidders, prior to
awarding the Contract.

INVITATION FOR BIDS   ONE PAGE
ASLA DOC. 11A   PAGE 1

Figure 7.2

INSTRUCTIONS TO BIDDERS

1. **Proposal Form:**

   These Contract Documents include a complete set of bidding and contract forms which are for the convenience of the bidders and are not to be detached, filled out, or executed. Separate copies of Bid Forms are furnished for that purpose. These must be enclosed and sealed in an

   envelope which states on the outside: Sealed Bid for (Name of Project)_____

   _____

2. **Interpretations and Addenda:**

   No oral interpretation will be made to any bidder as to the meaning of the specifications and drawings. Interpretations, if made, shall be written in the form of an addendum and sent to all bidders to whom specifications have been issued.

3. **Examination of the Site:**

   Each bidder shall visit the site of the proposed work to fully acquaint himself with the conditions and difficulties attending the performance of the Contract. No additional compensation nor relief from any obligations of the Contract will be granted because of a lack of knowledge of the site or the conditions under which the work be accomplished.

4. **Time:**

   Proposals will be received at _____

   _____ until _____. Standard _____ time,

   _____ Daylight Saving

   _____ , 19_____ ......tted to be withdrawn after the time set for bid opening.

5. **Opening Bids:**

   All bids received prior to the opening time shall be securely kept until the day and the hour above stated at which time all bids will be publicly opened and read. No bids will be received after the above stated time.

6. **Right to Reject Bids:**

   The Owner reserves the right to accept any part, or all of any bid, and to reject any and all or parts of any and all bids. Any proposal which contains items not specified, or which does not complete all the items scheduled for bid, shall be considered informal and shall be rejected on this basis. may

7. **Signature and Legibility:**

   The prices for work and the names, addresses and signatures of the Bidders shall be clearly and legibly written. Signatures shall be signed in the space provided and in compliance with all legal requirements.

Figure 7.3

11B

8. Bid Guarantee:

Each proposal must be accompanied by a certified check, bank draft, or bid bond in an amount equal to ______________(%) percent of the amount of the bid. This guarantee shall be executed in favor of and guarantee to the Owner that the bidder will execute the Agreement and furnish the Performance and Labor and Material Bonds as required by the Contract Documents.

The aforesaid guarantee deposits of unsuccessful Bidders will be returned as soon as practical after the opening of the Bids.

9. Execution of Contract and Delivery of Bonds:

The successful Bidder shall within ____________ days after notice that his proposal has been accepted enter into a contract and deliver to the Owner a Performance Bond and a Labor and Material Bond each respectively issued by an approved surety company satisfactory to the Owner in an amount equal to the total price bid.

10. Special Conditions: ____

These sample forms are for reference only. For current ASLA Standard Forms of Agreement and guidelines on their use, contact the American Society of Landscape Architects, 1733 Connecticut Ave. NW, Washington, D.C. 20009.

INSTRUCTIONS TO BIDDERS — TWO PAGES

ASLA DOC. 11B — PAGE 2

Figure 7.4

BID FORM

Name of Project _____

Location _____

Gentlemen:

Pursuant to and in compliance with the advertisement for bids dated _____ 19__, and

Instructions to Bidders and other documents related thereto, the undersigned, having familiarized _____

self   with the existing conditions on the site and the conditions under which the work is to be
selves
done, hereby proposes to furnish all labor, materials, equipment, and services to perform all
specified work for the Site Improvement on the above named project in strict accordance with the

Contract Documents and all addenda issued thereto at the prices set forth on the accompanying bid
                                                         price
form sheets attached hereto.

If written notice of acceptance of this bid is mailed, telegraphed, or delivered to the undersigned

within _____ days after the opening of bids, or at any time thereafter before this bid is
withdrawn, the undersigned agrees to execute and deliver a contract in the form specified and

furnish the required bonds within _____ days afte_____ ed forms are presented to him
for signature.

Security in the sum of _____ _____) Dollars in the

form of _____   tted herewith in accordance
with the Instructions to Bid

                       a corporation
The bidder is a partnership and   ery person interested in this bid is as follows: _____
                       an individual

_____

Notice of acceptance of this Bid shall be mailed to the undersigned at the following address:

By _____

Title _____

_____

By _____

Title _____

Address _____

_____

Phone No. _____

BID FORM   ONE PAGE
ASLA DOC. 11C   PAGE 1

Figure 7.5

BID FORM—LUMP SUM BID

Lump Sum Price _____ ($ _____) Dollars

The above price includes completion of all the work called for under this Contract. All of the work

shall be installed and ready for the use of the Owner within _____ (____) calendar days, weather permitting, after notice to proceed. It is understood that it is the Contractor's obligation to have thoroughly familiarized himself with the site, the conditions under which the work will be done, and the actual quantities required to complete the work in accordance with the intent of the plans and specifications and that the above stated lump sum price, as bid, covers the complete work as required. It is further understood that prior to commencement of work, the Contractor shall furnish to the Owner for the purpose of adjusting the lump sum price in the event of additions, deletions or changes in the scope of the work, an itemized list of unit prices for the various parts of the work.

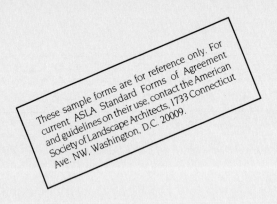

Figure 7.6

170

BID FORM—UNIT PRICE BID

Total Bid Price _____ ($ _____) Dollars

All of the work shall be installed ready for the Owner to use within _____ (____)
calendar days, weather permitting, after notice to proceed.

It is understood that the itemized quantities herein listed are not guaranteed as to accuracy but are
to be used for the purpose of comparing bids. Bid comparisons will be made on the basis of total
amounts derived from the unit prices bid at the quantities herein shown. The final amount to be
paid the Contractor for the work shall be the sum of the actual quantities of installed work at the
unit prices bid.

ITEM   QUANTITY   UNIT PRICE   AMOUNT

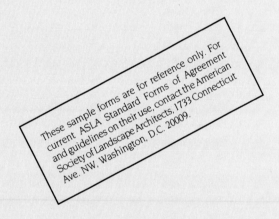

Figure 7.7

BID FORM—UNIT PRICE BID

Total Bid Price <u>Ten thousand Four hundred Twenty-two & 50/100</u> ($ <u>10,422.50</u>) Dollars

All of the work shall be installed ready for the Owner to use within _____ (____) calendar days, weather permitting, after notice to proceed.

It is understood that the itemized quantities herein listed are not guaranteed as to accuracy but are to be used for the purpose of comparing bids. Bid comparisons will be made on the basis of total amounts derived from the unit prices bid at the quantities herein shown. The final amount to be paid the Contractor for the work shall be the sum of the actual quantities of installed work at the unit prices bid.

ITEM	QUANTITY	UNIT PRICE	AMOUNT
1. Site Clearing	2.5 Acres	$ 1825.00/Acre	$ 4562.50
2. Wildflower Seeding	16,000 S.Y.	$ 0.26/S.Y.	4160.00
3. Acer Rubrum 1½"	10 Ea.	$ 170.00/Ea.	1700.00

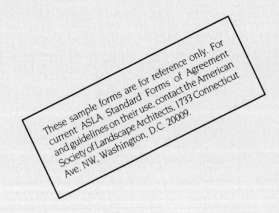

Figure 7.8

Putting Together A Bid

Bidding a large project means getting to know the person(s) connected with the project as well as the site. The matter of a qualifications statement is discussed in Chapter 1. The development of the lowest possible costs is explained in Chapters 4 and 5.

The bidder's work on the package begins with a complete review of the package itself. The cost estimate is the first item to be checked. Verifying the estimate requires another review of the drawings and specs. This is the time to search for oversights and contradictions in the cost information and for potential problems in the drawings and specs. Make a thorough analysis of the work proposed. If any problems are discovered, contract requirements and obligations will have to be clarified.

An ideal bid is made up entirely of detailed, accurate estimated costs and firm, reliable, subcontractor quotes. An actual bid may be something less than ideal and may contain costs representing budgets, "guesstimates", and allowances. These types of costs should be kept to a minimum. Unfortunately, bidding schedules do not always allow enough time to perform proper estimates. When putting a bid together for a job, the bidder may be forced by time constraints to use cost information that is not as accurate and dependable as a detailed estimate would be. Until the last moment, however, every effort should be made to confirm costs and receive commitments for both subcontract and material prices.

The basic requirements of the bidder are to respond to and complete the bid documents and requests, and to provide an offer to perform specific work often within a stated time frame in return for a specified price. The contractor's bid consists of all known costs, compiled and analyzed as carefully as possible. Included in this figure is a crucial amount for overhead and profit, and the bid bond if one is required. The bid bond cost is calculated last because it is always based on the total amount of the bid. For example, a 0.6% bid bond on a $100,000.00 contract would cost $600.00.

Submitting a Bid

When a bid package indicates a formal bid time and procedure, the instructions must be followed closely. Formal bid openings usually begin at the exact minute of the opening deadline. As a rule, a bid arriving after the opening ritual will not be accepted. At formal, public bid openings, it is a good idea to record all the bids submitted for the project. A review of competitors' bidding patterns can guide you on future projects.

The Bid Award

Only one bidder will be awarded the sought-after contract, and congratulations are in order for the company that is chosen. Acceptance of a bid is the maximum vote of confidence in a bidder's work. Knowledge gained from the experience is the only reward of the unsuccessful bidder. In such a case, one should put this hindsight to work on the next bid. The lessons of the current market, competition, profit margins, and bidding procedures cannot be completely learned from books.

Chapter Eight

JOB PLANNING

Chapter Eight

JOB PLANNING

After the estimating and bidding processes bring in a desirable contract, management takes over and job planning begins. Planning and scheduling should be considered by the estimator — throughout the estimating process — when obtaining costs for materials, equipment, and labor.

Proper job planning — of both time and costs — is an essential ingredient for job profit. Without proper schedules and cost planning, decisions made on the job could result in an interruption of progress and work flow. Down time and confusion may be the costly effects.

The Planning Team

Work scheduling often becomes a combination of juggling and precise planning. Experienced contractors try to rely on sound planning efforts to reduce the juggling act. Planning consists of designing a series of activities to occur in such a way as to bring about the most efficient and effective performance of a job. These goals are accomplished by arranging the activities in a logical order and assigning each a starting time, a duration time, and a completion time. Most contracting companies develop a routine of some sort for planning. For example, the management team should use all the information from the estimator and put together a plan and a schedule to construct the landscape job. From this point, the responsibility for planning and scheduling the project belongs to company management. The quantity takeoff prepared by the estimator becomes an information resource for management to use when planning the job.

The objectives of job planning include foreseeing any problems and establishing the following:
- Critical paths
- The *logical* sequence of events.
- The *best* work sequence.
- The impact of deviations ("What happens if . . . ?").
- Material requirements and delivery schedules.
- Ability to meet the completion date.

The Job Outline

Scheduling involves drawing up an outline or a simple bar chart to describe the general sequence of construction. Where and when will the work begin? In the sample project (Chapter 6), the major components of the work will start with the stone rip-rap and the placing of paving materials on the site. Activity begins at the stream level, progressing upward from there to the top of the bank. The work ends with the lawn seeding and a final cleanup and removal of debris.

Lists are made of the tasks required to complete each activity. Many companies make up their own checklist forms in order to avoid oversights. For some jobs "planting" may be too general a description and might need to be more specifically broken down into: "tree planting", "staking", "wrapping", and "mulching". Then on to "shrub planting" as a separate activity. For each of these activities, a crew make-up and an appropriate amount of time must be designated. Figure 8.1 is an example of how preliminary job planning might begin.

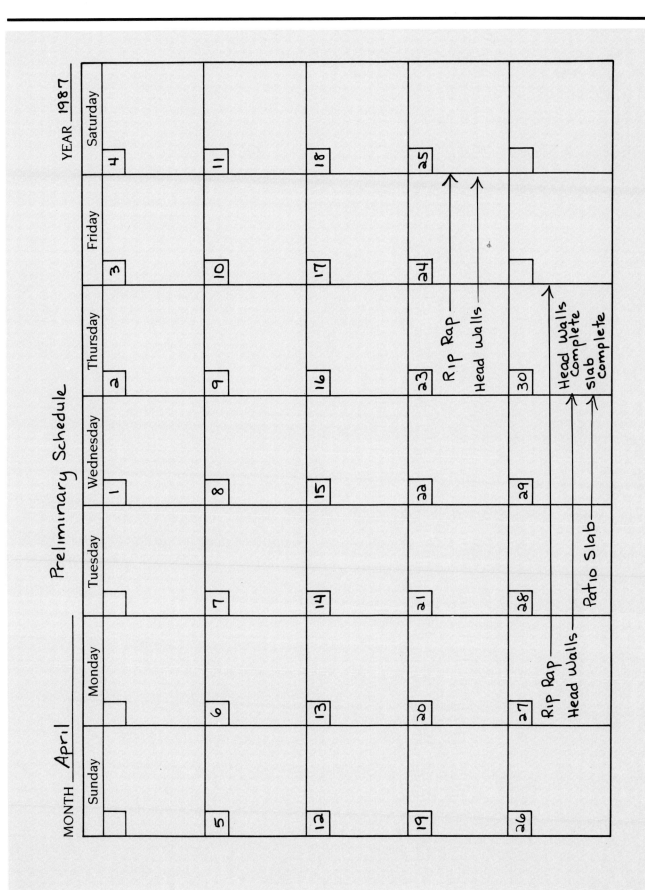

Figure 8.1

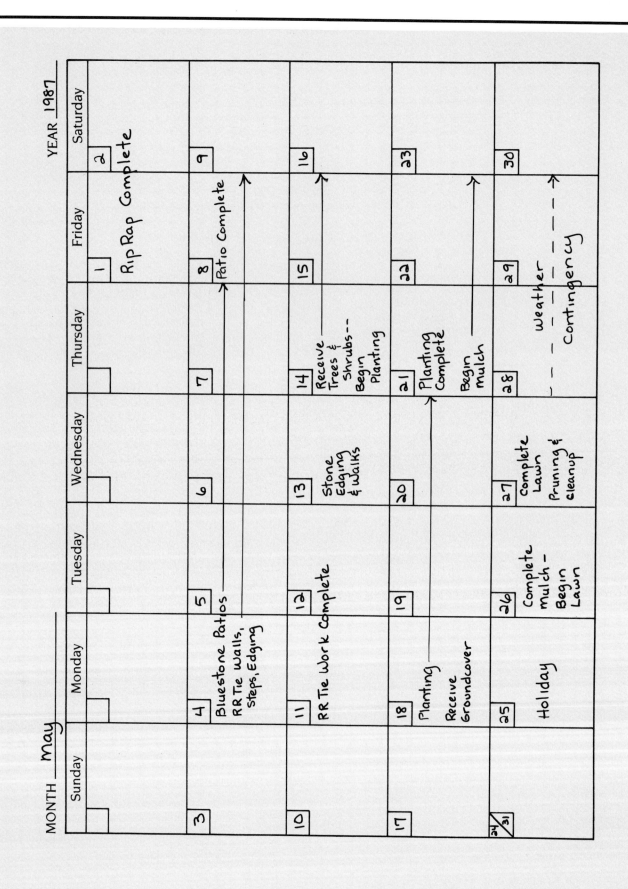

Figure 8.1 (cont.)

Plan. . .Coordinate . . .Target

When the basic time frames have been established, the crews are planned on the basis of the skills required as well as the number of workers needed to perform the work within the required time frame. The planner must coordinate all work with the delivery times obtained from suppliers. Targets of specific work goals should be established and may be timed to a certain day. For example: May 8 — bluestone patios complete.

Duration Time

In order to arrive at a schedule for the project, the planner must determine the amount of time required to do the complete job. Part of this process is determining what work must be completed before other tasks can begin or proceed, and how many tasks can be done at the same time.

Activities will be directed on site and records kept by the well-informed supervisor or foreman. The schedule for and management of the job should be based on the labor hours determined in the estimate for each phase of the work. "In place" labor records from actual jobs will be used for future estimating purposes. Other important scheduling factors include:

- The owner's requirements for job start and completion dates.
- Material delivery dates (purchase orders should be processed with confirmation of guaranteed prices and delivery dates).
- Work by subcontractors (contracts must be let with firm agreements on the scope of work and the required job duration or date of completion).

Established landscape firms have learned the value of creating and using a chart and calendar to schedule large projects. These individual project calendars should be checked against a master calendar listing the company's other scheduled work. Figure 8.2 shows how such a calendar might be set up. This particular example might be used to schedule crews. Note that there are no more than two jobs scheduled on any day. This may reflect the available work force (supervisory and labor) for a particular company.

The methods of scheduling may be simple or sophisticated, depending on the requirements of the job and the preferences of the planner. Whatever method is used, experienced managers rely on three basic scheduling principles.

- Interconnected activities
- Restraints
- Sequence of installation and duration times

An *interconnected activity* is one which may run at the same time as another activity. Examples are tree planting and patio installation; these two different aspects of the job may occur on the same day or days if there are no conflicts and sufficient labor is available.

Master Project Calendar

MONTH __May__   YEAR __1987__

Sunday	Monday	Tuesday	Wednesday	Thursday	Friday	Saturday
					1 Med. Co. Quincy	2
3	4 Griffin Newton	5 Griffin Newton	6 Marks Hingham	7 Griffin Newton / / Marks Hingham	8 Johnson Braintree	9
10	11 Johnson Braintree / / Kojak Cambridge /	12 Johnson Braintree / / Kojak Cambridge /	13 Costs Co. Kingston / Johnson Braintree	14 Costs Co. Kingston	15 Costs Co. Kingston	16
17	18 Costs Co. Kingston	19 Costs Co. Kingston	20 Costs Co. Kingston	21 Costs Co. Kingston	22 Costs Co. Kingston	23
24/31 Holiday	25 Holiday	26 Costs Co. Kingston	27 Costs Co. Kingston	28 Costs Co. Kingston (Complete) / Larson Newton	29 Larson Newton	30

Figure 8.2

Restraints should be sought out and appropriate plans made to deal with them. There are various types of restraints, fitting into several categories. A simple example is an activity that cannot be started before another is finished, such as a crushed stone drip edge to be in place before the lawn sod installation. The following questions reflect some important considerations regarding restraints:

- Is site access a factor?
- Will material arrive on schedule?
- What facilities and utilities are required and available?
- Will subcontractors perform as required?
- What risks are present?

Some risk factors may occur only at certain phases of a project, while others, such as security of goods and materials, may exist for the duration. To make a schedule, management needs to know which activities must be completed before another can begin, and which activities can be run concurrently.

Sequence of installation and duration time for activities must be plotted on calendars and charts so that specific dates can be assigned. When charting work days, it is important to allow for a certain amount of loss time. Cold, heat, and rain are all factors that must be taken into consideration.

Determine and list the durations according to actual time sequence as determined by the restraints. For example, when using a bar chart, the durations of listed activities are drawn on a time scaled chart. Each activity is reviewed with respect to the previously defined restraints. The following questions are posed:

Which, if any, activity must begin prior to this one?
Which activity must run at the same time?
Which activity must proceed after this one?

If the crew, equipment, and materials cannot all be effectively utilized during the scheduled time frame, then the schedule must be adjusted. Figure 8.3 is a bar chart that lists the various work activities for the sample project in Chapter 6. The activities are listed in the order they are scheduled with appropriate durations.

This chart lists the number of working days which can be determined using the methods described in Chapter 6. The bar chart is a refinement of the calendar, and lists the activities individually. The working days should also be shown on a calendar (Figure 8.1) with target dates. Adjustments for Saturdays, Sundays, holidays, and weather days should be taken into account when target dates are set up.

Job scheduling should be done by the manager and verified by the job foreman. Experienced managers provide foremen with written job activities and do not depend on memory for all of the details and required sequences. Management responsibilities regarding scheduling are handled in the following sequence:

1. Visualizing the installation process
2. Interpreting the project requirements
3. Preliminary scheduling

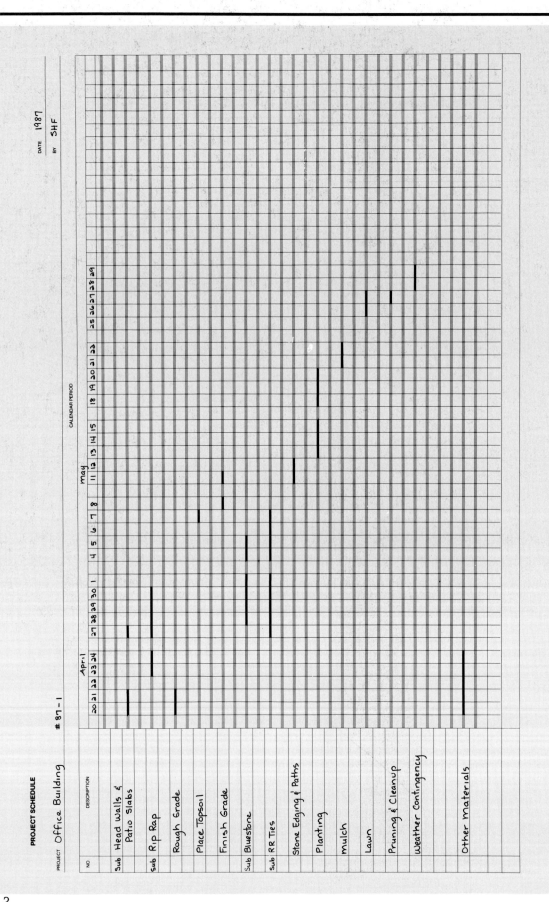

Figure 8.3

184

4. Making preparations
5. Scheduling
6. Determining the methods of construction
7. Allocating equipment and workers
8. Planning implementation
9. Arranging mobilization
10. Determining and arranging the cash flow

In scheduling, it is important to be aware of the effects of adjacent work carried out by the other trades involved in the project. For example, the installation of fence by others may involve excavation that could result in damage to nearby plantings. The responsibility should be established for 'cleaning up' or repairing and replacing damage to the landscaper's work. If conflicts arise regarding materials or other factors, the conditions of the contract generally describe the procedures that should be used to resolve these questions.

While it is important to establish a schedule at the start, there is room for adjustment in the course of the project. In case of crisis, a well developed schedule can give a broad overview of the options for adjusting work activities and salvaging work time. The best schedule makes the best use of these four major factors in the landscape industry: *manpower, materials, machinery,* and *money.* Keep in mind that none of these factors is available on immediate notice. Throughout the project, all four of these resources must be individually controlled. As the project progresses, records should be kept of time spent and materials used. Adjustments should be made, if necessary, to improve efficiency.

Planning is essential on jobs where payments depend upon specific completion dates. When the contractor's payment schedule relies upon certain timely activities, a chart listing and "timing" those activities may help control costly restraints, oversights, and delayed payments. Planning is especially critical when financial penalties may be imposed on the contractor for failure to perform by the established contract deadlines. Figure 8.4 is a projected payment chart from *Means Scheduling Manual* by F. William Horsley. This chart can be used to determine cash flow requirements for a particular project. Expanded, this method can be used to help predict requirements for a season or year.

Money is a primary consideration in job planning and activity scheduling. An important part of scheduling may be submitting invoices for completed work or for delivered materials. Scheduling may be tied to the payment agreement. If anticipated or required, the cost of borrowing money must also be considered — in estimating as well as planning. Contract agreements usually control payment requisitions. Typical contract requirements are: 1) specific dates (deadlines) for requisitions, 2) work periods that may be invoiced, 3) required inventories and acceptance of work and materials in place.

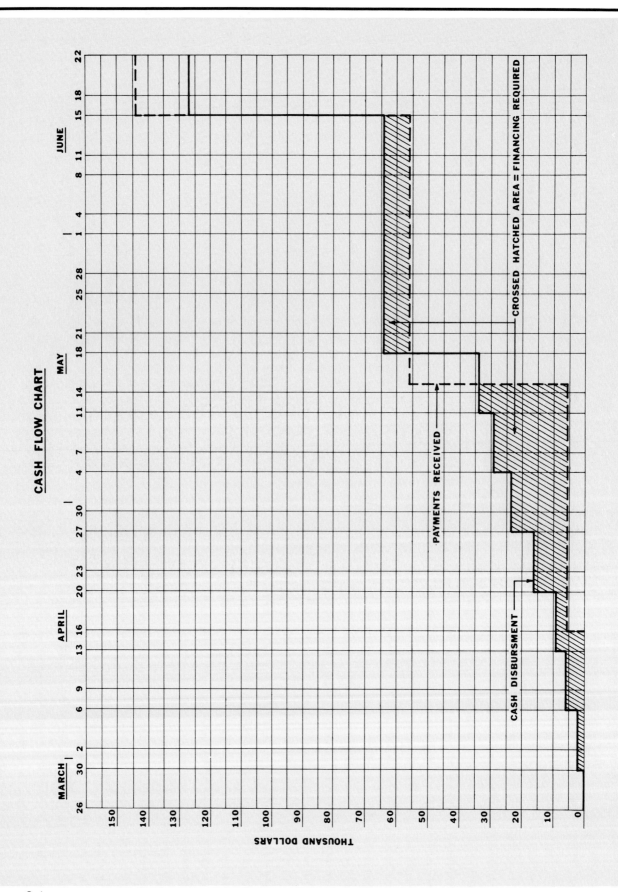

Figure 8.4

Schedule Review

Job planning is only effective if it has the agreement of all who are involved in the work or who are in a position to influence the progress of the work. When the schedule or job plan is finally drawn up on paper, it is vital that it be thoroughly checked over by the concerned parties for any potential problems or limitations. A problem involving any of the four major factors (manpower, materials, machinery, or money) has the potential to adversely affect the work schedule and therefore, successful completion of the project. A careful review should identify any such problems or restrictions at an early stage and should help to achieve a proper rate of production. If there are unavoidable constraints, the schedule must be adapted.

Success in job planning requires not only an initial review, but also an ongoing process of checking off completed work. Communication regarding current and future activities between management and other personnel is a vital component. Construction sites are always in a state of change, and potential problems which may arise at any time, must be recognized and resolved early. Adjusting schedules should not mean merely extending the time duration. Better solutions may involve allocating more resources or using manpower, machinery, materials, or money more productively.

Like many other activities discussed in this book, job planning builds upon prior experience and information gathering. Records of past job performance are important, as are old schedules with notations of actual versus anticipated production. These are the truest and most accurate measures of work capacity.

Chapter Nine

USING MEANS
SITE WORK
COST DATA

Chapter Nine

USING MEANS SITE WORK COST DATA

The previous chapters of this book are directed to the principles of landscape estimating — from an overview of the entire process to a detailed discussion of techniques for surveying the site, recording information, pricing, bidding, and scheduling. Chapter 6, the sample takeoff and estimate, demonstrates these principles and techniques in practice. Many of the prices used in the sample estimate are from *Means Site Work Cost Data*. This chapter describes the components and uses of this annual cost source, along with the methods by which these costs are obtained and organized.

Format and Data

Users of *Means Site Work Cost Data* are chiefly interested in obtaining quick, reasonable, average prices for site work and landscape estimates. This data is especially useful for items about which the estimator is unfamiliar. This is the primary purpose of the annual book — to eliminate guesswork when pricing unknowns. Many persons use the cost data, whether for bids or verification of quotations or budgets, without being fully aware of how the prices are obtained and derived. Without this knowledge, this resource is not being used to fullest advantage. In addition to the basic cost data, the book also contains a wealth of information to aid the estimator, the contractor, the designer, and the owner to better plan and manage landscape projects. Productivity data is provided in order to assist with scheduling, and national union labor rates are analyzed. Tables and charts for location and time adjustments are also included to help the estimator tailor the prices to a specific location. The costs in *Means Site Work Cost Data* consist of thousands of unit price line items and systems, or assembly prices. In addition to providing a complete, all-inclusive price, the assemblies systems can also be used as checklists to assure that all required items are included in a particular segment of the project.

The first section of *Means Site Work Cost Data* lists **unit prices**. This data is organized according to the 16 Divisions of the Masterformat as created by the Construction Specifications Institute, Inc. (see the list of divisions below). This index was developed with cooperation from representatives of all parties concerned with the building construction industry and has been accepted by the American Institute of Architects (AIA) and the Associated General Contractors of America, Inc. (AGC), as well as most manufacturers of building materials. In *Means Site Work Cost Data*, relevant parts of other divisions are included along with Division 2 - Site Work.

Construction Specifications Institute, Inc. Masterformat Divisions

Division 1 - General Requirements
Division 2 - Site Work
Division 3 - Concrete
Division 4 - Masonry
Division 5 - Metals
Division 6 - Wood & Plastics
Division 7 - Moisture-Thermal Control
Division 8 - Doors, Windows & Glass
Division 9 - Finishes
Division 10 - Specialties
Division 11 - Equipment
Division 12 - Furnishings
Division 13 - Special Construction
Division 14 - Conveying Systems
Division 15 - Mechanical
Division 16 - Electrical

The second section contains "**Reference Notes**", a collection of technical tables and reference information. It also provides estimating procedures for some types of work and explanations of cost development which support and supplement the unit price and assemblies systems cost data.

The third section, "**Assemblies**", contains thousands of costs for landscape and other site work systems. Components of the systems are fully detailed and accompanied by illustrations.

The prices presented in *Means Site Work Cost Data* are national averages. Material and equipment costs are developed through annual contact with manufacturers, dealers, distributors, and contractors throughout the United States. Means' staff of engineers is constantly updating prices and keeping abreast of changes and fluctuations within the industry. Labor rates are the national average of each trade as determined from union agreements from thirty major U. S. cities. Labor costs for each item are derived from productivity data which reflect actual working conditions and normal worker performance. Following is a list of factors and assumptions on which the Means costs are based:

Quality
The costs are based on methods, materials and workmanship in accordance with U.S. Government standards and represent good, sound construction practice.

Overtime
The costs as presented include *no* allowance for overtime. If overtime or premium time is anticipated, labor costs must be factored accordingly.

Productivity
The daily output figures are based on an eight-hour workday, during daylight hours. The chart in Figure 9.1 shows that as the number of hours worked per day (over eight) increases, and as the days per week (over five) increase, production efficiency decreases.

Size of Project
Costs in *Means Site Work Cost Data* are based on commercial and industrial buildings which cost $400,000 and up for the total projects including the landscape portion. Large residential projects are also included.

Days per Week	Hours per Day	Production Efficiency					Payroll Cost Factors	
		1 Week	2 Weeks	3 Weeks	4 Weeks	Average 4 Weeks	@ 1-1/2 times	@ 2 times
5	8	100%	100%	100%	100%	100%	100%	100%
	9	100	100	95	90	96.25	105.6	111.1
	10	100	95	90	85	91.25	110.0	120.0
	11	95	90	75	65	81.25	113.6	127.3
	12	90	85	70	60	76.25	116.7	133.3
6	8	100	100	95	90	96.25	108.3	116.7
	9	100	95	90	85	92.50	113.0	125.9
	10	95	90	85	80	87.50	116.7	133.3
	11	95	85	70	65	78.75	119.7	139.4
	12	90	80	65	60	73.75	122.2	144.4
7	8	100	95	85	75	88.75	114.3	128.6
	9	95	90	80	70	83.75	118.3	136.5
	10	90	85	75	65	78.75	121.4	142.9
	11	85	80	65	60	72.50	124.0	148.1
	12	85	75	60	55	68.75	126.2	152.4

Figure 9.1

Local Factors

Weather conditions, season of the year, local labor restrictions, and unusual zoning requirements can all have a significant impact on site work costs. The availability of a skilled labor force, sufficient materials, and even adequate energy and utilities will also affect costs. These factors vary in impact and are not necessarily dependent upon location. They must be reviewed for each project in every area.

In presenting prices in *Means Site Work Cost Data*, certain rounding rules are employed to make the numbers easy to use without significantly affecting accuracy. The rules are used consistently and are as follow:

PRICES		Rounded
From	To	to nearest
$ 0.01	$ 5.00	$ 0.01
5.01	20.00	0.05
20.01	100.00	1.00
100.01	1000.00	5.00
1,000.01	10,000.00	25.00
10,000.01	50,000.00	100.00
50,000.01	up	500.00

Unit Price Section

The Unit Price section of *Means Site Work Cost Data* contains a great deal of information in addition to unit costs for landscape and site work construction components. Figure 9.2 is a typical page, showing a partial listing of costs for ground cover. Note that prices are included for several types of ground cover, with separate listings for bare root or potted, one or two year old plants. In addition, a suggested crew of workers is indicated for the job. The crews are the basis of the installed costs and man-hour units. Productivity and cost data are broken down and itemized in this way to provide for the most detailed pricing possible. This price breakdown also allows for the opportunity to adjust for local variations on individual cost elements.

Within each individual line item, there is a description of the construction component, information regarding typical crews designated to perform the work, and productivity shown in man-hours. Costs are presented as "bare", or unburdened, as well as with mark-ups for overhead and profit. Figure 9.3 is a graphic representation of how to read a Unit Price page from *Means Site Work Cost Data*.

Line Numbers

Every construction item in the Means unit price cost data books has a unique line number. This line number acts as an address so that each item can be quickly located and/or referenced. The numbering system is based on the classification by division. In Figure 9.3, note the bold number in reverse type, 2.3. This number represents the major subdivision, in this case "Earthwork", of Division 2 — Site Work. All 16 divisions are organized in this manner. Within each subdivision, the data is broken down into major classifications. These major classifications are listed alphabetically and are designated by bold type for both numbers and descriptions. Each item, or line, is further defined by an individual number. As shown in Figure 9.3, the full line number for each item consists of: a major subdivision number — a major classification number

		Lawns & Planting	CREW	DAILY OUTPUT	MAN-HOURS	UNIT	MAT.	LABOR	EQUIP.	TOTAL	TOTAL INCL O&P	
		2.8 Lawns & Planting						BARE COSTS				
070	0010	**EROSION CONTROL** Jute mesh, 100 S.Y. per roll, 4' wide, stapled	B-1	2,500	.010	S.Y.	.59	.16		.75	.89	070
	0100	Plastic netting, stapled, 2" x 1" mesh, 20 mil		2,500	.010		.32	.16		.48	.59	
	0200	Polypropylene mesh, stapled, 6.5 oz/S.Y.		2,500	.010		1.55	.16		1.71	1.95	
	0300	Tobacco netting, #2, stapled		2,500	.010		.03	.16		.19	.27	
	1000	Silt fence, polypropylene, ideal conditions	2 Clab	1,600	.010	L.F.	2.30	.16		2.46	2.77	
	1100	Adverse conditions	"	950	.017	"	2.30	.27		2.57	2.93	
110	0010	**GROUND COVER** Planting only, no preparation										
	0020											
	0100	Ajuga, 1 year	B-1	9	2.670	C	45	45		90	115	
	0150	Potted, 2 year		6	4		210	67		277	330	
	0200	Bearberry, potted, 2 year		6	4		190	67		257	305	
	0250	Cotoneaster, 15"-18", shady areas		.60	40		550	670		1,220	1,600	
	0300	Boston ivy, on bank, 1 year		6	4		85	67		152	190	
	0350	Potted, 2 year		6	4		250	67		317	375	
	0400	English ivy, 1 year		9	2.670		50	45		95	120	
	0450	Potted, 2 year		6	4		100	67		167	210	
	0500	Halls honeysuckle, bare root, 1 year		5	4.800		35	80		115	155	
	0550	Potted, 2 year		4	6		250	100		350	425	
	0600	Memorial rose, 9"-12", 1 gallon		3	8		125	135		260	335	
	0650	Potted, 2 gallon		2	12		235	200		435	555	
	0700	Pachysandra, 1 year		10	2.400		10	40		50	70	
	0750	Potted, 2 year		6	4		60	67		127	165	
	0800	Vinca minor, 1 year		10	2.400		39	40		79	100	
	0850	Potted, 2 year		6	4		60	67		127	165	
	0900	Woodbine, on bank, ½ year		6	4		85	67		152	190	
	0950	Potted, 2 year		4	6		200	100		300	370	
	2000	Alternate method of figuring										
	2100	Ajuga, field division, 4000/M.S.F.	B-1	.23	104	M.S.F.	1,800	1,750		3,550	4,550	
	2300	Boston ivy, 1 year, 60/M.S.F.		10	2.400		51	40		91	115	
	2400	English ivy, 1 yr., 500/M.S.F.		1.80	13.330		250	225		475	605	
	2500	Halls honeysuckle, 1 yr., 333/M.S.F.		1.50	16		135	270		405	540	
	2600	Memorial rose, 9"-12", 1 gal., 333/M.S.F.		.90	26.670		415	445		860	1,125	
	2700	Pachysandra, 1 yr., 4000/M.S.F.		.25	96		400	1,600		2,000	2,800	
	2800	Vinca minor, rooted cutting, 2000/M.S.F.		1	24		700	400		1,100	1,350	
	2900	Woodbine, 1 yr., 60/M.S.F.		10	2.400		51	40		91	115	
240	0010	**LAWN BED PREPARATION**										240
	0020											
	0100	Rake topsoil, site material, harley rock rake, ideal	B-6	33	.727	M.S.F.		12.55	4.90	17.45	24	
	0200	Adverse	"	7	3.430			59	23	82	110	
	0300	Screened loam, york rake and finish, ideal	B-62	24	1			17.25	3.47	20.72	29	
	0400	Adverse	"	20	1.200			21	4.16	25.16	35	
	1000	Remove topsoil & stock pile on site, 75 HP dozer, 6" deep, 50' haul	B-10L	30	.400			7.70	6.90	14.60	18.85	
	1050	300' haul		6.10	1.970			38	34	72	93	
	1100	12" deep, 50' haul		15.50	.774			14.85	13.40	28.25	36	
	1150	300' haul		3.10	3.870			74	67	141	180	
	1200	200 HP dozer, 6" deep, 50' haul	B-10B	125	.096			1.84	5.45	7.29	8.70	
	1250	300' haul		30.70	.391			7.50	22	29.50	35	
	1300	12" deep, 50' haul		62	.194			3.72	10.95	14.67	17.50	
	1350	300' haul		15.40	.779			14.95	44	58.95	70	
	1400	Alternate method, 75 HP dozer, 50' haul	B-10L	860	.014	C.Y.		.27	.24	.51	.66	
	1450	300' haul	"	114	.105			2.02	1.82	3.84	4.96	
	1500	200 HP dozer, 50' haul	B-10B	2,660	.005			.09	.26	.35	.41	
	1600	300' haul	"	570	.021			.40	1.19	1.59	1.90	
	1800	Rolling topsoil, push roller	1 Clab	3,555	.002			.04		.04	.05	
	1850	Tractor drawn roller	B-66	210	.038			.75	.58	1.33	1.73	
	2000	Root raking and loading, residential, no boulders	B-6	53.30	.450	M.S.F.		7.75	3.04	10.79	14.75	
	2100	With boulders		32	.750			12.95	5.05	18	25	
	2200	Municipal, no boulders		200	.120			2.07	.81	2.88	3.93	
	2300	With boulders		120	.200			3.45	1.35	4.80	6.55	

75

Figure 9.2

HOW TO USE UNIT PRICE PAGES

Important
Prices in this section are listed in two ways: as bare costs and as costs including overhead and profit of the installing contractor. In most cases, if the work is to be subcontracted, it is best for a general contractor to add an additional 10% to the figures found in the column titled **"TOTAL INCL. O&P".**

Unit
The unit of measure listed here reflects the material being used in the line item. For example: gravel fill is defined in cubic yards.

Productivity
The daily output represents typical total daily amount of work that crew will produce. Man-hours are a unit of measure for the labor involved in performing a task. To derive the total man-hours for a task, multiply the quantity of the item involved times the man-hour figure shown.

Line Number Determination
Major CSI subdivision is **2.3** (two digits plus decimal point plus last digit)

Major classification within CSI subdivision is **200** (three digits)

Item line number is **1100** (four digits)

Complete line number is **2.3-200-1100**

Description
This line number indicates compacted gravel fill will be installed by a B-14 crew at a rate of 160 cubic yards a day, or .300 man-hours per cubic yard.

Crew B-14

Crew No.	Bare Costs		Incl. Subs O & P		Cost Per Man-hour	
Crew B-14	Hr.	Daily	Hr.	Daily	Bare Costs	Incl. O&P
1 Labor Foreman (outside)	$18.10	$144.80	$26.55	$212.40	$17.01	$24.96
4 Building Laborers	16.10	515.20	23.65	756.80		
1 Equip. Oper. (light)	19.60	156.80	28.65	229.20		
1 Backhoe Loader, 48 H.P.		161.80		178.00	3.37	3.70
48 M.H. Daily Totals		$978.60		$1376.40	$20.38	$28.66

Bare Costs are developed as follows for line no. **2.3-200-1100**

Mat. is **Bare Material Cost ($8.50)**

Labor for Crew B-14 = Man-hour Cost **($17.01)** × Man-hour Units **(.300)** = **$5.10**

Equip. for Crew B-14 = Equip. Hour Cost **($3.37)** × Man-hour Units **(.300)** = **$1.01**

Total = **Mat. Cost ($8.50)** + **Labor Cost ($5.10)** + **Equip. Cost ($1.01)** = **$14.61** per cubic yard of fill.

(**Note:** Equipment and Labor costs are derived from the Crew Tables. See example at the top of this page.)

Total Costs Including O&P are developed as follows:

Mat. is **Bare Material Cost** + 10% = **$8.50** + **$.85** = **$9.35**

Labor for Crew B-14 = Man-hour Cost **($24.96)** × Man-hour Units **(.300)** = **$7.49**

Equip. for Crew B-14 = Equip. Hour Cost **($3.70)** × Man-hour Units **(.300)** = **$1.11**

Total = **Mat. Cost ($9.35)** + **Labor Cost ($7.49)** + **Equip. Cost $1.11** = **$17.95**.

(**Note:** Equipment and Labor costs are derived from the Crew Tables. See example at top of this page. Total line follows the rounding rules.)

2.3 Earthwork

			CREW	DAILY OUTPUT	MAN-HOURS	UNIT	MAT.	LABOR	EQUIP.	TOTAL	TOTAL INCL O&P	
190	2700	12" wide trench and backfill, 12" deep	B-54	975	.008	L.F.	.16	.20		.36	.45	190
	2750	18" deep		860	.009		.18	.22		.40	.51	
	2800	24" deep		800	.010		.20	.24		.44	.55	
	2850	36" deep		725	.011		.22	.27		.49	.61	
	3000	16" wide trench and backfill, 12" deep		900	.009		.17	.21		.38	.49	
	3050	18" deep		750	.011		.21	.26		.47	.59	
	3100	24" deep		700	.011		.22	.28		.50	.63	
	3200	Compaction with vibratory plate, add								50%	50%	
200	0010	FILL Spread dumped material, no compaction, by dozer	B-10B	1,000	.012	C.Y.		.23	.68	.91	1.09	200
	0100	By hand	1 Clab	12	.667	"		10.75		10.75	15.75	
	0150	Spread fill, from stockpile with loader crawler,										
	0170	130 H.P. 300' haul	B-10P	600	.020	C.Y.		.38	1	1.38	1.66	
	0190	With dozer 300 H.P. 300' haul	B-10M	600	.020	"		.38	1.50	1.88	2.21	
	0500	Gravel fill, compacted, under floor slabs, 3" deep	B-14	10,000	.005	S.F.	.05	.08	.02	.15	.20	
	0600	6" deep		9,000	.005		.10	.09	.02	.21	.26	
	0700	9" deep	"	7,200	.007		.15	.11	.02	.28	.36	
	0800	12" deep		6,000	.008		.20	.14	.03	.37	.45	
	1000	Alternate pricing method, 3" deep		90	.533	C.Y.	8.50	9.10	1.80	19.40	25	
	1100	6" deep		160	.300		8.50	5.10	1.01	14.61	17.95	
	1200	9" deep		200	.240		8.50	4.08	.81	13.39	16.25	
	1300	12" deep		220	.218		8.50	3.71	.74	12.95	15.60	
	1501	For fill under exterior paving, see division 2.6-071										
220	0010	GRADING Site excav. & fill, not incl. mobilization, demobilization or										220
	0020	compaction. Includes ¼ push dozer per scraper.										
	0100	Dozer 300' haul, 75 H.P., = 20 C.Y./hr.	B-10L	160	.075	C.Y.		1.44	1.30	2.74	3.53	
	0200	300 H.P., 70 C.Y./hr.	B-10M	560	.021			.41	1.60	2.01	2.37	
	0400	Scraper, towed, 7 C.Y. 300' haul, 55 C.Y./hr.	B-33A	440	.032			.62	2.77	3.39	3.95	
	0500	1000' haul, 25 C.Y./hr.	"	200	.070			1.36	6.10	7.46	8.70	
	0700	10 C.Y. 300' haul, 85 C.Y./hr.	B-33B	680	.021			.40	1.84	2.24	2.61	
	0800	1000' haul, 50 C.Y./hr.	"	400	.035			.68	3.13	3.81	4.43	
	1000	Self-propelled scraper , 15 C.Y., 1000' haul, 95 C.Y./hr.	B-33D	760	.018			.36	1.60	1.96	2.29	
	1100	2000' haul, 70 C.Y./hr.	"	560	.025			.49	2.17	2.66	3.10	
	1300	25 C.Y. 1000' haul, 200 C.Y./hr.	B-33E	1,600	.009			.17	.84	1.01	1.17	
	1400	2000' haul, 160 C.Y./hr.	"	1,280	.011			.21	1.04	1.25	1.46	
	1600	For dozer with ripper, 200 H.P., add, minimum	B-11A	1,980	.008			.15	.34	.49	.60	
	1700	Add, maximum	"	990	.016			.30	.69	.99	1.19	
	1800	300 H.P., add, minimum	B-10M	3,670	.003			.06	.24	.30	.36	
	1900	Add, maximum	"	1,840	.007			.13	.49	.62	.72	
	2100	Fine grade, 3 passes with motor grader	B-11L	1,600	.010	S.Y.		.18	.30	.48	.60	
	2200	With grader plus rolling	B-32	1,600	.020			.39	.83	1.22	1.49	
	2400	Hand grading, finish	1 Clab	75	.107			1.72		1.72	2.52	
	2500	Rough		130	.062			.99		.99	1.45	
	2520	Alternate pricing method, finish		675	.012	S.F.		.19		.19	.28	
	2540	Rough		1,200	.007			.11		.11	.16	

Figure 9.3

—an item line number. Each full line number describes a unique construction element. For example, in Figure 9.3, the line number for "Fill, spread dumped material, no compaction, 6" deep" is 02.3-200-1100.

Line Description

Each line has a text description of the item for which costs are listed. The description may be self-contained and all inclusive as is the first line in Major Classification 02.3-200 in Figure 9.2, line 10. Lines that are indented rely on the complete description provided above. All indented items are delineations (by size, color, material, etc.) or breakdowns of previously described items. An extensive index is provided in the back of *Means Site Work Cost Data* to aid in locating particular items.

Crew

For each construction element (each line item), a minimum typical crew is designated as appropriate to perform the work. The crew may include one or more trades, foremen, craftsmen and helpers, and any equipment required for proper installation of the described item. If an individual trade installs the item using only hand tools, the smallest efficient number of tradesmen will be indicated; 1 Clab (common laborer), 1 Skwk (skilled worker), 1 Ston (stone mason), etc.). A complete list of abbreviations for trades is shown in Figure 9.4. If more than one trade is required to install the item and/or if powered equipment is needed, a crew number will be designated (B-18, B-36, etc.). A complete listing of crews is presented at the beginning of the Unit Price section of *Means Site Work Cost Data* (see Figure 9.5 for an example Crews page). On these pages, each crew is broken down into the following components:

1. Number and type of workers designated.
2. Number, size, and type of any equipment required.
3. Hourly labor costs listed two ways: "bare" — base rate including fringe benefits; and billing rate — including the installing contractor's overhead and profit. (See Figure 9.4 from the inside back cover of *Means Site Work Cost Data* for labor rate information).
4. Daily equipment costs, based on the weekly equipment rental cost divided by five, plus the hourly operating cost, times eight hours. This cost is listed two ways: as a bare cost, and with a 10% percent markup to cover handling and management costs.
5. Labor and equipment are further broken down into: cost per man-hour for labor, and cost per man-hour for equipment.
6. The total daily man-hours for the crew.
7. The total bare costs per day for the crew, including equipment.
8. The total daily cost of the crew including the installing contractor's overhead and profit.

   The total daily cost of the required crew is used to calculate the unit installation cost for each item (for both bare costs and cost including overhead and profit).

Installing Contractor's Overhead & Profit

Below are the **average** installing contractor's percentage mark-ups applied to base labor rates to arrive at typical billing rates.

Column A: Labor rates are based on union wages averaged for 30 major U.S. cities. Base rates including fringe benefits are listed hourly and daily. These figures are the sum of the wage rate, employer-paid fringe benefits such as vacation pay, employer-paid health and welfare costs, pension costs, plus appropriate training and industry advancement funds costs.

Column B: Workers' Compensation rates are the national average of state rates established for each trade.

Column C: Column C lists average fixed overhead figures for all trades. Included are Federal and State Unemployment costs set at 5.5%; Social Security Taxes (FICA) set at 7.15%; Builder's Risk Insurance costs set at 1.14%; and Public Liability costs set at 0.82%. All the percentages except those for Social Security Taxes vary from state to state as well as from company to company.

Column D and E: Percentages in Columns D and E are based on the presumption that the installing contractor has annual billing of $500,000 and up. Overhead percentages may increase with smaller annual billing. The overhead percentages for any given contractor may vary greatly and depend on a number of factors, such as the contractor's annual volume, engineering and logistical support costs, and staff requirements. The figures for overhead and profit will also vary depending on the type of job, the job location, and the prevailing economic conditions. All factors should be examined very carefully for each job.

Column F: Column F lists the total of columns B, C, D, and E.

Column G: Column G is Column A (hourly base labor rate) multiplied by the percentage in Column F (O&P percentage).

Column H: Column H is the total of Column A (hourly base labor rate) plus Column G (Total O&P).

Column I: Column I is Column H multiplied by eight hours.

		A		B	C	D	E	F		G	H	I
		Base Rate Incl. Fringes		Work-ers' Comp. Ins.	Average Fixed Over-head	Over-head	Profit	Total Overhead & Profit			Rate with O & P	
Abbr.	Trade	Hourly	Daily					%	Amount		Hourly	Daily
Skwk	Skilled Workers Average (35 trades)	$20.80	$166.40	10.4%	14.6%	12.6%	10%	47.6%	$ 9.90		$30.70	$245.60
	Helpers Average (5 trades)	15.90	127.20	11.1		12.7		48.4	7.70		23.60	188.80
	Foremen Average, Inside (50¢ over trade)	21.30	170.40	10.4		12.6		47.6	10.15		31.45	251.60
	Foremen Average, Outside ($2.00 over trade)	22.80	182.40	10.4		12.6		47.6	10.85		33.65	269.20
Clab	Common Building Laborers	16.10	128.80	11.4		10.8		46.8	7.55		23.65	189.20
Asbe	Asbestos Workers	23.00	184.00	8.8		15.7		49.1	11.30		34.30	274.40
Boil	Boilermakers	23.00	184.00	7.2		16.0		47.8	11.00		34.00	272.00
Bric	Bricklayers	20.55	164.40	8.5		10.7		43.8	9.00		29.55	236.40
Brhe	Bricklayer Helpers	16.15	128.40	8.5		10.7		43.8	7.05		23.20	185.60
Carp	Carpenters	20.55	164.40	11.4		10.8		46.8	9.60		30.15	241.20
Cefi	Cement Finishers	19.70	157.60	6.6		10.8		42.0	8.30		27.95	223.60
Elec	Electricians	22.65	181.20	4.5		15.9		45.0	10.20		32.85	262.80
Elev	Elevator Constructors	23.05	184.40	6.0		15.9		46.5	10.70		33.75	270.00
Eqhv	Equipment Operators, Crane or Shovel	21.20	169.60	7.8		13.8		46.2	9.80		31.00	248.00
Eqmd	Equipment Operators, Medium Equipment	20.75	166.00	7.8		13.8		46.2	9.60		30.35	242.80
Eqlt	Equipment Operators, Light Equipment	19.60	156.80	7.8		13.8		46.2	9.05		28.65	229.20
Eqol	Equipment Operators, Oilers	17.55	140.40	7.8		13.8		46.2	8.10		25.65	205.20
Eqmm	Equipment Operators, Master Mechanics	22.00	176.00	7.8		13.8		46.2	10.15		32.15	257.20
Glaz	Glaziers	20.75	166.00	8.7		10.8		44.1	9.15		29.90	239.20
Lath	Lathers	20.50	164.00	7.2		10.8		42.6	8.75		29.25	234.00
Marb	Marble Setters	20.25	162.00	8.5		10.7		43.8	8.85		29.10	232.80
Mill	Millwrights	21.25	170.00	7.2		10.8		42.6	9.05		30.30	242.40
Mstz	Mosaic and Terrazzo Workers	20.05	160.40	6.0		10.7		41.3	8.30		28.35	226.80
Pord	Painters, Ordinary	19.55	156.40	8.9		10.8		44.3	8.65		28.20	225.60
Psst	Painters, Structural Steel	20.20	161.60	29.4		10.1		64.1	12.95		33.15	265.20
Pape	Paper Hangers	19.75	158.00	8.9		10.8		44.3	8.75		28.50	228.00
Pile	Pile Drivers	20.35	162.80	18.3		15.7		58.6	11.95		32.30	258.40
Plas	Plasterers	20.25	162.00	8.7		10.9		44.2	8.95		29.20	233.60
Plah	Plasterer Helpers	16.65	133.20	8.7		10.9		44.2	7.35		24.00	192.00
Plum	Plumbers	23.00	184.00	5.3		15.9		45.8	10.55		33.55	268.40
Rodm	Rodmen (Reinforcing)	22.10	176.80	18.6		13.3		56.5	12.50		34.60	276.80
Rofc	Roofers, Composition	19.15	153.20	20.8		10.4		55.8	10.70		29.85	238.80
Rots	Roofers, Tile & Slate	19.25	154.00	20.8		10.4		55.8	10.75		30.00	240.00
Rohe	Roofer Helpers (Composition)	14.20	113.60	20.8		10.4		55.8	7.90		22.10	176.80
Shee	Sheet Metal Workers	23.10	184.80	7.0		15.8		47.4	10.95		34.05	272.40
Spri	Sprinkler Installers	23.85	190.80	6.1		15.9		46.6	11.10		34.95	279.60
Stpi	Steamfitters or Pipefitters	23.30	186.40	5.3		15.9		45.8	10.70		33.95	271.60
Ston	Stone Masons	20.60	164.80	8.5		10.7		43.8	9.00		29.60	236.80
Sswk	Structural Steel Workers	22.10	176.80	21.5		13.7		59.8	13.20		35.30	282.40
Tilf	Tile Layers (Floor)	20.00	160.00	6.0		10.7		41.3	8.25		28.25	226.00
Tilh	Tile Layer Helpers	16.10	128.80	6.0		10.7		41.3	6.65		22.75	182.00
Trlt	Truck Drivers, Light	16.70	133.60	9.8		10.7		45.1	7.55		24.25	194.00
Trhv	Truck Drivers, Heavy	16.95	135.60	9.8		10.7		45.1	7.65		24.60	196.80
Sswl	Welders, Structural Steel	22.10	176.80	21.5		13.7		59.8	13.20		35.30	282.40
Wrck	*Wrecking	16.10	128.80	23.1		10.4		58.1	9.35		25.45	203.60

*Not included in Averages.

Figure 9.4

198

CREWS

Crew B-10R

Crew No.	Hr.	Daily	Hr.	Daily	Bare Costs	Incl. O&P
1 Equip. Oper. (med.)	$20.75	$166.00	$30.35	$242.80	$19.20	$28.11
.5 Building Laborer	16.10	64.40	23.65	94.60		
F.E. Loader, W.M.1 C.Y.		212.40		233.65	17.70	19.47
12 M.H., Daily Totals		$442.80		$571.05	$36.90	$47.58

Crew B-10S

Crew No.	Hr.	Daily	Hr.	Daily	Bare Costs	Incl. O&P
1 Equip. Oper. (med.)	$20.75	$166.00	$30.35	$242.80	$19.20	$28.11
.5 Building Laborer	16.10	64.40	23.65	94.60		
F.E. Loader, W.M., 1.5 C.Y.		274.00		301.40	22.83	25.11
12 M.H., Daily Totals		$504.40		$638.80	$42.03	$53.22

Crew B-10T

Crew No.	Hr.	Daily	Hr.	Daily	Bare Costs	Incl. O&P
1 Equip. Oper. (med.)	$20.75	$166.00	$30.35	$242.80	$19.20	$28.11
.5 Building Laborer	16.10	64.40	23.65	94.60		
F.E. Loader, W.M., 2.5 C.Y.		446.00		490.60	37.16	40.88
12 M.H., Daily Totals		$676.40		$828.00	$56.36	$68.99

Crew B-10U

Crew No.	Hr.	Daily	Hr.	Daily	Bare Costs	Incl. O&P
1 Equip. Oper. (med.)	$20.75	$166.00	$30.35	$242.80	$19.20	$28.11
.5 Building Laborer	16.10	64.40	23.65	94.60		
F.E. Loader, W.M., 5.5 C.Y.		905.00		995.50	75.41	82.95
12 M.H., Daily Totals		$1135.40		$1332.90	$94.61	$111.06

Crew B-10W

Crew No.	Hr.	Daily	Hr.	Daily	Bare Costs	Incl. O&P
1 Equip. Oper. (med.)	$20.75	$166.00	$30.35	$242.80	$19.20	$28.11
.5 Building Laborer	16.10	64.40	23.65	94.60		
1 Dozer, 105 H.P.		353.60		388.95	29.46	32.41
12 M.H., Daily Totals		$584.00		$726.35	$48.66	$60.52

Crew B-10X

Crew No.	Hr.	Daily	Hr.	Daily	Bare Costs	Incl. O&P
1 Equip. Oper. (med.)	$20.75	$166.00	$30.35	$242.80	$19.20	$28.11
.5 Building Laborer	16.10	64.40	23.65	94.60		
1 Dozer, 410 H.P.		1189.00		1307.90	99.08	108.99
12 M.H., Daily Totals		$1419.40		$1645.30	$118.28	$137.10

Crew B-10Y

Crew No.	Hr.	Daily	Hr.	Daily	Bare Costs	Incl. O&P
1 Equip. Oper. (med.)	$20.75	$166.00	$30.35	$242.80	$19.20	$28.11
.5 Building Laborer	16.10	64.40	23.65	94.60		
1 Vibratory Drum Roller		278.60		306.45	23.21	25.53
12 M.H., Daily Totals		$509.00		$643.85	$42.41	$53.64

Crew B-11

Crew No.	Hr.	Daily	Hr.	Daily	Bare Costs	Incl. O&P
1 Equipment Oper. (med.)	$20.75	$166.00	$30.35	$242.80	$18.42	$27.00
1 Building Laborer	16.10	128.80	23.65	189.20		
16 M.H., Daily Totals		$294.80		$432.00	$18.42	$27.00

Crew B-11A

Crew No.	Hr.	Daily	Hr.	Daily	Bare Costs	Incl. O&P
1 Equipment Oper. (med.)	$20.75	$166.00	$30.35	$242.80	$18.42	$27.00
1 Building Laborer	16.10	128.80	23.65	189.20		
1 Dozer, 200 H.P.		680.00		748.00	42.50	46.75
16 M.H., Daily Totals		$974.80		$1180.00	$60.92	$73.75

Crew B-11B

Crew No.	Hr.	Daily	Hr.	Daily	Bare Costs	Incl. O&P
1 Equipment Oper. (med.)	$20.75	$166.00	$30.35	$242.80	$18.42	$27.00
1 Building Laborer	16.10	128.80	23.65	189.20		
1 Dozer, 200 H.P.		680.00		748.00		
1 Air Powered Tamper		12.95		14.25		
1 Air Compr. 365 C.F.M.		155.60		171.15		
2-50 Ft. Air Hoses, 1.5" Dia.		12.80		14.10	53.83	59.21
16 M.H., Daily Totals		$1156.15		$1379.50	$72.25	$86.21

Crew B-11C

Crew No.	Hr.	Daily	Hr.	Daily	Bare Costs	Incl. O&P
1 Equipment Oper. (med.)	$20.75	$166.00	$30.35	$242.80	$18.42	$27.00
1 Building Laborer	16.10	128.80	23.65	189.20		
1 Backhoe Loader, 48 H.P.		161.80		178.00	10.11	11.12
16 M.H., Daily Totals		$456.60		$610.00	$28.53	$38.12

Crew B-11K

Crew No.	Hr.	Daily	Hr.	Daily	Bare Costs	Incl. O&P
1 Equipment Oper. (med.)	$20.75	$166.00	$30.35	$242.80	$18.42	$27.00
1 Building Laborer	16.10	128.80	23.65	189.20		
1 Trencher, 8' D, 16" W.		433.20		476.50	27.07	29.78
16 M.H., Daily Totals		$728.00		$908.50	$45.49	$56.78

Crew B-11L

Crew No.	Hr.	Daily	Hr.	Daily	Bare Costs	Incl. O&P
1 Equipment Oper. (med.)	$20.75	$166.00	$30.35	$242.80	$18.42	$27.00
1 Building Laborer	16.10	128.80	23.65	189.20		
1 Grader, 30,000 Lbs.		473.40		520.75	29.58	32.54
16 M.H., Daily Totals		$768.20		$952.75	$48.00	$59.54

Crew B-11M

Crew No.	Hr.	Daily	Hr.	Daily	Bare Costs	Incl. O&P
1 Equipment Oper. (med.)	$20.75	$166.00	$30.35	$242.80	$18.42	$27.00
1 Building Laborer	16.10	128.80	23.65	189.20		
1 Backhoe Loader, 80 H.P.		227.20		249.90	14.20	15.61
16 M.H., Daily Totals		$522.00		$681.90	$32.62	$42.61

Crew B-12

Crew No.	Hr.	Daily	Hr.	Daily	Bare Costs	Incl. O&P
1 Equip. Oper. (crane)	$21.20	$169.60	$31.00	$248.00	$19.37	$28.32
1 Equip. Oper. Oiler	17.55	140.40	25.65	205.20		
16 M.H., Daily Totals		$310.00		$453.20	$19.37	$28.32

Crew B-12A

Crew No.	Hr.	Daily	Hr.	Daily	Bare Costs	Incl. O&P
1 Equip. Oper. (crane)	$21.20	$169.60	$31.00	$248.00	$19.37	$28.32
1 Equip. Oper. Oiler	17.55	140.40	25.65	205.20		
1 Hyd. Excavator, 1 C.Y.		435.60		479.15	27.22	29.94
16 M.H., Daily Totals		$745.60		$932.35	$46.59	$58.26

Crew B-12B

Crew No.	Hr.	Daily	Hr.	Daily	Bare Costs	Incl. O&P
1 Equip. Oper. (crane)	$21.20	$169.60	$31.00	$248.00	$19.37	$28.32
1 Equip. Oper. Oiler	17.55	140.40	25.65	205.20		
1 Hyd. Excavator, 1.5 C.Y.		565.60		622.15	35.35	38.88
16 M.H., Daily Totals		$875.60		$1075.35	$54.72	$67.20

Crew B-12C

Crew No.	Hr.	Daily	Hr.	Daily	Bare Costs	Incl. O&P
1 Equip. Oper. (crane)	$21.20	$169.60	$31.00	$248.00	$19.37	$28.32
1 Equip. Oper. Oiler	17.55	140.40	25.65	205.20		
1 Hyd. Excavator, 2 C.Y.		808.00		888.80	50.50	55.55
16 M.H., Daily Totals		$1118.00		$1342.00	$69.87	$83.87

Crew B-12D

Crew No.	Hr.	Daily	Hr.	Daily	Bare Costs	Incl. O&P
1 Equip. Oper. (crane)	$21.20	$169.60	$31.00	$248.00	$19.37	$28.32
1 Equip. Oper. Oiler	17.55	140.40	25.65	205.20		
1 Hyd. Excavator, 3.5 C.Y.		1414.00		1555.40	88.37	97.21
16 M.H., Daily Totals		$1724.00		$2008.60	$107.74	$125.53

Crew B-12E

Crew No.	Hr.	Daily	Hr.	Daily	Bare Costs	Incl. O&P
1 Equip. Oper. (crane)	$21.20	$169.60	$31.00	$248.00	$19.37	$28.32
1 Equip. Oper. Oiler	17.55	140.40	25.65	205.20		
1 Hyd. Excavator, .5 C.Y.		285.40		313.95	17.83	19.62
16 M.H., Daily Totals		$595.40		$767.15	$37.20	$47.94

Figure 9.5

The crew designation does not mean that this is the only crew that can perform the work. Crew size and content have been developed and chosen based on practical experience and feedback from contractors. These designations represent a labor and equipment make-up commonly found in the industry. The most appropriate crew for a given task is best determined based on particular project requirements. Unit costs may vary if crew sizes or content are significantly changed.

Figure 9.6 is a page from Division 1.5 of *Means Site Work Cost Data*. This type of page lists the equipment costs used in the presentation and calculation of the crew costs and unit price data. Rental costs are shown as daily, weekly, and monthly rates. The Hourly Operating Cost represents the cost of fuel, lubrication and routine maintenance. Equipment costs used in the crews are calculated as follows:

Line Number	1.5-050-5210
Equipment	Tree spade, self propelled
Rent per week	$1,310.00
Hourly Operating Cost:	$4.25

$$\frac{\text{Weekly rental}}{\text{5 days per week}} + (\text{Hourly Oper. Cost} \times 8 \text{ hrs/day}) = \text{Crews Equipment Cost}$$

$$\frac{\$1,310}{5} + (\$4.25 \times 8) = \$296.00$$

Units

The unit column (see Figure 9.3) defines the component for which the costs have been calculated. It is this "unit" on which Unit Price Estimating is based. The units as used represent standard estimating and quantity takeoff procedures. However, the estimator should always check to be sure that the units taken off are the same as those priced. A list of standard abbreviations is included at the back of *Means Site Work Cost Data*.

Bare Costs

There are four columns listed under "Bare Costs" (bare costs are listed for all unit prices except Division 1.5, Equipment). Bare costs are presented as: "Material", "Labor", "Equipment", and "Total", and represent the actual cost of construction items to the contractor. In other words, bare costs are those which *do not* include the overhead and profit of the installing contractor (a subcontractor or a general contracting company using its own crews).

Material: Material costs are based on the national average contractor purchase price delivered to the job site. Delivered costs are assumed to be within a 20 mile radius of metropolitan areas. No sales tax is included in the material prices because of variations from state to state.

The prices are based on quantities that would normally be purchased for landscape projects costing $5,000 to $10,000 and up. Material costs represent wholesale prices. Prices for small quantities must be adjusted accordingly. If more current costs for materials are available for the appropriate location, it is recommended that adjustments be made to the unit costs to reflect any cost difference.

Labor: Labor costs are calculated by multiplying the "Bare Labor Cost" per man-hour times the number of man-hours, from the "Man-Hours" column. The "Bare" labor rate is determined by adding the base rate plus

1.5 Contractor Equipment	UNIT	HOURLY OPER. COST.	RENT PER DAY	RENT PER WEEK	TOTAL PER MONTH	CREW EQUIPMENT COST	
050 3300 Sheepsfoot roller, self-propelled, 4 wheel, 130 H.P.	Ea.	10.40	345	1,040	3,125	291.20	050
3320 300 H.P.		15.50	445	1,340	4,025	392	
3350 Vibratory steel drum & pneumatic tire, diesel, 18,000 lb.		11.70	310	925	2,775	278.60	
3400 29,000 lb.		14.60	370	1,115	3,350	339.80	
3410 Rotary mower, brush, 60", with tractor	↓	.90	240	725	2,170	152.20	
3430							
3450 Scrapers, towed type, 7 to 9 C.Y. capacity	Ea.	2.73	120	365	1,100	94.85	
3500 12 to 17 C.Y. capacity		4.54	155	460	1,375	128.30	
3550 Self-propelled, 4 x 4 drive, 2 engine, 14 C.Y. capacity		37	1,160	3,485	10,450	993	
3600 1 engine, 24 C.Y. capacity		44	1,265	3,800	11,400	1,112	
3650 Self-loading, 11 C.Y. capacity		33	605	1,815	5,450	627	
3700 22 C.Y. capacity	↓	50	930	2,790	8,375	958	
3850 Shovels, see Cranes division 1.5-200							
3860 Shovel front attachment, mechanical, ½ C.Y. ⑯	Ea.	.63	60	180	535	41.05	
3870 ¾ C.Y.		2.60	95	285	855	77.80	
3880 1 C.Y.		2.82	145	435	1,300	109.55	
3890 1-½ C.Y.		3.07	165	490	1,475	122.55	
3910 3 C.Y.		5.70	305	910	2,725	227.60	
3950 Stump chipper, 18" deep, 30 H.P.		1.25	205	620	1,860	134	
4050 Tractor, 40 H.P.		3.35	210	625	1,880	151.80	
4110 Tractor, crawler, with bulldozer, torque converter, diesel 75 H.P.		6.80	255	765	2,300	207.40	
4150 105 H.P.		10.45	450	1,350	4,075	353.60	
4200 140 H.P.		13.90	550	1,650	4,950	441.20	
4260 200 H.P.		18.75	885	2,650	8,000	680	
4310 300 H.P.		26	1,150	3,450	10,400	898	
4360 410 H.P.		38	1,475	4,425	13,250	1,189	
4380 700 H.P.		67	2,340	7,165	21,500	1,969	
4400 Loader, crawler, torque conv., diesel, 1-½ C.Y., 80 H.P.		10.25	320	965	2,900	275	
4450 1-½ to 1-¾ C.Y., 95 H.P.		12.15	370	1,115	3,350	320.20	
4510 1-¾ to 2-¼ C.Y., 130 H.P.		15.90	510	1,525	4,550	432.20	
4530 2-½ to 3-¼ C.Y., 190 H.P.		24	675	2,025	6,100	597	
4560 4-½ to 5 C.Y., 275 H.P.		34	1,250	3,750	11,300	1,022	
4610 Tractor loader, wheel, torque conv 4 x 4, 1 to 1-¼ C.Y., 65 H.P. ⑰		8.05	245	740	2,225	212.40	
4620 1-½ to 1-¾ C.Y., 80 H.P.		10.40	315	940	2,825	271.20	
4650 1-¾ to 2 C.Y., 100 H.P.		12.20	380	1,135	3,400	324.60	
4710 2-½ to 3-½ C.Y., 130 H.P.		17.40	510	1,535	4,600	446.20	
4730 3 to 4-½ C.Y., 170 H.P.		21	560	1,675	5,025	503	
4760 5-¼ to 5-¾ C.Y., 270 H.P.		34	1,055	3,165	9,500	905	
4810 7 to 8 C.Y., 375 H.P.		58	1,210	3,635	10,900	1,191	
4870 12-½ C.Y., 690 H.P.		95	2,755	8,265	24,800	2,413	
4880 Wheeled, skid steer, 10 C.F., 30 H.P. gas		3.40	95	280	840	83.20	
4890 1 C.Y., 78 H.P., diesel		4.70	165	490	1,475	135.60	
4900 Trencher, chain, boom type, gas, operator walking, 12 H.P.		7.80	120	360	1,075	134.40	
4910 Operator riding, 40 H.P.		12.50	155	465	1,400	193	
5000 Wheel type, gas, 4' deep, 12" wide		11.25	250	750	2,250	240	
5100 Diesel, 6' deep, 20" wide		15	500	1,500	4,500	420	
5150 Ladder type, gas, 5' deep, 8" wide		8.55	315	950	2,850	258.40	
5200 Diesel, 8' deep, 16" wide		10.40	585	1,750	5,250	433.20	
5210 Tree spade, self-propelled	↓	4.25	435	1,310	3,930	296	
5230							
5250 Truck, dump, tandem, 12 ton payload	Ea.	12.75	190	575	1,725	217	
5300 Three axle dump, 16 ton payload		15.75	255	760	2,275	278	
5350 Dump trailer only, rear dump, 16-½ C.Y.		3.90	80	240	715	79.20	
5400 20 C.Y.		4.75	92	280	845	94	
5450 Flatbed, single axle, 1-½ ton rating		3.70	47	140	415	57.60	
5500 3 ton rating		4.25	57	170	505	68	
5550 Off highway rear dump, 25 ton capacity		25	750	2,250	6,750	650	
5600 35 ton capacity		34	1,055	3,160	9,475	904	
6000 Vibratory plow, 25 H.P., walking	↓	1.03	105	315	950	71.25	

For expanded coverage of these items see *Means Building Construction Cost Data 1987*

9

Figure 9.6

201

fringe benefits. The base rate is the actual hourly wage of a worker used in figuring payroll. It is from this figure that employee deductions are taken (Federal withholding, FICA, State withholding). Fringe benefits include all employer-paid benefits, above and beyond the payroll amount (employer-paid health, vacation pay, pension, profit sharing). The "Bare Labor Cost" is, therefore, the actual amount that the contractor must pay directly for construction workers. Figure 9.4, therefore, shows labor rates for the 35 construction trades plus skilled worker, helper, and foreman averages. These rates are the averages of union wage agreements effective January 1 of the current year from 30 major cities in the United States. The "Bare Labor Cost" for each trade, as used in *Means Site Work Cost Data*, is shown in column "A" as the base rate including fringes. Refer to the "Crew" column to determine what rate is used to calculate the "Bare Labor Cost" for a particular line item.

Equipment: Equipment costs are calculated by multiplying the "Bare Equipment Cost" per man-hour, from the appropriate "Crew" listing, times the man-hours in the "Man-Hours" column. The calculation of the equipment portion of installation costs is outlined earlier in this chapter.

Total Bare Costs: The Total Bare Costs are the arithmetical sum of the "Bare Material Cost", "Bare Labor Cost", and "Bare Equipment Cost" columns. The "Total Bare Cost" of any particular line item is the amount that a contractor will directly pay for that item. This is, in effect, the contractor's wholesale price.

Total Including Overhead and Profit

The prices in the "Total Including Overhead and Profit" column might also be called the "billing rate". These prices are, on the average, what the installing contractor would charge for the particular item of work.

The installing contractor could be either the general contractor or a subcontractor. If these costs are used for an item to be installed by a subcontractor, the general contractor should include an additional percentage (usually 10 % to 20%) to cover the expenses of supervision and management.

The costs in the "Total Including Overhead and Profit" column are the arithmetical sum of the following three calculations:

1. Bare Material Cost plus 10%
2. Labor Cost, including overhead and profit, per man-hour times the number of man-hours.
3. Equipment Cost (bare cost plus 10%) per man-hour times the number of man-hours.

In order to increase the crew cost to include overhead and profit, labor and equipment costs are treated separately. Ten percent is added to the bare equipment cost for handling, management, etc. Labor costs are increased by percentages for overhead and profit, depending upon trade as shown in Figure 9.4. The resulting rates are listed in the right hand columns of the same figure. The following items are included in the increase for overhead and profit, also shown in Figure 9.4:

Workers' Compensation and Employer's Liability:
Workers' Compensation and Employer's Liability Insurance rates vary from state to state and are tied into the construction trade safety records in that particular state. Rates also vary by trade according to the hazard involved. (See Figure 9.7 from *Means Site Work Cost Data*, 1987) The proper authorities will most likely keep the contractor well informed of the rates and obligations.

State and Federal Unemployment Insurance:
The employer's tax rate is adjusted by a merit-rating system according to the number of former employees applying for benefits. Contractors who find it possible to offer a maximum of steady employment can enjoy a reduction in the unemployment tax rate.

Employer-Paid Social Security (FICA):
The tax rate is adjusted annually by the federal government. It is a percentage of an employee's salary up to a maximum annual contribution.

Builder's Risk and Public Liability:
These insurance rates vary according to the trades involved and the state in which the work is done.

Overhead: The column listed as "Overhead" provides percentages to be added for office or operating overhead. This is the cost of doing business. The percentages are presented as national averages by trade as shown in Figure 9.4 (Note that the operating overhead costs are applied to *labor only* in *Means Site Work Cost Date.*)

Profit: The percentage is the fee added by the contractor to offer both a return on investment and an allowance to cover the risk involved in the type of construction being bid as well as a consideration for future growth of the company. The profit percentage may vary from 4% on large, staightforward projects to as much as 25% on smaller, high-risk jobs. Profit percentages are directly affected by economic conditions, the expected number of bidders, and the estimated risk involved in the project. For estimating purposes, *Means Site Work Cost Data* assumes 10% as a reasonable average profit factor (as applied to labor costs).

CIRCLE REFERENCE NUMBERS

⑦ Workers' Compensation (Div. 1.1)

The table below tabulates the national averages for Workers' Compensation insurance rates by trade and type of building. The average "Insurance Rate" is multiplied by the "% of Building Cost" for each trade. This produces the "Workers' Compensation Cost" by % of total labor cost, to be added for each trade by building type to determine the weighted average Workers' Compensation rate for the building types analyzed.

Trade	Insurance Rate (% of Labor Cost)		% of Building Cost			Workers' Compensation Cost		
	Range	Average	Office Bldgs.	Schools & Apts.	Mfg.	Office Bldgs.	Schools & Apts.	Mfg.
Excavation, Grading, etc.	2.4% to 28.9%	7.8%	4.8%	4.9%	4.5%	.37%	.38%	.35%
Piles & Foundations	4.9 to 47.6	18.3	7.1	5.2	8.7	1.30	.95	1.59
Concrete	2.7 to 28.2	10.3	5.0	14.8	3.7	.51	1.52	.38
Masonry	2.2 to 22.0	8.5	6.9	7.5	1.9	.59	.64	.16
Structural Steel	3.0 to 52.4	21.5	10.7	3.9	17.6	2.30	.84	3.78
Miscellaneous & Ornamental Metals	1.6 to 19.6	7.5	2.8	4.0	3.6	.21	.30	.27
Carpentry & Millwork	3.6 to 56.5	11.4	3.7	4.0	0.5	.42	.46	.06
Metal or Composition Siding	3.3 to 23.3	8.9	2.3	0.3	4.3	.20	.03	.38
Roofing	4.3 to 55.4	20.8	2.3	2.6	3.1	.48	.54	.64
Doors & Hardware	2.0 to 16.6	6.6	0.9	1.4	0.4	.06	.09	.03
Sash & Glazing	3.1 to 13.9	8.7	3.5	4.0	1.0	.30	.35	.09
Lath & Plaster	3.1 to 23.9	8.7	3.3	6.9	0.8	.29	.60	.07
Tile, Marble & Floors	1.3 to 23.3	6.0	2.6	3.0	0.5	.16	.18	.03
Acoustical Ceilings	1.8 to 16.0	7.2	2.4	0.2	0.3	.17	.01	.02
Painting	3.0 to 20.0	8.9	1.5	1.6	1.6	.13	.14	.14
Interior Partitions	3.6 to 56.5	11.4	3.9	4.3	4.4	.44	.49	.50
Miscellaneous Items	1.6 to 96.4	10.6	5.2	3.7	9.7	.55	.39	1.03
Elevators	2.1 to 16.2	6.0	2.1	1.1	2.2	.13	.07	.13
Sprinklers	2.0 to 17.5	6.1	0.5	—	2.0	.03	—	.12
Plumbing	1.5 to 13.9	5.3	4.9	7.2	5.2	.26	.38	.28
Heat., Vent., Air Conditioning	2.4 to 14.5	7.0	13.5	11.0	12.9	.95	.77	.90
Electrical	1.1 to 13.7	4.5	10.1	8.4	11.1	.45	.38	.50
Total	1.1% to 96.4%	—	100.0%	100.0%	100.0%	10.3%	9.51%	11.45%
Overall Weighted Average							10.42%	

The table below lists the weighted average Workers' Compensation base rate for each state with a factor comparing this with the national average of 10.4%.

State	Weighted Average	Factor	State	Weighted Average	Factor	State	Weighted Average	Factor
Alabama	7.1%	68	Kentucky	6.4%	62	North Dakota	6.8%	65
Alaska	13.5	130	Louisiana	8.4	81	Ohio	7.6	73
Arizona	11.4	110	Maine	13.1	126	Oklahoma	11.4	110
Arkansas	6.9	66	Maryland	14.6	140	Oregon	21.5	207
California	11.7	113	Massachusetts	13.1	126	Pennsylvania	11.4	110
Colorado	13.3	128	Michigan	11.3	109	Rhode Island	15.8	152
Connecticut	16.4	158	Minnesota	18.5	178	South Carolina	7.4	71
Delaware	10.6	102	Mississippi	6.1	59	South Dakota	7.2	69
District of Columbia	18.7	180	Missouri	6.3	61	Tennessee	5.8	56
Florida	13.9	134	Montana	16.7	161	Texas	7.3	70
Georgia	7.2	69	Nebraska	6.1	59	Utah	6.7	64
Hawaii	26.1	251	Nevada	10.8	104	Vermont	7.7	74
Idaho	8.5	82	New Hampshire	13.2	127	Virginia	8.3	80
Illinois	14.4	138	New Jersey	6.6	63	Washington	7.9	76
Indiana	2.9	28	New Mexico	14.4	138	West Virginia	7.7	74
Iowa	6.6	63	New York	9.4	90	Wisconsin	8.5	82
Kansas	6.8	65	North Carolina	5.4	52	Wyoming	5.4	52
Weighted Average for U.S. is 10.4% of payroll = 100								

Rates in the following table are the base or manual costs per $100 of payroll for Workers' Compensation in each state. Rates are usually applied to straight time wages only and not to premium time wages and bonuses.

The weighted average skilled worker rate for 35 trades is 10.4%. For bidding purposes, apply the full value of Workers' Compensation directly to total labor costs, or if labor is 32%, materials 48% and overhead and profit 20% of total cost, carry 32/80 x 10.4% = 4.2% of cost (before overhead and profit) into overhead. Rates vary not only from state to state but also with the experience rating of the contractor.

Rates are the most current available at the time of publication.

Figure 9.7

Assemblies Cost Tables

Means' assemblies data are divided into twelve "Uniformat" divisions, which organize the components of construction into logical groupings. The Assemblies approach was devised to provide a quick and easy method for estimating even when only preliminary design data are available. The groupings, or systems, are presented in such a way that the estimator can easily vary components within the systems as well as substituting one system for another. This arrangement is extremely useful when adapting to budget, design, or other considerations. Figure 9.8 shows how the data are presented in the Assemblies pages, and Figure 9.9 is an example system for headwalls.

Each system is illustrated and accompanied by a detailed description. The book lists the components and sizes of each system, usually in the order of construction. Alternates for the most commonly variable components are also listed. Further, each individual component can be found in the Unit Price Section, if a required alternate is not listed in Systems.

Quantity

A unit of measure is established for each system. For example, lawn systems are measured by the square foot area to be seeded or planted; retaining walls are measured by the linear foot; tree pits are measured as "each". Within each system, the components are measured by industry standard, using the same units as in the Unit Price section.

Material

The cost of each component in the Material column is the "Bare Material Cost", plus 10% handling, for the unit and quantity as defined in the "Quantity" column.

Installation

Installation costs as listed in the Systems pages contain both labor and equipment costs. The labor rate includes the "Bare Labor Cost" plus the installing contractor's overhead and profit. These rates are shown in Figure 9.4. The equipment rate is the "Bare Equipment Cost" plus 10%.

The Reference Section

Throughout the Unit Price and Systems sections are reference numbers within bold circles. These numbers serve as footnotes, referring the reader to illustrations, charts, and estimating reference tables in the "Circle Numbers" section. Figure 9.10 shows an example circle reference number (for trees) as it appears on a Unit Price page. Figure 9.11 shows the corresponding reference page from the Circle Reference section. The development of unit costs for many items is explained in these reference tables. Design criteria for many types of site work systems are also included to aid the designer/estimator in making appropriate choices.

HOW TO USE SYSTEMS PAGES

Illustration
At the top of each cost table is an illustration, brief description, and design criteria used to develop the cost.

System Components
The components of a system are listed separately to show the user a typical makeup of that system's price. The price for each system in the table below is calculated in a similar fashion.

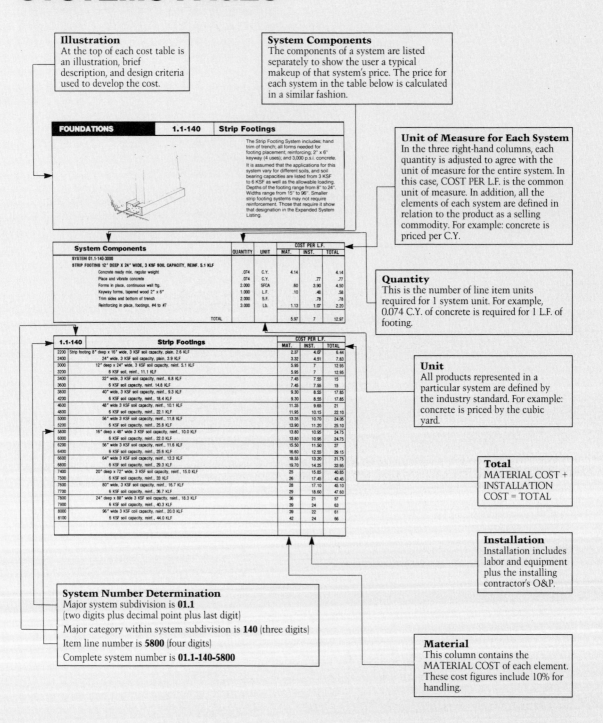

FOUNDATIONS	1.1-140	Strip Footings

The Strip Footing System includes; hand trim of trench; all forms needed for footing placement; reinforcing; 2" x 6" keyway (4 uses); and 3,000 p.s.i. concrete.

It is assumed that the applications for this system vary for different soils, and soil bearing capacities are listed from 3 KSF to 6 KSF as well as the allowable loading. Depths of the footing range from 8" to 24". Widths range from 15" to 96". Smaller strip footing systems may not require reinforcement. Those that require it show that designation in the Expanded System Listing.

System Components		QUANTITY	UNIT	COST PER L.F.		
				MAT.	INST.	TOTAL
SYSTEM 01.1-140-3000						
STRIP FOOTING 12" DEEP X 24" WIDE, 3 KSF SOIL CAPACITY, REINF. 5.1 KLF						
Concrete ready mix, regular weight		.074	C.Y.	4.14		4.14
Place and vibrate concrete		.074	C.Y.		.77	.77
Forms in place, continuous wall ftg.		2.000	SFCA	.60	3.90	4.50
Keyway forms, tapered wood 2" x 6"		1.000	L.F.	.10	.48	.58
Trim sides and bottom of trench		2.000	S.F.		.78	.78
Reinforcing in place, footings, #4 to #7		3.000	Lb.	1.13	1.07	2.20
	TOTAL			5.97	7	12.97

Unit of Measure for Each System
In the three right-hand columns, each quantity is adjusted to agree with the unit of measure for the entire system. In this case, COST PER L.F. is the common unit of measure. In addition, all the elements of each system are defined in relation to the product as a selling commodity. For example: concrete is priced per C.Y.

Quantity
This is the number of line item units required for 1 system unit. For example, 0.074 C.Y. of concrete is required for 1 L.F. of footing.

1.1-140	Strip Footings	COST PER L.F.		
		MAT.	INST.	TOTAL
2200	Strip footing 8" deep x 16" wide, 3 KSF soil capacity, plain, 2.6 KLF	2.37	4.07	6.44
2400	24" wide, 3 KSF soil capacity, plain, 3.9 KLF	3.32	4.51	7.83
3000	12" deep x 24" wide, 3 KSF soil capacity, reinf. 5.1 KLF	5.95	7	12.95
3200	6 KSF soil, reinf., 11.1 KLF	5.95	7	12.95
3400	32" wide, 3 KSF soil capacity, reinf., 6.8 KLF	7.45	7.55	15
3600	6 KSF soil capacity, reinf. 14.8 KLF	7.45	7.55	15
3800	40" wide, 3 KSF soil capacity, reinf., 9.3 KLF	9.30	8.55	17.85
4200	6 KSF soil capacity, reinf., 18.4 KLF	9.30	8.55	17.85
4600	48" wide 3 KSF soil capacity, reinf., 10.1 KLF	11.35	9.65	21
4800	6 KSF soil capacity, reinf., 22.1 KLF	11.95	10.15	22.10
5000	56" wide 3 KSF soil capacity, reinf., 11.8 KLF	13.35	10.70	24.05
5200	6 KSF soil capacity, reinf., 25.8 KLF	13.90	11.20	25.10
5800	16" deep x 48" wide, 3 KSF soil capacity, reinf., 10.0 KLF	13.80	10.95	24.75
6000	6 KSF soil capacity, reinf., 22.0 KLF	13.80	10.95	24.75
6200	56" wide 3 KSF soil capacity, reinf., 11.5 KLF	15.50	11.50	27
6400	6 KSF soil capacity, reinf., 25.6 KLF	16.60	12.55	29.15
6600	64" wide 3 KSF soil capacity, reinf., 13.3 KLF	18.55	13.20	31.75
6800	6 KSF soil capacity, reinf., 29.3 KLF	19.70	14.25	33.95
7400	20" deep x 72" wide, 3 KSF soil capacity, reinf., 15.0 KLF	25	15.85	40.85
7500	6 KSF soil capacity, reinf., 33 KLF	26	17.45	43.45
7600	80" wide, 3 KSF soil capacity, reinf., 16.7 KLF	28	17.10	45.10
7700	6 KSF soil capacity, reinf., 36.7 KLF	29	18.60	47.60
7800	24" deep x 88" wide 3 KSF soil capacity, reinf., 18.3 KLF	36	21	57
7900	6 KSF soil capacity, reinf., 40.3 KLF	39	24	63
8000	96" wide 3 KSF soil capacity, reinf., 20.0 KLF	39	22	61
8100	6 KSF soil capacity, reinf., 44.0 KLF	42	24	66

Unit
All products represented in a particular system are defined by the industry standard. For example: concrete is priced by the cubic yard.

Total
MATERIAL COST + INSTALLATION COST = TOTAL

Installation
Installation includes labor and equipment plus the installing contractor's O&P.

System Number Determination
Major system subdivision is **01.1** (two digits plus decimal point plus last digit)
Major category within system subdivision is **140** (three digits)
Item line number is **5800** (four digits)
Complete system number is **01.1-140-5800**

Material
This column contains the MATERIAL COST of each element. These cost figures include 10% for handling.

Figure 9.8

206

SITE WORK	12.3-750	Headwalls

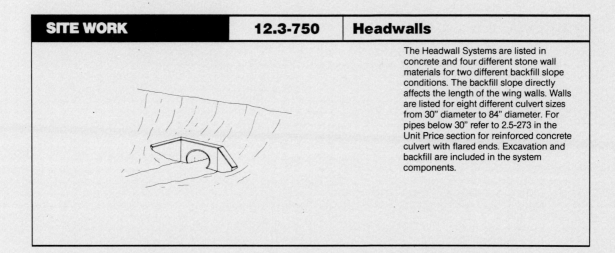

The Headwall Systems are listed in concrete and four different stone wall materials for two different backfill slope conditions. The backfill slope directly affects the length of the wing walls. Walls are listed for eight different culvert sizes from 30" diameter to 84" diameter. For pipes below 30" refer to 2.5-273 in the Unit Price section for reinforced concrete culvert with flared ends. Excavation and backfill are included in the system components.

System Components	QUANTITY	UNIT	COST PER EACH		
			MAT.	INST.	TOTAL
SYSTEM 12.3-750-2000					
HEADWALL C.I.P. CONCRETE FOR 30" PIPE, 3' LONG WING WALLS					
Excavation, hydraulic backhoe, ⅜ C.Y. bucket	2.500	C.Y.		65.24	65.24
Formwork, 2 uses	157.000	SFCA	152.05	827.64	979.69
Reinforcing in place including dowels	45.000	Lb.	17.55	54.90	72.45
Concrete, 3000 psi, in place	2.600	C.Y.	145.60	59.80	205.40
Backfill, dozer	2.500	C.Y.		25.20	25.20
TOTAL			315.20	1,032.78	1,347.98

12.3-750	Headwalls	COST PER EACH		
		MAT.	INST.	TOTAL
2000	Headwall, 1-½ to 1 slope soil, C.I.P. conc, 30"pipe, 3'long wing walls	315	1,025	1,340
2020	Pipe size 36", 3'-6" long wing walls	395	1,250	1,645
2040	Pipe size 42", 4' long wing walls	480	1,450	1,930
2060	Pipe size 48", 4'-6" long wing walls	575	1,700	2,275
2080	Pipe size 54", 5'-0" long wing walls	685	1,975	2,660
2100	Pipe size 60", 5'-6" long wing walls	800	2,275	3,075
2120	Pipe size 72", 6'-6" long wing walls	1,075	2,925	4,000
2140	Pipe size 84", 7'-6" long wing walls	1,375	3,600	4,975
2500	$16/ton stone, pipe size 30", 3' long wing walls	57	340	397
2520	Pipe size 36", 3'-6" long wing walls	74	410	484
2540	Pipe size 42", 4' long wing walls	92	490	582
2560	Pipe size 48", 4'-6" long wing walls	115	585	700
2580	Pipe size 54", 5' long wing walls	140	685	825
2600	Pipe size 60", 5'-6" long wing walls	165	795	960
2620	Pipe size 72", 6'-6" long wing walls	225	1,075	1,300
2640	Pipe size 84", 7'-6" long wing walls	295	1,375	1,670
3000	$32/ton stone, pipe size 30", 3' long wing walls	115	340	455
3020	Pipe size 36", 3'-6" long wing walls	145	410	555
3040	Pipe size 42", 4' long wing walls	185	490	675
3060	Pipe size 48", 4'-6" long wing walls	230	585	815
3080	Pipe size 54", 5' long wing walls	275	685	960
3100	Pipe size 60", 5'-6" long wing walls	325	795	1,120
3120	Pipe size 72", 6'-6" long wing walls	450	1,075	1,525
3140	Pipe size 84", 7'-6" long wing walls	595	1,375	1,970
3500	$48/ton stone, pipe size 30", 3' long wing walls	170	340	510
3520	Pipe size 36", 3'-6" long wing walls	220	410	630

273

Figure 9.9

207

2.8 Lawns & Planting	CREW	DAILY OUTPUT	MAN-HOURS	UNIT	BARE COSTS MAT.	LABOR	EQUIP.	TOTAL	TOTAL INCL O&P	
660 2400 Boston ivy, 2 year	B-1	600	.040	Ea.	2.70	.67		3.37	3.95	**660**
2500 Corylus, 3'-4'	B-17	75	.427		62	7.35	5.05	74.40	84	
2600 Cotoneaster, 15"-18"	B-1	80	.300		8.50	5.05		13.55	16.75	
2700 Deutzia, 12"-15"	"	96	.250		6.45	4.19		10.64	13.25	
2800 Dogwood, 3'-4'	B-17	40	.800		13	13.75	9.45	36.20	45	
2900 Euonymus, alatus compacta, 15" to 18"	B-1	80	.300		7.50	5.05		12.55	15.65	
3000 Flowering almond, 2'-3'	"	36	.667		7.50	11.20		18.70	25	
3100 Flowering currant, 3'-4'	B-17	75	.427		13	7.35	5.05	25.40	31	
3200 Forsythia, 2'-3'	B-1	60	.400		6.45	6.70		13.15	16.95	
3300 Hibiscus, 3'-4'	B-17	75	.427		14.05	7.35	5.05	26.45	32	
3400 Honeysuckle, 3'-4'	B-1	60	.400		8.55	6.70		15.25	19.25	
3500 Hydrangea, 2'-3', b&b	"	57	.421		7.50	7.05		14.55	18.60	
3600 Lilac, 3'-4', b&b	B-17	40	.800		13	13.75	9.45	36.20	45	
3700 Mockorange, 3'-4'	B-1	36	.667		7.50	11.20		18.70	25	
3800 Osier willow, 2'-3'		57	.421		17.15	7.05		24.20	29	
3900 Privet, bare root, 18"-24"		80	.300		2.20	5.05		7.25	9.80	
4000 Pyracantha, 2'-3'		80	.300		18.20	5.05		23.25	27	
4100 Quince, 2'-3'		57	.421		17.15	7.05		24.20	29	
4200 Russian olive, 3'-4'	B-17	75	.427		11.45	7.35	5.05	23.85	29	
4300 Snowberry, 2'-3'	B-1	57	.421		13	7.05		20.05	25	
4400 Spirea, 3'-4'	"	70	.343		19.25	5.75		25	30	
4500 Viburnum, 3'-4', b&b	B-17	40	.800		17.15	13.75	9.45	40.35	49	
4600 Weigela, 3'-4'	B-1	70	.343		17.15	5.75		22.90	27	
4700 Woodbine, 2 year	"	600	.040		4.25	.67		4.92	5.65	
670 0010 SHRUBS AND TREES Evergreen, planted in prepared beds ㉚										**670**
0100 Arborvitae pyramidal, 4'-5', balled & burlapped (B&B)	B-17	30	1.070	Ea.	21	18.35	12.65	52	64	
0150 Globe, 12"-15"	B-1	96	.250		7.40	4.19		11.59	14.30	
0200 Balsam, fraser, 6'-7'	B-17	30	1.070		94	18.35	12.65	125	145	
0300 Cedar, blue, 8'-10', b&b		18	1.780		104	31	21	156	180	
0350 Japanese, 4'-5'		55	.582		31	10	6.90	47.90	56	
0400 Cypress, hinoki, 15"-18", b&b	B-1	80	.300		14.05	5.05		19.10	23	
0500 Hemlock, canadian, 2-½'-3', b&b		36	.667		17.15	11.20		28.35	35	
0600 Juniper, andora, 18"-24"		80	.300		7.80	5.05		12.85	15.95	
0620 Wiltoni, 15"-18"		80	.300		13	5.05		18.05	22	
0640 Skyrocket, 4-½'-5', b&b	B-17	55	.582		26	10	6.90	42.90	51	
0660 Blue pfitzer, 2'-2-½'	B-1	44	.545		14.85	9.15		24	30	
0680 Ketleerie, 2-½'-3', b&b		50	.480		19.25	8.05		27.30	33	
0700 Pine, black, 2-½'-3', b&b		50	.480		15.10	8.05		23.15	28	
0720 Mugo, 18"-24"		60	.400		12.50	6.70		19.20	24	
0740 White, 4'-5'	B-17	75	.427		21	7.35	5.05	33.40	39	
0800 Spruce, blue, 18"-24"	B-1	60	.400		19.25	6.70		25.95	31	
0820 Dwarf alberta, 18"-24"	"	60	.400		19.25	6.70		25.95	31	
0840 Norway, 4'-5', b&b	B-17	75	.427		34	7.35	5.05	46.40	54	
0900 Yew, denisforma, 12"-15"	B-1	60	.400		8.85	6.70		15.55	19.60	
1000 Capitata, 18"-24"		30	.800		21	13.40		34.40	43	
1100 Hicksi, 2'-2-½'		30	.800		18.20	13.40		31.60	40	
680 0010 TREES Deciduous, in prep. beds, balled & burlapped (B&B)										**680**
0100 Ash, 2" caliper	B-17	8	4	Ea.	62	69	47	178	220	
0200 Beech, 5'-6' ㉚		50	.640		57	11	7.60	75.60	87	
0300 Birch, 6'-8', 3 stems		20	1.600		35	28	18.95	81.95	100	
0400 Cherry, 6'-8', 1" caliper		24	1.330		35	23	15.80	73.80	89	
0500 Crabapple, 6'-8'		20	1.600		34	28	18.95	80.95	98	
0600 Dogwood, 4'-5'		40	.800		19.25	13.75	9.45	42.45	52	
0700 Eastern redwood, 4'-5'		40	.800		21	13.75	9.45	44.20	54	
0800 Elm, 8'-10'		20	1.600		52	28	18.95	98.95	120	
0900 Ginkgo, 6'-7'		24	1.330		31	23	15.80	69.80	85	
1000 Hawthorn, 8'-10', 1" caliper		20	1.600		62	28	18.95	108.95	130	
1100 Honeylocust, 10'-12', 1-½" caliper		10	3.200		45	55	38	138	170	
1200 Laburnum, 6'-8', 1" caliper		24	1.330		34	23	15.80	72.80	88	
1300 Larch, 8'		32	1		21	17.20	11.85	50.05	61	

79

Figure 9.10

CIRCLE REFERENCE NUMBERS

㉗ Single Track R.R. Siding (Div. 2.9-150)

Description and Bare Costs	Bare Costs	Incl. Subs O&P
100 lb. rail @ $570 per ton, prime grade (Relayer rail cost $230 per ton)	$19.00	$20.90
Spikes, plates, bolts (36 plates @ $4.50 ea., 2 splices @ $30.00 ea., plus 8 bolts @ $2.00 per 33')	7.20	7.90
6" x 8" x 8'-6" treated timber ties 22" O.C. at $16.00 ea. (C.L. lots)	8.75	9.65
Ballast 1/2 C.Y. (crushed stone @ $9.50 per ton, delivered using 2/3 ton per L.F.)	6.33	6.97
Crew B14, $978.60 ÷ 57 L.F. per day	17.17	24.14
Total per L.F.	$58.45	$69.56

Add $3.10 per L.F. for curves over 14°.

Rail lighter than 100 lbs. per yard or special chemical or shape requirements cause price of rail to vary upwards from mill base price.

Light rail sections cost from $65 to $120 per ton more than heavy sections. Typical turnout quantities are 3700 B.F. timber, 5 tons of rail and 50 tons of ballast. A prefabricated #8 turnout with new 100 lb. rail costs $17,900.

㉘ Single Track, Steel Ties, Concrete Bed (Div. 2.9-150)

Description and Bare Costs	Bare Costs	Incl. Subs O&P
100 lb. rail @ $570 per ton	$19.00	$ 20.90
Fasteners and plates	7.20	7.90
6" WF beam @ 30" O.C., 6'-6" long, 15.5, 20, or 25#/L.F.	18.10	19.90
Concrete 9' wide x 10" thick incl. reinforcing and forms	15.90	17.50
Crew B14 , $978.60 ÷ 22 L.F. per day	44.48	62.55
Total per L.F.	$104.68	$128.75

Curves not included.

㉙ Seeding (Div. 2.8-450)

The type of grass is determined by light, shade and moisture content of soil plus intended use. Fertilizer should be disked 4" before seeding. For steep slopes disk five tons of mulch and lay two tons of hay or straw on surface per acre after seeding. Surface mulch can be staked, lightly disked or tar emulsion sprayed. Material for mulch can be wood chips, peat moss, partially rotted hay or straw, wood fibers and sprayed emulsions. Hemp seed blankets with fertilizer are also available. For spring seeding, watering is necessary. Late fall seeding may have to be reseeded in the spring. Hydraulic seeding, power mulching, and aerial seeding can be used on large areas.

㉚ Cost of Trees (Deciduous) (Div. 2.8-650)

Tree Diameter	Normal Height	Catalog List Price of Tree	Guying Material	Equipment Charge	Installation Labor	Total
2 to 3 inch	14 feet	$ 80	$ 10	$ 25	$ 66	$ 181
3 to 4 inch	16 feet	155	25	44	117	341
4 to 5 inch	18 feet	225	40	52	140	457
6 to 7 inch	22 feet	600	70	69	183	922
8 to 9 inch	26 feet	1200	85	90	238	1613

Installation Time & Cost for Planting Trees, Bare Costs													
Ball Size Diam. x Depth	Soil in Ball	Weight of Ball	Hole Diam. Req'd.	Hole Exca-vation	Amount of Soil Displ.	Topsoil Handled	Time Required in Man-Hours						Cost	
							Dig & Lace	Handle Ball	Dig Hole	Plant & Prune	Water & Guy	Total M.H.	Crew	Total per Tree
Inches	C.F.	Lbs.	Feet	C.F.	C.F.	C.F.								
12x12	.7	56	2	4	3	11	.25	.17	.33	.25	.07	1.1	1 Clab	$ 18
18x16	2	160	2.5	8	6	21	.50	.33	.47	.35	.08	1.7	2 Clab	27
24x18	4	320	3	13	9	38	1.00	.67	1.08	.82	.20	3.8	3 Clab	61
30x21	7.5	600	4	27	19.5	76	.82	.71	.79	1.22	.26	3.8		$ 91
36x24	12.5	980	4.5	38	25.5	114	1.08	.95	1.11	1.32	.30	4.76		114
42x27	19	1520	5.5	64	45	185	1.90	1.27	1.87	1.43	.34	6.8	B-6	163
48x30	28	2040	6	85	57	254	2.41	1.60	2.06	1.55	.39	8.0	@	192
54x33	38.5	3060	7	127	88.5	370	2.86	1.90	2.39	1.76	.45	9.4	$24.00	226
60x36	52	4160	7.5	159	107	474	3.26	2.17	2.73	2.00	.51	10.7	per	257
66x39	68	5440	8	196	128	596	3.61	2.41	3.07	2.26	.58	11.9	man-	285
72x42	87	7160	9	267	180	785	3.90	2.60	3.71	2.78	.70	13.7	hour	329

Figure 9.11

City Cost Indexes

The unit prices in *Means Site Work Cost Data* are national averages. When they are to be applied to a particular location, these prices must be adjusted to local conditions. R. S. Means Co., Inc. has developed the City Cost Indexes for just that purpose. *Means Site Work Cost Data* contains tables of indexes for 162 U.S. and Canadian cities based on a 30 major city average of 100. Please note that for each city there is a weighted average based on total project costs. This average is based on the relative contribution of each division to the construction process as a whole. Figure 9.12 is a sample page from the City Cost Index.

In addition to adjusting the figures in *Means Site Work Cost Data* for particular locations, the City Cost Index can also be used to adjust costs from one city to another. For example, the price of a certain landscape job is known for City A. In order to budget the costs for the same type of project in City B, the following calculation can be made:

$$\frac{\text{City B Index}}{\text{City A Index}} \text{ x City A Cost = City B Cost}$$

While City Cost Indexes provide a means to adjust prices for location, the Historical Cost Index, (also included in *Means Site Work Cost Data* and shown in Figure 9.13) provides a means to adjust for time. Using the same principle as above, a time-adjustment factor can be calculated:

$$\frac{\text{Index for Year X}}{\text{Index for Year Y}} \text{ x Time-adjustment Factor}$$

This time-adjustment factor can be used to determine the budget costs for a particular type of project in Year X, based on costs for a similar building type known from Year Y. Used together, the two indexes allow for cost adjustments from one city during a given year to another city in another year (the present or otherwise). For example, a project constructed in San Francisco in 1974, originally cost $50,000. How much will a similar project cost in Phoenix in 1987? Adjustment factors are developed as shown above using data from Figures 9.12 (City Cost Index) and 9.13 (Historical Cost Index):

$$\frac{\text{Phoenix Index}}{\text{San Francisco Index}} = \frac{92.8}{123.4} = 0.75$$

$$\frac{\text{1987 index}}{\text{1974 index}} = \frac{195.8}{94.7} = 2.07$$

Original cost x location adjustment x time adjustment = Proposed new cost.

$$\$50,000 \text{ x } 0.75 \text{ x } 2.07 = \$77,625$$

Understanding how *Means Site Work Cost Data* prices are obtained and organized makes this annual cost book a more valuable tool for the landscape estimator.

ALABAMA / ALASKA / ARIZONA

DIVISION		BIRMINGHAM MAT.	INST.	TOTAL	HUNTSVILLE MAT.	INST.	TOTAL	MOBILE MAT.	INST.	TOTAL	MONTGOMERY MAT.	INST.	TOTAL	ANCHORAGE MAT.	INST.	TOTAL	PHOENIX MAT.	INST.	TOTAL
2	SITE WORK	96.7	91.2	94.3	115.6	92.1	105.1	118.5	88.9	105.3	88.1	87.7	87.9	154.7	131.7	144.4	89.9	95.0	92.2
3.1	FORMWORK	90.5	72.6	76.5	92.7	73.4	77.6	97.0	78.7	82.7	102.1	70.2	77.2	114.1	146.3	139.3	108.4	91.8	95.4
3.2	REINFORCING	94.6	78.8	88.0	95.8	73.3	86.4	83.0	77.9	80.9	83.0	78.8	81.2	117.8	140.5	127.3	111.7	105.7	109.2
3.3	CAST IN PLACE CONC.	89.4	92.0	91.0	102.0	93.6	96.8	100.1	94.6	96.7	101.4	90.8	94.8	226.0	115.0	157.7	107.7	93.4	98.9
3	CONCRETE	90.7	83.2	85.9	98.8	83.9	89.2	95.7	86.9	90.1	97.5	81.7	87.3	180.4	129.5	147.7	108.7	93.9	99.2
4	MASONRY	79.9	76.7	77.5	86.1	69.8	73.7	92.2	84.5	86.3	85.2	56.9	63.6	137.0	149.3	146.4	93.3	69.5	75.1
5	METALS	95.8	84.0	91.6	100.4	80.1	93.1	93.7	84.2	90.3	96.1	83.9	91.7	116.7	130.9	121.7	98.7	101.1	99.6
6	WOOD & PLASTICS	91.7	73.7	81.5	104.1	73.6	86.8	92.0	80.4	85.5	101.4	73.9	85.9	117.9	141.2	131.1	99.6	90.7	94.6
7	MOISTURE PROTECTION	84.6	68.4	79.5	92.0	69.7	85.0	87.1	71.7	82.3	88.3	68.2	82.0	102.5	143.5	115.3	92.7	89.6	91.7
8	DOORS, WINDOWS, GLASS	91.0	74.3	82.3	101.5	67.4	83.8	99.0	78.8	88.5	98.3	72.1	84.7	129.4	136.8	133.3	103.8	89.3	96.3
9.1	LATH & PLASTER	96.1	71.2	77.2	87.0	73.3	76.6	91.9	86.0	87.5	108.4	73.7	82.1	120.4	148.3	141.6	93.1	93.5	93.4
9.2	DRYWALL	100.5	73.4	87.7	108.5	71.9	91.2	92.5	81.5	87.3	100.7	74.5	88.3	121.9	143.8	132.3	90.8	90.1	90.5
9.5	ACOUSTICAL WORK	98.7	73.3	84.9	101.1	73.2	86.0	94.2	80.0	86.5	94.2	73.0	82.7	125.6	142.7	134.9	103.1	89.8	95.9
9.6	FLOORING	112.0	79.6	103.5	97.4	70.7	90.4	114.0	86.4	106.8	100.4	50.7	87.4	117.3	149.3	125.6	93.0	74.5	88.2
9.8	PAINTING	104.5	71.9	78.4	110.7	70.5	78.5	121.5	81.6	89.5	119.7	80.2	88.0	123.2	146.3	141.7	96.5	91.2	92.3
9	FINISHES	103.3	73.2	87.1	105.1	71.5	87.0	100.4	82.0	90.5	102.2	74.7	87.4	121.3	145.3	134.2	92.9	89.6	91.1
10-14	TOTAL DIV. 10-14	100.0	75.4	92.6	100.0	73.2	91.9	100.0	82.7	94.8	100.0	71.4	91.4	100.0	143.2	112.9	100.0	89.8	96.9
15	MECHANICAL	96.5	77.7	86.9	99.6	77.4	88.3	97.5	79.8	88.4	99.2	74.6	86.6	107.5	136.6	122.4	98.5	85.4	91.8
16	ELECTRICAL	94.1	78.1	82.9	92.1	77.7	82.0	90.0	82.1	84.5	90.9	66.4	73.7	108.4	147.0	135.5	105.0	88.9	93.7
1-16	WEIGHTED AVERAGE	94.4	78.6	85.8	99.6	76.9	87.3	97.3	82.9	89.5	96.3	73.1	83.7	124.8	139.2	132.6	99.1	87.5	92.8

ARIZONA / ARKANSAS / CALIFORNIA

DIVISION		TUCSON MAT.	INST.	TOTAL	FORT SMITH MAT.	INST.	TOTAL	LITTLE ROCK MAT.	INST.	TOTAL	ANAHEIM MAT.	INST.	TOTAL	BAKERSFIELD MAT.	INST.	TOTAL	FRESNO MAT.	INST.	TOTAL
2	SITE WORK	106.6	97.0	102.3	96.6	91.8	94.4	103.3	94.1	99.2	101.0	113.1	106.4	93.1	111.2	101.2	91.7	120.5	104.5
3.1	FORMWORK	100.7	89.7	92.1	102.5	65.7	73.7	95.7	70.9	76.3	94.9	129.7	122.1	112.8	129.7	126.0	99.6	123.5	118.3
3.2	REINFORCING	95.1	105.7	99.5	124.6	71.3	102.3	117.8	69.1	97.5	99.3	130.1	112.2	96.1	130.1	110.3	106.5	130.1	116.3
3.3	CAST IN PLACE CONC.	105.7	97.7	100.7	90.6	91.9	91.4	98.5	92.3	94.7	109.5	109.2	109.3	103.4	109.4	107.1	93.1	107.3	101.9
3	CONCRETE	102.4	95.2	97.8	100.4	79.8	87.2	102.2	81.9	89.2	104.4	119.1	113.8	103.6	119.2	113.6	97.3	115.7	109.1
4	MASONRY	90.2	69.4	74.3	93.5	78.4	81.9	89.8	78.8	81.4	106.6	127.3	122.4	98.8	115.8	111.8	114.7	111.9	112.6
5	METALS	91.1	102.7	95.3	96.9	79.0	90.5	106.6	77.7	96.3	99.5	122.1	107.6	99.7	122.4	107.8	95.3	123.5	105.3
6	WOOD & PLASTICS	107.5	87.9	96.4	106.9	65.8	83.6	94.4	72.2	81.9	95.9	126.5	113.2	95.2	126.5	112.9	96.9	120.1	110.0
7	MOISTURE PROTECTION	105.6	77.5	96.8	84.7	67.3	79.2	84.2	68.3	79.2	108.2	131.6	115.5	84.7	117.6	95.0	107.7	108.2	107.8
8	DOORS, WINDOWS, GLASS	88.4	88.3	88.4	93.2	61.6	76.8	95.7	65.3	79.9	93.8	127.3	111.2	100.4	123.4	112.4	101.4	120.6	111.4
9.1	LATH & PLASTER	109.1	93.8	97.5	93.0	76.0	80.1	98.5	78.4	83.3	97.1	132.4	123.8	95.4	110.3	106.7	101.9	126.3	120.4
9.2	DRYWALL	82.1	88.7	85.2	95.1	64.6	80.7	114.8	71.3	94.2	97.4	127.9	111.9	98.0	121.7	109.2	98.7	124.0	110.7
9.5	ACOUSTICAL WORK	114.9	87.4	99.9	84.5	64.5	73.6	84.5	71.2	77.3	82.2	127.5	106.8	94.1	127.5	112.3	97.4	121.1	110.3
9.6	FLOORING	109.9	74.0	100.5	89.3	78.8	86.6	88.5	80.1	86.3	117.3	126.5	119.7	111.9	112.5	112.1	88.5	106.3	93.2
9.8	PAINTING	98.6	84.1	87.0	111.1	52.9	64.4	104.7	66.8	74.3	108.3	123.9	120.8	120.2	108.1	110.5	108.0	121.8	119.0
9	FINISHES	93.3	86.3	89.5	94.5	62.2	77.1	105.0	70.8	86.5	101.8	126.6	115.2	103.0	116.1	110.1	97.3	121.9	110.6
10-14	TOTAL DIV. 10-14	100.0	87.4	96.2	100.0	74.6	92.4	100.0	75.4	92.6	100.0	128.4	108.5	100.0	125.2	107.5	100.0	146.2	113.8
15	MECHANICAL	98.9	85.4	92.7	97.5	69.3	83.1	97.1	73.6	85.1	96.9	126.2	111.9	95.1	107.5	101.4	92.7	120.9	107.1
16	ELECTRICAL	102.3	87.9	92.2	99.3	76.6	83.3	93.6	80.2	84.2	98.7	139.7	127.5	106.0	103.4	104.2	109.5	101.0	103.5
1-16	WEIGHTED AVERAGE	98.5	86.9	92.2	96.7	74.2	84.5	98.5	77.2	86.9	100.6	126.1	114.5	98.4	114.7	107.3	98.9	117.0	108.7

CALIFORNIA

DIVISION		LOS ANGELES MAT.	INST.	TOTAL	OXNARD MAT.	INST.	TOTAL	RIVERSIDE MAT.	INST.	TOTAL	SACRAMENTO MAT.	INST.	TOTAL	SAN DIEGO MAT.	INST.	TOTAL	SAN FRANCISCO MAT.	INST.	TOTAL
2	SITE WORK	96.1	115.7	104.9	97.9	106.2	101.6	95.1	111.7	102.5	82.9	105.4	93.0	94.9	108.3	100.9	102.6	114.6	108.0
3.1	FORMWORK	112.9	130.1	126.4	90.1	130.0	121.3	102.5	129.7	123.8	101.0	123.7	118.7	105.2	127.5	122.6	104.9	133.7	127.4
3.2	REINFORCING	64.4	130.1	91.8	99.3	130.1	112.2	124.6	130.1	126.9	99.3	130.1	112.2	119.3	130.1	123.8	124.1	130.1	126.6
3.3	CAST IN PLACE CONC.	97.9	112.3	106.8	102.5	109.9	107.1	102.5	109.6	106.9	116.1	106.5	110.2	100.4	105.3	103.4	105.6	116.3	112.1
3	CONCRETE	93.5	120.8	111.1	99.4	119.6	112.4	107.3	119.3	115.0	109.5	115.3	113.2	105.5	116.1	112.3	109.5	124.3	119.0
4	MASONRY	108.8	127.3	122.9	98.4	120.9	115.7	102.8	121.1	116.8	101.4	105.6	104.6	111.3	118.4	116.7	128.6	143.4	139.9
5	METALS	101.8	123.1	109.4	105.6	122.4	111.6	99.6	122.2	107.7	111.4	123.4	115.7	99.0	121.1	106.9	104.2	126.5	112.2
6	WOOD & PLASTICS	100.6	127.6	115.9	92.7	127.1	112.2	94.8	126.5	112.8	78.4	120.4	102.2	97.1	123.8	112.2	94.0	132.6	115.9
7	MOISTURE PROTECTION	103.9	133.5	113.2	89.8	132.4	103.1	90.3	130.7	102.9	85.1	122.6	96.8	94.4	120.1	102.4	113.4	132.3	109.3
8	DOORS, WINDOWS, GLASS	102.2	127.3	115.2	103.0	127.3	115.6	103.0	127.3	115.9	92.2	120.1	106.7	108.1	123.6	116.1	113.4	132.3	123.2
9.1	LATH & PLASTER	95.8	132.5	123.6	97.6	134.0	125.1	97.6	128.3	120.9	98.9	120.1	115.0	102.2	119.7	115.5	101.5	147.1	136.0
9.2	DRYWALL	89.1	127.9	107.5	92.7	130.0	113.5	94.7	127.9	110.5	97.3	120.5	108.3	101.4	124.4	112.3	81.1	136.6	107.4
9.5	ACOUSTICAL WORK	98.7	127.5	114.4	88.4	127.5	109.7	88.4	127.5	109.7	86.6	121.1	105.4	100.7	124.8	113.8	100.7	134.2	118.9
9.6	FLOORING	96.3	126.5	104.2	95.6	126.5	103.7	95.6	126.5	103.7	85.8	133.3	98.3	98.5	121.7	104.6	107.4	140.0	115.9
9.8	PAINTING	84.3	126.3	118.0	92.2	117.8	112.8	100.8	123.9	119.3	112.3	132.4	128.4	92.1	127.9	120.8	102.8	143.5	135.5
9	FINISHES	91.2	127.5	110.7	96.5	125.5	112.1	95.1	126.4	112.0	95.4	125.6	111.6	99.8	125.2	113.5	91.3	139.7	117.4
10-14	TOTAL DIV. 10-14	100.0	128.9	108.6	100.0	128.3	108.5	100.0	128.3	108.5	100.0	147.9	114.3	100.0	126.8	108.0	100.0	153.0	115.9
15	MECHANICAL	97.7	128.8	113.6	98.8	127.4	113.4	96.6	130.9	114.2	98.2	124.1	111.5	103.1	127.6	115.6	100.5	158.4	130.2
16	ELECTRICAL	101.8	132.5	123.4	98.7	157.9	140.3	98.2	134.9	124.0	109.5	99.1	102.2	105.8	108.9	108.0	107.9	151.9	138.8
1-16	WEIGHTED AVERAGE	98.7	126.4	113.7	98.8	127.4	114.3	99.0	125.4	113.3	99.2	116.5	108.6	101.9	119.6	111.5	103.9	139.9	123.4

161

Figure 9.12

19.1 CITY COST INDEXES

Historical Cost Indexes

The table below lists both the Means City Cost Index based on Jan. 1, 1975 = 100 as well as the computed value of an index based on January 1, 1987 costs. Since the Jan. 1, 1987 figure is estimated, space is left to write in the actual index figures as they become available thru either the quarterly "Means Construction Cost Indexes" or as printed in the "Engineering News-Record". To compute the actual index based on Jan. 1, 1987 = 100, divide the Quarterly City Cost Index for a particular year by the actual Jan. 1, 1987 Quarterly City Cost Index. Space has been left to advance the index figures as the year progresses.

Year	"Quarterly City Cost Index" Jan. 1, 1975 = 100		Current Index Based on Jan. 1, 1987 = 100	
	Est.	Actual	Est.	Actual
Oct. 1987				
July 1987				
April 1987				
Jan. 1987	195.8		100.0	100.0
July 1986		192.8	98.5	
1985		189.1	96.6	
1984		187.6	95.8	
1983		183.5	93.7	
1982		174.3	89.0	
1981		160.2	81.8	
1980		144.0	73.5	
1979		132.3	67.6	
1978		122.4	62.5	
1977		113.3	57.9	
1976		107.3	54.8	
1975		102.6	52.4	

Year	"Quarterly City Cost Index" Jan. 1, 1975 = 100	Current Index Based on Jan. 1, 1987 = 100	
	Actual	Est.	Actual
July 1974	94.7	48.4	
1973	86.3	44.1	
1972	79.7	40.7	
1971	73.5	37.5	
1970	65.8	33.6	
1969	61.6	31.5	
1968	56.9	29.1	
1967	53.9	27.5	
1966	51.9	26.5	
1965	49.7	25.4	
1964	48.6	24.8	
1963	47.3	24.2	
1962	46.2	23.6	
1961	45.4	23.2	
1960	45.0	23.0	
1959	44.2	22.6	

Year	"Quarterly City Cost Index" Jan. 1, 1975 = 100	Current Index Based on Jan. 1, 1987 = 100	
	Actual	Est.	Actual
July 1958	43.0	22.0	
1957	42.2	21.6	
1956	40.4	20.6	
1955	38.1	19.5	
1954	36.7	18.7	
1953	36.2	18.5	
1952	35.3	18.0	
1951	34.4	17.6	
1950	31.4	16.0	
1949	30.4	15.5	
1948	30.4	15.5	
1947	27.6	14.1	
1946	23.2	11.8	
1945	20.2	10.3	
1944	19.3	9.9	
1943	18.6	9.5	

City Cost Indexes

Tabulated on the following pages are average construction cost indexes for 162 major U.S. and Canadian cities. Index figures for both material and installation are based on the 30 major city average of 100 and represent the cost relationship as of April 1, 1986. The index for each division is computed from representative material and labor quantities for that division. The weighted average for each city is a weighted total of the components listed above it, but does not include relative productivity between trades or cities.

The material index for the weighted average includes about 100 basic construction materials with appropriate quantities of each material to represent typical "average" building construction projects.

The installation index for the weighted average includes the contribution of about 30 construction trades with their representative man-days in proportion to the material items installed. Also included in the installation costs are the representative equipment costs for those items requiring equipment.

Since each division of the book contains many different items, any particular item multiplied by the particular city index may give incorrect results. However, when all the book costs for a particular division are summarized and then factored, the result should be very close to the actual costs for that particular division for that city.

If a project has a preponderance of materials from any particular division (say structural steel), then the weighted average index should be adjusted in proportion to the value of the factor for that division.

Figure 9.13

APPENDIX

Appendix

TABLE OF CONTENTS

Metric Conversion Factors

Description: This table is primarily for converting customary U.S. units in the left hand column to SI metric units in the right hand column. In addition, conversion factors for some commonly encountered Canadian and non-SI metric units are included.

	If You Know		Multiply By	To Find
Length	Inches	x	25.4[a]	= Millimeters
	Feet	x	0.3048[a]	= Meters
	Yards	x	0.9144[a]	= Meters
	Miles (statute)	x	1.609	= Kilometers
Area	Square inches	x	645.2	= Square millimeters
	Square feet	x	0.0929	= Square meters
	Square yards	x	0.8361	= Square meters
Volume (Capacity)	Cubic inches	x	16,387	= Cubic millimeters
	Cubic feet	x	0.02832	= Cubic meters
	Cubic yards	x	0.7646	= Cubic meters
	Gallons (U.S. liquids)[b]	x	0.003785	= Cubic meters[c]
	Gallons (Canadian liquid)[b]	x	0.004546	= Cubic meters[c]
	Ounces (U.S. liquid)[b]	x	29.57	= Milliliters[c,d]
	Quarts (U.S. liquid)[b]	x	0.9464	= Liters[c,d]
	Gallons (U.S. liquid)[b]	x	3.785	= Liters[c,d]
Force	Kilograms force[d]	x	9.807	= Newtons
	Pounds force	x	4.448	= Newtons
	Pounds force	x	0.4536	= Kilograms force[d]
	Kips	x	4448	= Newtons
	Kips	x	453.6	= Kilograms force[d]
Pressure, Stress, Strength (Force per unit area)	Kilograms force per square centimeter[d]	x	0.09807	= Megapascals
	Pounds force per square inch (psi)	x	0.006895	= Megapascals
	Kips per square inch	x	6.895	= Megapascals
	Pounds force per square inch (psi)	x	0.07031	= Kilograms force per square centimeter[d]
	Pounds force per square foot	x	47.88	= Pascals
	Pounds force per square foot	x	4.882	= Kilograms force per square meter[d]
Bending Moment Or Torque	Inch-pounds force	x	0.01152	= Meter-kilograms force[d]
	Inch-pounds force	x	0.1130	= Newton-meters
	Foot-pounds force	x	0.1383	= Meter-kilograms force[d]
	Foot-pounds force	x	1.356	= Newton-meters
	Meter-kilograms force[d]	x	9.807	= Newton-meters
Mass	Ounces (avoirdupois)	x	28.35	= Grams
	Pounds (avoirdupois)	x	0.4536	= Kilograms
	Tons (metric)	x	1000[a]	= Kilograms
	Tons, short (2000 pounds)	x	907.2	= Kiloprams
	Tons, short (2000 pounds)	x	0.9072	= Megagrams[e]
Mass per Unit Volume	Pounds mass per cubic foot	x	16.02	= Kilograms per cubic meter
	Pounds mass per cubic yard	x	0.5933	= Kilograms per cubic meter
	Pounds mass per gallon (U.S. liquid)[b]	x	119.8	= Kilograms per cubic meter
	Pounds mass per gallon (Canadian liquid)[b]	x	99.78	= Kilograms per cubic meter
Temperature	Degrees Fahrenheit	(F-32)/1.8	=	Degrees Celsius
	Degrees Fahrenheit	(F+459.67)/1.8	=	Degrees Kelvin
	Degrees Celsius	C+273.15	=	Degrees Kelvin

[a]The factor given is exact
[b]One U.S. gallon = 0.8327 Canadian gallon
[c]1 liter = 1000 milliliters = 1000 cubic centimeters
1 cubic decimeter = 0.001 cubic meter

[d]Metric but not SI unit
[e]Called "tonne" in England and "metric ton" in other metric countries

AREA CALCULATIONS

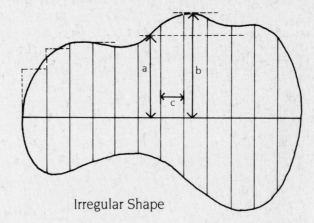

Irregular Shape

For each segment:

$$\text{Area} = \frac{(a + b)c}{2}$$

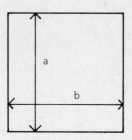

Square Area = ab

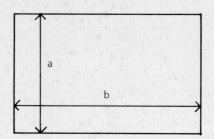

Rectangle Area = ab

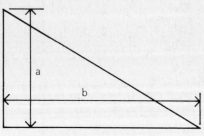

Triangle Area = $\dfrac{ab}{2}$

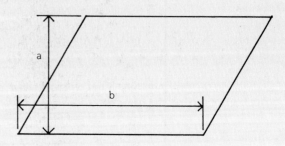

Parallelogram Area = ab

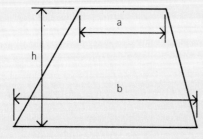

Trapezoid Area = $\dfrac{(a + b)h}{2}$

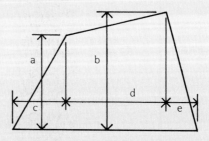

Trapezium Area = $\dfrac{bd - ad - be + ac}{2}$

| Conversion of Inches to Decimal Parts per Foot | | | | | | | | | | | |
	0	1″	2″	3″	4″	5″	6″	7″	8″	9″	10″	11″
0	0	.08	.17	.25	.33	.42	.50	.58	.67	.75	.83	.92
1/8″	.01	.09	.18	.26	.34	.43	.51	.59	.68	.76	.84	.93
1/4″	.02	.10	.19	.27	.35	.44	.52	.60	.69	.77	.85	.94
3/8″	.03	.11	.20	.28	.36	.45	.53	.61	.70	.78	.86	.95
1/2″	.04	.12	.21	.29	.37	.46	.54	.62	.71	.79	.87	.96
5/8″	.05	.14	.22	.30	.39	.47	.55	.64	.72	.80	.89	.97
3/4″	.06	.15	.23	.31	.40	.48	.56	.65	.73	.81	.90	.98
7/8″	.07	.16	.24	.32	.41	.49	.57	.66	.74	.82	.91	.99

Design Weight for Various Materials

Type		Description	Weight Per C.F.	Type		Description	Weight Per C.F.
Bituminous	Coal	Anthracite	97	Masonry	Ashlar	Granite	168
		Bituminous	84			Limestone, crystalline	168
		Peat, turf, dry	47			Limestone, oolitic	135
		Coke	75			Marble	173
						Sandstone	144
	Petroleum	Unrefined	54		Rubble, in mortar	Granite	153
		Refined	50			Limestone, crystalline	147
		Gasoline	42			Limestone, oolitic	138
	Pitch		69			Marble	156
	Tar	Bituminous	75			Sandstone	137
Concrete	Plain	Stone aggregate	144		Brick	Pressed	140
		Slag aggregate	132			Common	120
		Expanded slag aggregate	100			Soft	100
		Haydite (burned clay agg.)	90		Cement	Portland, loose	90
		Vermiculite/perlite, load bearing	70-105			Portland set	183
		Vermiculite & perlite, non load bear	25-50		Lime	Gypsum, loose	53-64
	Rein-forced	Stone aggregate	150		Mortar	Set	103
		Slag aggregate	138	Metals	Aluminum	Cast, hammered	165
		Lightweight aggregates	30-106		Brass	Cast, rolled	534
Earth	Clay	Dry	63		Bronze	7.9 to 14% Sn	509
		Damp, plastic	110		Copper	Cast, rolled	556
		and gravel, dry	100		Iron	Cast, pig	450
	Dry	Loose	76			Wrought	485
		Packed	95		Lead		710
	Moist	Loose	78		Monel		556
		Packed	96		Steel	Rolled	490
	Mud	Flowing	108		Tin	Cast, hammered	459
		Packed	115		Zinc	Cast rolled	440
	Riprap	Limestone	80-85	Timber	Cedar	White or red	22
		Sandstone	90		Fir	Douglas	32
		Shale	105			Eastern	25
	Sand & gravel	Dry, loose	90-105		Maple	Hard	43
		Dry, packed	100-120			White	33
		Wet	118-120		Oak	Red or Black	41
Gases	Air	0°C., 760 mm.	.0807			White	46
	Gas	Natural	.0385		Pine	White	26
Liquids	Alcohol	100%	49			Yellow, long leaf	44
	Water	4°C., maximum density	62.5			Yellow, short leaf	38
		Ice	56		Redwood	California	26
		Snow, fresh fallen	8		Spruce	White or Black	27
		Sea water	64				

Reinforcing Bars				
		Nominal Dimensions - Round Sections		
Bar Size Designation	Weight Pounds Per Foot	Diameter Inches	Cross-Sectional Area-Sq. Inches	Perimeter Inches
#3	.376	.375	.11	1.178
#4	.668	.500	.20	1.571
#5	1.043	.625	.31	1.963
#6	1.502	.750	.44	2.356
#7	2.044	.875	.60	2.749
#8	2.670	1.000	.79	3.142
#9	3.400	1.128	1.00	3.544
#10	4.303	1.270	1.27	3.990
#11	5.313	1.410	1.56	4.430
#14	7.650	1.693	2.25	5.320
#18	13.600	2.257	4.00	7.090

	Common Stock Styles of Welded Wire Fabric							
	New Designation	Old Designation	Steel Area Per Foot				Approximate Weight Per 100 Sq. Ft.	
			Longitudinal		Transverse			
	Spacing - Cross Sectional Area (IN.)-(Sq. IN. 100)	Spacing Wire Gauge (IN.)-(AS & W)	IN.	CM	IN.	CM	LB	KG
Rolls	6 x 6-W1.4 x W1.4	6 x 6-10 x 10	0.028	0.071	0.028	0.071	21	9.53
	6 x 6-W2.0 x W2.0	6 x 6-8 x 8 (1)	0.040	0.102	0.040	0.102	29	13.15
	6 x 6-W2.9 x W2.9	6 x 6-6 x 6	0.058	0.147	0.053	0.147	42	19.05
	6 x 6-W4.0 x W4.0	6 x 6-4 x 4	0.080	0.203	0.080	0.203	58	26.31
	4 x 4-W1.4 x W1.4	4 x 4-10 x 10	0.042	0.107	0.042	0.107	31	14.06
	4 x 4-W2.0 x W2.0	4 x 4-8 x 8 (1)	0.060	0.152	0.060	0.152	43	19.50
	4 x 4-W2.9 x W2.9	4 x 4-6 x 6	0.087	0.221	0.087	0.221	62	28.12
	4 x 4-W4.0 x W4.0	4 x 4-4 x 4	0.120	0.305	0.120	0.305	85	38.56
Sheets	6 x 6-W2.9 x W2.9	6 x 6-6 x 6	0.058	0.147	0.058	0.147	42	19.05
	6 x 6-W4.0 x W4.0	6 x 6-4 x 4	0.080	0.203	0.080	0.203	58	26.31
	6 x 6-W5.5 x W5.5	6 x 6-2 x 2 (2)	0.110	0.279	0.110	0.279	80	36.29
	6 x 6-W4.0 x W4.0	4 x 4-4 x 4	0.120	0.305	0.120	0.305	85	38.56

NOTES
1. Exact W-number size for 8 gauge is W2.1
2. Exact W-number size for 2 gauge is W5.4

Brick Quantities for Use in Paving (Courtesy Brick Institute of America)			
Estimating Mortarless Paving Units			
Paver Face Dimensions (actual inches) *w x l*		Paver Face Area (in sq. in.)	Paver Units (per sq. ft.)
4	8	32.0	4.5
3¾	8	30.0	4.8
3⅝	7⅝	27.6	5.2
3⅞	8¼	32.0	4.5
3⅞	7¾	30.0	4.8
3¾	7½	28.2	5.1
3¾	7¾	29.1	5.0
3⅝	11⅝	42.1	3.4
3⅝	8	29.0	5.0
3⅝	11¾	42.6	3.4
3⁹⁄₁₆	8	28.5	5.1
3½	7¾	27.1	5.3
3½	7½	26.3	5.5
3⅜	7½	25.3	5.7
4	4	16.0	9.0
6	6	36.0	4.0
7⅝	7⅝	58.1	2.5
7¾	7¾	60.1	2.4
8	8	64.0	2.3
8	16	128.0	1.1
12	12	144.0	1.0
16	16	256.0	0.6
6	6 Hexagon	31.2	4.6
8	8 Hexagon	55.4	2.6
12	12 Hexagon	124.7	1.2

NOTE: The above table does not include waste.
Allow at least 5% for waste and breakage.

Brick Quantities For Use In Paving

Brick Paver Units*

Face Dimensions (actual size in inches)		Thickness
w	x l	
4	8	The unit thickness of brick pavers varies. The most popular thicknesses are 2¼ in. and 1⅝ in. The range of thickness is generally from ¾ in. to 2½ in.
3¾	8	
3¾	7½	
3⅝	7⅝	
3½	7½	
6	6	
8	8	
6	6 Hexagon	
8	8 Hexagon	

*Table 1 is based on BIA survey conducted in 1973. According to the survey approximately 38 sizes are manufactured.

Brick Paving Units and Mortar Quantities

Brick Paver Units		Cubic Feet of Mortar Joints per 1000 Units	
w x l x t	Paver Units per sq. ft.	⅜-in. Joint	½-in. Joint
3⅝ x 8 x 2¼[a]	4.3	5.86	—
3⅝ x 7⅝ x 2¼	4.5	5.68	—
3¾ x 8 x 2¼	4.0	—	8.0
3⅝ x 7⅝ x 1¼	4.5	3.15	—
3¾ x 8 x 1⅛	4.0	—	4.0

[a]Running bond pattern only

NOTE: No waste was included for brick and mortar in above quantities. Allow 5% for brick and 25% for mortar.

Mortar Bed and Soft Cushion Base of Sand and Portland Cement

Material	Cubic per 100 sq. ft.	Weight of Material lb. per cu. ft.
½-in. cushion of: cement-sand (1:6)	4.17	
portland cement		15.67
sand		80.00
½-in. Type N mortar bed (1:1:6)	4.17	
portland cement		15.67
hydrated lime		6.67
sand		80.00

(*courtesy Brick Institute of America*)

Calculations For Lawn and Soil Maintenance

Pounds Per 1000 S.F. Nomograph

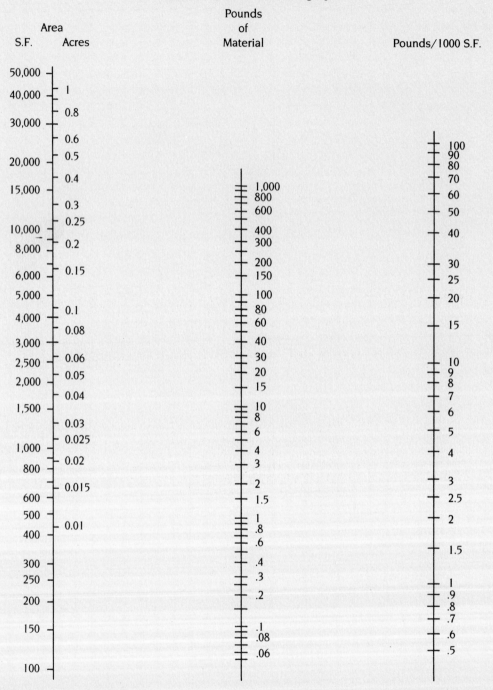

Area
| S.F. | Acres |

Pounds
of
Material

Pounds/1000 S.F.

Use by placing a straight edge to known or given points on any 2 scales and reading the unknown on the remaining scale. Example: How many pounds of material will be needed to treat an 8000 S.F. lawn at 5 lbs/1000 S.F.?

Answer: 40 lbs.

Prepared By: Harold Davidson, Department of Horticulture, Michigan State University

(courtesy of the National Landscape Association, "Landscape Designer and Estimator's Guide")

Calculations For Lawn and Soil Maintenance

Pounds Per Acre Nomograph

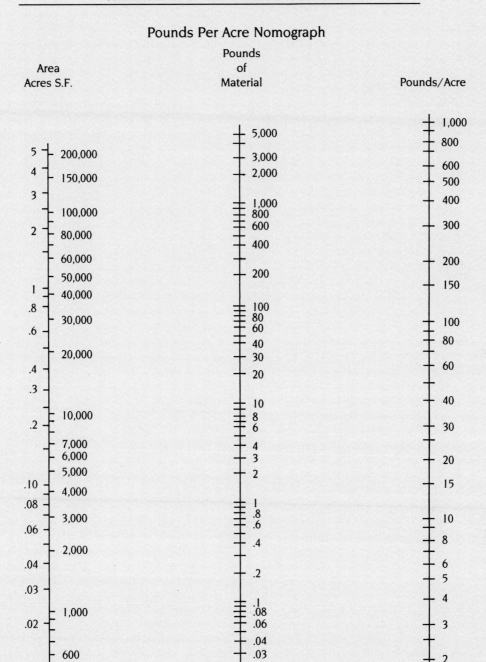

Use by placing a straight edge to known or given points on any 2 scales and reading the unknown on the remaining scale. Example: 80 pounds of material applied at 200 lbs./acre will treat .4 acre.

Prepared By: Harold Davidson, Department of Horticulture, Michigan State University

(courtesy of the National Landscape Association, "Landscape Designer and Estimator's Guide"

Appendix A

Computation
Volume of Excavated Material

(Depth in inches and feet)	(Cubic yards per square surface foot)
2"	.006
4"	.012
6"	.018
8"	.025
10"	.031
1'	.037
2'	.074
3'	.111
4'	.148
5'	.185
6'	.222
7'	.259
8'	.296
9'	.332
10'	.369

*(No swellage factor applied)

Example: Excavation required: 20' x 30' x 4" = 600 times .148 = 88.8 Cu. Yds.

224

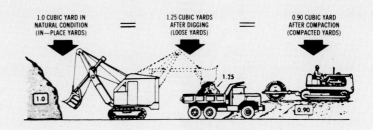

Approximate Material Characteristics*				
Material	Loose (lb/cu yd)	Bank (lb/cu yd)	Swell (%)	Load Factor
Clay, dry	2,100	2,650	26	0.79
Clay, wet	2,700	3,575	32	0.76
Clay and gravel, dry	2,400	2,800	17	0.85
Clay and gravel, wet	2,600	3,100	17	0.85
Earth, dry	2,215	2,850	29	0.78
Earth, moist	2,410	3,080	28	0.78
Earth, wet	2,750	3,380	23	0.81
Gravel, dry	2,780	3,140	13	0.88
Gravel, wet	3,090	3,620	17	0.85
Sand, dry	2,600	2,920	12	0.89
Sand, wet	3,100	3,520	13	0.88
Sand and gravel, dry	2,900	3,250	12	0.89
Sand and gravel, wet	3,400	3,750	10	0.91

*Exact values will vary with grain size, moisture content, compaction, etc. Test to determine exact values for specific soils.

Typical Soil Volume Conversion Factors				
Soil Type	Initial Soil Condition	Bank	Converted to: Loose	Compacted
Clay	Bank	1.00	1.27	0.90
	Loose	0.79	1.00	0.71
	Compacted	1.11	1.41	1.00
Common earth	Bank	1.00	1.25	0.90
	Loose	0.80	1.00	0.72
	Compacted	1.11	1.39	1.00
Rock (blasted)	Bank	1.00	1.50	1.30
	Loose	0.67	1.00	0.87
	Compacted	0.77	1.15	1.00
Sand	Bank	1.00	1.12	0.95
	Loose	0.89	1.00	0.85
	Compacted	1.05	1.18	1.00

Conversion Chart for Loam, Baled Peat, and Mulch

Loam Requirements		Mulch Requirements (Bulk Peat, Crushed Stone, Shredded Bark, Wood Chips)	
Depth per 10,000 S.F.	Cubic yards required	Depth per 1,000 S.F.	Cubic yards required
2 inches	70	1 inch	3-1/2
4 "	140	2 inches	7
6 "	210	3 "	10-1/2
		4 "	14
Per 1,000 S.F.		Per 100 S.F.	
2 inches	7	1 inch	1/3
4 "	14	2 inches	2/3
6 "	21	3 "	1
		4 "	1-1/3

Baled (or Compressed) Peat

Per 100 S.F.	Bales Required
1 inch	one 4 cubic foot bale
2 inches	two 4 cubic foot bales
3 "	two 6 cubic foot bales
4 "	one 4 cubic foot bales and two 6 cubic foot bales

Note: Opened and spread, peat from bales will be about 2-1/2 times the volume of the unopened bale.

					Surtee's Landscape Service Charts				

					Ball Sizes — Weight, Etc.				

Diam.	Depth	Area S.F.	Cubic Feet	Weight Lbs.	Diam.	Depth	Area S.F.	Cubic Feet	Weight Lbs.
8"	6"	0.35	0.15	13	26"	20"	''	5.37	457
8"	8"	''	0.21	18	26"	21"	''	5.64	480
10"	6"	0.54	0.24	21	27"	12"	3.98	3.49	297
10"	8"	''	0.32	28	27"	15"	''	4.36	370
10"	10"	''	0.39	34	27"	18"	''	5.23	444
12"	6"	0.78	0.34	29	27"	20"	''	5.81	491
12"	9"	''	0.52	45	27"	22"	''	6.39	532
12"	12"	''	0.68	58	27"	24"	''	6.97	588
14"	6"	1.08	0.47	40	28"	14"	4.28	4.36	370
14"	8"	''	0.63	53	28"	16"	''	4.99	424
14"	10"	''	0.78	66	28"	18"	''	5.62	477
14"	12"	''	0.94	80	28"	20"	''	6.24	530
14"	14"	''	1.10	94	28"	22"	''	6.87	583
15"	8"	1.23	0.72	62	28"	24"	''	7.49	637
15"	10"	''	0.90	76	30"	15"	4.91	5.37	456
15"	12"	''	1.07	91	30"	18"	''	6.44	547
15"	14"	''	1.26	107	30"	21"	''	7.51	638
15"	15"	''	1.35	115	30"	24"	''	8.58	729
16"	10"	1.40	1.13	96	30"	27"	''	9.65	820
16"	12"	''	1.21	103	33"	15"	5.94	6.50	552
16"	14"	''	1.42	120	33"	18"	''	7.80	663
16"	15"	''	1.52	129	33"	21"	''	9.10	773
18"	12"	1.77	1.54	131	33"	24"	''	10.40	884
18"	14"	''	1.81	155	33"	27"	''	11.69	994
18"	16"	''	2.05	175	36"	18"	7.07	9.27	788
20"	12"	2.18	1.91	163	36"	21"	''	10.83	920
20"	14"	''	2.24	191	36"	24"	''	12.37	1052
20"	15"	''	2.39	203	36"	27"	''	13.91	1183
20"	16"	''	2.54	216	36"	30"	''	15.46	1314
20"	18"	''	2.87	244	39"	18"	8.30	10.77	916
21"	12"	2.40	2.10	178	39"	21"	''	12.69	1079
21"	15"	''	2.63	224	39"	24"	''	14.52	1129
21"	18"	''	3.15	268	39"	27"	''	16.35	1270
21"	20"	''	3.50	298	39"	30"	''	18.15	1411
22"	12"	2.64	2.31	196	39"	33"	''	19.97	1550
22"	15"	''	2.89	246	40"	18"	8.73	11.46	974
22"	16"	''	3.08	262	40"	21"	''	13.38	1137
22"	18"	''	3.46	294	40"	24"	''	15.29	1300
22"	21"	''	4.04	343	40"	27"	''	17.19	1461
24"	12"	3.14	2.74	233	40"	30"	''	19.10	1623
24"	15"	''	3.44	292	40"	33"	''	21.00	1785
24"	16"	''	3.65	310	40"	36"	''	22.92	1948
24"	18"	''	4.13	351	42"	18"	9.62	12.63	1074
24"	21"	''	4.80	408	42"	21"	''	14.74	1253
26"	12"	3.69	3.23	275	42"	24"	''	16.85	1432
26"	14"	''	3.77	320	42"	27"	''	18.95	1610
26"	15"	''	4.03	343	42"	30"	''	21.05	1789
26"	16"	''	4.30	365	42"	33"	''	23.15	1970
26"	18"	''	4.83	411	42"	36"	''	25.25	2146

		Surtee's Landscape Service Charts							
		Ball Sizes — Weight, Etc.							
Diam.	Depth	Area S.F.	Cubic Feet	Weight Lbs.	Diam.	Depth	Area S.F.	Cubic Feet	Weight Lbs.
45″	18″	11.05	14.51	1234	60″	33″	19.64	47.26	4017
45″	21″	ʺ	16.93	1439	60″	36″	ʺ	51.56	4383
45″	24″	ʺ	19.35	1644	60″	39″	ʺ	55.86	4748
45″	27″	ʺ	21.77	1849	60″	42″	ʺ	60.15	5113
45″	30″	ʺ	24.18	2054	66″	21″	23.75	36.38	3092
45″	33″	ʺ	26.59	2260	66″	24″	ʺ	41.56	3533
45″	36″	ʺ	29.00	2465	66″	27″	ʺ	46.75	3974
48″	21″	12.57	19.24	16.35	66″	30″	ʺ	51.96	4417
48″	24″	ʺ	22.00	1870	66″	33″	ʺ	57.15	4858
48″	27″	ʺ	24.75	2104	66″	36″	ʺ	62.34	5299
48″	30″	ʺ	27.50	2337	66″	39″	ʺ	67.54	5741
48″	33″	ʺ	30.25	2571	66″	42″	ʺ	72.74	6183
48″	36″	ʺ	33.00	2804	72″	24″	28.28	49.49	4207
48″	39″	ʺ	35.75	3038	72″	27″	ʺ	55.67	4732
50″	21″	13.64	20.89	1776	72″	30″	ʺ	61.85	5257
50″	24″	ʺ	23.87	2029	72″	33″	ʺ	68.04	5784
50″	27″	ʺ	26.86	2283	72″	36″	ʺ	74.23	6310
50″	30″	ʺ	29.84	2536	72″	39″	ʺ	80.42	6836
50″	33″	ʺ	32.82	2790	72″	42″	ʺ	86.62	7363
50″	36″	ʺ	35.80	3043	78″	24″	33.18	58.06	4935
50″	39″	ʺ	38.79	3296	78″	27″	ʺ	65.32	5552
50″	42″	ʺ	41.78	3550	78″	30″	ʺ	72.58	6170
51″	21″	14.18	21.72	1846	78″	33″	ʺ	79.84	6786
51″	24″	ʺ	24.82	2110	78″	36″	ʺ	87.11	7404
51″	27″	ʺ	27.92	2373	78″	39″	ʺ	94.36	8021
51″	30″	ʺ	31.02	2637	78″	42″	ʺ	101.61	8637
51″	33″	ʺ	34.12	2900	78″	45″	ʺ	108.86	9253
51″	36″	ʺ	37.22	3163	78″	48″	ʺ	116.11	9870
51″	39″	ʺ	40.33	3428	84″	24″	38.49	67.36	5725
51″	42″	ʺ	43.43	3692	84″	27″	ʺ	75.78	6441
54″	21″	15.91	24.36	2071	84″	30″	ʺ	84.20	7157
54″	24″	ʺ	27.84	2367	84″	33″	ʺ	92.62	7873
54″	27″	ʺ	31.32	2663	84″	36″	ʺ	101.04	8588
54″	30″	ʺ	34.80	2959	84″	39″	ʺ	109.46	9304
54″	33″	ʺ	38.28	3255	84″	42″	ʺ	117.88	10020
54″	36″	ʺ	41.76	3559	84″	45″	ʺ	126.30	10736
54″	39″	ʺ	45.24	3846	84″	48″	ʺ	134.72	11451
54″	42″	ʺ	48.73	4142	90″	24″	44.18	77.32	6572
57″	21″	17.71	27.11	2305	90″	27″	ʺ	86.98	7393
57″	24″	ʺ	31.00	2635	90″	30″	ʺ	96.64	8214
57″	27″	ʺ	34.88	2965	90″	33″	ʺ	106.30	9036
57″	30″	ʺ	38.76	3294	90″	36″	ʺ	115.96	9857
57″	33″	ʺ	42.63	3623	90″	39″	ʺ	125.63	10679
57″	36″	ʺ	46.50	3952	90″	42″	ʺ	135.30	11500
57″	39″	ʺ	50.37	4281	90″	45″	ʺ	144.97	12323
57″	42″	ʺ	54.24	4610	90″	48″	ʺ	154.63	13144
60″	21″	19.64	30.07	2556	96″	30″	50.27	109.96	9347
60″	24″	ʺ	34.37	2921	96″	33″	ʺ	120.96	10282
60″	27″	ʺ	38.67	3286	96″	36″	ʺ	131.96	11217
60″	30″	ʺ	42.96	3652	96″	39″	ʺ	142.96	12152

Diam.	Depth	Area S.F.	Cubic Feet	Weight Lbs.	Diam.	Depth	Area S.F.	Cubic Feet	Weight Lbs.
96″	42″	50.27	153.96	13087	138″	39″	103.87	295.38	25107
96″	45″	″	164.96	14022	138″	42″	″	318.11	27039
96″	48″	″	175.96	14957	138″	45″	″	340.83	28971
102″	30″	56.75	124.14	10552	138″	48″	″	363.55	30902
102″	33″	″	136.55	11607	138″	54″	″	409.08	34764
102″	36″	″	148.96	12662	138″	60″	″	454.43	38627
102″	39″	″	161.37	13717	144″	36″	113.09	269.86	25233
102″	42″	″	173.78	14771	144″	39″	″	321.60	27336
102″	45″	″	186.20	15827	144″	42″	″	346.34	29439
102″	48″	″	198.62	16883	144″	45″	″	371.08	31542
108″	30″	63.62	139.17	11830	144″	48″	″	395.82	33645
108″	33″	″	153.09	13013	144″	54″	″	445.30	37850
108″	36″	″	167.01	14196	144″	60″	″	494.77	42055
108″	39″	″	180.93	15379	150″	36″	122.72	322.14	27382
108″	42″	″	194.85	16562	150″	39″	″	348.99	29664
108″	45″	″	208.76	17745	150″	42″	″	375.84	31946
108″	48″	″	222.67	18927	150″	45″	″	402.69	34228
114″	30″	70.88	155.05	13179	150″	48″	″	429.53	36510
114″	33″	″	170.56	14498	150″	54″	″	480.22	41074
114″	36″	″	186.07	15816	150″	60″	″	536.90	45637
114″	39″	″	201.58	17135	156″	36″	132.73	348.42	29616
114″	42″	″	217.08	18452	156″	39″	″	377.45	32083
114″	45″	″	232.58	19770	156″	42″	″	406.48	34551
114″	48″	″	248.08	21087	156″	45″	″	435.51	37019
120″	30″	78.54	171.81	14603	156″	48″	″	464.54	39487
120″	33″	″	188.98	16063	156″	54″	″	522.61	44423
120″	36″	″	206.16	17524	156″	60″	″	580.69	49359
120″	39″	″	223.34	18984	162″	36″	143.14	375.74	31938
120″	42″	″	240.52	20444	162″	39″	″	407.06	34600
120″	45″	″	257.70	21905	162″	42″	″	438.38	37262
120″	48″	″	274.89	23366	162″	45″	″	469.69	39924
126″	30″	86.59	189.42	16101	162″	48″	″	501.00	42586
126″	33″	″	208.36	17711	162″	54″	″	563.62	47908
126″	36″	″	227.30	19321	162″	60″	″	626.24	53230
126″	39″	″	246.24	20931	168″	36″	153.94	404.09	34348
126″	42″	″	265.18	22541	168″	39″	″	437.77	37212
126″	45″	″	284.12	24150	168″	42″	″	471.45	40072
126″	48″	″	303.06	25760	168″	45″	″	505.13	42934
126″	54″	″	340.94	28980	168″	48″	″	538.80	45796
126″	60″	″	378.83	32200	168″	54″	″	606.14	51521
132″	36″	95.03	249.46	21204	168″	60″	″	673.48	57246
132″	39″	″	270.24	22970	180″	36″	176.71	463.86	39428
132″	42″	″	291.03	24736	180″	39″	″	502.52	42714
132″	45″	″	311.81	26503	180″	42″	″	541.17	46000
132″	48″	″	332.60	28270	180″	45″	″	579.83	49286
132″	54″	″	374.16	31805	180″	48″	″	618.48	52572
132″	60″	″	415.76	35340	180″	54″	″	695.80	59143
138″	36″	103.87	272.65	23175	180″	60″	″	773.11	65714

Surtee's Landscape Service Charts — Ball Sizes — Weight, Etc.

Surtee's Tree Pits and Tree Balls
Cubic Feet Per Tree
For Estimating Excavation and Top Soil

Diameters / Depths		1'	1¼'	1½'	1¾'	2'	2¼'	2½'	2¾'	3'	3¼'	3½'
Tree Pit	1'	.94	1.47	2.13	2.88	3.77	4.78	5.89	7.13	8.48	9.96	11.5
Ball		.68	1.07	1.54	2.10	2.73	3.42	4.30	5.20	6.19	7.38	8.4
Tree Pit	1¼'	1.16	1.85	2.65	3.60	4.71	5.93	7.37	8.90	10.6	12.4	14.4
Ball		.85	1.35	1.93	2.63	3.42	4.29	5.36	6.49	7.7	9.2	10.5
Tree Pit	1½'	1.40	2.22	3.08	4.32	5.65	7.16	8.83	10.7	12.7	15.0	17.3
Ball		1.02	1.62	2.32	3.15	4.10	5.19	6.39	7.8	9.2	10.9	12.7
Tree Pit	1¾'	1.65	2.58	3.70	5.04	6.60	8.20	10.3	12.5	14.8	17.4	20.2
Ball		1.20	1.88	3.72	3.68	4.78	6.03	7.5	9.1	10.7	12.7	14.7
Tree Pit	2'	1.87	2.95	4.26	5.76	7.54	9.55	11.8	14.3	17.0	19.9	23.0
Ball		1.38	2.15	3.10	4.20	5.49	6.92	8.5	10.4	12.3	14.5	16.8
Tree Pit	2¼'	2.10	3.32	4.78	6.48	8.48	10.7	13.2	16.0	19.1	22.4	26.0
Ball		1.55	2.43	3.48	4.73	6.19	7.5	9.6	11.7	13.8	16.4	18.9
Tree Pit	2½'	2.34	3.69	5.30	7.20	9.42	11.9	14.7	17.8	21.2	24.9	28.9
Ball		1.70	2.70	3.87	5.25	6.89	8.7	10.7	13.0	15.4	18.2	21.0
Tree Pit	2¾'	2.57	4.06	5.83	7.92	10.3	13.1	16.2	19.6	23.3	27.4	31.8
Ball		1.87	2.98	4.25	5.77	7.6	9.6	11.8	14.3	17.0	20.0	23.1
Tree Pit	3'	2.81	4.43	6.37	8.64	11.3	14.3	17.7	21.4	25.4	29.9	34.6
Ball		2.05	3.24	4.65	6.30	8.3	10.5	12.9	15.6	18.6	21.8	25.2
Tree Pit	3¼'	3.00	4.80	6.90	9.36	12.2	15.5	19.2	23.2	27.5	32.4	37.5
Ball		2.21	3.50	5.03	6.83	8.9	11.4	14.0	16.9	20.1	23.6	27.3
Tree Pit	3½'	3.28	5.17	7.41	10.1	13.2	16.7	20.7	25.0	29.6	34.9	40.4
Ball		2.39	3.77	5.42	7.4	9.6	12.2	15.0	18.2	21.7	25.4	29.4
Tree Pit	3¾'	3.50	5.53	7.96	10.8	14.2	17.9	22.2	26.7	31.7	37.1	43.3
Ball		2.56	4.04	3.80	7.9	10.3	13.1	16.1	19.5	23.2	27.2	31.5
Tree Pit	4'	3.74	5.90	8.50	11.5	15.1	19.1	23.7	28.5	33.8	39.9	46.2
Ball		2.73	4.31	6.19	8.4	11.0	14.0	17.2	20.8	24.8	29.0	33.6
Tree Pit	4¼'	3.97	6.28	9.01	12.3	16.0	20.3	25.1	30.3	36.0	42.3	49.1
Ball		2.90	4.58	6.58	8.9	11.8	14.8	18.3	22.1	26.3	30.8	35.7
Tree Pit	4½'	4.20	6.64	9.55	13.0	17.0	21.5	26.6	32.0	38.1	44.8	52.0
Ball		3.07	4.85	6.97	9.5	12.4	15.7	19.4	23.4	27.8	32.6	37.8
Tree Pit	4¾'	4.43	7.00	10.0	13.7	17.9	22.7	28.0	33.8	40.2	47.3	54.9
Ball		3.24	5.12	7.4	10.0	13.0	16.5	20.4	24.7	29.1	34.2	40.0
Tree Pit	5'	4.68	7.38	10.6	14.4	18.8	23.9	29.8	35.6	42.3	49.9	57.7
Ball		3.41	5.38	7.8	10.5	13.7	17.4	21.5	26.0	30.9	36.1	42.1
Tree Pit	5½'	5.14	8.12	11.7	15.8	20.7	26.3	32.4	39.2	46.7	54.8	63.5
Ball		3.76	5.93	8.5	11.6	15.1	19.1	23.7	28.6	34.0	40.0	46.3
Tree Pit	6'	5.41	8.86	12.7	17.3	22.6	28.7	35.4	42.8	50.9	57.8	69.3
Ball		4.10	6.46	9.3	12.6	16.5	20.9	25.9	31.2	37.1	43.6	50.5

Surtee's Tree Pits and Tree Balls
Cubic Feet Per Tree
For Estimating Excavation and Top Soil

Diameters Depths		3¾'	4'	4¼'	4½'	4¾'	5'	5½'	6'	6½'	7'	7½'
Tree Pit Ball	1'	13.3 9.7	15.1 11.0	17.0 12.4	19.1 13.9	21.2 15.5	23.6 17.4	28.5 20.8	33.9 24.7	39.8 29.0	46.2 33.7	53.0 38.7
Tree Pit Ball	1¼'	16.6 12.2	18.8 13.8	21.3 15.5	23.8 17.4	26.5 19.4	29.5 21.7	35.6 26.0	42.4 30.9	49.8 36.3	57.7 42.1	66.3 48.3
Tree Pit Ball	1½'	19.9 14.5	22.6 16.5	25.5 18.6	28.6 20.9	31.9 23.2	35.4 25.8	42.8 31.2	50.9 37.1	59.7 43.6	69.3 50.5	79.5 58.0
Tree Pit Ball	1¾'	23.2 16.9	26.4 19.1	29.7 21.7	33.4 24.4	37.2 27.1	41.2 30.1	49.9 36.4	59.4 43.4	69.7 50.8	80.8 58.9	92.8 67.7
Tree Pit Ball	2'	26.5 19.2	30.2 21.9	34.0 24.8	38.2 27.8	42.0 31.0	47.1 34.4	57.0 41.6	67.9 49.5	79.6 58.1	92.4 67.4	106.3 77.3
Tree Pit Ball	2¼'	29.8 21.6	33.9 24.6	38.3 27.9	43.0 31.3	47.8 34.9	53.0 39.7	64.1 46.8	76.4 55.7	89.6 65.3	103.9 75.8	119.3 87.0
Tree Pit Ball	2½'	33.1 24.1	37.7 27.3	42.5 31.0	47.7 34.7	53.1 38.8	59.0 43.0	71.3 52.0	84.9 61.9	99.6 72.6	115.5 84.2	132.6 96.7
Tree Pit Ball	2¾'	36.5 26.4	41.5 30.0	46.8 34.1	52.5 38.1	58.5 42.6	64.8 47.3	78.4 57.2	93.3 68.0	109.5 79.9	127.0 92.6	145.8 106.3
Tree Pit Ball	3'	39.8 28.8	45.3 32.8	51.0 37.0	57.3 41.5	63.8 46.5	70.6 51.6	85.5 62.3	101.8 74.2	119.5 87.1	138.5 101.0	159.0 116.0
Tree Pit Ball	3¼'	43.1 31.4	49.0 35.7	55.3 40.1	62.0 45.0	69.1 50.4	76.5 55.9	92.6 67.5	110.3 80.4	129.4 94.4	150.1 109.5	172.3 125.6
Tree Pit Ball	3½'	46.4 33.9	52.8 38.5	59.6 43.2	66.8 48.5	74.3 54.4	82.5 60.2	99.7 72.7	118.7 86.6	139.4 101.6	161.7 112.9	185.6 135.3
Tree Pit Ball	3¾'	49.7 36.4	56.6 41.2	63.8 46.3	71.6 52.2	79.7 58.1	88.4 64.4	106.8 77.5	127.3 92.3	149.3 108.7	173.8 126.3	198.8 145.0
Tree Pit Ball	4'	53.0 38.9	60.3 44.0	68.1 49.4	76.3 55.7	85.0 62.0	94.2 68.7	113.0 82.8	135.7 98.5	159.3 116.1	184.8 134.7	212.1 154.6
Tree Pit Ball	4¼'	56.3 41.4	64.1 46.8	72.3 52.5	81.1 59.2	90.3 65.9	100.1 73.0	121.0 88.1	144.2 104.8	169.2 123.0	196.3 142.4	225.3 163.4
Tree Pit Ball	4½'	59.6 43.9	67.9 49.5	76.6 55.6	85.9 62.7	95.6 69.8	106.2 77.4	128.2 93.4	152.7 111.0	179.2 130.3	207.9 150.9	238.6 172.9
Tree Pit Ball	4¾'	63.0 46.0	71.6 52.3	80.9 58.8	90.7 66.2	101.0 73.7	112.0 81.7	135.3 98.6	161.2 117.2	189.1 137.6	219.4 159.7	265.1 182.4
Tree Pit Ball	5'	66.3 48.5	75.4 55.0	85.2 62.0	95.5 69.7	106.3 77.5	117.9 86.0	142.5 103.9	169.7 123.4	199.1 144.9	230.9 168.2	265.1 192.0
Tree Pit Ball	5½'	72.9 53.2	83.0 60.5	93.6 68.3	105.2 76.6	116.9 85.2	129.6 94.6	156.8 114.2	186.7 135.9	219.0 159.6	254.0 184.6	291.6 211.0
Tree Pit Ball	6'	79.5 58.0	90.5 66.0	102.1 74.5	114.5 83.5	127.5 93.0	141.5 103.1	171.0 124.7	203.6 148.5	238.9 174.2	277.1 202.0	318.1 230.0

φ	P	A	C	W	N	G	D	L	P'	W'
Angle of Stall	Parking Depth	Aisle Width	Curb Length	Width Overall	Net Car Area	Gross Car Area	Distance Last Car	Lost Area	Parking Depth	Width Overall
90°	19'	24'	9'	62'	171 S.F.	171 S.F.	9'	0	19'	62'
60°	21'	18'	10.4'	60'	171 S.F.	217 S.F.	7.8'	205 S.F.	18.8'	55.5'
45°	19.8'	13'	12.8'	52.7'	171 S.F.	252 S.F.	6.4'	286 S.F.	16.6'	46.2'

Parking Lot Specifications
Layout Data Based on 9' x 19' Parking Stall Size

Note: Square foot per car areas do not include the area of the travel lane.

90° Stall Angle: The main reason for use of this stall angle is to achieve the highest car capacity. This may be sound reasoning for employee lots with all day parking, but in most (in & out) lots there is difficulty in entering the stalls and no traffic lane direction. This may outweigh the advantage of high capacity.

60° Stall Angle: This layout is used most often due to the ease of entering and backing out, also the traffic aisle may be smaller.

45° Stall Angle: Requires a small change of direction from the traffic aisle to the stall, so the aisle may be reduced in width.

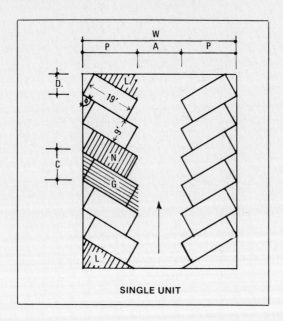

SINGLE UNIT

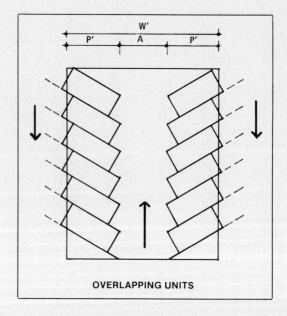

OVERLAPPING UNITS

The following information on plant containers and tree and shrub calipers, heights, root spreads, and ball sizes is from the *American Standard for Nursery Stock*, courtesy the American Association of Nurserymen.

Volumes and Weights of Plants in Containers

Pot Size	Volume	Weight
2¼″ pot	0.10 liter	³/₁₀ lb. each
2½″ rose pot	0.20 liter	½ lb. each
3″ pot	0.24 liter	¾ lb each
4″ pot	0.50 liter	1 lb. each
2″ x 5″ tree pot	0.50 liter	1 lb. each
1 gallon can	3.00 liters	6 lbs. each
2 gallon can	6.00 liters	14 lbs. each
3 gallon can	11.00 liters	21 lbs. each
egg can	16.00 liters	35 lbs. each
7 gallon can	34.00 liters	65 lbs each
14 gallon can	52.00 liters	100 lbs. each

Tree Heights and Acceptable Container Sizes
Shade and Flowering Trees

Tree Height	Container Size
12 in. 18 in. 2 ft. 3 ft.	1 gal. (trade designation). Minimum of 5½″ across top and height of 6″ or equivalent volume.
2 ft. 3 ft. 4 ft.	2 gal. (trade designation). Minimum of 7″ across top and height of 7½″ or equivalent volume.
4 ft. 5 ft. 6 ft.	5 gal., egg can or square can (trade designation). Minimum of 9″ across top and height of 10″ or equivalent volume.

Tree Heights and Acceptable Container Sizes (Cont.)	
Conifers - Spreading, Semi-Spreading, Globe or Dwarf Type	
Height (Globe or Dwarf Conifers) or Spread (Spreading or Semi-spreading)	**Container Size**
6 in. 9 in. 12 in.	1 gal. (trade designation). Minimum of 5½" across top and height of 6" or equivalent volume.
12 in. 15 in.	2 gal. (trade designation). Minimum of 7" across top and height of 7½" or equivalent volume.
18 in. 2 ft. 2½ ft.	5 gal., egg can or square can (trade designation). Minimum of 9" across top and height of 10" or equivalent volume.

Cone, Broad Upright, and Columnar Conifers*	
Height	**Container Size**
6 in. 9 in. 12 in. 15 in. 18 in.	1 gal. (trade designation). Minimum of 5½" across top and height of 6" or equivalent volume.
12 in. 15 in. 18 in. 2 ft.	2 gal. (trade designation). Minimum of 7" across top and height of 7½" or equivalent volume.
18 in. 2 ft. 2½ ft. 3 ft. 3½ ft.	5 gal., egg can or square can (trade designation). Minimum of 9" across top and height of 10" or equivalent volume.

*Extreme columnar types, such as Cupressus sempervirens (Italian Cypress) are acceptable in one or two sizes taller than the standard for a given container.

Broadleaf Evergreens	
Spreading, Semi-Spreading, Dwarf or Globe	
Spread (Spreading & Semi-Spreading) Height (Dwarf or Globe)	**Container Size**
6 in. 9 in. 12 in.	1 gal. (trade designation). Minimum of 5½″ across top and height of 6″ or equivalent volume.
12 in. 15 in.	2 gal. (trade designation). Minimum of 7″ across top and height of 7½″ or equivalent volume.
12 in. 2 ft. 2½ ft.	5 gal., egg can or square can (trade designation). Minimum of 9″ across top and height of 10″ or equivalent volume.

Broad Upright and Cone Type* Broadleaf Evergreens	
Height	**Container Size**
6 in. 9 in. 12 in. 15 in. 18 in.	1 gal. (trade designation). Minimum of 5½″ across top and height of 6″ or equivalent volume.
12 in. 15 in. 18 in. 2 ft.	2 gal. (trade designation). Minimum of 7″ across top and height of 7½″ or equivalent volume.
18 in. 2 ft. 2½ ft. 3 ft. 3½ ft.	5 gal., egg can or square can (trade designation). Minimum of 9″ across top and height of 10″ or equivalent volume.

*Extreme columnar types, such as Prunus laurocerasus (Cherry Laurel) and Ligustrum japonicum (Japanese Privet) are acceptable in one or two sizes taller than the standard for a given container.

Tree Caliper Measurements Relative to Height

Standard Shade Trees - Normal Growth Rate
Examples:

Acer rubrum, saccharinum
Betula
Cinnamomum camphora
Fraxinus americana, pennsylvanica, uhdei
Ginkgo
Gleditsia
Liriodendron
Platanus
Populus
Quercus borealis, macrocarpa, palustris, phellos, virginiana
Salix
Tilia americana
Ulmus americana

Caliper	Average Height Range	Maximum Heights
½ in.	5 to 6 ft.	8 ft.
¾ in.	6 to 8 ft.	10 ft.
1 in.	8 to 10 ft.	11 ft.
1¼ in.	8 to 10 ft.	12 ft.
1½ in.	10 to 12 ft.	14 ft.
1¾ in.	10 to 12 ft.	14 ft.
2 in.	12 to 14 ft.	16 ft.
2½ in.	12 to 14 ft.	16 ft.
3 in.	14 to 16 ft.	18 ft.
3½ in.	14 to 16 ft.	18 ft.
4 in.	16 to 18 ft.	22 ft.
5 in.	18 ft. and up	26 ft.

SHADE TREES OF SLOWER GROWTH usually do not attain the height measurement in relation to caliper as listed above. The height of these slower growing trees should not be less than two thirds of those described above.

Examples: Aesculus
Celtis
Cladrastic lutea
Fagus sylvatica
Koelreuteria
Laburnum
Liquidambar
Magnolia grandiflora
Nyssa
Olea europaea
Quercus alba
Sorbus
Tilia cordata, euchlora

Tree Caliper Measurements Relative to Height (Cont.)

SMALL UPRIGHT TREES

Examples: Acer campestre, circinatum
            Cercis
            Crataegus
            Halesia
            Malus (most crabapples)
            Prunus cerasifera "Thundercloud"
            Prunus serrulata, subhirtella
            Styrax
            Syringa amurensis "Japonica"

Height	Caliper	Number of Branches
2 ft.	$5/16''$	3 or more
3 ft.	$7/16''$	4 or more
4 ft.	$9/16''$	5 or more
5 ft.	$11/16''$	6 or more
	$3/4''$	7 or more

SMALL SPREADING TREES

Examples: Acer palmatum, griseum
            Cornus
            Lagerstromia indica
            Magnolia, soulangeana, stellata
            Malus sargentii
            Viburnum prunifolium

Height shall be the governing measurement for small spreading trees, up to a height of six feet. Sizing is in one foot increments. At six feet and over, caliper takes precedence. A height relative to caliper may be specified, but shall not be considered in determining minimum diameter ball sizes.

Root Spread Relative to Height and Caliper		
(Approved Minimum Root Spread for Nursery Grown Shade Trees, Courtesy of the National Association of Nurserymen)		
Caliper	Average Height Range	Minimum Root Spread
½ in.	5 to 6 ft.	12 in.
¾ in.	6 to 8 ft.	16 in.
1 in.	8 to 10 ft.	18 in.
1¼ in.	8 to 10 ft.	20 in.
1½ in.	10 to 12 ft.	22 in.
1¾ in.	10 to 12 ft.	24 in.
2 in.	12 to 14 ft.	28 in.
2½ in.	12 to 14 ft.	32 in.
3 in.	14 to 16 ft.	38 in.

Minimum Root Spreads for Nursery Grown Deciduous Shrubs						
Height of plant	18 in.	2 ft.	3 ft.	4 ft.	5 ft.	6 ft.
Minimum Root Spread	10 in.	11 in.	14 in.	16 in.	18 in.	20 in.

Recommended Minimum Ball Sizes for Balled and Burlapped Trees			
Shade Trees		Small Upright and Spreading Trees	
Caliper	Minimum Diameter Ball	Up to 6 ft.- Height 6 ft. & Over-	Minimum Diameter Ball
Inches	Inches	Caliper	Inches
½	12	2 ft.	10
¾	14	3 ft.	12
1	16	4 ft.	14
1¼	18	5 ft.	16
1½	20	¾ in.	16
1¾	22	1 in.	18
2	24	1½ in.	20
2½	28	1¾ in.	22
3	32	2 in.	24
3½	38	2½ in.	28
4	42	3 in.	32
4½	48	3½ in.	38
5	54	4 in.	42
		4½ in.	48
		5 in.	54

All multi-stem trees shall have a minimum ball size of one size larger than the size presently specified for single-stem trees.

It is recognized that plants having a coarse or wide-spreading root system because of natural habit of growth, soil condition, infrequent transplanting practice, or that are moved out of season, would require a size of ball in excess of the recommended sizes.

Ball Depth Ratio

Diameter Less Than 20 in. Depth Not Less Than 75% of Diameter of 3/4 of Width

Diameter 20 to 30 in. Depth Not Less Than 66-2/3% or 2/3 of Width

Diameter 31 to 48 in. Depth Not Less Than 60% or 3/5 of Width Balls With a Diameter of 30 in. or More Should be Drum-Laced

Height and Ball Diameter of Nursery Grown Deciduous Shrubs

Height	Minimum Diameter Ball Inches
12 in.	8
18 in.	9
2 ft.	10
3 ft.	12
4 ft.	14
5 ft.	16
6 ft.	18
7 ft.	20
8 ft.	22
9 ft.	24
10 ft.	26

Minimum Recommended Ball Diameters for Nursery Grown Conifers

Spreading, Semi-Spreading and Globe or Dwarf Type Conifers		Cone and Broad Upright Type Conifers	
Spread	Minimum Diameter Ball	Height	Minimum Diameter Ball
18 in.	10 in.	18 in.	10 in.
2 ft.	12 in.	2 ft.	12 in.
2½ ft.	14 in.	3 ft.	14 in.
3 ft.	16 in.	4 ft.	16 in.
3½ ft.	18 in.	5 ft.	20 in.
4 ft.	21 in.	6 ft.	22 in.
5 ft.	24 in.	7 ft.	24 in.
6 ft.	28 in.	8 ft.	27 in.
7 ft.	32 in.	9 ft.	30 in.
8 ft.	36 in.	10 ft.	34 in.
		12 ft.	38 in.
		14 ft.	42 in.
		16 ft.	46 in.
		18 ft.	50 in.

Columnar Conifers

Regular growing kinds		Rapid growing kinds*	
Height	Minimum Diameter Ball	Height	Minimum Diameter Ball
18 in.	10 in.	18 in.	8 in.
2 ft.	12 in.	2 ft.	9 in.
3 ft.	13 in.	3 ft.	11 in.
4 ft.	14 in.	4 ft.	12 in.
5 ft.	16 in.	5 ft.	14 in.
6 ft.	18 in.		
7 ft.	20 in.		
8 ft.	22 in.		
9 ft.	24 in.		
10 ft.	27 in.		
12 ft.	30 in.		
14 ft.	33 in.		
16 ft.	36 in.		
18 ft.	40 in.		

*Rapid growing kinds as: Thuja orientalis (Oriental Arborvitae), Juniperus communis 'Stricta' (Irish Juniper).

Minimum Recommended Ball Sizes for Nursery Grown Broadleaf Evergreens			
Spreading, Semi-Spreading and Globe or Dwarf Broadleaf Evergreens		Cone and Broad Upright Type Broadleaf Evergreens	
Spread	Minimum Diameter Ball	Height	Minimum Diameter Ball
18 in.	10 in.	18 in.	10 in.
2 ft.	12 in.	2 ft.	12 in.
2½ ft.	14 in.	3 ft.	14 in.
3 ft.	16 in.	4 ft.	16 in.
3½ ft.	18 in.	5 ft.	20 in.
4 ft.	21 in.	6 ft.	22 in.
		7 ft.	24 in.
		8 ft.	27 in.
		9 ft.	30 in.
		10 ft.	34 in.
		12 ft.	38 in.
		14 ft.	42 in.
		16 ft.	46 in.
		18 ft.	50 in.

Major Trees

Silhouettes indicate specimens of natural form, but varieties or forced forms possessing compact, spreading, columnar or pyramidal characteristics are available. The height at the ten year stage of development is given as an architectural design factor to be considered in the selection of tree sizes.

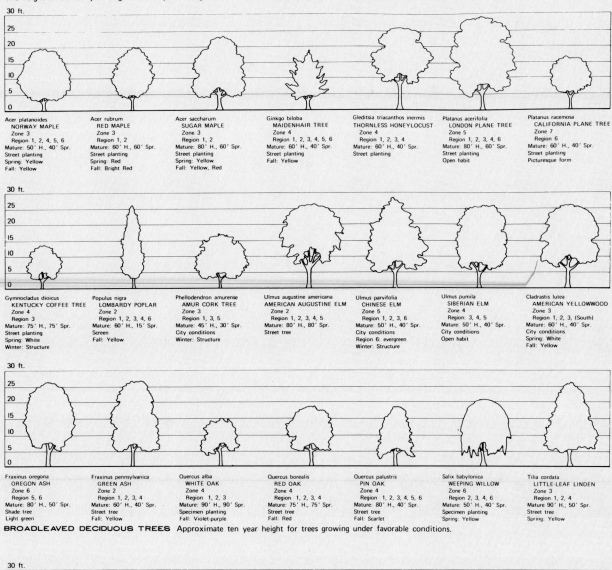

Acer platanoides
NORWAY MAPLE
Zone 3
Region 1, 2, 4, 5, 6
Mature: 50′ H., 40′ Spr.
Street planting
Spring: Yellow
Fall: Yellow

Acer rubrum
RED MAPLE
Zone 3
Region 1, 2
Mature: 60′ H., 60′ Spr.
Street planting
Spring: Red
Fall: Bright Red

Acer saccharum
SUGAR MAPLE
Zone 3
Region 1, 2
Mature: 80′ H., 60′ Spr.
Street planting
Spring: Yellow
Fall: Yellow, Red

Ginkgo biloba
MAIDENHAIR TREE
Zone 4
Region 1, 2, 3, 4, 5, 6
Mature: 60′ H., 40′ Spr.
Street planting
Fall: Yellow

Gleditsia triacanthos inermis
THORNLESS HONEYLOCUST
Zone 4
Region 1, 2, 3, 4
Mature: 60′ H., 40′ Spr.
Street planting

Platanus acerifolia
LONDON PLANE TREE
Zone 5
Region 1, 2, 3, 4, 6
Mature: 80′ H., 60′ Spr.
Street planting
Open habit

Platanus racemosa
CALIFORNIA PLANE TREE
Zone 7
Region 6
Mature: 60′ H., 40′ Spr.
Street planting
Picturesque form

Gymnocladus dioicus
KENTUCKY COFFEE TREE
Zone 4
Region 3
Mature: 75′ H., 75′ Spr.
Street planting
Spring: White
Winter: Structure

Populus nigra
LOMBARDY POPLAR
Zone 2
Region 1, 2, 3, 4, 6
Mature: 60′ H., 15′ Spr.
Screen
Fall: Yellow

Phellodendron amurense
AMUR CORK TREE
Zone 3
Region 1, 3, 5
Mature: 45′ H., 30′ Spr.
City conditions
Winter: Structure

Ulmus augustine americana
AMERICAN AUGUSTINE ELM
Zone 2
Region 1, 2, 3, 4, 5
Mature: 80′ H., 80′ Spr.
Street tree

Ulmus parvifolia
CHINESE ELM
Zone 5
Region 1, 2, 3, 6
Mature: 50′ H., 40′ Spr.
City conditions
Region 6: evergreen
Winter: Structure

Ulmus pumila
SIBERIAN ELM
Zone 4
Region: 3, 4, 5
Mature: 50′ H., 40′ Spr.
City conditions
Open habit

Cladrastis lutea
AMERICAN YELLOWWOOD
Zone 3
Region 1, 2, 3, (South)
Mature: 60′ H., 40′ Spr.
City conditions
Spring: White
Fall: Yellow

Fraxinus oregona
OREGON ASH
Zone 6
Region 5, 6
Mature: 80′ H., 50′ Spr.
Shade tree
Light green

Fraxinus pennsylvanica
GREEN ASH
Zone 2
Region 1, 2, 3, 4
Mature: 60′ H., 40′ Spr.
Street tree
Fall: Yellow

Quercus alba
WHITE OAK
Zone 4
Region 1, 2, 3
Mature: 90′ H., 90′ Spr.
Specimen planting
Fall: Violet-purple

Quercus borealis
RED OAK
Zone 4
Region 1, 2, 3, 4
Mature: 75′ H., 75′ Spr.
Street tree
Fall: Red

Quercus palustris
PIN OAK
Zone 4
Region 1, 2, 3, 4, 5, 6
Mature: 80′ H., 40′ Spr.
Street tree
Fall: Scarlet

Salix babylonica
WEEPING WILLOW
Zone 6
Region 2, 3, 4, 6
Mature: 50′ H., 40′ Spr.
Specimen planting
Spring: Yellow

Tilia cordata
LITTLE-LEAF LINDEN
Zone 3
Region 1, 2, 4
Mature 90′ H., 50′ Spr.
Street tree
Spring: Yellow

BROADLEAVED DECIDUOUS TREES Approximate ten year height for trees growing under favorable conditions.

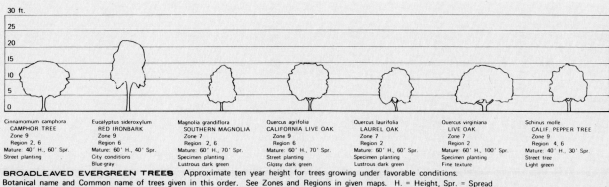

Cinnamomum camphora
CAMPHOR TREE
Zone 9
Region 2, 6
Mature: 40′ H., 60′ Spr.
Street planting

Eucalyptus sideroxylum
RED IRONBARK
Zone 9
Region 6
Mature: 60′ H., 40′ Spr.
City conditions
Blue-gray

Magnolia grandiflora
SOUTHERN MAGNOLIA
Zone 7
Region 2, 6
Mature: 60′ H., 70′ Spr.
Specimen planting
Lustrous dark green

Quercus agrifolia
CALIFORNIA LIVE OAK
Zone 9
Region 6
Mature: 60′ H., 70′ Spr.
Street planting
Glossy dark green

Quercus laurifolia
LAUREL OAK
Zone 7
Region 2
Mature: 60′ H., 60′ Spr.
Specimen planting
Lustrous dark green

Quercus virginiana
LIVE OAK
Zone 7
Region 2
Mature: 60′ H., 100′ Spr.
Specimen planting
Fine texture

Schinus molle
CALIF. PEPPER TREE
Zone 9
Region 4, 6
Mature: 40′ H., 30′ Spr.
Street tree
Light green

BROADLEAVED EVERGREEN TREES Approximate ten year height for trees growing under favorable conditions.
Botanical name and Common name of trees given in this order. See Zones and Regions in given maps. H. = Height, Spr. = Spread

Laurence & Beatriz Coffin, Urban Planners & Landscape Architects; Washington, D. C.

(courtesy *Architectural Graphic Standards*, John Wiley & Sons, 6th edition, 1970)

Major Trees

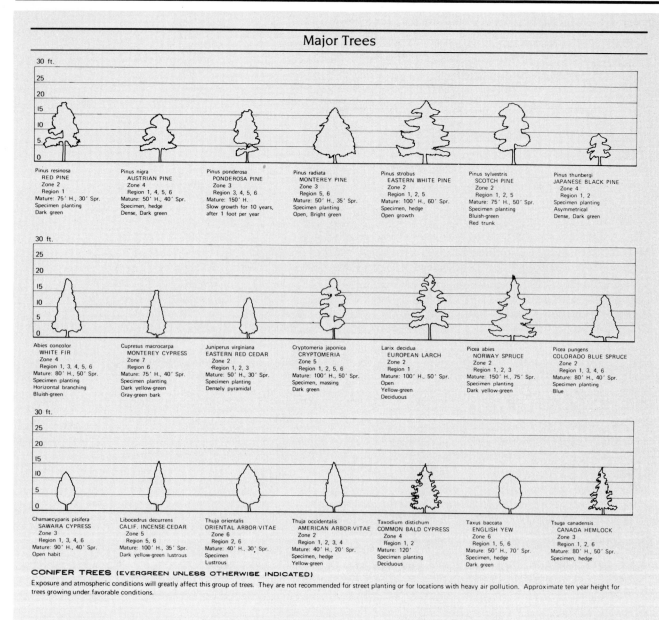

Pinus resinosa
RED PINE
Zone 2
Region 1
Mature: 75' H., 30' Spr.
Dark green

Pinus nigra
AUSTRIAN PINE
Zone 4
Region 1, 4, 5, 6
Mature: 50' H., 40' Spr.
Specimen, hedge
Dense, Dark green

Pinus ponderosa
PONDEROSA PINE
Zone 3
Region 3, 4, 5, 6
Mature: 150' H.
Slow growth for 10 years,
after 1 foot per year

Pinus radiata
MONTEREY PINE
Zone 3
Region 5, 6
Mature: 50' H., 35' Spr.
Specimen planting
Open, Bright green

Pinus strobus
EASTERN WHITE PINE
Zone 2
Region 1, 2, 5
Mature: 100' H., 60' Spr.
Specimen, hedge
Open growth

Pinus sylvestris
SCOTCH PINE
Zone 2
Region 1, 2, 5
Mature: 75' H., 50' Spr.
Specimen planting
Bluish-green
Red trunk

Pinus thunbergi
JAPANESE BLACK PINE
Zone 4
Region 1, 2, 6
Specimen planting
Asymmetrical
Dense, Dark green

Abies concolor
WHITE FIR
Zone 4
Region 1, 3, 4, 5, 6
Mature: 80' H., 50' Spr.
Specimen planting
Horizontal branching
Bluish-green

Cupresus macrocarpa
MONTEREY CYPRESS
Zone 7
Region 6
Mature: 75' H., 40' Spr.
Specimen planting
Dark yellow-green
Gray-green bark

Juniperus virginiana
EASTERN RED CEDAR
Zone 2
Region 1, 2, 3
Mature: 50' H., 30' Spr.
Specimen planting
Densely pyramidal

Cryptomeria japonica
CRYPTOMERIA
Zone 5
Region 1, 2, 5, 6
Mature: 100' H., 50' Spr.
Specimen, massing
Dark green

Larix decidua
EUROPEAN LARCH
Zone 2
Region 1
Mature: 100' H., 50' Spr.
Open
Yellow-green
Deciduous

Picea abies
NORWAY SPRUCE
Zone 2
Region 1, 2, 3
Mature: 150' H., 75' Spr.
Specimen planting
Dark yellow-green

Picea pungens
COLORADO BLUE SPRUCE
Zone 2
Region 1, 3, 4, 6
Mature: 80' H., 50' Spr.
Specimen planting
Blue

Chamaecyparis pisifera
SAWARA CYPRESS
Zone 3
Region 1, 3, 4, 6
Mature: 90' H., 40' Spr.
Open habit

Libocedrus decurrens
CALIF. INCENSE-CEDAR
Zone 5
Region 5, 6
Mature: 100' H., 35' Spr.
Dark yellow-green lustrous

Thuja orientalis
ORIENTAL ARBOR-VITAE
Zone 6
Region 2, 6
Mature: 40' H., 30' Spr.
Specimen
Lustrous

Thuja occidentalis
AMERICAN ARBOR-VITAE
Zone 2
Region 1, 2, 3, 4
Mature: 40' H., 20' Spr.
Specimen, hedge
Yellow-green

Taxodium distichum
COMMON BALD CYPRESS
Zone 4
Region 1, 2
Mature: 120'
Specimen planting
Deciduous

Taxus baccata
ENGLISH YEW
Zone 6
Region 1, 5, 6
Mature: 50' H., 70' Spr.
Specimen, hedge
Dark green

Tsuga canadensis
CANADA HEMLOCK
Zone 3
Region 1, 3, 6
Mature: 80' H., 50' Spr.
Specimen, hedge

CONIFER TREES (EVERGREEN UNLESS OTHERWISE INDICATED)

Exposure and atmospheric conditions will greatly affect this group of trees. They are not recommended for street planting or for locations with heavy air pollution. Approximate ten year height for trees growing under favorable conditions.

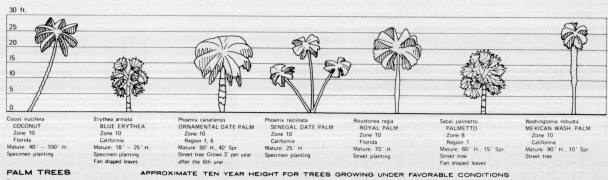

Cocos nucifera
COCONUT
Zone 10
Florida
Mature: 40' – 100' H.
Specimen planting

Erythea armata
BLUE ERYTHEA
Zone 10
California
Mature: 18' – 25' H.
Specimen planting
Fan shaped leaves

Phoenix canariensis
ORNAMENTAL DATE PALM
Zone 10
Region 1, 6
Mature: 50' H., 40' Spr.
Street tree Grows 3' per year
after the 6th year

Phoenix reclinata
SENEGAL DATE PALM
Zone 10
California
Mature: 25' H.
Specimen planting

Roystonea regia
ROYAL PALM
Zone 10
Florida
Mature: 70' H.
Street planting

Sabal palmetto
PALMETTO
Zone 8
Region 1
Mature: 60' H., 15' Spr.
Street tree
Fan shaped leaves

Washingtonia robusta
MEXICAN WASH. PALM
Zone 10
California
Mature: 90' H., 10' Spr.
Street tree

PALM TREES   APPROXIMATE TEN YEAR HEIGHT FOR TREES GROWING UNDER FAVORABLE CONDITIONS

Botanical name and Common name given in this order. See Zones and Regions in given maps. H. = Height Spr. = Spread.

Laurence & Beatriz Coffin, Urban Planners & Landscape Architects; Washington, D. C.

(*courtesy Architectural Graphic Standards*, John Wiley & Sons, 6th edition, 1970)

MINOR TREES AND SHRUBS

Betula populifolia
GREY BIRCH
Zone 2
Region 1, 2, 3, 4, 5
Mature: 30' H., 20' Spr.
White bark
Fall: Yellow

Cornus florida
FLOWERING DOGWOOD
Zone 4
Region 1, 2, 3(East)
Mature: 20' H., 25' Spr.
Spring: White or Pink
Fall: Red

Cornus nutalli
PACIFIC DOGWOOD
Zone 7
Region 5, 6
Mature: 30' H., 30' Spr.
Spring: White
Fall: Scarlet and Yellow

Cercis canadensis
EASTERN REDBUD
Zone 4
Region 1, 2, 4
Mature: 30' H., 30' Spr.
Spring: Purplish Pink
Fall: Yellow

Crataegus phaenopyrum
WASHINGTON HAWTHORN
Zone 4
Region 1, 2
Mature: 30' H., 30' Spr.
Spring: White
Fall: Orange

Ilex opaca
AMERICAN HOLLY
Zone 5
Region 1, 2
Mature: 40' H., 25' Spr.
Dark green, Red fruit
Evergreen

Lagerstroemia indica
CRAPE MYRTLE
Zone 7
Region 2, 6
Mature: 20' H., 20' Spr.
Spring: Pink, Bluish
Dense

Acer palmatum
JAPANESE MAPLE
Zone 5
Region 1, 2, 6
Mature: 20' H., 20' Spr.
Spring: Red
Fall: Red

Delonix regia
FLAME TREE
Zone 10
Florida
Mature: 40' H., 40' Spr.
Summer: Red flowers
Fern-like folliage

Myrica californica
CALIFORNIA BAYBERRY
Zone 7
Region 5, 6
Mature: 30' H., 15' Spr.
Bronze colored
Evergreen

Magnolia soulangeana
SAUCER MAGNOLIA
Zone 5
Region 1, 2, 6
Mature: 25' H., 25' Spr.
Spring: White - Pink
Coarse texture

Malus (species)
FLOWERING CRAB
Zone 4
Region 1, 2, 4
Mature: 20' H., 25' Spr.
Spring: White, Pink, Red
Dense

Prunus serrulata
ORIENTAL CHERRY
Zone 5, 6
Region 1, 2, 5, 6
Mature: 25' H., 25' Spr.
Spring: White, Pink
Glossy bark

Photinia serrulata
CHINESE PHOTINIA
Zone 7
Region 2, 6
Mature: 36' H., 25' Spr.
Spring: New growth Red
Lustrous evergreen

Botanical name and Common name of trees and shrubs given in this order. See Zones and Regions in given maps.
H. = Height   Spr. = Spread
MINOR TREES—ADAPTED TO CITY CONDITIONS, DECIDUOUS UNLESS OTHERWISE SPECIFIED.

SIZE	DECIDUOUS SHRUBS—WITHSTANDING CITY CONDITIONS				EVERGREEN SHRUBS—WITHSTANDING CITY CONDITIONS		
10' to 15' HIGH Scale 1" = 30'	Cornus racemosa GRAY DOGWOOD Zone 4 Region 1, 2 Red stalks Hedge	Hamamells virginiana COMMON WITCH HAZEL Zone 4 Region 1, 2, 3 Fall: Yellow	Ligustrum amurense AMUR PRIVET Zone 3 Region 1, 2, 3, 5, 6 Nearly evergreen Hedge or specimen	Syringa vulgaris COMMON LILAC Zone 3 Region 1, 4, 5 Spring: Lilac Massing	Juniperus chinensus columnaris CHINESE JUNIPER Zone 4 Region 1, 2, 3 Hedge specimen	Taxus cupidata capitata JAPANESE YEW Zone 4 Region 1, 2, 3, 4, 5, 6 Specimen Dark green	Rhododendron maximum ROSEBAY RHODODENDRON Zone 3 Region 1, 2, 5 Spring: Pink Dark green, dense
6' to 10' HIGH Scale 1" = 20'	Aronia arbutifolia RED CHOKEBERRY Zone 5 Region 1, 2 Spring: White Fall: Red	Fremontia californica FLANNEL BUSH Zone 7 California Spring: Yellow Massing	Spirea prunifolia plena BRIDALWREATH SPIREA Zone 4 Region 1, 2, 3 Spring: White	Vibornum tomentosum DOUBLEFILE VIBURNUM Zone 2 Region 1, 2, 3, 4, 5, 6 Spring: White Massing	Taxus cuspidata JAPANESE YEW Zone 4 Region 1, 2, 3, 4, 5, 6 Hedge Dark green	Myrtus communis MYRTLE Zone 8–9 Region 2, 6 Hedge, Specimen Massing	Nerium oleander NERIUM Zone 7–8 Region 2, 3, 4, 6 Bamboo-like Light green—white flower
2' to 6' HIGH Scale 1" = 20'	Berberis thunbergi JAPANESE BARBERRY Zone 5 Region 1, 2, 3, 4, 5, 6 Fall: Scarlet Hedge	Forsythia intermediaspetabilis SHOWY BORDER FORSYTHIA Zone 5 Region 1, 2, 3, 4, 5, 6 Spring: Yellow Massing	Euonymus alata WINGED EUONYMUS Zone 3 Region 1, 2, 5, 6 Fall: Scarlet Hedge: Massing	Rosa rugosa RUGOSA ROSE Zone 2 Region 1, 2 Fall: Orange Hedge	Juniperus chinensis pfitzeriana PFITZER'S JUNIPER Zone 4 Region 1, 2 Feathery texture	Buxus suffruticosa DWARF BOX Zone 5 Region 2, 3, 6 Dark lustrous	Pinus mugo mughus MUGO PINE Zone 2 Region 1, 2, 4, 5, 6 Bright green Specimen, Massing
6' to 24' HIGH Used as ground cover	Cotoneaster horizontalis ROCK SPRAY Zone 4 Region 1, 2, 3, 4, 5, 6	Cytisus albus PORTUGUESE BROOM Zone 5 Region 1, 5 White flowers	Euonymus fortunei WINTER CREEPER Zone 2 Region 1, 2, 3, 4, 5, 6	Juniperus sabina tamariscifolia TAMARIX JUNIPER Zone 4 Region 3, 4, 5, 6	Juniperus chinensis sargenti SARGENT JUNIPER Zone 4 Region 1, 2	Hedera helix vars. ENGLISH IVY Zone 4 Region 1, 2	Pachistima cambyi CAMBYI PACHISTIMA Zone 5 Region 1, 2 Fall: Bronze

Silhouettes indicate specimens of natural form. Shrubs are adaptable to different height and forms by pruning. A wide range of varieties and exotic shrubs can be found throughout the plant regions. A few shrubs commonly used are listed here.

Laurence & Beatriz Coffin, Urban Planners & Landscape Architects; Washington, D. C.

(courtesy Architectural Graphic Standards, John Wiley & Sons, 6th edition, 1970)

Planting References and Books

This list is made up of standard references as well as personal recommendations. Also consider advice from your local nurseryman, landscape architect or landscape gardener, depending upon where your information gap may be. Note that some nurseryman's catalogs are widely used as references within the industry: some of these are listed here. Your most relevant and accurate sources are local suppliers.

America's Garden Book
James and Louise Bush-Brown
Scribner's, Revised 1980

Taylor's Encyclopedia of Gardening
Norman Taylor, editor
Houghton Mifflin
Fourth edition 1976

Specific Topics:

Tree Maintenance
P.P. Pirone
Oxford, 1978

Trees for Every Purpose
Joseph Hudak
McGraw-Hill, 1980

Shrubs in the Landscape
Joseph Hudak
McGraw-Hill, 1984

Brooklyn Botanic Garden booklets
These publications address plants, gardens structures, and other horticultural subjects. A catalogue can be obtained from:

Gift Shop
Brooklyn Botanic Garden
1000 Washington Ave.
Brooklyn, N.Y. 11225

American Nurseryman Magazine
U.S. Govt. Printing Office
Washington, D.C. 20402
Numerous publications, the best catalogues are:
SB-301 "Gardening"
SB-041 "The Home"

Monrovia Nurseries
P.O. Box Q
Azusa, CA 91702

Schichtel's Illustrated Tree Catalog
An excellent illustrated catalog of tree form and growth characteristics.
8745 Chestnut Ridge Rd.
Orchard Park, NY 14127

Wayside Gardens Catalog
Colored illustrations
Hodges, S.C. 29695

Weston Nurseries Catalog
E. Main St.
P.O. Box 186
Hopkinton, MA 01748

Professional Landscape Organizations

For a complete list of landscaping trade associations in your area, contact these organizations at their national headquarters.

American Society of Landscape Architects   (203) 466-7730
1733 Connecticut Avenue, N.W.
Washington, D.C. 20009

American Associations of Nurserymen, Inc.   (202) 789-2900
1250 I St., N.W., Suite 500
Washington, D.C. 20005

Associated Landscape Contractors of America   (703) 241-4004
405 Washington Street
North Falls Church, VA 22046

Masonry Organizations

Brick Institute of America
1750 Old Meadow Road
McLean, Virginia 22102

Indiana Limestone Institute
Stone City Bank Bldg. S-400
Bedford, Indiana 47421

International Masonry Institute
823 15th Street, N.W.
Suite 1001
Washington, D.C. 20005

International Union of Bricklayers and Allied Craftsmen
815 15th Street, N.W.
Washington D.C. 20005

Wood References

American Institute of Timber Construction
333 W. Hampden Ave.
Englewood, CO 80110

American Plywood Association
7011 S. 19th St.
Tacoma, WA 22206

American Wood Preservers Bureau
2772 S. Randolph St.
Arlington, VA 22200

American Wood Preservers Institute
1945 Old Gallows Rd.
Vienna, VA 22180

California Redwood Association
591 Redwood Highway
Suite 3100
Mill Valley, CA 94941

National Forest Products Association
1619 Mass Ave., N.W.
Washington, D.C. 20036

Southern Forest Products Association
2900 Indiana Ave.
Kenner, LA 70065

Western Wood Products Association
Yeon Bldg.
522 S.W. 5th Ave.
Portland, OR 97204

U.S. Forest Service
Forest Products Laboratory
P.O. Box 5130
Madison, WI 53705

Forest Service Office of Information
P.O. Box 2417
Washington, D.C. 20013

THE ZONES OF PLANT HARDINESS

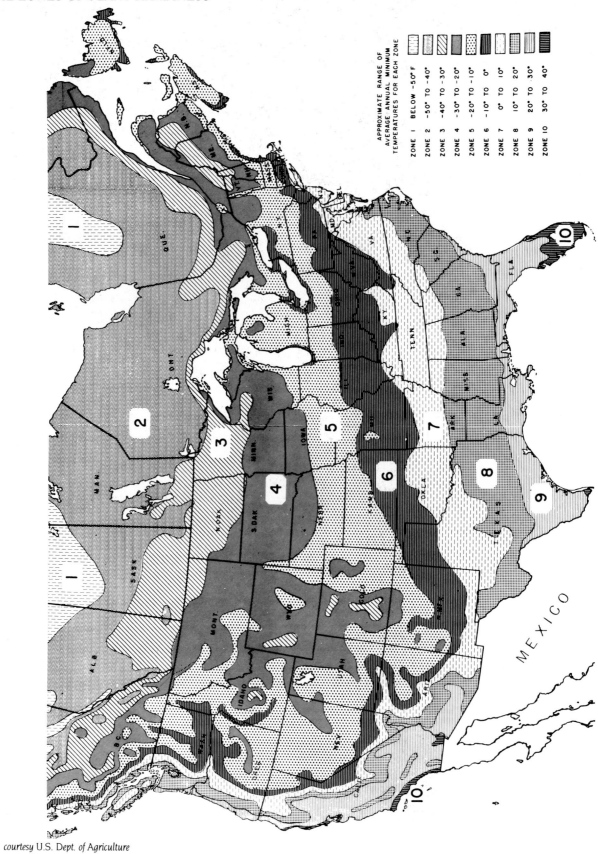

courtesy U.S. Dept. of Agriculture

Maximum Depth of Frost Penetration in Inches

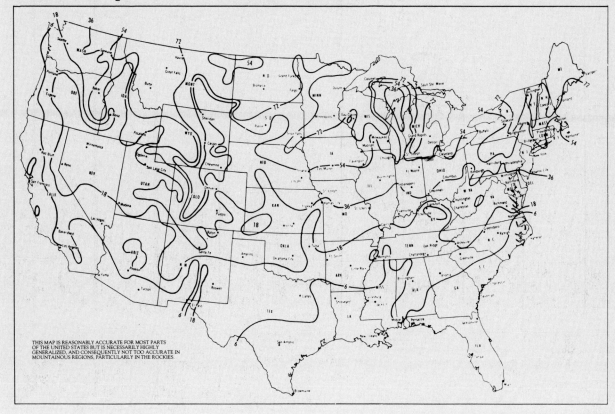

THIS MAP IS REASONABLY ACCURATE FOR MOST PARTS
OF THE UNITED STATES BUT IS NECESSARILY HIGHLY
GENERALIZED, AND CONSEQUENTLY NOT TOO ACCURATE IN
MOUNTAINOUS REGIONS, PARTICULARLY IN THE ROCKIES.

Weather Data and Design Conditions

City	Latitude[1] 0	Latitude[1] 1	Winter Temperatures[1] Med. of Annual Extremes	99%	97½%	Winter Degree Days[2]	Summer Temperatures (Design Dry Buld) 1%	2½%	5%
UNITED STATES									
Albuquerque, NM	35	0	6	14	17	4,400	96	94	92
Atlanta, GA	33	4	14	18	23	3,000	95	92	90
Baltimore, MD	39	2	12	16	20	4,600	94	92	89
Birmingham, AL	33	3	14	19	22	2,600	97	94	93
Bismarck, ND	46	5	-31	-24	-19	8,800	95	91	88
Boise, ID	43	3	0	4	10	5,800	96	93	91
Boston, MA	42	2	-1	6	10	5,600	91	88	85
Burlington, VT	44	3	-18	-12	-7	8,200	88	85	83
Charleston, WV	38	2	1	9	14	4,400	92	90	88
Charlotte, NC	35	1	13	18	22	3,200	96	94	92
Casper, WY	42	5	-20	-11	-5	7,400	92	90	87
Chicago, IL	41	5	-5	-3	1	6,600	94	91	88
Cincinnati, OH	39	1	2	8	12	4,400	94	92	90
Cleveland, OH	41	2	-2	2	7	6,400	91	89	86
Columbia, SC	34	0	16	20	23	2,400	98	96	94
Dallas, TX	32	5	14	19	24	2,400	101	99	97
Denver, CO	39	5	-9	-2	3	6,200	92	90	89
Des Moines, IA	41	3	-13	-7	-3	6,600	95	92	89
Detroit, MI	42	2	0	4	8	6,200	92	88	85
Great Falls, MT	47	3	-29	-20	-16	7,800	91	88	85
Hartford, CT	41	5	-4	1	5	6,200	90	88	85
Houston, TX	29	5	24	29	33	1,400	96	94	92
Indianapolis, IN	39	4	-5	0	4	5,600	93	91	88
Jackson, MS	32	2	17	21	24	2,200	98	96	94
Kansas City, MO	39	1	-2	4	8	4,800	100	97	94
Las Vegas, NV	36	1	18	23	26	2,800	108	106	104
Lexington, KY	38	0	0	6	10	4,600	94	92	90
Little Rock, AR	34	4	13	19	23	3,200	99	96	94
Los Angeles, CA	34	0	38	42	44	2,000	94	90	87
Memphis, TN	35	0	11	17	21	3,200	98	96	94
Miami, FL	25	5	39	44	47	200	92	90	89
Milwaukee, WI	43	0	-11	-6	-2	7,600	90	87	84
Minneapolis, MN	44	5	-19	-14	-10	8,400	92	89	86
New Orleans, LA	30	0	29	32	35	1,400	93	91	90
New York, NY	40	5	6	11	15	5,000	94	91	88
Norfolk, VA	36	5	18	20	23	3,400	94	91	89
Oklahoma City, OK	35	2	4	11	15	3,200	100	97	95
Omaha, NE	41	2	-12	-5	-1	6,600	97	94	91
Philadelphia, PA	39	5	7	11	15	4,400	93	90	87
Phoenix, AZ	33	3	25	31	34	1,800	108	106	104
Pittsburgh, PA	40	3	1	7	11	6,000	90	88	85
Portland, ME	43	4	-14	-5	0	7,600	88	85	81
Portland, OR	45	4	17	21	24	4,600	89	85	81
Portsmouth, NH	43	1	-8	-2	3	7,200	88	86	83
Providence, RI	41	4	0	6	10	6,000	89	86	83
Rochester, NY	43	1	-5	2	5	6,800	91	88	85
Salt Lake City, UT	40	5	-2	5	9	6,000	97	94	92
San Francisco, CA	37	5	38	42	44	3,000	80	77	83
Seattle, WA	47	4	22	28	32	5,200	81	79	76
Sioux Falls, SD	43	4	-21	-14	-10	7,800	95	92	89
St. Louis, MO	38	4	1	7	11	5,000	96	94	92
Tampa, FL	28	0	32	36	39	680	92	91	90
Trenton, NJ	40	1	7	12	16	5,000	92	90	87
Washington, DC	38	5	12	16	19	4,200	94	92	90
Wichita, KS	37	4	-1	5	9	4,600	102	99	96
Wilmington, DE	39	4	6	12	15	5,000	93	93	20
ALASKA									
Anchorage	61	1	-29	-25	-20	10,800	73	70	67
Fairbanks	64	5	-59	-53	-50	14,280	82	78	75
CANADA									
Edmonton, Alta.	53	3	-30	-29	-26	11,000	86	83	80
Halifax, N.S.	44	4	-4	0	4	8,000	83	80	77
Montreal, Que.	45	3	-20	-16	-10	9,000	88	86	84
Saskatoon, Sask.	52	1	-37	-34	-30	11,000	90	86	83
St. John, Nwf.	47	4	1	2	6	8,600	79	77	75
Saint John, N.B.	45	2	-15	-12	-7	8,200	81	79	77
Toronto, Ont.	43	4	-10	-3	1	7,000	90	87	85
Vancouver, B.C.	49	1	13	15	19	6,000	80	78	76
Winnipeg, Man.	49	5	-31	-28	-25	10,800	90	87	84

[1]Handbook of Fundamentals, ASHRAE, Inc., NY 1972
[2]Local Climatological Annual Survey, USDC Env. Science Services Administration, Ashville, SC

EARTHWORK EQUIPMENT

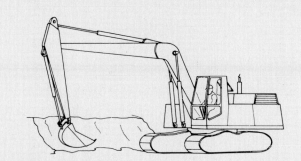

Backhoe - Crawler Type

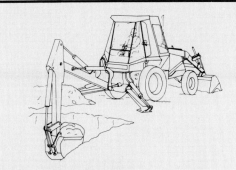

Backhoe/Loader - Wheel Type

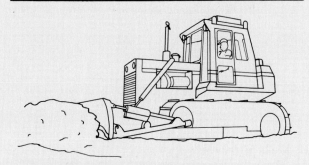

Tractor - Crawler Type

Tractor Loader - Wheel Type

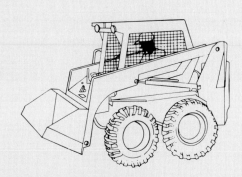

Tractor Loader - Wheel Type, Small

Dump Truck

EARTHWORK EQUIPMENT

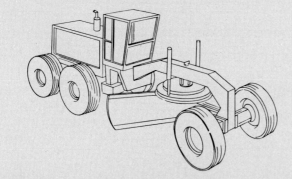

Grader

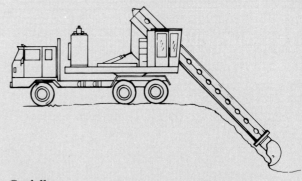

Gradall

Roller

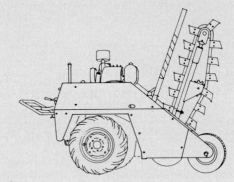

Trencher

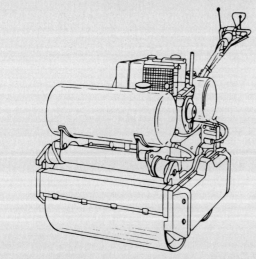

Compactor Roller

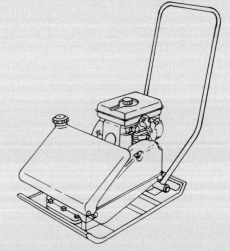

Compactor - Vibratory Plate

CONCRETE EQUIPMENT

Ready Mix Truck

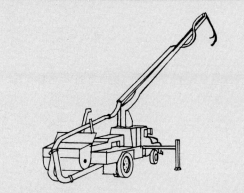

Concrete Pump

Concrete Bucket

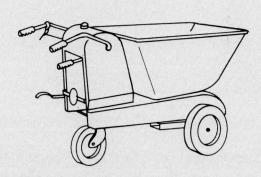

Concrete Cart

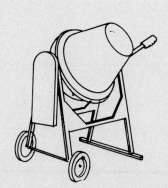

Concrete Mixer

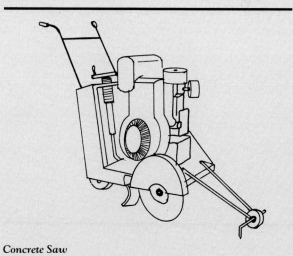

Concrete Saw

CONCRETE EQUIPMENT

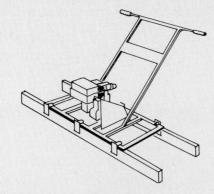

Power Screed

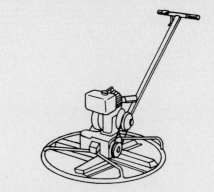

Concrete Finisher

Magnesium Screed

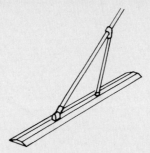

Magnesium Darby

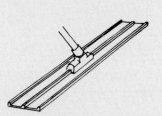

Bull Float

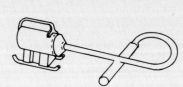

Concrete Vibrator

Finishing Broom

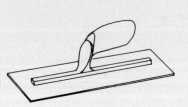

Steel Trowel

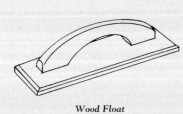

Wood Float

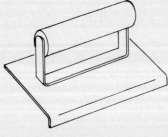

Edger

Bronze Groover

Hand Finishing Tools

DEWATERING

Excavation dewatering is the process of removing surface and ground water which may interfere with the excavation and construction of a structure. Methods used for removal of surface water are ditching, or gravity flow, and pumping.

The use of ditches to remove surface water by gravity flow may be economical where the angle of repose of the earth is steep and the amount of required excavation of the site is minimal. Where surface water is a common feature in the geographic location, the dewatering ditch may be planned as part of the final landscaping or topographical design of the site.

The removal of surface water by pumping is the alternative to the ditching method. Depending on the condition and the amount of the water to be removed, diaphragm or centrifugal pumps may be used. Where the water contains large amounts of solids, the diaphragm type is recommended. The more efficient centrifugal pumps should be used in cases which require removal of large volumes of surface water. Regardless of the type of pump selected, it should be located as close to the water as possible to minimize lift. Ideally, it should rest in a sump at a low point of the excavation. The inlet to the pump should be fitted with a trash screen to protect the pump and be set in a mesh enclosure to prevent clogging. Placing the inlet in a wooden box may keep it from settling in mud and sludge.

Water may be removed prior to excavation by lowering the water table around the site with the installation of well points or deep wells and pumping. A well point is a section of perforated pipe that is jetted vertically into place below the ground water level and then connected by riser pipes to a horizontal header at the ground surface. Well points and their accompanying risers are spaced along the header at intervals ranging from 2-1/2' to 10' on center. A pump is then connected to the header pipe, and the ground water is drawn from the water table, which, in time, is lowered to the depth of the well points (usually a maximum of 15'). Deeper well points are installed by locating headers at successively lower levels and operating the pump at the lowest of these levels. The flow of ground water into the well points depends on the porosity of the soil surrounding them. Where the soil is comprised of clay or consists of material which restricts its porosity, sand fill may be placed around the well points to facilitate the flow of water into them. The deep well system is a more complex and costly operation than the well point system because of the depth of installation involved and the drilling and lining of the shafts. Deep wells can be driven to depths of 50' and deeper and are spaced at wider intervals than well points.

Because all types of dewatering operations may require continuous pumping, a standby pump and extra operating equipment should be readily available to cope with breakdowns. To save on overtime wages for uninterrupted pumping operations that last for a week or longer, the assignment of four men rotating six-hour shifts computes to a total of only eight hours overtime wages per man per week.

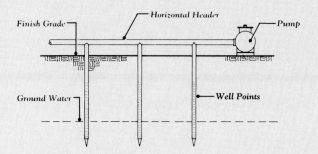

Man-hours

Description	m/hr	Unit
Excavate Drainage Trench, 2' Wide		
2' Deep	.178	cu yd
3' Deep	.160	cu yd
Sump Pits, By Hand		
Light Soil	1.130	cu yd
Heavy Soil	2.290	cu yd
Pumping 8 Hours, Diaphragm or Centrifugal Pump		
Attended 2 hours per Day	3.000	day
Attended 8 hours per Day	12.000	day
Pumping 24 Hours, Attended 24 Hours, 4 Men at 6 Hour Shifts, 1 Week Minimum	25.140	day
Relay Corrugated Metal Pipe, Including Excavation, 3' Deep		
12" Diameter	.209	lf
18" Diameter	.240	lf
Sump Hole Construction, Including Excavation, with 12" Gravel Collar		
Corrugated Pipe		
12" Diamter	.343	lf
18" Diameter	.480	lf
Wood Lining, Up to 4' x 4'	.080	sfca
Well-point System, Single Stage, Install and Remove, per Length of Header		
Minimum	.750	lf
Maximum	2.000	lf
Wells, 10' to 20' Deep with Steel Casing 2' Diameter		
Minimum	.145	vlf
Average	.245	vlf
Maximum	.490	vlf

TRENCH DRAINS

Trench drains are used to remove surface water and to serve as a linear boundary to retain surface drainage. Situations where trench drains may be called for include: a sloped driveway entering a building, a stairway intersecting a plaza, or a sloping landscape where surface water may collect. Trench drains are often constructed from formed concrete with a cast iron grating cover, but other natural and man-made materials may also be used.

Trench drains are designed for open-channel flow. The cover of the drain is recessed to the level of the surrounding grade to allow for unobstructed crossing by foot or wheeled traffic. The cover can be manufactured from light- or heavy-duty material, depending on the amount of support required by the expected traffic flow. A framing angle is embedded into the perimeter of the trench to receive the cover.

Prefabricated concrete trench drains can be installed much faster than poured-in-place concrete drains. One type, for example, is manufactured from polymer concrete with sections that snap together for relatively easy and quick installation. The polymer concrete material used in the drain also resists chemicals and is not affected by the freeze-thaw cycle. Modular catch basins are also available with this prefabricated drainage system.

Materials other than concrete are used occasionally to create trench drains in lawns and/or other landscaped or site areas where concrete drains are not desired for aesthetic or other reasons. One alternative method of trench drain installation is to place drainage stone in an envelope of geotextile fabric, usually 4- to 6-ounce nonwoven polyester. The fabric is unrolled into an open trench, filled with the stone, and then overlapped. Additional stone or suitable landscaping materials may then be used to cover the drain.

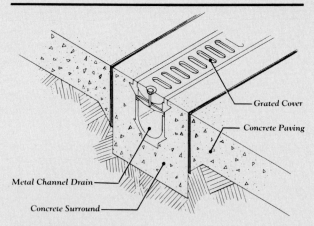

Embedded Trench Drain

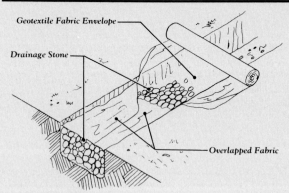

Stone Trench Drain

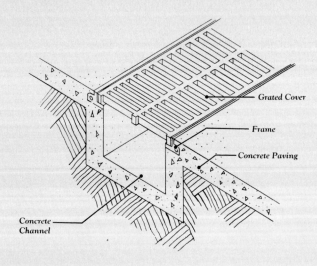

Man-hours

Description	m/hr	Unit
Trench Forms		
1 Use	.200	sfca
4 Uses	.173	sfca
Reinforcing	15.240	ton
Concrete		
Direct Chute	.320	cu yd
Pumped	.492	cu yd
With Crane and Bucket	.533	cu yd
Trench Cover, Including Angle Frame		
To 18" Wide	.400	lf
Cover Frame Only		
For 1" Grating	.178	lf
For 2" Grating	.229	lf
Geotextile Fabric in Trench		
Ideal Conditions	.007	sq yd
Adverse Conditions	.010	sq yd
Drainage Stone		
3/4"	.092	cu yd
Pea Stone	.092	cu yd

OPEN SITE DRAINAGE SYSTEMS

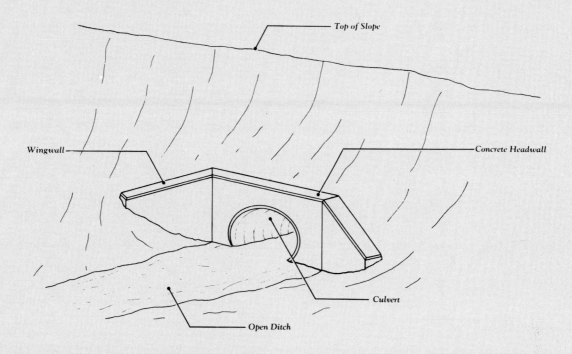

The flow of storm water runoff on the surfaces of slopes and the embankments of swales and ditches must be controlled to prevent erosion and the undermining of site structures and pavements. Where the vegetative cover is insufficient to control surface erosion, transverse water diversion ditches should be placed at the top of the slope. Where the end of the intercepting ditch becomes too steep or must follow the slope, a paved spillway section may be installed to conduct the flow. Paving may be required where the flow in a ditch or swale exceeds the runoff limits for bare earth or turf grass. The paving materials commonly used for these installations include stone rubble, asphalt, and concrete. Concrete drop structures, which are similar in construction to catch basins, may also be installed at critical locations along the ditch to reduce the volume of the flow and to allow some of the runoff to be carried by pipe to safe remote discharge locations.

Culverts may also be employed to conduct storm water runoff, especially under roads, highways, and railroad beds. Small culverts of only a few feet in diameter may be constructed from sections of reinforced concrete pipe, corrugated metal, or plastic. Large culverts require more complex installations which may be constructed from reinforced concrete pipe of up to 8′ in diameter, precast box culverts of up to 12′ in height, corrugated steel or aluminum arches of up to 6′ in radius, or multi-plate steel arches. Poured-in-place concrete bridges may even be required for extremely large-scale culvert installations. Regardless of the size of the culvert, the structure, wherever possible, should be placed at right angles to the roadway or rail bed to minimize the length of the structure and to reduce its cost.

Care should be exercised in planning and constructing the entrances and exits of culverts so that appropriately designed and installed headwalls will protect and retain the surrounding fill. For small culverts which are correctly aligned on slight slopes, a simple straight headwall constructed perpendicular to the flow serves as adequate protection. For larger culverts and moderate to steep slopes, wing walls must be placed alongside the straight headwall to prevent erosion of the sloped fill and undermining of the culvert itself. In situations where the flow changes abruptly at a culvert, the wing walls must be skewed in a direction to coincide with the natural stream. In addition to the headwall, a paved apron may also be required where high intake or exit flow velocities can cause further erosion or undermining.

The materials used for the construction of culverts, headwalls and culvert piping vary according to the size of the structure and the conditions of its placement. Large field constructed headwalls are normally constructed from poured-in-place concrete or from building stones set in mortar. Precast culvert boxes may be ordered with custom end walls at an additional cost. Some types of small culvert piping can be ordered with special sections with flared ends which can function as headwalls. Concrete culvert pipe may be ordered with a vitreous lining which greatly improves the pipe's hydraulic characteristics. Corrugated metal pipe also achieves greater hydraulic efficiency with the addition of a specially ordered paved invert.

OPEN SITE DRAINAGE SYSTEMS (CONT.)

Man-hours

Description	m/hr	Unit
Paving, Asphalt, Ditches	.185	sq yd
Concrete, Ditches	.360	sq yd
Filter Stone Rubble	.258	cu yd
Paving, Ashpalt, Aprons	.320	sq yd
Concrete, Aprons	.620	sq yd
Drop Structure	8.000	Ea.
Culverts, Reinforced Concrete, 12″ Diameter	.162	lf
24″ Diameter	.183	lf
48″ Diameter	.280	lf
72″ Diameter	.431	lf
96″ Diameter	.560	lf
Flared Ends, 12″ Diameter	1.080	Ea.
24″ Diameter	1.750	Ea.
Corrugated Metal, 12″ Diameter	.114	lf
24″ Diameter	.175	lf
48″ Diameter	.560	lf
72″ Diameter	1.240	lf
Reinforced Plastic, 12″ Diameter	.280	lf
Precast Box Culvert, 6′ x 3′	.343	lf
8′ x 8′	.480	lf
12′ x 8′	.716	lf
Aluminum Arch Culvert, 17″ x 11″	.150	lf
35″ x 24″	.300	lf
57″ x 38″	.800	lf
Multi-plate Arch, Steel	.014	lb

Corrugated Metal Culvert

Man-hours (cont.)

Description	m/hr	Unit
Headwall, Concrete, 30″ Diameter Pipe,		
3′ Wing Walls	28.750	Ea.
4′-3″ Wing Walls	33.500	Ea.
60″ Diameter Pipe, 5′-6″ Wing Walls	63.250	Ea.
8′-0″ Wing Walls	76.650	Ea.
Stone, 30″ Diameter Pipe, 3′ Wing Walls	12.650	Ea.
4′-3″ Wing Walls	14.800	Ea.
60″ Diameter Pipe, 5′-6″ Wing Walls	30.200	Ea.
8′-0″ Wing Walls	37.200	Ea.

SEWAGE AND DRAINAGE COLLECTION SYSTEMS

Sewage and drainage usually flow by gravity from the source of collection, through service lines, into mains, and eventually to a point of treatment. However, force mains are not uncommonly substituted for gravity mains in sewage systems in which the fluid head must be augmented with pumping stations to assist the drainage flow. Manholes are spaced at regular intervals along the main lines to provide access for repair and maintenance. Sewage and drainage systems operate in the same manner, but their components vary in the types of materials used, because their functions are different.

Sewage-collection systems conduct biological waste to a treatment facility. Gravity sewer mains are usually manufactured from reinforced concrete, but plastic piping can also be used. Asbestos cement piping, at one time the most commonly used form of main piping material, has declined in use due to the hazards of handling asbestos. Force sewer mains (under pressure) are usually manufactured from ductile iron or reinforced plastic pipe. Service lines to individual users consist of vitrified clay or plastic piping. The fittings used in tying the service lines into the main should be made of the same material as that of the service line.

Drainage systems are used to collect stormwater and surface drainage from roadways and parking areas and to conduct the flow away to a suitable outfall. Drainage piping is usually manufactured from reinforced concrete or corrugated metal, although plastic piping has become increasingly popular. Catch basins, which are located at the sump, or low point, of the area to be drained, are sized to handle the maximum volume of rainfall for that area. A catch basin is protected from clogging by a cast iron grating that is removed for maintaining and periodic cleaning. Because the basin outlet pipe is located several feet above the lowest level of the basin, silt and debris settle and accumulate at the bottom of the structure. This material must be cleaned out at regular intervals to prevent buildup and the eventual clogging of the outlet pipe.

Although manholes may require the installation of steps, and may differ from catch basins in function, size, and type of cover, both structures are commonly constructed in the same way and of the same materials. Both structures are fabricated from brick, concrete blocks, c.i.p. concrete or precast concrete sections that are assembled on a poured-in-place concrete slab or on a precast base. A typical manhole or catch basin is a cylinder $4' \pm$ in diameter and 6' high (internal dimensions) at the lower section. The cylinder tapers into an upper section, 2' in diameter by 2' high, that receives the cover. The cover, and the frame, range from 4" to 10" in depth and may be adjusted to grade with brick.

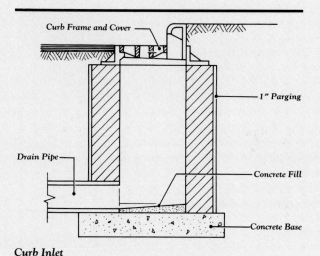

Curb Inlet

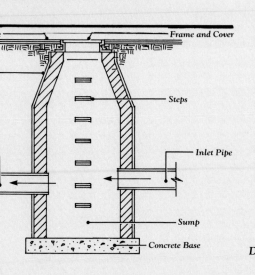

Catch Basin

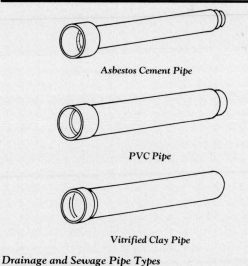

Drainage and Sewage Pipe Types

SEWAGE AND DRAINAGE COLLECTION SYSTEMS (CONT.)

Man-hours

Description	m/hr	Unit
Catch Basins or Manholes, Not Including Excavation and Backfill, Frame and Cover		
Brick, 4′ I.D., 6′ Deep	23.881	Ea.
8′ Deep	32.000	Ea.
10′ Deep	44.444	Ea.
Concrete Block, 4′ I.D., 6′ Deep	16.000	Ea.
8′ Deep	21.333	Ea.
10′ Deep	29.630	Ea.
Precast Concrete, 4′ I.D., 6′ Deep	3.000	Ea.
8′ Deep	4.000	Ea.
10′ Deep	6.000	Ea.
Cast in Place Concrete, 4′ I.D., 6′ Deep	10.667	Ea.
8′ Deep	16.000	Ea.
10′ Deep	32.000	Ea.
Frames and Covers, 18″ Square, 160 lbs	2.400	Ea.
270 lbs	2.791	Ea.
24″ Square, 220 lbs	2.667	Ea.
400 lbs	3.077	Ea.
26″ D Shape, 600 lbs	3.429	Ea.
Roll Type Curb, 24″ Square, 400 lbs	3.077	Ea.
Light Traffic, 18″ Diameter, 100 lbs	2.526	Ea.
24″ Diameter, 300 lbs	2.759	Ea.
36″ Diameter, 900 lbs	4.138	Ea.
Heavy Traffic, 24″ Diameter, 400 lbs	3.077	Ea.
36″ Diameter, 1150 lbs.	8.000	Ea.
Raise Frame and Cover 2″, for Resurfacing,		
20″ to 26″ Frame	3.640	Ea.
30″ to 36″ Frame	4.440	Ea.

Description	m/hr	Unit
Drainage and Sewage Piping, Not Including Excavation and Backfill		
Asbestos Cement, 6″ to 8″ Diameter	.073	lf
12″ Diameter	.100	lf
16″ Diameter	.140	lf
24″ Diameter	.261	lf
Concrete, up to 8″ Diameter	.140	lf
10″ to 18″ Diameter	.168	lf
21″ to 24″ Diameter	.183	lf
30″ Diameter	.212	lf
36″ Diameter	.250	lf
Corrugated Metal, 8″ Diameter	.073	lf
12″ Diameter	.114	lf
18″ Diameter	.147	lf
24″ Diameter	.175	lf
30″ Diameter	.233	lf
36″ Diameter	.280	lf
Ductile Iron, 6″ Diameter	.190	lf
8″ Diameter	.259	lf
12″ Diameter	.389	lf
16″ Diameter	.609	lf
Polyvinyl Chloride, 4″ Diameter	.064	lf
8″ Diameter	.072	lf
12″ Diameter	.088	lf
15″ Diameter	.147	lf
Vitrified Clay, 4″ Diameter	.063	lf
6″ Diameter	.071	lf
8″ Diameter	.093	lf
12″ Diameter	.147	lf

EROSION CONTROL

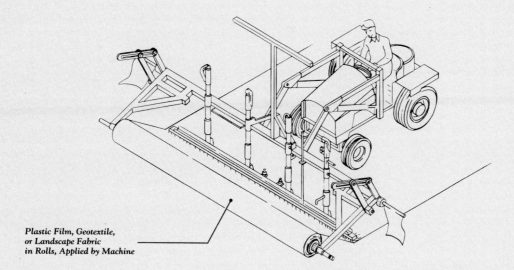

Plastic Film, Geotextile,
or Landscape Fabric
in Rolls, Applied by Machine

Erosion control may be used when top soil, subsoil, or fill tends to run off with the rapid flow of water down a sloped surface. The type of erosion control selected varies for different situations and is determined by the size and severity of the erosion problem, the amount of time available to establish the control system, cost factors, and the final landscaping design of the site. Natural controls, mulches of all types, fiber grids, and rip rap stone are among the many erosion control materials used to keep soil in place.

For moderate slopes and swales, the planting of natural materials may serve as an adequate method for slowing runoff. The root systems of shrubbery, ground cover, and, especially, grass provide a constantly growing and expanding source of natural erosion control. This method of control, however, often takes a long time to establish and may require regular maintenance of mowing and pruning after the vegetation takes root. More immediate controls, even if they are temporary, can be implemented to hold the soil in place while grass or other vegetation gets established.

Included among these faster methods of erosion control are many different types of organic and stone mulches which can be spread over large areas to control runoff. Most organic mulches are relatively inexpensive and can be easily distributed by wheelbarrow or light-duty loader. Wood chips, often a by-product of site clearing, can be placed to a depth of 1″ to 2″. Straw can be placed by itself or as a cover to protect seeded banks. Blankets of excelsior, held together with biodegradable plastic netting, can be unrolled and stapled into place on the slope. For rapid installation, mulch may also be applied by the hydro-spraying method from a distribution truck. This slurry consists of water and wood cellulose alone or mixed with grass seed and fertilizer. Expensive organic mulches, which include peat and bark in shreaded or nugget form, should be installed where the aesthetic impact of the site is a prime consideration.

Stone mulches provide permanent protection against slope erosion, but they are harder to install and more expensive than most organic erosion control materials. Quarry stone is the most economical type of stone mulch, but other types of decorative stone are available at costs of ten to thirty times that of quarry stone. The size of stone mulch ranges from pea stone to boulders.

To control weeds and other unwanted growth which may establish themselves beneath and between the mulch, several methods may be employed. For example, two mil black plastic film can be installed on the slope prior to the spreading of the mulch. Geotextile and landscaping fabric can be substituted for the plastic film if a porous material is needed to allow water penetration into the slope. Lightweight polypropylene fabric can be installed prior to the placing of small stone mulch, but heavier stones may require a heavier fabric or a light fabric with a granular bedding layer.

Several types of organic and synthetic fiber grids, nettings, and fabric materials may also be used alone or in conjunction with mulches or with ground covers and plantings to control slope erosion. Recycled tobacco cloth, which is used for shading tobacco fields, is available from landscaping wholesalers in many parts of the country. Jute mesh and woven polyethylene mesh cost a little more than tobacco cloth, but they can serve as an adequate substitute in areas where tobacco cloth is not available.

Polypropylene, which is often used in the manufacture of geotextiles, has been adapted for use in erosion control as a flat, loosely bonded film that allows air and moisture to pass freely while inhibiting weed growth. Flexible three-dimensional matting, which is fabricated from bonded vinyl, nylon, or polypropylene filaments, becomes permanently interlocked in vegetation growth after it has been placed.

EROSION CONTROL (CONT.)

For more severe erosion control situations, such as shorelines, the banks of channels, and very steep slopes, heavier materials are required. Rip rap stone, which ranges in size from 8″ to 1/3 of a cubic yard and larger, can be installed by a variety of methods. Small rip rap may be distributed by truck or loader and then spread or placed by hand or machine. Large rip rap must be placed a stone at a time, often with a crane. The stone may be set in a gravel bedding or a geotextile base, grouted in place with concrete, or dry grouted by filling voids with smaller stone.

Several other materials and methods besides rip rap can be employed for severe erosion control. Precast interlocking concrete blocks, which are installed like rip rap, can be employed as a heavy-duty paving material on eroded slopes. A unique concrete forming system for interconnected modular blocks is also available. This system consists of a heavy fabric which can be unrolled in place and then pumped full of concrete. Gabion revetment mats can be set on banks, filled with stone, and then coated with an asphaltic slurry.

A final method of severe erosion control includes the installation of a barrier or a series of barriers set at right angles to the direction of flow to interrupt the runoff. These barriers consist of materials which filter out and retain the sediment in the runoff but allow the water to pass. Hay bales supported by wood stakes comprise the most commonly installed barrier of this type. Another type of barrier, called a silt fence, is constructed from sections of woven polypropylene strip fabric that are reinforced and drawn between posts located at intervals of 8′ to 10′.

Man-hours

Description	m/hr	Unit
Mulch		
Hand Spread		
Wood Chips, 2″ Deep	.004	sf
Oat Straw, 1″ Deep	.002	sf
Excelsior w/Netting	.001	sf
Polyethylene Film	.001	sf
Shredded Bark, 3″ Deep	.009	sf
Pea Stone	.643	cu yd
Marble Chips	2.400	cu yd
Polypropylene Fabric	.001	sf
Jute Mesh	.001	sf
Machine Spread		
Wood Chips, 2″ Deep	1.970	MSF
Oat Straw, 1″ Deep	.089	MSF
Shreded Bark, 3″ Deep	2.960	MSF
Pea Stone	.047	cu yd
Hydraulic Spraying		
Wood Cellulose	.200	MSF
Rip Rap		
Filter Stone, Machine Placed	.258	cu yd
1/3 cu yd Pieces, Crane Set Grouted	.700	sq yd
18″ Thick, Crane Set, Not Grouted	1.060	sq yd
Gabion Revetment Mats, Stone Filled, 12″ Deep	.366	sq yd
Precast Interlocking Concrete Block Pavers	.078	sf

ASPHALT PAVEMENT

Asphalt pavements transfer and distribute traffic loads to the subgrade. The pavement is made up of two layers of material, the wearing course and the base course. The wearing course consists of two layers: the thin surface course and the thicker binder course that bonds the surface course to the heavy base layer underneath. The base consists of one layer that varies in thickness, type of material, and design, according to the bearing value of the subgrade material. If the subgrade material has a low-bearing value, either the thickness or the flexural strength of the base must be increased to spread the load over a larger area.

Increasing the flexural strength of the base course can be accomplished in two ways, one of which is to mix asphalt with the base material. The addition of the asphalt doubles the load distributing ability of a conventional granular base. A second method of increasing flexural strength is to add a layer of geotextile stabilization fabric between the base and the subgrade. This fabric not only adds tensile strength to the base, but also prevents the subgrade material from pumping up and contaminating the base during load cycles.

The thicknesses of the various courses within the pavement vary with each layer, according to the intended use of the pavement and, as noted earlier for the base course, the bearing value of the subgrade. For example, pavement may contain a 1″ surface course, a 2″-3″ binder course, and a 5″ or more base course. Standard commercial parking lot pavement may consist of 2-1/2″ of wearing surface and 8″ of granular base, while a highway may require a full-depth pavement with 5-1/2″ of asphalt base and 4″ of wearing surface. Granular base courses usually range from 6″ to 18″ in thickness. The cost of the asphalt mix for a pavement depends on the quality of the aggregate used in the various layers. Generally, the surface mixes contain smaller, higher-grade aggregates and, therefore, cost more than the heavier base mixes.

The installation of pavement material involves several steps and requires highly specialized equipment. Asphalt mix is delivered by truck to the hopper on the front end of the paver and is carried back to the spreading screws by bar feeders. The screws deposit a continuous flow of mix in front of the screed unit, which controls the thickness of the course being spread by the machine. The width of the mat may be increased with extensions added to the screed unit. Automatic sensors, which follow a previously set string line or a ski that rides on an adjacent grade, guide the screed unit to maintain the correct grade of the paved surface. After the pavement has been spread, steel-wheeled or pneumatic-tired rollers compact the asphalt in three separate rollings: the first, to achieve the desired density; the second, to seal the surface; and the third, to remove compactor roller marks and to smooth the wearing surface.

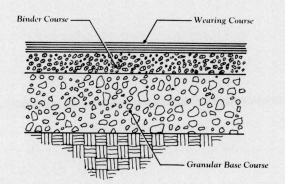

Asphalt Pavement

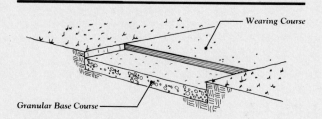

Bituminous Sidewalk

MAN-HOURS

Description	m/hr	Unit
Subgrade, Grade and Roll		
Small Area	.024	sq yd
Large Area	.011	sq yd
Base Course		
Bank Run Gravel, Spread Compact		
6″ Deep	.004	sq yd
18″ Deep	.013	sq yd
Crushed Stone, Spread Compact		
6″ Deep	.016	sq yd
18″ Deep	.029	sq yd
Asphalt Concrete Base		
4″ Thick	.053	sq yd
8″ Thick	.089	sq yd
Stabilization Fabric, Polypropylene, 6 oz./sq yd	.002	sq yd
Asphalt Pavement, Wearing Course		
1-1/2″ Thick	.026	sq yd
3″ Thick	.052	sq yd

PAVEMENT RECYCLING

The process of recycling used asphalt pavement provides a means of reclaiming and rejuvenating old pavement materials so that they can be respread. Generally, all of the methods of recycling involve the tearing up or breaking of the old material, pulverizing it into uniform consistency at a treatment plant or with on-site machines, combining it with new materials, and reinstalling the paving mixture.

The reclaiming part of the recycling process includes the loosening and removing of all or part of the worn-out asphalt pavement. The method used for removal of the existing paved surface depends on the thickness of the pavement to be recycled and the nature of the underlying base. If the base is concrete and the entire layer of pavement above it is to be removed, a ripper or scarifier, which has been mounted on a dozer, loader, or motor grader, can be used. If the base is composed of gravel, the total pavement can be removed with a pavement breaker. Another method, which can be implemented with any type of base material, is to sawcut the pavement into manageable sized strips that can be removed with a backhoe or gradall. Regardless of the method used in tearing up or breaking the old pavement, the loosened, variously sized pieces must be loaded for stockpiling and eventual pulverization.

The pulverization of the old asphalt pavement material can be accomplished on the site with three types of machines designed for this procedure: the stabilizer, the cold planer, or the miller. The actual pulverizing of the old material is performed by a rotating drum with inlaid carbide cutting teeth, called the "cutter," within the planer unit. If the planer is track-mounted, material with depths of just above 0" to a maximum of 5" to 12" can be processed; for wheel-mounted machines, the maximum falls between 3" and 7" in depth. The width of the cutter varies.

After the material has been pulverized, several methods of handling it can be employed, depending on how it is to be used when respread. The recycled pavement may be blended with the base as it is being pulverized to upgrade the strength of the base; it may be left behind in a windrow; or it may be deposited into a truck with an elevating loader. The pulverized material may also be deposited into a traveling hammermill or portable crushing plant and processed into a uniformly graded mixture that is suitable for respreading.

Two operations may be implemented for rejuvenating the pulverized old pavement: cold-mix recycling and hot-mix recycling. Cold-mix recycling involves the combining-in-place of asphalt emulsions or cutbacks with the reclaimed pavement materials at the installation site. If, as often happens, the reclaimed pavement has been respread over the roadway after pulverization, asphaltic emulsion is sprayed on the material from a distribution tanker and then blade-mixed with motor graders. In another cold-mix method, the emulsion is added during the mixing with a stabilizer connected to the tanker. Some planers are also equipped with blending and asphalt emulsion spray bars, and therefore perform three tasks—pulverization, addition of emulsion, and mixing—and function as self-contained, mobile recycling plants.

The hot-mix recycling process is carried out at an asphalt recycling facility, rather than at the removal and/or installation site. In the hot-mix recycling operation, stockpiled recycled pavement must be crushed and screened before being mixed with new aggregate and asphalt. The proportion of old to new material depends on the new mix design and type of plant in which the recycling operation is taking place. In a batch plant, the new mix usually consists of 30% old material and 70% new; in a continuous mix plant, the new mix is usually composed of 70% old material and 30% new. The reason for the superior efficiency of continuous mix plants is that both the recycled material and the new aggregate are directly heated. In the batch plant operation, the recycled pavement is heated only mixing it with superheated new aggregate. Additional savings in both operations can be realized by utilizing recycled aggregate materials in addition to the recycled pavement.

Man-hours

Description	m/hr	Unit
Asphalt Pavement Demolition		
Hydraulic Hammer	.035	sq yd
Ripping Pavement, Load and Sweep	.007	sq yd
Crush and Screen, Traveling Hammermill		
3" Deep	.004	sq yd
6" Deep	.007	sq yd
12" Deep	.012	sq yd
Pulverizing, Crushing, and Blending into Base		
4" Pavement		
Over 15,000 sq yd	.027	sq yd
5,000 to 15,000 sq yd	.029	sq yd
8" Pavement		
Over 15,000 sq yd	.029	sq yd
5,000 to 15,000 sq yd	.032	sq yd
Remove, Rejuvenate and Spread, Mixer-Paver	.026	sq yd
Profiling, Load and Sweep		
1" Deep	.002	sq yd
3" Deep	.006	sq yd
6" Deep	.011	sq yd
12" Deep	.019	sq yd

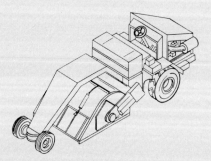

Pulverizer

CURBS

Curbs are set along the sides of roadways to protect the unpaved roadside and to provide erosion-free means of drainage for the road surface. Commonly used curb materials include cast-in-place concrete, precast concrete, bituminous concrete, asphalt, and stone (usually granite). The methods of curb installation vary with the type of curbing material.

Cast-in-place concrete curbs can be formed and cast or placed monolithically with a form-and-place machine. In the latter method, the concrete is placed into a large retaining bin on the machine, formed into the shape of the curb, and then placed as the machine moves along at a set pace. Bituminous concrete curbing can be formed and placed in the same way. In both the cast-in-place and monolithic methods, gutters can be placed as an integral part of the curb.

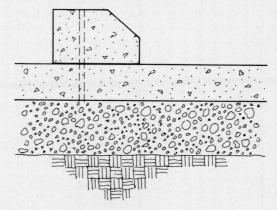

Precast Concrete Parking Bumper

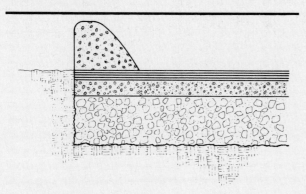

Bituminous Curb

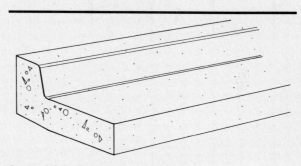

Cast-in-Place Concrete Curb and Gutter

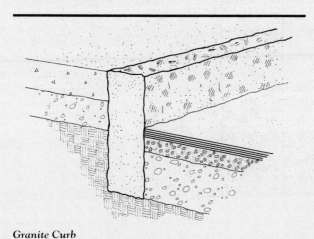

Granite Curb

Man-hours

Description	m/hr	Unit
Curbs, Bituminous, Plain, 8" Wide, 6" High, 50 lf/ton	.032	lf
8" Wide, 8" High, 44 lf/ton	.036	lf
Bituminous Berm, 12" Wide, 3" to 6" High, 35 lf/ton, before Pavement	.046	lf
12" Wide, 1-1/2" to 4" High, 60 lf/ton, Laid with Pavement	.030	lf
Concrete, 6" x 18", Cast-in-place, Straight	.096	lf
6" x 18" Radius	.107	lf
Precast, 6" x 18", Straight	.160	lf
6" x 18" Radius	.172	lf
Granite, Split Face, Straight, 5" x 16"	.112	lf
6" x 18"	.124	lf
Radius Curbing, 6" x 18", Over 10' Radius	.215	lf
Corners, 2' Radius	.700	Ea.
Edging, 4-1/2" x 12", straight	.187	lf
Curb inlets, (guttermouth) straight	1.366	Ea.
Monolithic concrete curb and gutter, cast in place with 6' high curb and 6" thick gutter		
24" wide, .055 cy per lf	.128	lf
30" wide, .066 cy per lf	.141	lf

BRICK, STONE AND CONCRETE PAVING

Brick and stone provide durable, weather-resistant surfaces for exterior pavements. Many types of hard brick and stone are available to meet the practical and cosmetic needs of a given surface. The patterns in which the brick or stone is placed should be determined according to the surface's use and its desired appearance.

Both brick and stone may be set in a sand or concrete bed and grouted with mortar or watered and tamped sand. Regardless of the type of bed material, the subbase must first be leveled and thoroughly compacted to prevent cracking and settling of the finished surface. Wire mesh reinforcing may be required in concrete beds that are large in area or subjected to heavy traffic.

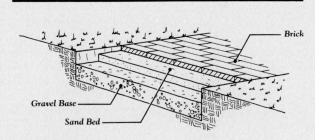

Brick Sidewalk

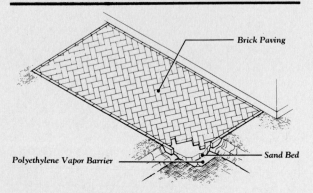

Brick Paving on Sand Bed

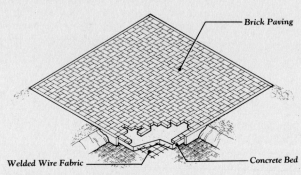

Brick Paving on Concrete Bed

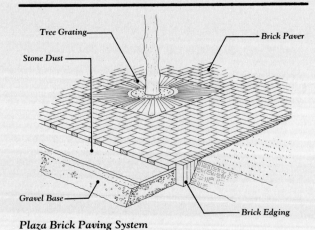
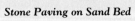

Plaza Brick Paving System

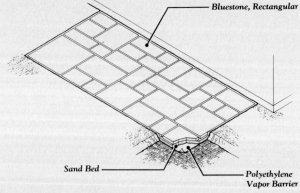

Stone Paving on Sand Bed

BRICK, STONE AND CONCRETE PAVING

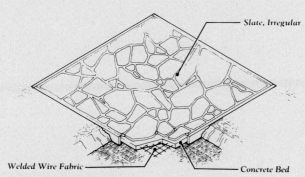

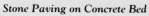

Stone Paving on Concrete Bed

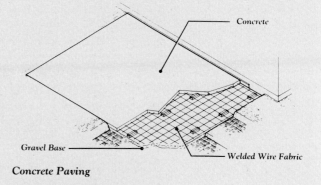

Concrete Paving

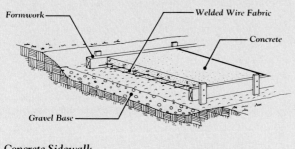

Concrete Sidewalk

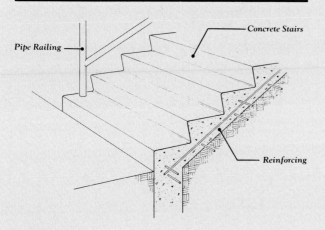

Concrete Stairs

Man-hours

Description	m/hr	Unit
Brick Paving without Joints (4.5 Brick/sf)	.145	sf
Grouted, 3/8" Joints (3.9 Brick/sf)	.178	sf
Sidewalks		
Brick on 4" Sand Bed		
Laid on Edge (7.2/sf)	.229	sf
Flagging		
Bluestone, Irregular, 1" Thick	.198	sf
Snapped Randon Rectangular 1" Thick	.174	sf
1-1/2" Thick	.188	sf
2" Thick	.193	sf
Slate		
Natural Cleft, Irregular, 3/4" Thick	.174	sf
Random Rectangular, Gauged, 1/2" Thick	.152	sf
Random Rectangular, Butt Joint, Gauged,		
1/4" Thick	.107	sf
Granite Blocks, 3-1/2" x 3-1/2" x 3-1/2"	.174	sf
4" to 12" Long, 3" to 5" Wide, 3" to 5" Thick	.163	sf
6" to 15" Long, 3" to 6" Wide, 3" to 5" Thick	.152	sf

BULKHEAD RETAINING WALLS

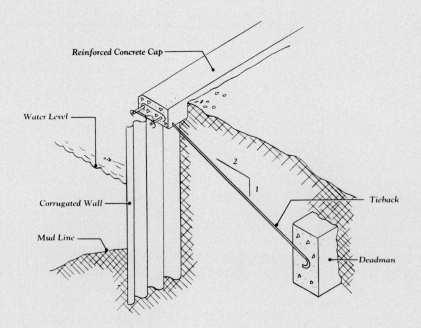

Bulkhead retaining walls are usually used for canal bank and shoreline protection. Sheet piling is installed with a continuous cap that is anchored at regular intervals with tiebacks connected to a deadman buried in the retained bank. Three types of sheet piling are used for these walls: asbestos-cement, aluminum, and steel. The choice of anchor material to be used depends on a number of variables, including the amount of force to be withstood by the wall, its height, and climate considerations. Aluminum and steel sheet piling can be installed with either a pile driving hammer or jetting; asbestos-cement can be erected only with jetting.

Asbestos-cement sheeting, because it does not have the strength of aluminum or steel sheeting, is restricted in its use to sheltered waterways with tidal variations of less than 2'. It is available in panels measuring 3'-6" in width and 3' to 10' in length. The maximum allowable exposed face is 5' in height or less, with a maximum embedment of 6'-6". It resists corrosion, but it cannot be used in climates that experience a regular freeze-thaw cycle. After the piling is installed and anchored with tie rods at spacings of 10', a reinforced concrete cap is formed and placed to maintain wall alignment. Asbestos-cement sheeting can also be used as a knee wall to protect the toe of a larger bulkhead where severe tidal and erosion forces must be resisted.

Aluminum sheet piling, because it is stronger than asbestos-cement piling, can be used in waterways and bays where wave action is considerable. Also, this sheeting is not restricted by climate or corrosive environments. It is available in panels measuring 5' in width and 13' in length which can be installed with a maximum exposed face of 8'. Longer aluminum sheet piling is available in interlocking Z and U shaped sections which can be used in conjunction with walers when the exposed face must be 12' or more in

height. After the piling is installed and secured, a concrete cap, similar to the cap used for asbestos-cement walls, or an aluminum cap, is installed to maintain alignment and to anchor one end of the tieback.

Steel sheet piling possesses the greatest strength of the three types. With appropriate use of walers, steel sheeting can be used to heights of 30' and can withstand severe tidal and wave forces. Galvanized or aluminum coatings can be applied to provide corrosion protection when needed. The sheeting profile is only 3" deep, as compared with 9" to 16" for Z shaped steel sheeting. The thickness ranges from 5 to 12 gauge to suit the specific application. Successive panels interlock to simplify alignment during driving. Steel sheeting is superior to other types when difficult driving conditions are encountered.

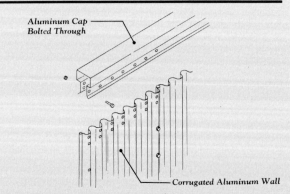

Aluminum Bulkhead Retaining Wall - Aluminum Cap

BULKHEAD RETAINING WALLS

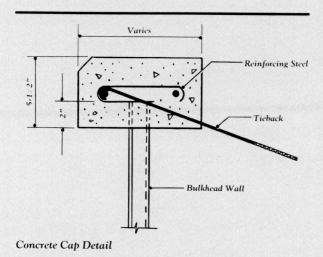

Concrete Cap Detail

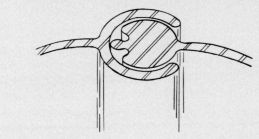

Connection Detail

Man-hours

Description	m/hr	Unit
Asbestos-Cement Sheeting, by Jetting, Including Cap and Anchors, Coarse Compact Sand,		
2'-6" Embedment	.267	lf
5'-6" Embedment	.533	lf
Loose Silty Sand		
2'-6" Embedment	.200	lf
5'-6" Embedment	.400	lf
Aluminum Panel Sheeting, Vibratory Hammer Driven, Including Cap and Anchors, Coarse Compact Sand,		
2'-0" Embedment	.320	lf
5'-6" Embedment	.674	lf
Loose Silty Sand,		
3'-0" Embedment	.312	lf
5'-6" Embedment	.492	lf
Steel Sheet Piling, Exposed Face		
Shore Driven	.067	sf
Barge Driven	.116	sf

CONCRETE RETAINING WALLS

Concrete retaining walls are freestanding structures used to retain earth. They take up much less space than bin- or crib-type wall structures and can be used in situations where very high retaining walls are needed. When soil conditions are normal and the backfill is level, the forces of earth pressure on the wall vary with the height. However, normal earth pressure forces can be increased several times by special conditions such as water, sloped backfill, and building, highway, or railroad bed surcharges. Concrete retaining walls must be built to resist the tendency for sliding and overturning which these forces generate.

There are two basic types of concrete retaining walls: gravity and cantilever. A gravity wall resists sliding and overturning by its mass alone. The cross-sectional shape is usually trapezoidal—narrowest at the top and widest at the base where the forces of the retained earth are greatest. Since the width at the base is greater than 50% of the wall's height, the volume of concrete and related cost become prohibitive if the wall rises above 10′.

A cantilever wall consists of two segments: a vertical wall stem and a horizontal base slab. The wall stem acts as a cantilever fixed at the base. Vertical reinforcing bars resist bending in the stem, and horizontal bars resist bending in the base. Cantilever wall thickness may be constant for structures of less than 10′ in height. Higher walls may require a section that increases in width toward the base by means of a 1:12 slope on the inside face. This slope may also be included on the outside face for aesthetic effect. The wall stem is usually keyed into the base, and the base may be keyed into the underlying, undisturbed earth to resist sliding.

Because retaining walls are not usually designed to withstand hydraulic pressure, provisions must be made to remove any groundwater that might collect behind the structure. This condition can be prevented by placing a blanket of drainage stone backfill behind the wall and placing weep holes at about 10′ intervals at the bottom of the wall. To remove the water entirely, perforated pipe, surrounded by drainage stone, can be installed along the inside face at the base of the wall prior to backfilling.

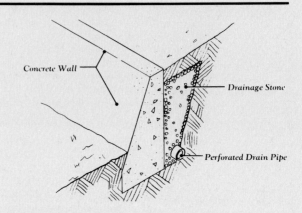

Gravity Retaining Wall

Man-hours

Description	m/hr	Unit
Concrete Retaining Wall		
Footing Formwork	.066	sfca
Wall Formwork, Under 8′ High	.049	sfca
Under 16′ High	.079	sfca
Wall Formwork, Battered to 16′ High	.150	sfca
Footing Reinforcing Bars	15.240	ton
Wall Reinforcing Bars	10.670	ton
Footing Concrete, Direct Chute	.400	cu yd
Pumped	.640	cu yd
Crane and Bucket	.711	cu yd
Wall Concrete, Direct Chute	.480	cu yd
Pumped	.674	cu yd
Crane and Bucket	.711	cu yd
Perforated, Clay, 4″ Diameter	.060	lf
6″ Diameter	.076	lf
8″ Diameter	.083	lf
Bituminous, 4″ Diameter	.032	lf
6″ Diameter	.035	lf
Porous Concrete, 4″ Diameter	.072	lf
6″ Diameter	.076	lf
8″ Diameter	.090	lf
Drainage Stone, 3/4″ Diameter	.092	cu yd
Backfill, Dozer	.010	cu yd
Compaction, Vibrating Plate, 12″ Lifts	.044	cu yd

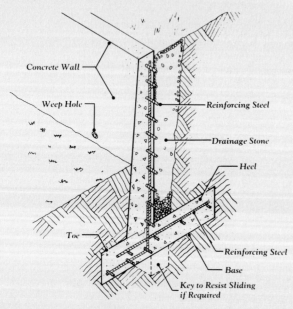

Cantilever Retaining Wall

GABION RETAINING WALLS

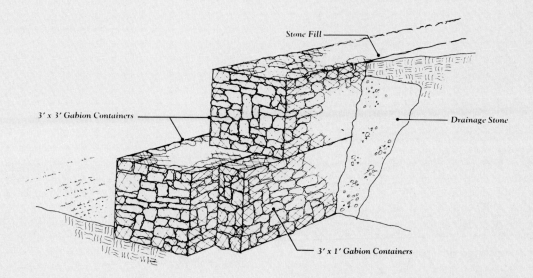

Stone Fill

3' x 3' Gabion Containers

Drainage Stone

3' x 1' Gabion Containers

Gabion retaining walls are designed and built to hold back earth with their weight and mass. Although they have the greatest mass of retaining wall types, they are among the least expensive to erect. The basic components of the walls include individual gabion containers, wire or plastic, and the 4" to 8" stone with which the containers are filled. The containers are 3' in width and range from 1' to 3' in height and 6' to 12' in length.

The process of installing the walls involves several steps. Empty containers are arranged, one course at a time and one or more deep, and then filled. During the installation and filling process, care must be taken not to damage the galvanized or plastic coating on the wire mesh. The stone on the exposed face of the wall may be set by hand with the balance of each of the containers filled by machine. Voids within the container average about 35% of its total volume.

Special construction techniques may add to the life and effectiveness of gabion walls. Either face of the wall may be stepped, for example, and added stability may be realized by tilting the wall into the retained earth at a 1:6 slope. In clay soils, additional gabions, spaced from 13' to 30' on center, should run traverse to the wall line, from the outside face to beyond the slip plane of the retained bank. If drainage is a problem, especially in instances where the retained earth supports a highway or railroad bed, a blanket of drainage stone should be placed behind the wall. This drainage system helps in preventing fines from washing through and undermining the wall's backfill.

Man-hours

Description	m/hr	Unit
Gabion with stone fill		
3' x 6' x 1'	.280	Ea.
3' x 6' x 3'	1.020	Ea.
3' x 9' x 1'	.431	Ea.
3' x 9' x 3'	1.510	Ea.
3' x 12' x 1'	.560	Ea.
3' x 12' x 3'	2.240	Ea.
Drainage stone, 3/4" diameter	.092	cu yd
Backfill Dozer	.010	cu yd
Compaction, roller, 12" lifts	.014	cu yd

MASONRY RETAINING WALLS

Masonry retaining walls may be constructed of block, brick or stone.

Brick or block walls are usually placed on a concrete footing that acts as a leveling pad and distributes imposed loads to the subsoil. Both the wall and the footing may be reinforced. Voids in the masonry are usually filled with mortar or grout, and the wall capped with a suitable material. Solid masonry walls should include porous backfill against the back of the wall and weep holes or drainage piping to eliminate hydrostatic head.

Stone retaining walls may be constructed dry or mortar set with or without a suitable concrete footing. All masonry retaining walls should be placed a sufficient depth below grade to eliminate the danger of frost heave. Mortar set walls should include an adequate drainage system.

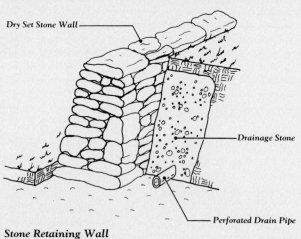

Stone Retaining Wall

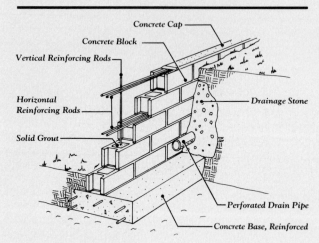

Masonry Retaining Wall

Man-hours

Description	m/hr	Unit
Masonry Retaining Wall, 8″ Thick, 4′ High		
Continous Wall Footing	.140	lf
Concrete Block Wall Including Reinforcing		
and Grouting	.610	lf
Fill in Trench Crushed Bank Run	.010	lf
Perforated Asbestos Cement Drain,		
4″ Diameter	.062	lf
Masonry Retaining Wall, 10″ Thick, 6′ High		
Continuous Wall Footing	.218	lf
Concrete Block Wall Including Reinforcing		
and Grouting	.957	lf
Fill in Trench Crushed Bank Run	.015	lf
Perforated Asbestos Cement Drain,		
4″ Diameter	.062	lf
Masonry Retaining Wall, 12″ Thick, 8′ High		
Continuous Wall Footing	.278	lf
Concrete Block Wall Including Reinforcing		
and Grouting	1.548	lf
Fill in Trench Crushed Bank Run	.020	lf
Perforated Asbestos Cement Drain,		
4″ Diameter	.062	lf
Stone Retaining Wall, 3′ Above Grade, Dry Set	2.742	lf
Mortar Set	2.400	lf
6′ Above Grade, Dry Set	4.114	lf
Mortar Set	3.600	lf

Note: Units are per lf of wall.

WOOD RETAINING WALLS

Wood retaining walls are usually constructed of redwood, cedar, pressure-treated lumber, or creosoted lumber.

The three systems normally used to construct these walls are wood post, post-and-board, and wood tie.

Wood post walls consist of posts placed side by side and anchored a suitable distance below the subgrade in order to resist overturning.

Post-and-board walls are erected of spaced, anchored posts, horizontal wood sheathing, and a wood cap.

Wood tie walls are constructed of railroad or landscape ties. These are anchored by steel rods driven thru holes in the ties.

Wood retaining walls are normally used for their pleasing aesthetic effect and are not suitable for high cuts or heavy surcharges.

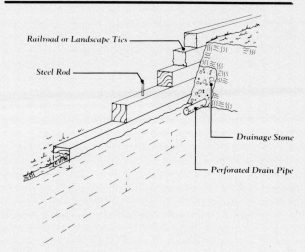

Wood Tie Retaining Wall

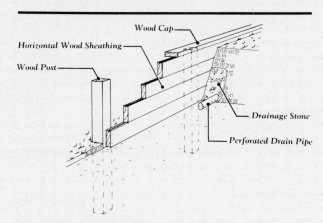

Wood Post and Board Retaining Wall

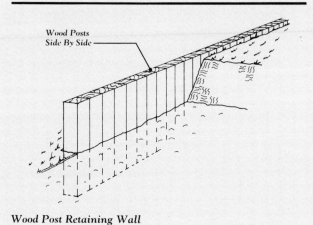

Wood Post Retaining Wall

Man-hours

Description	m/hr	Unit
Wood Post and Board Retaining Wall		
4' High		
Redwood Posts, Plank and Cap	.664	lf
Porous Backfill	.010	lf
Perforated Pipe	.062	lf
6' High		
Redwood Posts, Plank and Cap	.742	lf
Porous Backfill	.015	lf
Perforated Pipe	.062	lf
8' High		
Redwood Posts, Plank and Cap	1.307	lf
Porous Backfill	.020	lf
Perforated Pipe	.062	lf
Wood Post Retaining Wall		
2' High Redwood Posts	.358	lf
Porous Fill	.005	lf
Perforated Pipe	.062	lf
4' High Redwood Posts	1.074	lf
Porous Fill	.010	lf
Perforated Pipe	.062	lf
6' High Redwood Posts	2.505	lf
Porous Fill	.015	lf
Perforated Pipe	.062	lf
Wood Tie Retaining Wall		
4' High Redwood Ties	.689	lf
Porous Fill	.010	lf
Perforated Pipe	.062	lf
6' High Redwood Ties	1.034	lf
Porous Fill	.015	lf
Perforated Pipe	.062	lf

FENCING

Fences are usually composed of a series of vertical posts set into the earth and spanned with rails, panels, or stretched metal fencing fabric. They are installed for many reasons, including privacy, safety, security, weather protection, cosmetics, and mandate of local codes. Fence posts may be installed and secured by direct driving or by setting them in concrete or compacted fill in predug post holes. The most commonly used fencing materials are wood (usually cedar or redwood), galvanized steel, aluminum, and plastic-coated steel.

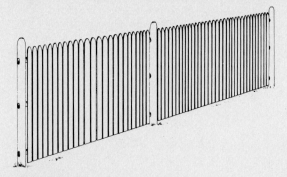

Stockade Fence

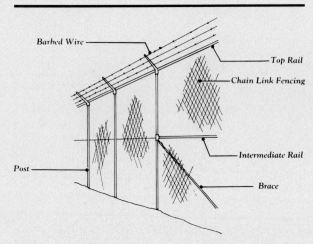

Chain Link Fence, Industrial

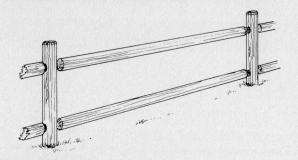

Open Rail Rustic Fence

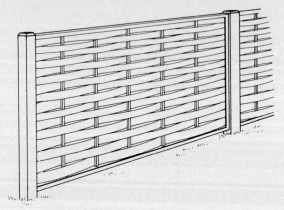

Basketweave Fence

Man-hours

Description	m/hr	Unit
Fence, Chain Link, Industrial Plus 3 Strands Barbed Wire, 2″ Line Post @ 10′ on Center		
1-5/8″ Top Rail, 6′ High	.096	lf
Corners, Add	.600	Ea.
Braces, Add	.300	Ea.
Gate, Add	.686	Ea.
Residential, 11 Gauge Wire, 1-5/8″ Line Post @ 10′ on Center 1-3/8″		
Top Rail, 3′ High	.048	lf
4′ High	.060	lf
Gate, Add	.400	Ea.
Tennis Courts, 11 Gauge Wire, 1-3/4″ Mesh, 2-1/2″ Line Posts, 1-5/8″ Top Rail,		
10′ High	.155	lf
12′ High	.185	lf
Corner Posts, 3″ Diameter, Add	.800	Ea.
Fence, Security, 12′ High	.960	lf
16′ High	1.200	lf
Fence, Wood, Cedar Picket, 2 Rail, 3′ High	.150	lf
Gate, 3′-6″, Add	.533	Ea.
Cedar Picket, 3 Rail, 4′ High	.160	lf
Gate, 3′-6″, Add	.585	Ea.
Open Rail Rustic, 2 Rail, 3′ High	.150	lf
Stockade, 6′ High	.150	lf
Board, Shadow Box, 1″ x 6″ Treated Pine, 6′ High	.150	lf

SITE IRRIGATION

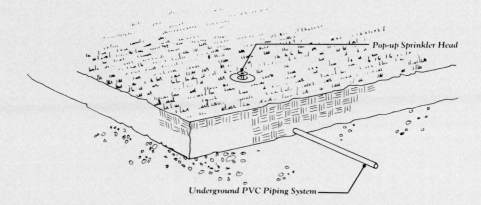

Pop-up Sprinkler Head

Underground PVC Piping System

Site irrigation is accomplished with sprinkler heads that are attached to a permanent underground piping system, usually of PVC pipe or flexible polyethylene tubing. The system may be controlled at a main valve, either manually or automatically, or at each individual sprinkler head.

Several types of sprinkler head operations are available: spray, impact, or rotary. Any of these heads may accommodate one of several types of mountings: pop-up, riser mount, or quick connect. The mountings are made of plastic or brass in both economy and heavy-duty models.

The area covered by a single sprinkler head can range in a circular or arc pattern from 10′ to 100′ in radius, or in a quadrilateral pattern, such as a 24′ square or a 40′ by 6′ rectangle. Radius pattern heads can be adjusted for irrigating areas along property boundaries. Since large radius sprays require great amounts of water, the local water pressure must be sufficient. If this is not the case, then booster pumps may be required to provide the necessary pressure. Generally, the larger-coverage sprinklers provide a more economical system.

The site served is usually divided into zones determined by the nature of the landscaping (turf or shrub), the amount of irrigation needed (sunny or shady), and the coverage of the sprinkler head (small or large). Each zone is controlled by a separate valve. In an automated system, each of these valves and the main valve from the water supply are electrically operated. The electrical service to each of these valves is connected to and controlled from a remote panel.

Man-hours

Description	m/hr	Unit
Sprinkler System, Golf Course, Fully Automatic	.600	9 holes
12′ Radius Heads, 15′ Spacing		
Minimum	.343	head
Maximum	.600	head
30′ Radius Heads, Automatic		
Minimum	.857	head
Maximum	1.040	head
Sprinkler Heads		
Minimum	.267	head
Maximum	.320	head
Trenching, Chain Trencher, 12 hp		
4″ Wide, 12″ Deep	.010	lf
6″ Wide, 24″ Deep	.015	lf
Backfill and Compact		
4″ Wide, 12″ Deep	.010	lf
6″ Wide, 24″ Deep	.030	lf
Trenching and Backfilling, Chain Trencher, 40 hp		
6″ Wide, 12″ Deep	.007	lf
8″ Wide, 36″ Deep	.010	lf
Compaction		
6″ Wide, 12″ Deep	.003	lf
8″ Wide, 36″ Deep	.005	lf
Vibrating Plow		
8″ Deep	.004	lf
12″ Deep	.006	lf
Automatic Valves, Solenoid		
3/4″ Diameter	.363	Ea.
2″ Diameter	.500	Ea.
Automatic Controllers		
4 Station	1.500	Ea.
12 Station	2.000	Ea.

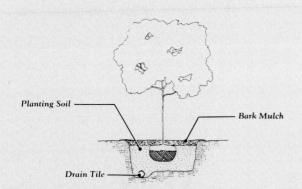

Planting Soil

Bark Mulch

Drain Tile

Tree/Shrub Irrigation and Drainage

Appendix H

Cross Reference List of Plants by Common Names
Courtesy of Monrovia Nursery Company

A
African Daisy .....................................OSTEOSPERMUM
African Iris...MORAEA
African Sumac..RHUS
Alaskan Fern......................................POLYSTICHUM
Alder...ALNUS
Arborvitae..THUJA
Arron's Beard...HYPERICUM
Ash...FRAXINUS
Aspen...POPULUS
Australian Tree Fern...............................ALSOPHILA
Australian Willow.......................................GEIJERA
Autumn Fern..DRYOPTERIS

B
Bamboo.............NANDINA PHYLLOSTACHYS, SASA
Bamboo Palm..................................CHAMAEDOREA
Banana Shrub..MICHELIA
Banana Tree..ENSETE
Barberry..BERBERIS
Beauty Bush...KOLKWITZIA
Big Tree......................................SEQUOIADENDRON
Birch...BETULA
Bird of Paradise, Bird of Paradise Tree ......STRELITZIA
Bird's Eye Bush..OCHNA
Black Gum...NYSSA
Black Laurel...GORDONIA
Blue Hair Grass......................................KOELERIA
Blue Hibiscus...ALYOGYNE
Bluebeard..CARYOPTERIS
Boston Ivy......................................PARTHENOCISSUS
Bottle-brush.......................................CALLISTEMON
Bottle Tree......................................BRACHYCHITON
Bower Vine..PANDOREA
Boxwood...BUXUS
Bridal Wreath..SPIRAEA
Brisbane Box...TRISTANIA
Broom............................CYTISUS, SPARTIUM
Brush Cherry............EUGENIA (SYZGIUM)
Bunya-Bunya..ARAUCARIA
Bush Germander....................................TEUCRIUM
Buttercup Shrub....................................POTENTILLA
Butterfly Bush...BUDDLEIA

C
Cajeput Tree..MELALEUCA
California Christmas Tree.............................CEDRUS
California Lilac.......................................CEANOTHUS
Camphor Tree..................................CINNAMOMUM
Candytuft..IBERIS
Cape Honeysuckle...............................TECOMARIA
Carob Tree..CERATONIA
Carolina Jessamine...............................GELSEMIUM
Carrotwood Tree.................................CUPANIOPSIS
Cat's Claw Vine..................................MACFADYENA
Cedar.........CALOCEDRUS, CEDRUS, CRYPTOMERIA
Cherry Tree (ornamental)...........................PRUNUS
Chilean Jasmine...................................MANDEVILLA
Chinese Gooseberry.................................ACTINIDIA
Chinese Lantern.....................................ABUTILON
Cinquefoils..POTENTILLA
Coast Redwood..SEQUOIA
Confederate Jasmine................TRACHELOSPERMUM
Confederate Rose...................(HARDY) HIBISCUS
Coral Tree..ERYTHRINA
Coral Vine..ANTIGONON
Cottonwood..POPULUS
Crab Apple Tree (ornamental)........................MALUS
Crape Myrtle...................................LAGERSTROEMIA
Crenate Chinese Croton.......................EXCOECARIA
Crested Lady Fern...................................ATHYRIUM
Cupid's Dart..CATANANCHE
Cypress.............CHAMAECYPARIS, CUPRESSOCYPARIS,
CUPRESSUS

D
Date Palm..PHOENIX
Dawn Redwood.................................METASEQUOIA
Daylillies.......................................HEMEROCALLIS
Desert Willow...CHILOPSIS
Dogwood..CORNUS
Dracaena Palm.......................................CORDYLINE
Dusty Miller...CENTRAUREA
Dwarf Keffirboom...................................ERYTHRINA
Dwarf Karo..PITTOSPORUM

E
Elm..ULMUS
Emu Bush..EREMOPHILA
English Fern..POLYSTICHUM
Evergreen Wisteria....................................MILLETTIA

F
False Holly...OSMANTHUS
Ferns ....ALSOPHILA, ASPLENIUM, ATHYRIUM, CYRTOMIUM,
DICKSONIA, DRYOPTERIS, NEPHROLEPIS, ONOCLEA,
OSMUNDA, POLYSTICHUM, RUMOHRA
Fescue ....FESTUCA
Fig (Ornamental and Fruit Bearing)................FICUS
Firethorn..PYRACANTHA
Flame Bottle Tree.............................BRACHYCHITON
Floss Silk Tree...CHORISIA
Flowering Quince...............................CHAENOMELES
Flowering Maple.....................................ABUTILON
Flowering Willow....................................CHILOPSIS
Fortnight Lily...MORAEA
Fountain Grass....................................PENNISETUM
Franklin Tree...FRANKLINIA

G
Geraldton Wax Flower.......................CHAMAELAUCIUM
Giant Sequoia.............................SEQUOIADENRON
Gold Medallion Tree..................................CASSIA
Golden Bells...FORSYTHIA
Golden Rain Tree...............................KOELREUTERIA
Golden Shrub Daisy.................................EURYOPS
Grape (Fruiting)...VITIS
Grape Ivy..CISSUS
Grapefruit..CITRUS
Grasses............CAREX, CHONDROPETALUM, CORTADERIA,
FESTUCA, KOELERIA, MISCANTHUS, PENNISETUM
Grecian Pattern Plant..............................ACANTHUS
Guadalupe Palm..BRAHEA
Guava................................FEIJOA, PSIDIUM
Guinea Gold Vine...................................HIBBERTIA
Gum Tree..EUCALYPTUS

H
Heart-leaf Flame Pea..............................CHORIZEMA
Heath, Heather...ERICA
Heavenly Bamboo.....................................NANDINA
Heliotrope.......................................HELIOTROPIUM
Hemlock..TSUGA
Himalayan Sweet Box ....SARCOCOCCA
Holly...ILEX
Holly Fern...CYRTOMIUM
Honeysuckle..LONICERA
Hopseed Bush...DODONAEA
Horse Chestnut......................................AESCULUS
Horsetail Reed Grass.............................EQUISETUM
Hummingbird Bush...............................GREVILLEA

I
Incense Cedar.....................................CALOCEDRUS
Indian Hawthorn...............................RAPHIOLEPIS
Indian Laurel Fig...FICUS
Indian Rhododendron.........................MELASTOMA
Indigo...INDIGOFERA
Ironbark...EUCALYPTUS
Ivy...HEDERA

J
Japanese Aralia..FATSIA
Japanese Lace Fern...............................POLYSTICHUM
Japanese Plum......................................ERIOBOTRYA
Japanese Sedge Grass..................................CAREX
Japanese Silver Grass.............................MISCANTHUS
Japanese Spurge.................................PACHYSANDRA
Japanese Sword Fern.............................DRYOPTERIS
Japanese Umbrella Pine.........................SCIADOPITYS
Jasmine................JASMINUM, MANDEVILLA, STEPHANOTIS,
TRACHELOSPERMUM
Jessamine..........CESTRUM, GELSEMIUM, MURRAYA
Juniper..JUNIPERUS

K
Kaffir Lilly...CLIVIA
King Plam...................................ARCHONTOPHOENIX
Kiwi Vine..ACTINIDIA
Kumquat........................CITRUS (FORTUNELLA)

L
Lace Fern..POLYSTICHUM
Larch..LARIX
Laurel...PRUNUS
Lavender...LAVANDULA
Lavender Cotton....................................SANTOLINA
Lavender Star Plant...................................GREWIA

Cross Reference List of Plants by Common Names (Continued)

L Leatherleaf Fern ....RUMOHRA
Lemon ....CITRUS
Lemon Leaf ....GAULTHERIA
Lilac..................BUDDLEIA, CEANOTHUS, SYRINGA
Lilac Hibiscus ....ALYOGYNE
Lily of the Nile ....AGAPANTHUS
Lily of the Valley Shrub ....PIERIS
Lily Turf ....LIRIOPE, OPHIOPOGON
Lime ....CITRUS
Loblolly Bay ....GORDONIA
Loquat ....ERIOBOTRYA
Loosestrife ....LYTHRUM

M Madagascar Jasmine ....STEPHANOTIS
Malden Grass ....MISCANTHUS
Maidenhair Tree ....GINKGO
Mallet Flower ....TUPIDANTHUS
Manzanita ...............................ARCTOSTAPHYLOS
Maple ....ACER
Marmalade Bush ....STRETOSOLEN
Marsupial Lobelia ....DAMPIERA
Mediterranean Fan Palm ....CHAMAEROPS
Mescal Bean ....SOPHORA
Mesquite ....PROSOPIS
Mexican Fan Palm .......................WASHINGTONIA
Mimosa Tree ....ALBIZIA
Mock Orange .........PHILADELPHUS, PITTOSPORUM
Mondo Grass ....OPHIOPOGON
Mother Fern ....ASPLENIUM
Mountain Ash ....SORBUS
Mulberry ....MORUS
Myrtle ....MYRTUS

N Natal Plum...CARISSA
Neanthe Bella Palm ....CHAMAEDOREA
Night Blooming Jessamine ....CESTRUM
Nightshade ....SOLANUM
Ninebark ....PHYSOCARPUS
Norfolk Island Pine ....ARAUCARIA

N Oak...QUERCUS
Oleander ....NERIUM, THEVETIA
Olive ....OLEA
Orange ....CITRUS
Orange Clock Vine ....THUNBERGIA
Orange Jessamine ....MURRAYA
Orchid Tree ....BAUHINIA
Oregon Grape Holly.............................MAHONIA

P Palms .........ARCHONTOPHOENIX, ARECASTRUM, BRAHEA,
CHAMAEDOREA, CHAMAEROPS, CYCAS, PHOENIX,
TRACHYCARPUS, WASHINGTONIA
Pampas Grass ....CORTADERIA
Paraguay Nightshade ....SOLANUM
Passion Flower, Passion Vine.................PASSIFLORA
Pear (Ornamental) ....PYRUS
Pepperidge Tree ....NYSSA
Pepper Tree...SCHINUS
Periwinkle ....VINCA
Pine ....PINUS
Pistachio ....PISTACIA
Plumbago ....................................CERATOSTIGMA
Pomegranate ....PUNICA
Potato Vine ....SOLANUM
Poplar ....POPULUS
Powder Puff ....CALLIANDRA
Princess Flower ....TIBOUCHINA
Privet..LIGUSTRUM
Pussy Willow ....SALIX

Q Quaking Aspen ....POPULUS
Queen Palm ....ARECASTRUM
Queen's Wreath ....ANTIGONON

R Redbud ....CERCIS
Red Bird of Paradise Bush ....CAESALPINIA
Red Clusterberry ....COTONEASTER
Red-Leaf Plum ....PRUNUS
Red Yucca ....HESPERALOB
Redwood ....METASEQUOIA, SEQUOIA
Rock Rose ....CISTUS
Rose...ROSA

Rose of Sharon ....HIBISCUS (ALTHAEA)
Rosemary ....ROSMARINUS
Royal Fern ....OSMUNDA
Rubber Tree ....FICUS
Ruffled Leaf Wonder ....FATSHEDERA

S Sago Palm ....CYCAS
Salal ....GAULTHERIA
Sand Cherry ....PRUNUS
Satinwood..MURRAYA
Saxifrage ....SAXIFRAGA
Scotch Broom..CYTISUS
Sea Lavender ....LIMONIUM
Sedge Grass ....CAREX
Senisa ....LEUCOPHYLLUM
Sensitive Fern ....ONOCLEA
Shaddock ....CITRUS
Shrimp Plant ....JUSTICIA
Siberian Gooseberry.............................ACTINIDIA
Silk Oak ....GREVILLEA
Silk Tree ....ALBIZIA
Silverberry ....ELAEAGNUS
Silver Dollar Tree ....EUCALYPTUS
Silver Lace Vine ....POLYGONUM
Snail Vine ....VIGNA
Snowball ....VIBURNUM
Spanish Broom ....SPARTIUM
Spring Bouquet ....VIBURNUM
Spruce ....PICEA
Spurge ....PACHYSANDRA
St. John's Bread Tree...........................CERATONIA
St. John's-Wort ....HYPERICUM
Star Jasmine...............................TRACHELOSPERMUM
Star Pine...ARAUCARIA
Stonecrop ....SEDUM
Strawberry Bush ....ARBUTUS
Summer Lilac ....BUDDLEIA
Swamp Tea Tree ....MELALEUCA
Sweet Broom ....CYTISUS
Sweet Gum ....LIQUIDAMBAR
Sweet Olive ....OSMANTHUS
Sweet Pea Shrub....................................POLYGALA
Sword Fern ....NEPHROLEPIS
Sycamore ....PLATANUS

T Tangelo ....CITRUS
Tangerine ....CITRUS
Tasmanian Tree Fern ....DICKSONIA
Tea Plant ....CAMELLIA
Tea Tree ......................................LEPTOSPERMUM
Texas Mountain Laurel ....SOPHORA
Texas Sage .................................LEUCOPHYLLUM
Thyme ....THYMUS
Trailing African Daisy.....................OSTEOSPERMUM
Trailing Hop Bush ....DODONAEA
Trumpet Creeper ....CAMPSIS
Trumpet Tree ....TABEBUIA
Trumpet Vine..............CAMPSIS, CLYTOSTOMA, DISTICTUS,
MACFADYENA
Tulip Tree ......................................LIRIODENDRON

U Umbrella Plant ....SCHEFFLERA
V Victorian Box....................................PITTOSPORUM
Vine Lilac .....................................HARDENBERGIA
Virginia Creeper ..........................PARTHENOCISSUS

W Wattles ....ACACIA
Wax Leaf Privet...................................LIGUSTURM
Western Sword Fern ....POLYSTICHUM
White Sapote ....CASIMIROA
Willow Leaved Peppermint ....EUCALYPTUS
Windmill Palm ...............................TRACHYCARPUS
Woodbine ....LONICERA
Woadwaxen ....GENISTA

Y Yarrow ....ACHILLEA
Yellow Bells, Yellow Elder......................TECOMA
Yellow Oleander...................................THEVETIA
Yellow Poplar .................................LIRIODENDRON
Yesterday, Today, Tomorrow.................BRUNFELSIA

Abbreviations

A	Area Square Feet; Ampere
	Asbestos Bonded Steel
A.C.	Alternating Current; Air Conditioning; Asbestos Cement
Ac	Acre
A.C.I.	American Concrete Institute
Addit.	Additional
Adj.	Adjustable
Agg.	Aggregate
A hr	Ampere-hour
A.I.A.	American Institute of Architects
Allow.	Allowance
alt.	Altitude
Alum.	Aluminum
a.m.	ante meridiem
Amp.	Ampere
Approx.	Approximate
Apt.	Apartment
Asb.	Asbestos
A.S.B.C.	American Standard Building Code
Asbe.	Asbestos Worker
A.S.M.E.	American Society of Mechanical Engineers
A.S.T.M.	American Society for Testing and Materials
Attchmt.	Attachment
Avg.	Average
Bbl.	Barrel
	Balled & Burlapped
BCF	Bank Cubic Foot
BCY	Bank Cubic Yard
B.&W.	Black and White
B.F.	Board Feet
Bg. Cem.	Bag of Cement
B.I.	Black Iron
Bit.; Bitum.	Bituminous
Bldg.	Building
Blk.	Block
Bm.	Beam
Brg.	Bearing
Brhe.	Bricklayer Helper
Bric.	Bricklayer
Brk.	Brick
Brng.	Bearing
Brs.	Brass
Brz.	Bronze
Bsn.	Basin
Btr.	Better
BTU	British Thermal Unit
BTUH	BTU per Hour
BU	Bushel
BX	Interlocked Armored Cable
c	Conductivity
C	Hundred; Centigrade
C/C	Center to Center
Cair.	Air Tool Laborer
Cal.	Caliper
Calc	Calculated
Cap.	Capacity
Carp.	Carpenter
C.B.	Circuit Breaker
C.C.F.	Hundred Cubic Feet
cd	Candela
CD	Grade of Plywood Face & Back
CDX	Plywood, grade C&D, exterior glue
Cefi.	Cement Finisher
Cem.	Cement
CF	Hundred Feet
C.F.	Cubic Feet
CFM	Cubic Feet per Minute
c.g.	Center of Gravity
CHW	Commercial Hot Water
C.I.	Cast Iron
C.I.P.	Cast in Place
Circ.	Circuit
C.L.	Carload Lot
Clab.	Common Laborer
C.L.F.	Hundred Linear Feet
cm	Centimeter
CMP	Corr. Metal Pipe
C.M.U.	Concrete Masonry Unit
Col.	Column
CO_2	Carbon Dioxide
Comb.	Combination
Compr.	Compressor
Conc.	Concrete
Cont.	Continuous; Continued
Corr.	Corrugated
Cov.	Cover
Cplg.	Coupling
C.P.M.	Critical Path Method
CPVC	Chlorinated Polyvinyl Chloride
C. Pr.	Hundred Pair
Creos.	Creosote
C.S.F.	Hundred Square Feet
C.S.I.	Construction Specification Institute
Cu	Cubic
Cu. Ft.	Cubic Foot
Cwt.	100 Pounds
C.Y.	Cubic Yard (27 cubic feet)
C.Y./Hr.	Cubic Yard per Hour
Cyl.	Cylinder
d	Penny (nail size)
D	Deep; Depth; Discharge
Dis.; Disch.	Discharge
Dbl.	Double
DC	Direct Current
Demob.	Demobilization
Diag.	Diagonal
Diam.	Diameter
Distrib.	Distribution
Dk.	Deck
Do.	Ditto
Dp.	Depth
D.P.S.T.	Double Pole, Single Throw
Dr.	Driver
Drink.	Drinking
Dty.	Duty
E	Equipment Only; East
Ea.	Each
Econ.	Economy
EDP	Electronic Data Processing
Eq.	Equation
Elec.	Electrician; Electrical
Elev.	Elevator; Elevating
	Thin Wall Conduit
Eng.	Engine
Eqhv.	Equip. Oper., heavy
Eqlt.	Equip. Oper., light
Eqmd.	Equip. Oper., medium
Eqmm.	Equip. Oper., Master Mechanic
Eqol.	Equip. Oper., oilers
Equip.	Equipment
Est.	Estimated
E.W.	Each Way
Excav.	Excavation
F	Fahrenheit; Female; Fill
Fab.	Fabricated
FBGS	Fiberglass
F.C.	Footcandles
f'c.	Compressive Stress in Concrete; Extreme Compressive Stress
F.G.	Flat Grain
FH	Feet Head
F.H.A.	Federal Housing Administration
Fig.	Figure
Fin.	Finished
Fixt.	Fixture
Fl. Oz.	Fluid Ounces
Flr.	Floor
Fmg.	Framing
Fndtn.	Foundation
Fori.	Foreman, inside
Foro.	Foreman, outside
Fount.	Fountain
4 PST	Four Pole, Single Throw
FPM	Feet per Minute
FPT	Female Pipe Thread
Fr.	Frame
Ft.	Foot; Feet
Ftng.	Fitting
Ftg.	Footing
Ft. Lb.	Foot Pound
Furn.	Furniture
g	Gram
Ga.	Gauge
Gal.	Gallon
Gal./Min.	Gallon Per Minute
Galv.	Galvanized
Gen.	General
Glaz.	Glazier
GPD	Gallons per Day
GPH	Gallons per Hour
GPM	Gallons per Minute
GR	Grade
Gran.	Granular
Grnd.	Ground
H.D.	Heavy Duty; High Density
Hdr.	Header
Hdwe.	Hardware
Help.	Helper average
Hg	Mercury
H.O.	High Output
Horiz.	Horizontal
H.P.	Horsepower; High Pressure
H.P.F.	High Power Factor
Hr.	Hour
Hrs./Day	Hours Per Day
HSC	High Short Circuit
Ht.	Height
Htg.	Heating
Htrs.	Heaters
HVAC	Heating, Ventilating & Air Conditioning
Hvy.	Heavy
HW	Hot Water
Hyd.; Hydr.	Hydraulic
ID	Inside Diameter
I.D.	Inside Dimension; Identification
I.F.	Inside Frosted
I.M.C.	Intermediate Metal Conduit
In.	Inch
Incan.	Incandescent
Incl.	Included; Including
Int.	Interior
Inst.	Installation
Insul.	Insulation
I.P.	Iron Pipe
I.P.S.	Iron Pipe Size; Inside Pipe Size
I.P.T.	Iron Pipe Threaded
K.	Thousand; Thousand Pounds
K.D.A.T.	Kiln Dried After Treatment
kg	Kilogram
Kip.	1000 Pounds
Km	Kilometer
K.L.F.	Kips per Linear Foot
K.S.F.	Kips per Square Foot
K.S.I.	Kips per Square Inch
KW	Kilo Watt

Abbreviations

KWh	Kilowatt-hour	Mult.	Multi; Multiply	Sched.	Schedule
L	Labor Only; Length; Long	MYD	Thousand yards	S.C.R.	Modular Brick
Lab.	Labor	N	Natural; North	S.E.	Surfaced Edge
lat	Latitude	NA	Not Available; Not Applicable	S.F.	Square Foot
Lath.	Lather	N.B.C.	National Building Code	S.F.C.A.	Square Foot Contact Area
Lav.	Lavatory	N.L.B.	Non-Load-Bearing	S.F.G.	Square Foot of Ground
lb.; #	Pound	No.	Number	S.F. Hor.	Square Foot Horizontal
L.B.	Load Bearing; L Conduit Body	NPS	Nominal Pipe Size	Shee.	Sheet Metal Worker
L. & E.	Labor & Equipment	OC	On Center	Sin.	Sine
lb./hr.	Pounds per Hour	OD	Outside Diameter	Skwk.	Skilled Worker
lb./L.F.	Pounds per Linear Foot	O.D.	Outside Dimension	S.P.	Static Pressure; Single Pole;
lbf/sq in.	Pound-force per Square Inch	O & P	Overhead and Profit		Self Propelled
LCF	Loose Cubic Foot	Oper.	Operator	Spri.	Sprinkler Installer
LCY	Loose Cubic Yard	Opng.	Opening	Sq.	Square; 100 square feet
L.C.L.	Less than Carload Lot	Orna.	Ornamental	S.P.D.T.	Single Pole, Double Throw
Ld.	Load	Ovhd	Overhead	S.P.S.T.	Single Pole, Single Throw
L.F.	Linear Foot	Oz.	Ounce	SPT	Standard Pipe Thread
Lg.	Long; Length; Large	P.	Pole; Applied Load; Projection	S.S.	Single Strength; Stainless Steel
L.J.	Long Span Standard Strength	p.	Page	St; Stl.	Steel
	Bar Joist	Pc.	Piece	Std.	Standard
L.L.	Live Load	P.C.	Portland Cement;	Str.	Strength; Starter; Straight
L.L.D.	Lamp Lumen Depreciation		Power Connector	Struct.	Structural
lm	Lumen	P.C.F.	Pounds per Cubic Foot	Sty.	Story
lm/sf	Lumber Square Foot	P.E.	Professional Engineer;	Subj.	Subject
lm/W	Lumen Per Watt		Porcelain Enamel; Polyethylene;	Subs.	Subcontractors
L.O.A.	Length Over All		Plain End	Surf.	Surface
log	Logarithm	Perf.	Perforated	Sw.	Switch
L.P.	Liquefied Petroleum;	Ph.	Phase	S.Y.	Square Yard
	Low Pressure	P.I.	Pressure Injected	Sys.	System
L.P.F.	Low Power Factor	Pile.	Pile Driver	t	Thickness
Lt.	Light	Pkg.	Package	T	Temperature; Ton
L.T.L.	Less than Truckload Lot	Pl.	Plate	T.C.	Terra Cotta
Lt. Wt.	Lightweight	PLS	Pure Live Seed	T. & G.	Tongue & Groove;
L.V.	Low Voltage	Pluh.	Plumbers Helper		Tar & Gravel
M	Thousand; Material; Male;	Plum.	Plumber	Th.; Thk.	Thick
	Light Wall Copper	Ply.	Plywood	Thn.	Thin
m/hr	Man-hour	Pord.	Painter, Ordinary	Thrded	Threaded
Mach.	Machine	pp	Pages	Tilf.	Tile Layer Floor
Maint.	Maintenance	PP; PPL	Polypropylene	Tilh.	Tile Layer Helper
Marb.	Marble Setter	P.P.M.	Parts per Million	T.L.	Truckload
Mat.	Material	Pr.	Pair	T/M	Tan/Mile
Mat'l.	Material	Prefab.	Prefabricated	Tot.	Total
Max.	Maximum	Prefin.	Prefinished	Tr.	Trade
MBF	Thousand Board Feet	PSF; psf	Pounds per Square Foot	Transf.	Transformer
M.C.F.	Thousand Cubic Feet	PSI; psi	Pounds per Square Inch	Trhv.	Truck Driver, Heavy
M.C.F.M.	Thousand Cubic Feet	PSIG	Pounds per Square Inch Gauge	Trir.	Trailer
	per Minute	PSP	Plastic Sewer Pipe	Trlt.	Truck Driver, Light
MD	Medium Duty	Pspr.	Painter, Spray	UCI	Uniform Construction Index
Med.	Medium	P.T.	Potential Transformer	U.L.	Underwriters Laboratory
MF	Thousand Feet	P. & T.	Pressure & Temperature	Unfin.	Unfinished
M.F.B.M.	Thousand Feet Board Measure	Ptd.	Painted	V	Volt
Mfg.	Manufacturing	Ptns.	Partitions	VA	Volt/amp
Mfrs.	Manufacturers	PVC	Polyvinyl Chloride	Vent.	Ventilating
mg	Milligram	Pvmt.	Pavement	Vert.	Vertical
MH	Manhole; Metal-	Pwr.	Power	V.G.	Vertical Grain
	Halide; Man Hour	Quan.; Qty.	Quantity	Vib.	Vibrating
MHz	Megahertz	Qt.	Quart	Vol.	Volume
Mi.	Mile	R.C.P.	Reinforced Concrete Pipe	W	Wire; Watt; Wide; West
MI	Malleable Iron; Mineral Insulated	Rect.	Rectangle	w/	With
mm	Millimeter	Reg.	Regular	Wldg.	Welding
Min.	Minimum	Reinf.	Reinforced	Wrck.	Wrecker
Misc.	Miscellaneous	Req'd.	Required	W.S.P.	Water, Steam, Petroleum
M.L.F.	Thousand Linear Feet	Resi	Residential	WT, Wt.	Weight
Mo.	Month	Rgh.	Rough	WWF	Welded Wire Fabric
Mobil.	Mobilization	R.H.W.	Rubber, Heat & Water Resistant	XFMR	Transformer
MPH	Miles per Hour		Residential Hot Water	XHD	Extra Heavy Duty
MPT	Male Pipe Thread	Rnd.	Round	yd	Yard
MRT	Mile Round Trip	Rodm.	Rodman	yr	Year
M.S.F.	Thousand Square Feet	R.O.W.	Right of Way	%	Percent
Mstz.	Mosaic & Terrazzo Worker	RPM	Revolutions per Minute	~	Approximately
M.S.Y.	Thousand Square Yards	R.S.	Rapid Start	Ø	Phase
Mtd.	Mounted	RT	Round Trip	@	At
Mthe.	Mosaic & Terrazzo Helper	S.	Suction; Single Entrance;	#	Pound; Number
Mtng.	Mounting		South	<	Less Than
		Scaf.	Scaffold	>	Greater Than
		Sch.;			